SITE CARPENTRY

LEVEL 3 DIPLOMA

PATRICK JOSEPH CLANCY
STEVEN LEAVERLAND
PAUL MURRAY

Leeds College of Building

Nelson Thornes

Published in 2013 by:
Nelson Thornes Ltd
Delta Place
27 Bath Road
CHELTENHAM
GL53 7TH
United Kingdom

13 14 15 16 17 / 10 9 8 7 6 5 4 3 2 1

A catalogue record for this book is available from the British Library

ISBN 978 1 4085 2127 4

Cover photograph: tuja66/Fotolia

Page make-up by GreenGate Publishing Services, Tonbridge, Kent

Printed in Croatia by Zrinski

Note to learners and tutors

This book clearly states that a risk assessment should be undertaken and the correct PPE worn for the particular activities before any practical activity is carried out. Risk assessments were carried out before photographs for this book were taken and the models are wearing the PPE deemed appropriate for the activity and situation. This was correct at the time of going to print. Colleges may prefer that their learners wear additional items of PPE not featured in the photographs in this book and should instruct learners to do so in the standard risk assessments they hold for activities undertaken by their learners. Learners should follow the standard risk assessments provided by their college for each activity they undertake which will determine the PPE they wear.

CONTENTS

Introduction   iv

Contributors to this book   v

1 Health, Safety and Welfare in
Construction and Associated Industries   **1**

2 Analysing Technical Information,
Quantities and Communication with
Others   **39**

3 Analysing the Construction Industry
and Built Environment   **77**

4 Carry Out First Fixing Operations   **113**

5 Carry Out Second Fixing Operations   **173**

6 Set Up and Operate Cutting and
Shaping Machinery   **233**

7 Erect Complex Structural Carcassing
Components   **255**

8 Install and Maintain Non-structural and
Structural Components   **299**

Index   351

Acknowledgements   354

INTRODUCTION

About this book

This book has been written for the Cskills Awards Level 3 Diploma in Site Carpentry. It covers all the units of the qualification, so you can feel confident that your book fully covers the requirements of your course.

This book contains a number of features to help you acquire the knowledge you need. It also demonstrates the practical skills you will need to master to successfully complete your qualification. We've included additional features to show how the skills and knowledge can be applied in the workforce, as well as tips and advice on how you can improve your chances of gaining employment.

The features include:

* chapter openers which list the learning outcomes you must achieve in each unit

* key terms that provide explanations of important terms that you will need to know and understand

* Did you know? margin notes to provide key facts that are helpful to your study

* practical tips to explain facts or skills to remember when undertaking practical tasks

* Reed tips to offer advice about work, building your CV and how to apply the skills and knowledge you have learnt in the workplace

* case studies that are based on real tradespeople who have undertaken apprenticeships and explain why the skills and knowledge you learn during college are useful in the workforce.

* practical tasks that provide step-by-step directions and illustrations for a range of projects you may do during your course

* Test yourself multiple choice questions that appear at the end of each unit to give you the chance to revise what you have learnt and practise your assessment (your tutor will give you the answers to these questions).

Further support for this book can be found at our website, www.planetvocational.com/subjects/build

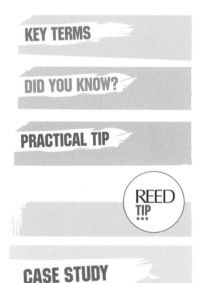

KEY TERMS

DID YOU KNOW?

PRACTICAL TIP

REED
TIP

CASE STUDY

PRACTICAL TASK

TEST YOURSELF

Planet
Vocational

CONTRIBUTORS TO THIS BOOK

Reed Property & Construction

Reed Property & Construction specialises in placing staff at all levels, in both temporary and permanent positions, across the complete lifecycle of the construction process. Our consultants work with most major construction companies in the UK and our clients are involved with the design, build and maintenance of infrastructure projects throughout the UK.

Expert help

As a leading recruitment consultancy for mid–senior level construction staff in the UK, Reed Property & Construction is ideally placed to advise new workers entering the sector, from building a CV to providing expertise and sharing our extensive sector knowledge with you. That's why, throughout this book, you will find helpful hints from our highly experienced consultants, all designed to help you find that first step on the construction career ladder. These tips range from advice on CV writing to interview tips and techniques, and are all linked in with the learning material in this book.

Work-related advice

Reed Property & Construction has gained insights from some of our biggest clients – leading recruiters within the industry – to help you understand the mind-set of potential employers. This includes the traits and skills that they would like to see in their new employees, why you need the skills taught in this book and how they are used on a day to day basis within their organisations.

Getting your first job

This invaluable information is not available anywhere else and is all geared towards helping you gain a position with an employer once you've completed your studies. Entry level positions are not usually offered by recruitment companies, but the advice we've provided will help you to apply for jobs in construction and hopefully gain your first position as a skilled worker.

CONTRIBUTORS TO THIS BOOK

The case studies in this book feature staff from Laing O'Rourke and South Tyneside Homes.

Laing O'Rourke is an international engineering company that constructs large-scale building projects all over the world. Originally formed from two companies, John Laing (founded in 1848) and R O'Rourke and Son (founded in 1978) joined forces in 2001.

At Laing O'Rourke, there is a strong and unique apprenticeship programme. It runs a four-year 'Apprenticeship Plus' scheme in the UK, combining formal college education with on-the-job training. Apprentices receive support and advice from mentors and experienced tradespeople, and are given the option of three different career pathways upon completion: remaining on site, continuing into a further education programme, or progressing into supervision and management.

The company prides itself on its people development, supporting educational initiatives and investing in its employees. Laing O'Rourke believes in collaboration and teamwork as a path to achieving greater success, and strives to maintain exceptionally high standards in workplace health and safety.

South Tyneside Council's
Housing Company

South Tyneside Homes was launched in 2006, and was previously part of South Tyneside Council. It now works in partnership with the council to repair and maintain 18,000 properties within the borough, including delivering parts of the Decent Homes Programme.

South Tyneside Homes believes in putting back into the community, with 90 per cent of its employees living in the borough itself. Equality and diversity, as well as health and wellbeing of staff, is a top priority, and it has achieved the Gold Status Investors in People Award.

South Tyneside Homes is committed to the development of its employees, providing opportunities for further education and training and great career paths within the company – 80 per cent of its management team started as apprentices with the company. As well as looking after its staff and their community, the company looks after the environment too, running a renewable energy scheme for council tenants in order to reduce carbon emissions and save tenants money.

The apprenticeship programme at South Tyneside Homes has been recognised nationally, having trained over 80 young people in five main trade areas over the past six years. One of the UK's Top 100 Apprenticeship Employers, it is an Ambassador on the panel of the National Apprentice Service. It has won the Large Employer of the Year Award at the National Apprenticeship Awards and several of its apprentices have been nominated for awards, including winning the Female Apprentice of the Year for the local authority.

Chapter 1

Unit CSA–L1Core01

HEALTH, SAFETY AND WELFARE IN CONSTRUCTION AND ASSOCIATED INDUSTRIES

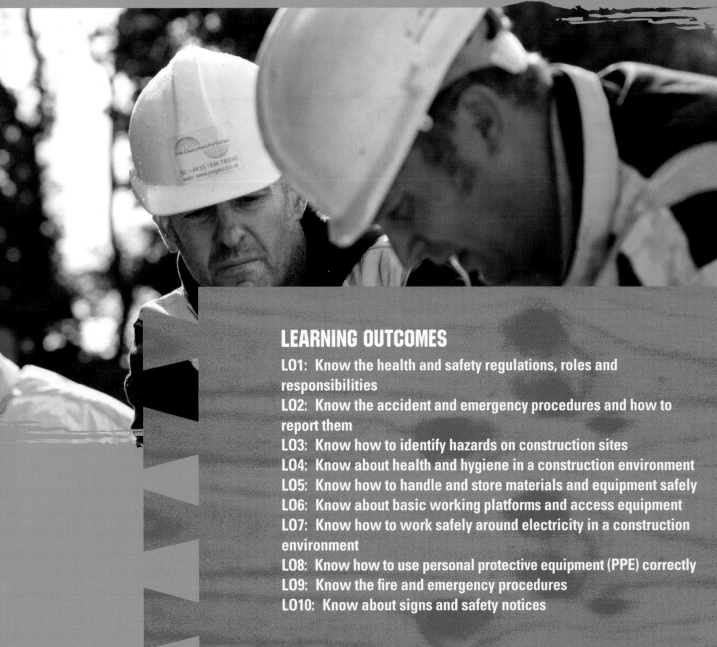

LEARNING OUTCOMES

LO1: Know the health and safety regulations, roles and responsibilities

LO2: Know the accident and emergency procedures and how to report them

LO3: Know how to identify hazards on construction sites

LO4: Know about health and hygiene in a construction environment

LO5: Know how to handle and store materials and equipment safely

LO6: Know about basic working platforms and access equipment

LO7: Know how to work safely around electricity in a construction environment

LO8: Know how to use personal protective equipment (PPE) correctly

LO9: Know the fire and emergency procedures

LO10: Know about signs and safety notices

INTRODUCTION

The aim of this chapter is to:

* help you to source relevant safety information

* help you to use the relevant safety procedures at work.

HEALTH AND SAFETY REGULATIONS, ROLES AND RESPONSIBILITIES

The construction industry can be dangerous, so keeping safe and healthy at work is very important. If you are not careful, you could injure yourself in an accident or perhaps use equipment or materials that could damage your health. Keeping safe and healthy will help ensure that you have a long and injury-free career.

Although the construction industry is much safer today than in the past, more than 2,000 people are injured and around 50 are killed on site every year. Many others suffer from long-term ill-health such as deafness, spinal damage, skin conditions or breathing problems.

Key health and safety legislation

Laws have been created in the UK to try to ensure safety at work. Ignoring the rules can mean injury or damage to health. It can also mean losing your job or being taken to court.

The two main laws are the Health and Safety at Work etc. Act **(HASAWA)** and the Control of Substances Hazardous to Health Regulations **(COSHH)**.

The Health and Safety at Work etc. Act (HASAWA) (1974)

This law applies to all working environments and to all types of worker, sub-contractor, employer and all visitors to the workplace. It places a duty on everyone to follow rules in order to ensure health, safety and welfare. Businesses must manage health and safety risks, for example by providing appropriate training and facilities. The Act also covers first aid, accidents and ill health.

Reporting of Injuries, Diseases and Dangerous Occurrences Regulations (RIDDOR) (1995)

Under RIDDOR, employers are required to report any injuries, diseases or dangerous occurrences to the **Health and Safety Executive (HSE)**. The regulations also state the need to maintain an **accident book**.

Control of Substances Hazardous to Health (COSHH) (2002)

In construction, it is common to be exposed to substances that could cause ill health. For example, you may use oil-based paints or preservatives, or work in conditions where there is dust or bacteria.

Employers need to protect their employees from the risks associated with using hazardous substances. This means assessing the risks and deciding on the necessary precautions to take.

Any control measures (things that are being done to reduce the risk of people being hurt or becoming ill) have to be introduced into the workplace and maintained; this includes monitoring an employee's exposure to harmful substances. The employer will need to carry out health checks and ensure that employees are made aware of the dangers and are supervised.

Control of Asbestos at Work Regulations (2012)

Asbestos was a popular building material in the past because it was a good insulator, had good fire protection properties and also protected metals against corrosion. Any building that was constructed before 2000 is likely to have some asbestos. It can be found in pipe insulation, boilers and ceiling tiles. There is also asbestos cement roof sheeting and there is a small amount of asbestos in decorative coatings such as Artex.

Asbestos has been linked with lung cancer, other damage to the lungs and breathing problems. The regulations require you and your employer to take care when dealing with asbestos:

* You should always assume that materials contain asbestos unless it is obvious that they do not.

* A record of the location and condition of asbestos should be kept.

* A risk assessment should be carried out if there is a chance that anyone will be exposed to asbestos.

The general advice is as follows:

* Do not remove the asbestos. It is not a hazard unless it is removed or damaged.

* Remember that not all asbestos presents the same risk. Asbestos cement is less dangerous than pipe insulation.

* Call in a specialist if you are uncertain.

Provision and Use of Work Equipment Regulations (PUWER) (1998)

PUWER concerns health and safety risks related to equipment used at work. It states that any risks arising from the use of equipment must either be prevented or controlled, and all suitable safety measures must have been taken. In addition, tools need to be:

* suitable for their intended use

* safe

* well maintained

* used only by those who have been trained to do so.

Manual Handling Operations Regulations (1992)

These regulations try to control the risk of injury when lifting or handling bulky or heavy equipment and materials. The regulations state as follows:

* Hazardous manual handling should be avoided if possible.

* An assessment of hazardous manual handling should be made to try to find alternatives.

* You should use mechanical assistance where possible.

* The main idea is to look at how manual handling is carried out and finding safer ways of doing it.

Personal Protection at Work Regulations (PPE) (1992)

This law states that employers must provide employees with personal protective equipment **(PPE)** at work whenever there is a risk to health and safety. PPE needs to be:

* suitable for the work being done

* well maintained and replaced if damaged

* properly stored

* correctly used (which means employees need to be trained in how to use the PPE properly).

Work at Height Regulations (2005)

Whenever a person works at any height there is a risk that they could fall and injure themselves. The regulations place a duty on employers or anyone who controls the work of others. This means that they need to:

* plan and organise the work

* make sure those working at height are **competent**

* assess the risks and provide appropriate equipment

* manage work near or on fragile surfaces

* ensure equipment is inspected and maintained.

In all cases the regulations suggest that, if it is possible, work at height should be avoided. Perhaps the job could be done from ground level? If it is not possible, then equipment and other measures are needed to prevent the risk of falling. When working at height measures also need to be put in place to minimise the distance someone might fall.

KEY TERMS

PPE

– personal protective equipment can include gloves, goggles and hard hats.

Competent

– to be competent an organisation or individual must have:

* sufficient knowledge of the tasks to be undertaken and the risks involved

* the experience and ability to carry out their duties in relation to the project, to recognise their limitations and take appropriate action to prevent harm to those carrying out construction work, or those affected by the work.

(*Source* HSE)

Figure 1.1 Examples of personal protective equipment

Employer responsibilities under HASAWA

HASAWA states that employers with five or more staff need their own health and safety policy. Employers must assess any risks that may be involved in their workplace and then introduce controls to reduce these risks. These risk assessments need to be reviewed regularly.

Employers also need to supply personal protective equipment (PPE) to all employees when it is needed and to ensure that it is worn when required.

Specific employer responsibilities are outlined in Table 1.1.

Employee responsibilities under HASAWA

HASAWA states that all those operating in the workplace must aim to work in a safe way. For example, they must wear any PPE provided and look after their equipment. Employees should not be charged for PPE or any actions that the employer needs to take to ensure safety.

Specific employer responsibilities are outlined in Table 1.1. Table 1.2 identifies the key employee responsibilities.

KEY TERMS

Risk

– the likelihood that a person may be harmed if they are exposed to a hazard.

Hazard

– a potential source of harm, injury or ill-health.

Near miss

– any incident, accident or emergency that did not result in an injury but could have done so.

Employer responsibility	Explanation
Safe working environment	Where possible all potential risks and hazards should be eliminated.
Adequate staff training	When new employees begin a job their induction should cover health and safety. There should be ongoing training for existing employees on risks and control measures.
Health and safety information	Relevant information related to health and safety should be available for employees to read and have their own copies.
Risk assessment	Each task or job should be investigated and potential risks identified so that measures can be put in place. A risk assessment and method statement should be produced. The method statement will tell you how to carry out the task, what PPE to wear, equipment to use and the sequence of its use.
Supervision	A competent and experienced individual should always be available to help ensure that health and safety problems are avoided.

Table 1.1 Employer responsibilities under HASAWA

Employee responsibility	Explanation
Working safely	Employees should take care of themselves, only do work that they are competent to carry out and remove obvious hazards if they are seen.
Working in partnership with the employer	Co-operation is important and you should never interfere with or misuse any health and safety signs or equipment. You should always follow the site rules.
Reporting hazards, near misses and accidents correctly	Any health and safety problems should be reported and discussed, particularly a near miss or an actual accident.

Table 1.2 Employee responsibilities under HASAWA

Improvement notice

– this is issued by the HSE if a health or safety issue is found and gives the employer a time limit to make changes to improve health and safety.

Prohibition notice

– this is issued by the HSE if a health or safety issue involving the risk of serious personal injury is found and stops all work until the improvements to health and safety have been made.

Sub-contractor

– an individual or group of workers who are directly employed by the main contractor to undertake specific parts of the work.

Health and Safety Executive

The Health and Safety Executive (HSE) is responsible for health, safety and welfare. It carries out spot checks on different workplaces to make sure that the law is being followed.

HSE inspectors have access to all areas of a construction site and can also bring in the police. If they find a problem then they can issue an **improvement notice**. This gives the employer a limited amount of time to put things right.

In serious cases, the HSE can issue a **prohibition notice**. This means all work has to stop until the problem is dealt with. An employer, the employees or **sub-contractors** could be taken to court.

The roles and responsibilities of the HSE are outlined in Table 1.3.

Responsibility	Explanation
Enforcement	It is the HSE's responsibility to reduce work-related death, injury and ill health. It will use the law against those who put others at risk.
Legislation and advice	The HSE will use health and safety legislation to serve improvement or prohibition notices or even to prosecute those who break health and safety rules. Inspectors will provide advice either face-to-face or in writing on health and safety matters.
Inspection	The HSE will look at site conditions, standards and practices and inspect documents to make sure that businesses and individuals are complying with health and safety law.

Table 1.3 HSE roles and responsibilities

Sources of health and safety information

There is a wide variety of health and safety information. Most of it is available free of charge, while other organisations may make a charge to provide information and advice. Table 1.4 outlines the key sources of health and safety information.

Source	Types of information	Website
Health and Safety Executive (HSE)	The HSE is the primary source of work-related health and safety information. It covers all possible topics and industries.	www.hse.gov.uk
Construction Industry Training Board (CITB)	The national training organisation provides key information on legislation and site safety.	www.citb.co.uk
British Standards Institute (BSI)	Provides guidelines for risk management, PPE, fire hazards and many other health and safety-related areas.	www.bsigroup.com
Royal Society for the Prevention of Accidents (RoSPA)	Provides training, consultancy and advice on a wide range of health and safety issues that are aimed to reduce work related accidents and ill health.	www.rospa.com
Royal Society for Public Health (RSPH)	Has a range of qualifications and training programmes focusing on health and safety.	www.rsph.org.uk

Table 1.4 Health and safety information

Informing the HSE

The HSE requires the reporting of:

* deaths and injuries – any **major injury**, **over 7-day injury** or death

* occupational disease

* dangerous occurrence – a collapse, explosion, fire or collision

* gas accidents – any accidental leaks or other incident related to gas.

Enforcing guidance

Work-related injuries and illnesses affect huge numbers of people. According to the HSE, 1.1 million working people in the UK suffered from a work-related illness in 2011 to 2012. Across all industries, 173 workers were killed, 111,000 other injuries were reported and 27 million working days were lost.

The construction industry is a high risk one and, although only around 5 per cent of the working population is in construction, it accounts for 10 per cent of all major injuries and 22 per cent of fatal injuries.

The good news is that enforcing guidance on health and safety has driven down the numbers of injuries and deaths in the industry. Only 20 years ago over 120 construction workers died in workplace accidents each year. This is now reduced to fewer than 60 a year.

However, there is still more work to be done and it is vital that organisations such as the HSE continue to enforce health and safety and continue to reduce risks in the industry.

On-site safety inductions and toolbox talks

The HSE suggests that all new workers arriving on site should attend a short induction session on health and safety. It should:

* show the commitment of the company to health and safety

* explain the health and safety policy

* explain the roles individuals play in the policy

* state that each individual has a legal duty to contribute to safe working

* cover issues like excavations, work at height, electricity and fire risk

* provide a layout of the site and show evacuation routes

* identify where fire fighting equipment is located

* ensure that all employees have evidence of their skills

* stress the importance of signing in and out of the site.

KEY TERMS

Major injury

– any fractures, amputations, dislocations, loss of sight or other severe injury.

Over 7-day injury

– an injury that has kept someone off work for more than seven days.

DID YOU KNOW?

Workplace injuries cost the UK £13.4bn in 2010 to 2011.

Behaviour and actions that could affect others

It is the responsibility of everyone on site not only to look after their own health and safety, but also to ensure that their actions do not put anyone else at risk.

Trying to carry out work that you are not competent to do is not only dangerous to yourself but could compromise the safety of others.

Simple actions, such as ensuring that all of your rubbish and waste is properly disposed of, will go a long way to removing hazards on site that could affect others.

Just as you should not create a hazard, ignoring an obvious one is just as dangerous. You should always obey site rules and particularly the health and safety rules. You should follow any instructions you are given.

ACCIDENT AND EMERGENCY PROCEDURES

All sites will have specific procedures for dealing with accidents and emergencies. An emergency will often mean that the site needs to be evacuated, so you should know in advance where to assemble and who to report to. The site should never be re-entered without authorisation from an individual in charge or the emergency services.

Types of emergencies

Emergencies are incidents that require immediate action. They can include:

* fires
* spillages or leaks of chemicals or other hazardous substances, such as gas
* failure of a scaffold
* collapse of a wall or trench
* a health problem
* an injury
* bombs and security alerts.

Legislation and reporting accidents

RIDDOR (1995) puts a duty on employers, anyone who is self-employed, or an individual in control of the work, to report any serious workplace accidents, occupational diseases or dangerous occurrences (also known as near misses).

The report has to be made by these individuals and, if it is serious enough, the responsible person may have to fill out a RIDDOR report.

Figure 1.2 It's important that you know where your company's fire-fighting equipment is located

Injuries, diseases and dangerous occurrences

Construction sites can be dangerous places, as we have seen. The HSE maintains a list of all possible injuries, diseases and dangerous occurrences, particularly those that need to be reported.

Injuries

There are two main classifications of injuries: minor and major. A minor injury can usually be handled by a competent first aider, although it is often a good idea to refer the individual to their doctor or to the hospital. Typical minor injuries can include:

* minor cuts   * minor burns   * exposure to fumes.

Major injuries are more dangerous and will usually require the presence of an ambulance with paramedics. Major injuries can include:

* bone fracture   * concussion

* unconsciousness   * electric shock.

Diseases

There are several different diseases and health issues that have to be reported, particularly if a doctor notifies that a disease has been diagnosed. These include:

* poisoning   * infections

* skin diseases   * occupational cancer

* lung diseases   * hand/arm vibration syndrome.

Dangerous occurrences

Even if something happens that does not result in an injury, but could easily have done so, it is classed as a dangerous occurrence. It needs to be reported immediately and then followed up by an accident report form. Dangerous occurrences can include:

* accidental release of a substance that could damage health

* anything coming into contact with overhead power lines

* an electrical problem that caused a fire or explosion

* collapse or partial collapse of scaffolding over 5 m high.

> **PRACTICAL TIP**
>
> An up-to-date list of dangerous occurrences is maintained by the Health and Safety Executive.

Recording accidents and emergencies

The Reporting of Injuries, Diseases and Dangerous Occurrences Regulations (RIDDOR) (1995) requires employers to:

* report any relevant injuries, diseases or dangerous occurrences to the Health and Safety Executive (HSE)

* keep records of incidents in a formal and organised manner (for example, in an accident book or online database).

After an accident, you may need to complete an accident report form – either in writing or online. This form may be completed by the person who was injured or the first aider.

On the accident report form you need to note down:

* the casualty's personal details, e.g. name, address, occupation

* the name of the person filling in the report form

* the details of the accident.

In addition, the person reporting the accident will need to sign the form.

On site a trained first aider will be the first individual to try and deal with the situation. In addition to trying to save life, stop the condition from getting worse and getting help, they will also record the occurrence.

On larger sites there will be a health and safety officer, who would keep records and documentation detailing any accidents and emergencies that have taken place on site. All companies should keep such records; it may be a legal requirement for them to do so under RIDDOR and it is good practice to do so in case the HSE asks to see it.

Importance of reporting accidents and near misses

Reporting incidents is not just about complying with the law or providing information for statistics. Each time an accident or near miss takes place it means lessons can be learned and future problems avoided.

The accident or near miss can alert the business or organisation to a potential problem. They can then take steps to ensure that it does not occur in the future.

Major and minor injuries and near misses

RIDDOR defines a major injury as:

* a fracture (but not to a finger, thumb or toes)

* a dislocation

* an amputation

* a loss of sight in an eye

* a chemical or hot metal burn to the eye

* a penetrating injury to the eye

* an electric shock or electric burn leading to unconsciousness and/or requiring resuscitation

* hyperthermia, heat-induced illness or unconsciousness

* asphyxia

* exposure to a harmful substance

* inhalation of a substance

* acute illness after exposure to toxins or infected materials.

A minor injury could be considered as any occurrence that does not fall into any of the above categories.

A near miss is any incident that did not actually result in an injury but which could have caused a major injury if it had done so. Non-reportable near misses are useful to record as they can help to identify potential problems. Looking at a list of near misses might show patterns for potential risk.

Accident trends

We have already seen that the HSE maintains statistics on the number and types of construction accidents. The following are among the 2011/2012 construction statistics:

* There were 49 fatalities.

* There were 5,000 occupational cancer patients.

* There were 74,000 cases of work-related ill health.

* The most common types of injury were caused by falls, although many injuries were caused by falling objects, collapses and electricity. A number of construction workers were also hurt when they slipped or tripped, or were injured while lifting heavy objects.

Accidents, emergencies and the employer

Even less serious accidents and injuries can cost a business a great deal of money. But there are other costs too:

* Poor company image – if a business does not have health and safety controls in place then it may get a reputation for not caring about its employees. The number of accidents and injuries may be far higher than average.

* Loss of production – the injured individual might have to be treated and then may need a period of time off work to recover. The loss of production can include those who have to take time out from working to help the injured person and the time of a manager or supervisor who has to deal with all the paperwork and problems.

* Insurance – each time there is an accident or injury claim against the company's insurance the premiums will go up. If there are many accidents and injuries the business may find it impossible to get insurance. It is a legal requirement for a business to have insurance so in the end that company might have to close down.

* Closure of site – if there is a serious accident or injury then the site may have to be closed while investigations take place to discover the reason, or who was responsible. This could cause serious delays and loss of income for workers and the business.

DID YOU KNOW?

RoSPA (the Royal Society for the Prevention of Accidents) uses many of the statistics from the HSE. The latest figures that RoSPA has analysed date back to 2008/2009. In that year, 1.2 million people in the UK were suffering from work-related illnesses. With fewer than 132,000 reportable injuries at work, this is believed to be around half of the real figure.

DID YOU KNOW?

An employee working in a small business broke two bones in his arm. He could not return to proper duties for eight months. He lost out on wages while he was off sick and, in total, it cost the business over £45,000.

REED TIP

On some construction sites, you may get a Health and Safety Inspector come to look round without any notice – one more reason to always be thinking about working safely.

Accident and emergency authorised personnel

Several different groups of people could be involved in dealing with accident and emergency situations. These are listed in Table 1.5.

Authorised personnel	Role
First aiders and emergency responders	These are employees on site and in the workforce who have been trained to be the first to respond to accidents and injuries. The minimum provision of an appointed person would be someone who has had basic first aid training. The appointment of a first aider is someone who has attained a higher or specific level of training. A construction site with fewer than 5 employees needs an appointed first aider. A construction site with up to 50 employees requires a trained first aider, and for bigger sites at least one trained first aider is required for every 50 people.
Supervisors and managers	These have the responsibility of managing the site and would have to organise the response and contact emergency services if necessary. They would also ensure that records of any accidents are completed and up to date and notify the HSE if required.
Health and Safety Executive	The HSE requires businesses to investigate all accidents and emergencies. The HSE may send an inspector, or even a team, to investigate and take action if the law has been broken.
Emergency services	Calling the emergency services depends on the seriousness of the accident. Paramedics will take charge of the situation if there is a serious injury and if they feel it necessary will take the individual to hospital.

Table 1.5 People who deal with accident and emergency situations

The basic first aid kit

BS 8599 relates to first aid kits, but it is not legally binding. The contents of a first aid box will depend on an employer's assessment of their likely needs. The HSE does not have to approve the contents of a first aid box but it states that where the work involves low level hazards the minimum contents of a first aid box should be:

* a copy of its leaflet on first aid – *HSE Basic advice on first aid at work*

* 20 sterile plasters of assorted size

* 2 sterile eye pads

* 4 sterile triangular bandages

* 6 safety pins

* 2 large sterile, unmedicated wound dressings

* 6 medium-sized sterile unmedicated wound dressings

* 1 pair of disposable gloves.

The HSE also recommends that no tablets or medicines are kept in the first aid box.

Figure 1.3 A typical first aid box

What to do if you discover an accident

When an accident happens it may not only injure the person involved directly, but it may also create a hazard that could then injure others. You need to make sure that the area is safe enough for you or someone else to help the injured person. It may be necessary to turn off the electrical supply or remove obstructions to the site of the accident.

The first thing that needs to be done if there is an accident is to raise the alarm. This could mean:

* calling for the first aider

* phoning for the emergency services

* dealing with the problem yourself.

How you respond will depend on the severity of the injury.

You should follow this procedure if you need to contact the emergency services:

* Find a telephone away from the emergency.

* Dial 999.

* You may have to go through a switchboard. Carefully listen to what the operator is saying to you and try to stay calm.

* When asked, give the operator your name and location, and the name of the emergency service or services you require.

* You will then be transferred to the appropriate emergency service, who will ask you questions about the accident and its location. Answer the questions in a clear and calm way.

* Once the call is over, make sure someone is available to help direct the emergency services to the location of the accident.

IDENTIFYING HAZARDS

As we have already seen, construction sites are potentially dangerous places. The most effective way of handling health and safety on a construction site is to spot the hazards and deal with them before they can cause an accident or an injury. This begins with basic housekeeping and carrying out risk assessments. It also means having a procedure in place to report hazards so that they can be dealt with.

Good housekeeping

Work areas should always be clean and tidy. Sites that are messy, strewn with materials, equipment, wires and other hazards can prove to be very dangerous. You should:

* always work in a tidy way

* never block fire exits or emergency escape routes

* never leave nails and screws scattered around

* ensure you clean and sweep up at the end of each working day

* not block walkways

* never overfill skips or bins

* never leave food waste on site.

Risk assessments and method statements

It is a legal requirement for employers to carry out risk assessments. This covers not only those who are actually working on a particular job, but other workers in the immediate area, and others who might be affected by the work.

It is important to remember that when you are carrying out work your actions may affect the safety of other people. It is important, therefore, to know whether there are any potential hazards. Once you know what these hazards are you can do something to either prevent or reduce them as a risk. Every job has potential hazards.

There are five simple steps to carrying out a risk assessment, which are shown in Table 1.6, using the example of repointing brickwork on the front face of a dwelling.

Step	Action	Example
1	Identify hazards	The property is on a street with a narrow pavement. The damaged brickwork and loose mortar need to be removed and placed in a skip below. Scaffolding has been erected. The road is not closed to traffic.
2	Identify who is at risk	The workers repointing are at risk as they are working at height. Pedestrians and vehicles passing are at risk from the positioning of the skip and the chance that debris could fall from height.
3	What is the risk from the hazard that may cause an accident?	The risk to the workers is relatively low as they have PPE and the scaffolding has been correctly erected. The risk to those passing by is higher, as they are unaware of the work being carried out above them.
4	Measures to be taken to reduce the risk	Station someone near the skip to direct pedestrians and vehicles away from the skip while the work is being carried out. Fix a secure barrier to the edge of the scaffolding to reduce the chance of debris falling down. Lower the bricks and mortar debris using a bucket or bag into the skip and not throwing them from the scaffolding. Consider carrying out the work when there are fewer pedestrians and less traffic on the road.
5	Monitor the risk	If there are problems with the first stages of the job, you need to take steps to solve them. If necessary consider taking the debris by hand through the building after removal.

Table 1.6 A five-step risk assessment for repointing brickwork

Your employer should follow these working practices, which can help to prevent accidents or dangerous situations occurring in the workplace:

* *Risk assessments* look carefully at what could cause an individual harm and how to prevent this. This is to ensure that no one should be injured or become ill as a result of their work. Risk assessments identify how likely it is that an accident might happen and the consequences of it happening. A risk factor is worked out and control measures created to try to offset them.

* *Method statements,* however brief, should be available for every risk assessment. They summarise risk assessments and other findings to provide guidance on how the work should be carried out.

* *Permit to work systems* are used for very high risk or even potentially fatal activities. They are checklists that need to be completed before the work begins. They must be signed by a supervisor.

* *A hazard book* lists standard tasks and identifies common hazards. These are useful tools to help quickly identify hazards related to particular tasks.

Types of hazards

Typical construction accidents can include:

* fires and explosions

* slips, trips and falls.

* burns, including those from chemicals

* falls from scaffolding, ladders and roofs

* electrocution

* injury from faulty machinery

* power tool accidents

* being hit by construction debris

* falling through holes in flooring

We will look at some of the more common hazards in a little more detail.

Fires
Fires need oxygen, heat and fuel to burn. Even a spark can provide enough heat needed to start a fire, and anything flammable, such as petrol, paper or wood, provides the fuel. It may help to remember the 'triangle of fire' – heat, oxygen and fuel are all needed to make fire so remove one or more to help prevent or stop the fire.

Tripping

Leaving equipment and materials lying around can cause accidents, as can trailing cables and spilt water or oil. Some of these materials are also potential fire hazards.

Chemical spills

If the chemicals are not hazardous then they just need to be mopped up. But sometimes they do involve hazardous materials and there will be an existing plan on how to deal with them. A risk assessment will have been carried out.

Falls from height

A fall even from a low height can cause serious injuries. Precautions need to be taken when working at height to avoid permanent injury. You should also consider falls into open excavations as falls from height. All the same precautions need to be in place to prevent a fall.

Burns

Burns can be caused not only by fires and heat, but also from chemicals and solvents. Electricity and wet concrete and cement can also burn skin. PPE is often the best way to avoid these dangers. Sunburn is a common and uncomfortable form of burning and sunscreen should be made available. For example, keeping skin covered up will help to prevent sunburn. You might think a tan looks good, but it could lead to skin cancer.

Electrical

Electricity is hazardous and electric shocks can cause burns and muscle damage, and can kill.

Exposure to hazardous substances

We look at hazardous substances in more detail on pages 20–1. COSHH regulations identify hazardous substances and require them to be labelled. You should always follow the instructions when using them.

Plant and vehicles

On busy sites there is always a danger from moving vehicles and heavy plant. Although many are fitted with reversing alarms, it may not be easy to hear them over other machinery and equipment. You should always ensure you are not blocking routes or exits. Designated walkways separate site traffic and pedestrians – this includes workers who are walking around the site. Crossing points should be in place for ease of movement on site.

Reporting hazards

We have already seen that hazards have the potential to cause serious accidents and injuries. It is therefore important to report hazards and there are different methods of doing this.

The first major reason to report hazards is to prevent danger to others, whether they are other employees or visitors to the site. It is vital to prevent accidents from taking place and to quickly correct any dangerous situations.

Injuries, diseases and actual accidents all need to be reported and so do dangerous occurrences. These are incidents that do not result in an actual injury, but could easily have hurt someone.

Accidents need to be recorded in an accident book, computer database or other secure recording system, as do near misses. Again it is a legal requirement to keep appropriate records of accidents and every company will have a procedure for this which they should tell you about. Everyone should know where the book is kept or how the records are made. Anyone that has been hurt or has taken part in dealing with an occurrence should complete the details of what has happened. Typically this will require you to fill in:

* the date, time and place of the incident

* how it happened

* what was the cause

* how it was dealt with

* who was involved

* signature and date.

The details in the book have to be transferred onto an official HSE report form.

As far as is possible, the site, company or workplace will have set procedures in place for reporting hazards and accidents. These procedures will usually be found in the place where the accident book or records are stored. The location tends to be posted on the site notice board.

How hazards are created

Construction sites are busy places. There are constantly new stages in development. As each stage is begun a whole new set of potential hazards need to be considered.

At the same time, new workers will always be joining the site. It is mandatory for them to be given health and safety instruction during induction. But sometimes this is impossible due to pressure of work or availability of trainers.

Construction sites can become even more hazardous in times of extreme weather:

* Flooding – long periods of rain can cause trenches to fill with water, cellars to be flooded and smooth surfaces to become extremely wet and slippery.

* Wind – strong winds may prevent all work at height. Scaffolding may have become unstable, unsecured roofing materials may come loose, dry-stored materials such as sand and cement may have been blown across the site.

* Heat – this can change the behaviour of materials: setting quicker, failing to cure and melting. It can also seriously affect the health of the workforce through dehydration and heat exhaustion.

* Snow – this can add enormous weight to roofs and other structures and could cause collapse. Snow can also prevent access or block exits and can mean that simple and routine work becomes impossible due to frozen conditions.

Storing combustibles and chemicals

A combustible substance can be both flammable and explosive. There are some basic suggestions from the HSE about storing these:

* Ventilation – the area should be well ventilated to disperse any vapours that could trigger off an explosion.

* Ignition – an ignition is any spark or flame that could trigger off the vapours, so materials should be stored away from any area that uses electrical equipment or any tool that heats up.

* Containment – the materials should always be kept in proper containers with lids and there should be spillage trays to prevent any leak seeping into other parts of the site.

* Exchange – in many cases it can be possible to find an alternative material that is less dangerous. This option should be taken if possible.

* Separation – always keep flammable substances away from general work areas. If possible they should be partitioned off.

Combustible materials can include a large number of commonly used substances, such as cleaning agents, paints and adhesives.

HEALTH AND HYGIENE

Just as hazards can be a major problem on site, other less obvious problems relating to health and hygiene can also be an issue. It is both your responsibility and that of your employer to make sure that you stay healthy.

The employer will need to provide basic welfare facilities, no matter where you are working and these must have minimum standards.

Welfare facilities

Welfare facilities can include a wide range of different considerations, as can be seen in Table 1.7.

Facilities	Purpose and minimum standards
Toilets	If there is a lock on the door there is no need to have separate male and female toilets. There should be enough for the site workforce. If there is no flushing water on site they must be chemical toilets.
Washing facilities	There should be a wash basin large enough to be able to wash up to the elbow. There should be soap, hot and cold water and, if you are working with dangerous substances, then showers are needed.
Drinking water	Clean drinking water should be available; either directly connected to the mains or bottled water. Employers must ensure that there is no **contamination.**
Dry room	This can operate also as a store room, which needs to be secure so that workers can leave their belongings there and also use it as a place to dry out if they have been working in wet weather, in which case a heater needs to be provided.
Work break area	This is a shelter out of the wind and rain, with a kettle, a microwave, tables and chairs. It should also have heating.

Table 1.7 Welfare facilities in the workplace

CASE STUDY

South Tyneside Homes

South Tyneside Council's Housing Company

Staying safe on site

Johnny McErlane finished his apprenticeship at South Tyneside Homes a year ago.

'I've been working on sheltered accommodation for the last year, so there are a lot of vulnerable and elderly people around. All the things I learnt at college from doing the health and safety exams comes into practice really, like taking care when using extension leads, wearing high-vis and correct footwear. It's not just about your health and safety, but looking out for others as well.

On the shelters, you can get a health and safety inspector who just comes around randomly, so you have to always be ready. It just becomes a habit once it's been drilled into you. You're health and safety conscious all the time.

The shelters also have a fire alarm drill every second Monday, so you've got to know the procedure involved there. When it comes to the more specialised skills, such as mouth-to-mouth and CPR, you might have a designated first aider on site who will have their skills refreshed regularly. Having a full first aid certificate would be valuable if you're working in construction.

You cover quite a bit of the first aid skills in college and you really have to know them because you're not always working on large sites. For example, you might be on the repairs team, working in people's houses where you wouldn't have a first aider, so you've got to have the basic knowledge yourself, just in case. All our vans have a basic first aid kit that's kept fully stocked.

The company keeps our knowledge current with these "toolbox talks", which are like refresher courses. They give you any new information that needs to be passed on to all the trades. It's a good way of keeping everyone up to date.'

Noise

Ear defenders are the best precaution to protect the ears from loud noises on site. Ear defenders are either basic ear plugs or ear muffs, which can be seen in Fig 1.13 on page 32.

The long-term impact of noise depends on the intensity and duration of the noise. Basically, the louder and longer the noise exposure, the more damage is caused. There are ways of dealing with this:

* Remove the source of the noise.

* Move the equipment away from those not directly working with it.

* Put the source of the noise into a soundproof area or cover it with soundproof material.

* Ask a supervisor if they can move all other employees away from that part of the site until the noise stops.

Substances hazardous to health

COSHH Regulations (see page 3) identify a wide variety of substances and materials that must be labelled in different ways.

Controlling the use of these substances is always difficult. Ideally, their use should be eliminated (stopped) or they should be replaced with something less harmful. Failing this, they should only be used in controlled or restricted areas. If none of this is possible then they should only be used in controlled situations.

If a hazardous situation occurs at work, then you should:

* ensure the area is made safe

* inform the supervisor, site manager, safety officer or other nominated person.

You will also need to report any potential hazards or near misses.

Personal hygiene

Construction sites can be dirty places to work. Some jobs will expose you to dust, chemicals or substances that can make contact with your skin or may stain your work clothing. It is good practice to wear suitable PPE as a first line of defence as chemicals can penetrate your skin. Whenever you have finished a job you should always wash your hands. This is certainly true before eating lunch or travelling home. It can be good practice to have dedicated work clothing, which should be washed regularly.

Always ensure you wash your hands and face and scrub your nails. This will prevent dirt, chemicals and other substances from contaminating your food and your home.

Make sure that you regularly wash your work clothing and either repair it or replace it if it becomes too worn or stained.

Health risks

The construction industry uses a wide variety of substances that could harm your health. You will also be carrying out work that could be a health risk to you, and you should always be aware that certain activities could cause long-term damage or even kill you if things go wrong. Unfortunately not all health risks are immediately obvious. It is important to make sure that from time to time you have health checks, particularly if you have been using hazardous substances. Table 1.8 outlines some potential health risks in a typical construction site.

KEY TERMS

Dermatitis

– this is an inflammation of the skin. The skin will become red and sore, particularly if you scratch the area. A GP should be consulted.

Leptospirosis

– this is also known as Weil's disease. It is spread by touching soil or water contaminated with the urine of wild animals infected with the leptospira bacteria. Symptoms are usually flu-like but in extreme cases it can cause organ failure.

Health risk	Potential future problems
Dust	The most dangerous potential dust is, of course, asbestos, which **should only be handled by specialists under controlled conditions**. But even brick dust and other fine particles can cause eye injuries, problems with breathing and even cancer.
Chemicals	Inhaling or swallowing dangerous chemicals could cause immediate, long-term damage to lungs and other internal organs. Skin problems include burns or skin can become very inflamed and sore. This is known as **dermatitis**.
Bacteria	Contact with waste water or soil could lead to a bacterial infection. The germs in the water or dirt could cause infection which will require treatment if they enter the body. The most extreme version is **leptospirosis**.
Heavy objects	Lifting heavy, bulky or awkward objects can lead to permanent back injuries that could require surgery. Heavy objects can also damage the muscles in all areas of the body.
Noise	Failure to wear ear defenders when you are exposed to loud noises can permanently affect your hearing. This could lead to deafness in the future.
Vibrating tools	Using machines that vibrate can cause a condition known as hand/arm vibration syndrome (HAVS) or vibration white finger, which is caused by injury to nerves and blood vessels. You will feel tingling that could lead to permanent numbness in the fingers and hands, as well as muscle weakness.
Cuts	Any open wound, no matter how small, leaves your body exposed to potential infections. Cuts should always be cleaned and covered, preferably with a waterproof dressing. The blood loss from deep cuts could make you feel faint and weak, which may be dangerous if you are working at height or operating machinery.
Sunlight	Most construction work involves working outside. There is a temptation to take advantage of hot weather and get a tan. But long-term exposure to sunshine means risking skin cancer so you should cover up and apply sun cream.
Head injuries	You should seek medical attention after any bump to the head. Severe head injuries could cause epilepsy, hearing problems, brain damage or death.

Table 1.8 Health risks in construction

HANDLING AND STORING MATERIALS AND EQUIPMENT

On a busy construction site it is often tempting not to even think about the potential dangers of handling equipment and materials. If something needs to be moved or collected you will just pick it up without any thought. It is also tempting just to drop your tools and other equipment when you have finished with them to deal with later. But abandoned equipment and tools can cause hazards both for you and for other people.

Safe lifting

Lifting or handling heavy or bulky items is a major cause of injuries on construction sites. So whenever you are dealing with a heavy load, it is important to carry out a basic risk assessment.

The first thing you need to do is to think about the job to be done and ask:

* Do I need to lift it manually or is there another way of getting the object to where I need it?

Consider any mechanical methods of transporting loads or picking up materials. If there really is no alternative, then ask yourself:

1. Do I need to bend or twist?

2. Does the object need to be lifted or put down from high up?

3. Does the object need to be carried a long way?

4. Does the object need to be pushed or pulled for a long distance?

5. Is the object likely to shift around while it is being moved?

If the answer to any of these questions is 'yes', you may need to adjust the way the task is done to make it safer.

Think about the object itself. Ask:

1. Is it just heavy or is it also bulky and an awkward shape?

2. How easy is it to get a good hand-hold on the object?

3. Is the object a single item or are there parts that might move around and shift the weight?

4. Is the object hot or does it have sharp edges?

Again, if you have answered 'yes' to any of these questions, then you need to take steps to address these issues.

It is also important to think about the working environment and where the lifting and carrying is taking place. Ask yourself:

1. Are the floors stable?

2. Are the surfaces slippery?

3. Will a lack of space restrict my movement?

4. Are there any steps or slopes?

5. What is the lighting like?

Before lifting and moving an object, think about the following:

* Check that your pathway is clear to where the load needs to be taken.

* Look at the product data sheet and assess the weight. If you think the object is too heavy or difficult to move then ask someone to help you. Alternatively, you may need to use a mechanical lifting device.

When you are ready to lift, gently raise the load. Take care to ensure the correct posture – you should have a straight back, with your elbows tucked in, your knees bent and your feet slightly apart.

Once you have picked up the load, move slowly towards your destination. When you get there, make sure that you do not drop the load but carefully place it down.

DID YOU KNOW?

Although many people regard the weight limit for lifting and/or moving heavy or awkward objects to be 20 kg, the HSE does not recommend safe weights. There are many things that will affect the ability of an individual to lift and carry particular objects and the risk that this creates, so manual handling should be avoided altogether where possible.

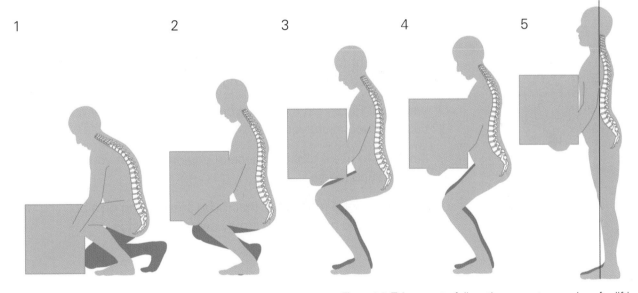

1   2   3   4   5

Figure 1.4 Take care to follow the correct procedure for lifting

Sack trolleys are useful for moving heavy and bulky items around. Gently slide the bottom of the sack trolley under the object and then raise the trolley to an angle of 45° before moving off. Make sure that the object is properly balanced and is not too big for the trolley.

Trailers and forklift trucks are often used on large construction sites, as are dump trucks. Never use these without proper training.

Figure 1.5 Pallet truck

Figure 1.6 Sack trolley

Site safety equipment

You should always read the construction site safety rules and when required wear your PPE. Simple things, such as wearing the right footwear for the right job, are important.

Safety equipment falls into two main categories:

* PPE – including hard hats, footwear, gloves, glasses and safety vests

* perimeter safety – this includes screens, netting and guards or clamps to prevent materials from falling or spreading.

Construction safety is also directed by signs, which will highlight potential hazards.

Safe handling of materials and equipment

All tools and equipment are potentially dangerous. It is up to you to make sure that they do not cause harm to yourself or others. You should always know how to use tools and equipment. This means either instruction from someone else who is experienced, or at least reading the manufacturer's instructions.

You should always make sure that you:

* use the right tool – don't be tempted to use a tool that is close to hand instead of the one that is right for the job

* wear your PPE – the one time you decide not to bother could be the time that you injure yourself

* never try to use a tool or a piece of equipment that you have not been trained to use.

You should always remember that if you are working on a building that was constructed before 2000 it may contain asbestos.

Correct storage

We have already seen that tools and equipment need to be treated with respect. Damaged tools and equipment are not only less effective at doing their job, they could also cause you to injure yourself.

Table 1.9 provides some pointers on how to store and handle different types of materials and equipment.

Materials and equipment	Safe storage and handling
Hand tools	Store hand tools with sharp edges either in a cover or a roll. They should be stored in bags or boxes. They should always be dried before putting them away as they will rust.
Power tools	Never carry them by the cable. Store them in their original carrying case. Always follow the manufacturer's instructions.
Wheelbarrows	Check the tyres and metal stays regularly. Always clean out after use and never overload.
Bricks and blocks	Never store more than two packs high. When cutting open a pack, be careful as the bricks could collapse.
Slabs and curbs	Store slabs flat on their edges on level ground, preferably with wood underneath to prevent damage. Store curbs the same way. To prevent weather damage, cover them with a sheet.
Tiles	Always cover them and protect them from damage as they are relatively fragile. Ideally store them in a hut or container.
Aggregates	Never store aggregates under trees as leaves will drop on them and contaminate them. Cover them with plastic sheets.
Plaster and plasterboard	Plaster needs to be kept dry, so even if stored inside you should take the precaution of putting the bags on pallets. To prevent moisture do not store against walls and do not pile higher than five bags. Plasterboard can be awkward to manage and move around. It also needs to be stored in a waterproof area. It should be stored flat and off the ground but should not be stored against walls as it may bend. Use a rotation system so that the materials are not stored in the same place for long periods.
Wood	Always keep wood in dry, well-ventilated conditions. If it needs to be stored outside it should be stored on bearers that may be on concrete. If wood gets wet and bends it is virtually useless. Always be careful when moving large cuts of wood or sheets of ply or MDF as they can easily become damaged.
Adhesives and paint	Always read the manufacturer's instructions. Ideally they should always be stored on clearly marked shelves. Make sure you rotate the stock using the older stock first. Always make sure that containers are tightly sealed. Storage areas must comply with fire regulations and display signs to advise of their contents.

Table 1.9 Safe storing and handling of materials and equipment

Waste control

The expectation within the building services industry is increasingly that working practices conserve energy and protect the environment. Everyone can play a part in this. For example, you can contribute by turning off hose pipes when you have finished using water, or not running electrical items when you don't need to.

Simple things, such as keeping construction sites neat and orderly, can go a long way to conserving energy and protecting the environment. A good way to remember this is Sort, Set, Shine, Standardise:

* Sort – sort and store items in your work area, eliminate clutter and manage deliveries.

* Set – everything should have its own place and be clearly marked and easy to access. In other words, be neat!

Figure 1.7 It's important to create as little waste as possible on the construction site

* Shine – clean your work area and you will be able to see potential problems far more easily.

* Standardise – by using standardised working practices you can keep organised, clean and safe.

Reducing waste is all about good working practice. By reducing wastage disposal, and recycling materials on site, you will benefit from savings on raw materials and lower transportation costs.

Planning ahead, and accurately measuring and cutting materials, means that you will be able to reduce wastage.

BASIC WORKING PLATFORMS AND ACCESS EQUIPMENT

Working at height should be eliminated or the work carried out using other methods where possible. However, there may be situations where you may need to work at height. These situations can include:

* roofing

* repair and maintenance above ground level

* working on high ceilings.

Any work at height must be carefully planned. Access equipment includes all types of ladder, scaffold and platform. You must always use a working platform that is safe. Sometimes a simple step ladder will be sufficient, but at other times you may have to use a tower scaffold.

Generally, ladders are fine for small, quick jobs of less than 30 minutes. However, for larger, longer jobs a more permanent piece of access equipment will be necessary.

Working platforms and access equipment: good practice and dangers of working at height

Table 1.10 outlines the common types of equipment used to allow you to work at heights, along with the basic safety checks necessary.

Equipment	Main features	Safety checks
Step ladder	Ideal for confined spaces. Four legs give stability	• Knee should remain below top of steps • Check hinges, cords or ropes • Position only to face work
Ladder	Ideal for basic access, short-term work. Made from aluminium, fibreglass or wood	• Check rungs, tie rods, repairs, and ropes and cords on stepladders • Ensure it is placed on firm, level ground • Angle should be no greater than 75° or 1 in 4
Mobile mini towers or scaffolds	These are usually aluminium and foldable, with lockable wheels	• Ensure the ground is even and the wheels are locked • Never move the platform while it has tools, equipment or people on it
Roof ladders and crawling boards	The roof ladder allows access while crawling boards provide a safe passage over tiles	• The ladder needs to be long enough and supported • Check boards are in good condition • Check the welds are intact • Ensure all clips function correctly
Mobile tower scaffolds	These larger versions of mini towers usually have edge protection	• Ensure the ground is even and the wheels are locked • Never move the platform while it has tools, equipment or people on it • Base width to height ratio should be no greater than 1:3
Fixed scaffolds and edge protection	Scaffolds fitted and sized to the specific job, with edge protection and guard rails	• There needs to be sufficient braces, guard rails and scaffold boards • The tubes should be level • There should be proper access using a ladder
Mobile elevated work platforms	Known as scissor lifts or cherry pickers	• Specialist training is required before use • Use guard rails and toe boards • Care needs to be taken to avoid overhead hazards such as cables

Table 1.10 Equipment for working at height and safety checks

You must be trained in the use of certain types of access equipment, like mobile scaffolds. Care needs to be taken when assembling and using access equipment. These are all examples of good practice:

* Step ladders should always rest firmly on the ground. Only use the top step if the ladder is part of a platform.

* Do not rest ladders against fragile surfaces, and always use both hands to climb. It is best if the ladder is steadied (footed) by someone at the foot of the ladder. Always maintain three points of contact – two feet and one hand.

* A roof ladder is positioned by turning it on its wheels and pushing it up the roof. It then hooks over the ridge tiles. Ensure that the access ladder to the roof is directly beside the roof ladder.

* A mobile scaffold is put together by slotting sections until the required height is reached. The working platform needs to have a suitable edge protection such as guard-rails and toe-boards. Always push from the bottom of the base and not from the top to move it, otherwise it may lean or topple over.

Figure 1.8 A tower scaffold

WORKING SAFELY WITH ELECTRICITY

It is essential whenever you work with electricity that you are competent and that you understand the common dangers. Electrical tools must be used in a safe manner on site. There are precautions that you can take to prevent possible injury, or even death.

Precautions

Whether you are using electrical tools or equipment on site, you should always remember the following:

* Use the right tool for the job.

* Use a transformer with equipment that runs on 110V.

* Keep the two voltages separate from each other. You should avoid using 230V where possible but, if you must, use a residual current device (RCD) if you have to use 230V.

* When using 110V, ensure that leads are yellow in colour.

* Check the plug is in good order.

* Confirm that the fuse is the correct rating for the equipment.

* Check the cable (including making sure that it does not present a tripping hazard).

* Find out where the mains switch is, in case you need to turn off the power in the event of an emergency.

* Never attempt to repair electrical equipment yourself.

* Disconnect from the mains power before making adjustments, such as changing a drill bit.

* Make sure that the electrical equipment has a sticker that displays a recent test date.

Visual inspection and testing is a three-stage process:

1. The user should check for potential danger signs, such as a frayed cable or cracked plug.

2. A formal visual inspection should then take place. If this is done correctly then most faults can be detected.

3. Combined inspections and **PAT** should take place at regular intervals by a competent person.

Watch out for the following causes of accidents – they would also fail a safety check:

* damage to the power cable or plug

* taped joints on the cable

* wet or rusty tools and equipment

* weak external casing

* loose parts or screws

* signs of overheating

* the incorrect fuse

* lack of cord grip

* electrical wires attached to incorrect terminals

* bare wires.

When preparing to work on an electrical circuit, do not start until a permit to work has been issued by a supervisor or manager to a competent person.

Make sure the circuit is broken before you begin. A 'dead' circuit will not cause you, or anybody else, harm. These steps must be followed:

* Switch off – ensure the supply to the circuit is switched off by disconnecting the supply cables or using an isolating switch.

* Isolate – disconnect the power cables or use an isolating switch.

* Warn others – to avoid someone reconnecting the circuit, place warning signs at the isolation point.

* Lock off – this step physically prevents others from reconnecting the circuit.

* Testing – is carried out by electricians but you should be aware that it involves three parts:

  1. testing a voltmeter on a known good source (a live circuit) so you know it is working properly

  2. checking that the circuit to be worked on is dead

  3. rechecking your voltmeter on the known live source, to prove that it is still working properly.

It is important to make sure that the correct point of isolation is identified. Isolation can be next to a local isolation device, such as a plug or socket, or a circuit breaker or fuse.

The isolation should be locked off using a unique key or combination. This will prevent access to a main isolator until the work has been completed. Alternatively, the handle can be made detachable in the OFF position so that it can be physically removed once the circuit is switched off.

Dangers

You are likely to encounter a number of potential dangers when working with electricity on construction sites or in private houses. Table 1.11 outlines the most common dangers.

Danger	Identifying the danger
Faulty electrical equipment	Visually inspect for signs of damage. Equipment should be double insulated or incorporate an earth cable.
Damaged or worn cables	Check for signs of wear or damage regularly. This includes checking power tools and any wiring in the property.
Trailing cables	Cables lying on the ground, or worse, stretched too far, can present a tripping hazard. They could also be cut or damaged easily.
Cables and pipe work	Always treat services you find as though they are live. This is very important as services can be mistaken for one another. You may have been trained to use a cable and pipe locator that finds cables and metal pipes.
Buried or hidden cables	Make sure you have plans. Alternatively, use a cable and pipe locator, mark the positions, look out for signs of service connection cables or pipes and hand-dig trial holes to confirm positions.
Inadequate over-current protection	Check circuit breakers and fuses are the correct size current rating for the circuit. A qualified electrician may have to identify and label these.

Table 1.11 Common dangers when working with electricity

Each year there are around 1,000 accidents at work involving electric shocks or burns from electricity. If you are working in a construction site you are part of a group that is most at risk. Electrical accidents happen when you are working close to equipment that you think is disconnected but which is, in fact, live.

Another major danger is when electrical equipment is either misused or is faulty. Electricity can cause fires and contact with the live parts can give you an electric shock or burn you.

Different voltages

The two most common voltages that are used in the UK are 230V and 110V:

* 230V: this is the standard domestic voltage. But on construction sites it is considered to be unsafe and therefore 110V is commonly used.

* 110V: these plugs are marked with a yellow casement and they have a different shaped plug. A transformer is required to convert 230V to 110V.

Some larger homes, as well as industrial and commercial buildings, may have 415V supplies. This is the same voltage that is found on overhead electricity cables. In most houses and other buildings the voltage from these cables is reduced to 230V. This is what most electrical equipment works from. Some larger machinery actually needs 415V.

In these buildings the 415V comes into the building and then can either be used directly or it is reduced so that normal 230V appliances can be used.

Colour coded cables

Normally you will come across three differently coloured wires: Live, Neutral and Earth. These have standard colours that comply with European safety standards and to ensure that they are easily identifiable. However, in some older buildings the colours are different.

Wire type	Modern colour	Older colour
Live	Brown	Red
Neutral	Blue	Black
Earth	Yellow and Green	Yellow and Green

Table 1.12 Colour coding of cables

Working with equipment with different electrical voltages

You should always check that the electrical equipment that you are going to use is suitable for the available electrical supply. The equipment's power requirements are shown on its rating plate. The voltage from the supply needs to match the voltage that is required by the equipment.

Storing electrical equipment

Electrical equipment should be stored in dry and secure conditions. Electrical equipment should never get wet but – if it does happen – it should be dried before storage. You should always clean and adjust the equipment before connecting it to the electricity supply.

PERSONAL PROTECTIVE EQUIPMENT (PPE)

Personal protective equipment, or PPE, is a general term that is used to describe a variety of different types of clothing and equipment that aim to help protect against injuries or accidents. Some PPE you will use on a daily basis and others you may use from time to time. The type of PPE you wear depends on what you are doing and where you are. For example, the practical exercises in this book were photographed at a college, which has rules and requirements for PPE that are different to those on large construction sites. Follow your tutor's or employer's instructions at all times.

Types of PPE

PPE literally covers from head to foot. Here are the main PPE types.

Figure 1.9 A hi-vis jacket

Figure 1.10 Safety glasses and goggles

Figure 1.11 Hand protection

Figure 1.12 Head protection

Figure 1.13 Hearing protection

Protective clothing

Clothing protection such as overalls:

* provides some protection from spills, dust and irritants
* can help protect you from minor cuts and abrasions
* reduces wear to work clothing underneath.

Sometimes you may need waterproof or chemical-resistant overalls.

High visibility (hi-vis) clothing stands out against any background or in any weather conditions. It is important to wear high visibility clothing on a construction site to ensure that people can see you easily. In addition, workers should always try to wear light-coloured clothing underneath, as it is easier to see.

You need to keep your high visibility and protective clothing clean and in good condition.

Employers need to make sure that employees understand the reasons for wearing high visibility clothing and the consequences of not doing so.

Eye protection

For many jobs, it is essential to wear goggles or safety glasses to prevent small objects, such as dust, wood or metal, from getting into the eyes. As goggles tend to steam up, particularly if they are being worn with a mask, safety glasses can often be a good alternative.

Hand protection

Wearing gloves will help to prevent damage or injury to the hands or fingers. For example, general purpose gloves can prevent cuts, and rubber gloves can prevent skin irritation and inflammation, such as contact dermatitis caused by handling hazardous substances. There are many different types of gloves available, including specialist gloves for working with chemicals.

Head protection

Hard hats or safety helmets are compulsory on building sites. They can protect you from falling objects or banging your head. They need to fit well and they should be regularly inspected and checked for cracks. Worn straps mean that the helmet should be replaced, as a blow to the head can be fatal. Hard hats bear a date of manufacture and should be replaced after about 3 years.

Hearing protection

Ear defenders, such as ear protectors or plugs, aim to prevent damage to your hearing or hearing loss when you are working with loud tools or are involved in a very noisy job.

Respiratory protection

Breathing in fibre, dust or some gases could damage the lungs. Dust is a very common danger, so a dust mask, face mask or respirator may be necessary.

Make sure you have the right mask for the job. It needs to fit properly otherwise it will not give you sufficient protection.

Foot protection

Foot protection is compulsory on site, particularly if you are undertaking heavy work. Footwear should include steel toecaps (or equivalent) to protect feet against dropped objects, midsole protection (usually a steel plate) to protect against puncture or penetration from things like nails on the floor and soles with good grip to help prevent slips on wet surfaces.

Figure 1.14 Respiratory protection

Legislation covering PPE

The most important piece of legislation is the Personal Protective Equipment at Work Regulations (1992). It covers all sorts of PPE and sets out your responsibilities and those of the employer. Linked to this are the Control of Substances Hazardous to Health (2002) and the Provision and Use of Work Equipment Regulations (1992 and 1998).

Storing and maintaining PPE

All forms of PPE will be less effective if they are not properly maintained. This may mean examining the PPE and either replacing or cleaning it, or if relevant testing or repairing it. PPE needs to be stored properly so that it is not damaged, contaminated or lost. Each type of PPE should have a CE mark. This shows that it has met the necessary safety requirements.

Importance of PPE

PPE needs to be suitable for its intended use and it needs to be used in the correct way. As a worker or an employee you need to:

* make sure you are trained to use PPE

* follow your employer's instructions when using the PPE and always wear it when you are told to do so

* look after the PPE and if there is a problem with it report it.

Your employer will:

* know the risks that the PPE will either reduce or avoid

* know how the PPE should be maintained

* know its limitations.

Consequences of not using PPE

The consequences of not using PPE can be immediate or long-term. Immediate problems are more obvious, as you may injure yourself. The longer-term consequences could be ill health in the future. If your employer has provided PPE, you have a legal responsibility to wear it.

FIRE AND EMERGENCY PROCEDURES

If there is a fire or an emergency, it is vital that you raise the alarm quickly. You should leave the building or site and then head for the **assembly point.**

When there is an emergency a general alarm should sound. If you are working on a larger and more complex construction site, evacuation may begin by evacuating the area closest to the emergency. Areas will then be evacuated one-by-one to avoid congestion of the escape routes.

Figure 1.15 Assembly point sign

Three elements essential to creating a fire

Three ingredients are needed to make something combust (burn):

* oxygen   * heat   * fuel.

The fuel can be anything which burns, such as wood, paper or flammable liquids or gases, and oxygen is in the air around us, so all that is needed is sufficient heat to start a fire.

The fire triangle represents these three elements visually. By removing one of the three elements the fire can be prevented or extinguished.

Figure 1.16 The fire triangle

How fire is spread

Fire can easily move from one area to another by finding more fuel. You need to consider this when you are storing or using materials on site, and be aware that untidiness can be a fire risk. For example, if there are wood shavings on the ground the fire can move across them, burning up the shavings.

Heat can also transfer from one source of fuel to another. If a piece of wood is on fire and is against or close to another piece of wood, that too will catch fire and the fire will have spread.

On site, fires are classified according to the type of material that is on fire. This will determine the type of fire-fighting equipment you will need to use. The five different types of fire are shown in Table 1.13.

Class of fire	Fuel or material on fire
A	Wood, paper and textiles
B	Petrol, oil and other flammable liquids
C	LPG, propane and other flammable gases
D	Metals and metal powder
E	Electrical equipment

Table 1.13 Different classes of fire

There is also F, cooking oil, but this is less likely to be found on site, except in a kitchen.

Taking action if you discover a fire and fire evacuation procedures

During induction, you will have been shown what to do in the event of a fire and told about assembly points. These are marked by signs and somewhere on the site there will be a map showing their location.

If you discover a fire you should:

* sound the alarm

* not attempt to fight the fire unless you have had fire marshal training

* otherwise stop work, do not collect your belongings, do not run, and do not re-enter the site until the all clear has been given.

Different types of fire extinguishers

Extinguishers can be effective when tackling small localised fires. However, you must use the correct type of extinguisher. For example, putting water on an oil fire could make it explode. For this reason, you should not attempt to use a fire extinguisher unless you have had proper training.

When using an extinguisher it is important to remember the following safety points:

* Only use an extinguisher at the early stages of a fire, when it is small.

* The instructions for use appear on the extinguisher.

* If you do choose to fight the fire because it is small enough, and you are sure you know what is burning, position yourself between the fire and the exit, so that if it doesn't work you can still get out.

Type of fire risk	Fire class Symbol	White label Water	Cream label Foam	Black label Carbon dioxide	Blue label Dry powder	Yellow label Wet chemical
A – Solid (e.g. wood or paper)	A	✓	✓	✗	✓	✓
B – Liquid (e.g. petrol)	B	✗	✓	✓	✓	✗
C – Gas (e.g. propane)	C	✗	✗	✓	✓	✗
D – Metal (e.g. aluminium)	D METAL	✗	✗	✗	✓	✗
E – Electrical (i.e. any electrical equipment)	E	✗	✗	✓	✓	✗
F – Cooking oil (e.g. a chip pan)	F	✗	✗	✗	✗	✓

Table 1.14 Types of fire extinguishers

There are some differences you should be aware of when using different types of extinguisher:

* *CO_2 extinguishers* – do not touch the nozzle; simply operate by holding the handle. This is because the nozzle gets extremely cold when ejecting the CO_2, as does the canister. Fires put out with a CO_2 extinguisher may reignite, and you will need to ventilate the room after use.

* *Powder extinguishers* – these can be used on lots of kinds of fire, but can seriously reduce visibility by throwing powder into the air as well as on the fire.

SIGNS AND SAFETY NOTICES

In a well-organised working environment safety signs will warn you of potential dangers and tell you what to do to stay safe. They are used to warn you of hazards. Their purpose is to prevent accidents. Some will tell you what to do (or not to do) in particular parts of the site and some will show you where things are, such as the location of a first aid box or a fire exit.

Types of signs and safety notices

There are five basic types of safety sign, as well as signs that are a combination of two or more of these types. These are shown in Table 1.15.

Type of safety sign	What it tells you	What it looks like	Example
Prohibition sign	Tells you what you must *not* do	Usually round, in red and white	Do not use ladder
Hazard sign	Warns you about hazards	Triangular, in yellow and black	**Caution** Slippery floor
Mandatory sign	Tells you what you *must* do	Round, usually blue and white	Masks must be worn in this area
Safe condition or information sign	Gives important information, e.g. about where to find fire exits, assembly points or first aid kit, or about safe working practices	Green and white	First aid
Firefighting sign	Gives information about extinguishers, hydrants, hoses and fire alarm call points, etc.	Red with white lettering	Fire alarm call point
Combination sign	These have two or more of the elements of the other types of sign, e.g. hazard, prohibition and mandatory		**DANGER** Isolate before removing cover

Table 1.15 Different types of safety signs

TEST YOURSELF

1. Which of the following requires you to tell the HSE about any injuries or diseases?

   a. HASAWA

   b. COSHH

   c. RIDDOR

   d. PUWER

2. What is a prohibition notice?

   a. An instruction from the HSE to stop all work until a problem is dealt with

   b. A manufacturer's announcement to stop all work using faulty equipment

   c. A site contractor's decision not to use particular materials

   d. A local authority banning the use of a particular type of brick

3. Which of the following is considered a major injury?

   a. Bruising on the knee

   b. Cut

   c. Concussion

   d. Exposure to fumes

4. If there is an accident on a site who is likely to be the first to respond?

   a. First aider

   b. Police

   c. Paramedics

   d. HSE

5. Which of the following is a summary of risk assessments and is used for high risk activities?

   a. Site notice board

   b. Hazard book

   c. Monitoring statement

   d. Method statement

6. Some substances are combustible. Which of the following are examples of combustible materials?

   a. Adhesives

   b. Paints

   c. Cleaning agents

   d. All of these

7. What is dermatitis?

   a. Inflammation of the skin

   b. Inflammation of the ear

   c. Inflammation of the eye

   d. Inflammation of the nose

8. Screens, netting and guards on a site are all examples of which of the following?

   a. PPE

   b. Signs

   c. Perimeter safety

   d. Electrical equipment

9. Which of the following are also known as scissor lifts or cherry pickers?

   a. Bench saws

   b. Hand-held power tools

   c. Cement additives

   d. Mobile elevated work platforms

10. In older properties the neutral electricity wire is which colour?

    a. Black

    b. Red

    c. Blue

    d. Brown

Chapter 2

Unit CSA–L3Core07
ANALYSING TECHNICAL INFORMATION, QUANTITIES AND COMMUNICATION WITH OTHERS

LEARNING OUTCOMES

LO1: Know how to produce different types of drawings and information in the construction industry

LO2: Know how to estimate quantities and price work for contracts

LO3: Know how to ensure good working practices

INTRODUCTION

The aims of this chapter are to:

* help you to interpret information

* help you to estimate quantities

* help you to organise the building process and communicate the design work to colleagues and others.

PRODUCING DIFFERENT TYPES OF DRAWING AND INFORMATION

Accurate construction requires the creation of accurate drawings and matching supporting information. Supporting information can be found in a variety of different types of documents. These include:

* drawings and plans

* programmes of work

* procedures

* specifications

* policies

* schedules

* manufacturers' technical information

* organisational documentation

* training and development records

* risk and method statements

* Construction (Design and Management) (CDM) Regulations

* Building Regulations.

Each different type of construction plan has a definite look and purpose. Typical construction drawings focus in on floor plans or elevation.

Construction drawings are drawn to scale and need to be accurate, so that relative sizes are correct. The scale will be stated on the drawing, to avoid inaccuracies.

Working alongside these construction drawings are matched and linked specifications and schedules. It is these that outline all of the materials and tasks required to complete specific jobs.

In order to understand construction drawings you not only need to understand their purpose and what they are showing, but also a range of hatchings and symbols that act as shortcuts on the documents.

Electronic and traditional drawing methods

Construction drawings are only part of a long process in the design of buildings. In fact the construction drawings are the final stage or final version of these drawings. The design process begins with a basic concept, which is followed by outline drawings. By the end of the design stage working drawings, technical specifications and contract drawings have been completed.

The project is put out to tender. This is a process that involves companies bidding for the job based on the information that they have been given.

There are further changes just before the construction phase gets under way. The chosen construction company may have noted issues with the design, which means that the drawings may have to be amended. It is also at this stage that the construction company will begin the process of pricing up each phase of the job.

Electronic drawing methods

Many construction drawings are based on a system known as computer aided design (CAD). CAD basically produces two-dimensional electronic drawings using the similar lines, hatches and text that can be seen in traditional paper drawings.

Each different CAD drawing is created independently, so each design change has to be followed up on other CAD drawings.

Increasingly, however, a new electronic system is being used. It is known as building information modelling (BIM). This creates drawings in 3D. The buildings are virtually modelled from real construction elements, such as walls, windows and roofs. The big advantages are:

* it allows architects to design buildings in a similar way to the way in which the building will actually be built

* a central virtual building model stores all the data, so any changes to this are applied to individual drawings

* better coordinated designs can be created meaning that construction should be more straightforward.

Systems such as BIM provide 3D models, which can be viewed from any angle or perspective. It also includes:

* scheduling information

* labour required

* estimated costs

* a detailed breakdown of the construction phases.

Figure 2.1 BIM generated model

Traditional drawing methods

The development of the computer, laptops and hand-held tablets such as iPads is gradually making manual drafting of construction drawings obsolete. The majority of drawings are now created using CAD or BIM software.

Traditionally, drawings were limited to the available paper size and what would be convenient to transport.

As each of the traditional construction drawings were hand drawn, there was always a danger that the information on one drawing would not match the information on another. The only way to check that both were accurate was to cross-reference every detail.

One advantage is that paper plans are easier to carry around site, as computers can be broken or stolen. However, damaging or losing a paper plan can cause delays while it is replaced.

Types of supporting information

Drawings and plans

Drawings are an important part of construction work. You will need to understand how they provide you with the information you need to carry out the work. The drawings show what the building will look like and how it will be constructed. This means that there are several different drawings of the building from different viewpoints. In practice most of the drawings are shown on the same sheet.

Block plans

Block plans show the construction site and the surrounding area. Normally block plans are at a ratio of 1:1250 and 1:2500. This means that 1 millimetre on a block plan is equal to 1,250 mm (12.5 m) or 2,500 mm (25 m) or on the ground.

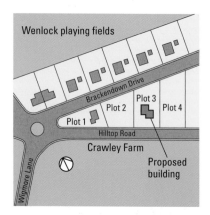

Figure 2.2 Block plan

Site plan

Often location drawings are also known as block plans or site plans. The site plan drawing shows what is planned for the site. It is often an important drawing because it has been created in order to get approval for the project from planning committees or funding sources. In most cases the site plan is actually an architectural plan, showing the basic arrangement of buildings and any landscaping.

The site plan will usually show:

* directional orientation (i.e. the north point)

* location and size of the building or buildings

* existing structures

* clear measurements.

General location

Location drawings show the site or building in relation to its surroundings. It will therefore show details such as boundaries, other buildings and roads. It will also contain other vital information, including:

* access

* drainage

* sewers

* the north point.

As with all plan drawings, the scale will be shown and the drawing will be given a title. It will be given a job or project number to help identify it easily, as well as an address, the date of the drawing and the name of the client. A version number will also be on the drawing with an amendment date if there have been any changes. You'll need to make sure you have the latest drawing.

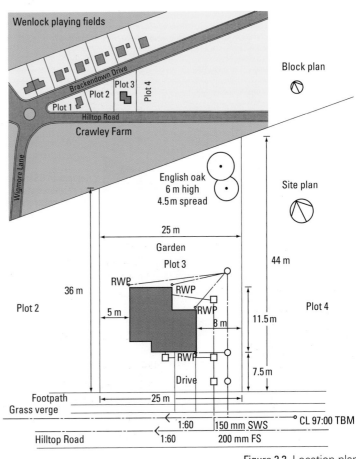

Figure 2.3 Location plan

Normally location drawings are either 1:200 or 1:500 (that is, 1 mm of the drawing represents 200 mm (2 m) or 500 mm (5 m) on the ground).

Assembly

These are detailed drawings that illustrate the different elements and components of the construction. They tend to be 1:5, 1:10 or 1:20 (1 mm of the drawing represents 5, 10 or 20 mm on the ground). This larger scale allows more detail to be shown, to ensure accurate construction.

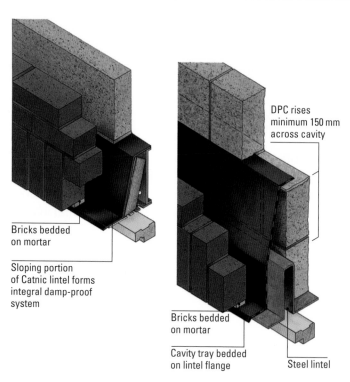

DPC rises minimum 150 mm across cavity

Bricks bedded on mortar

Sloping portion of Catnic lintel forms integral damp-proof system

Bricks bedded on mortar

Cavity tray bedded on lintel flange

Steel lintel

Figure 2.4 Assembly drawing

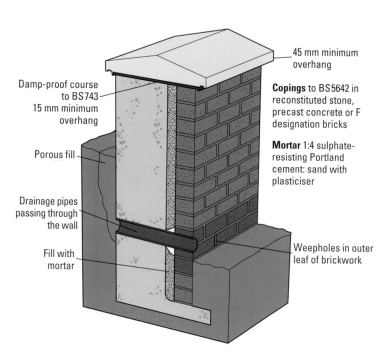

45 mm minimum overhang

Damp-proof course to BS 743 15 mm minimum overhang

Copings to BS 5642 in reconstituted stone, precast concrete or F designation bricks

Mortar 1:4 sulphate-resisting Portland cement: sand with plasticiser

Porous fill

Drainage pipes passing through the wall

Fill with mortar

Weepholes in outer leaf of brickwork

Figure 2.5 Section drawing of an earth retaining wall

Sectional

These drawings aim to provide:

* vertical and horizontal measurements and details

* constructional details.

They can be used to show the height of ground levels, damp-proof courses, foundations and other aspects of the construction.

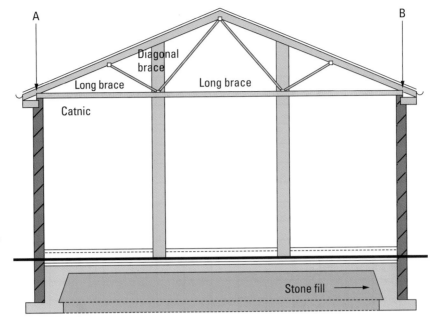

Figure 2.6 Section drawing of a garage

Details

These drawings show how a component needs to be manufactured. They can be shown in various scales, but mainly 1:10, 1:5 and 1:1 (the same size as the actual component if it is small).

Programmes of work

Programmes of work show the actual sequence of any work activities on a construction project. Part of the work programme plan is to show target times. They are usually shown in the form of a Gantt chart (a special type of bar chart), as can be seen in Fig 2.8.

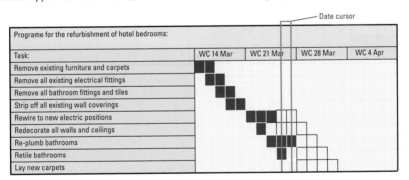

Figure 2.8 Single line contract plan Gantt chart

In this figure:

* on the left-hand side all of the tasks are listed – note this is in logical order

* on the right the blocks show the target start and end date for each of the individual tasks

* the timescale can be days, weeks or months.

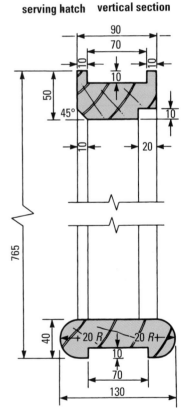

Figure 2.7 Detail drawing

Far more complex forms of work programmes can also be created. Fig 2.9 shows the planning for the construction of a house.

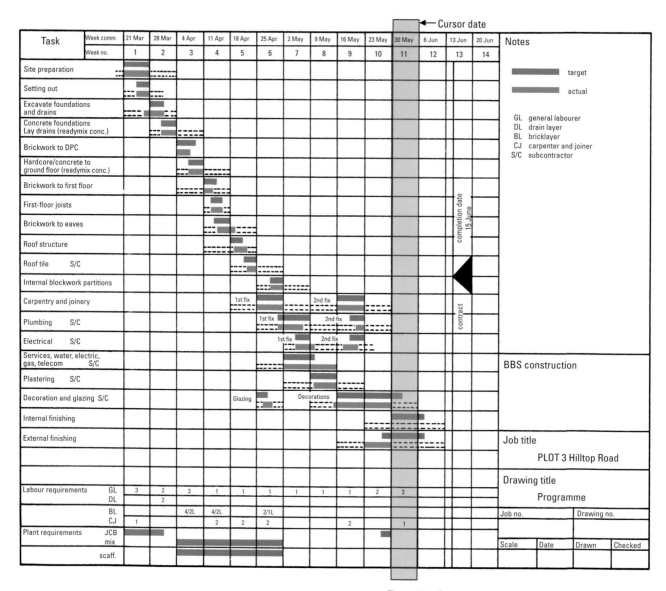

Figure 2.9 Gantt chart for the construction of a house

This more complex example shows the following:

- There are two lines – they show the target dates and actual dates. The actual dates are shaded, showing when the work actually began and how long it took.

- If this bar chart is kept up to date an accurate picture of progress and estimated completion time can be seen.

Procedures

When you work for a construction company they will have a series of procedures they will expect you to follow. A good example is the emergency procedure. This will explain precisely what is required in the case of an emergency on site and who will have responsibility to carry out particular duties. Procedures are there to show you the right way of doing something.

Another good example of a procedure is the procurement or buying procedure. This will outline:

* who is authorised to buy what, and how much individuals are allowed to spend

* any forms or documents that have to be completed when buying.

Specifications

In addition to drawings it is usually necessary to have documents known as specifications. These provide much more information, as can be seen in Fig 2.10.

The specifications give you a precise description. They will include:

* the address and description of the site

* on-site services (e.g. water and electricity)

* materials description, outlining the size, finish, quality and tolerances

* specific requirements, such as the individual that will authorise or approve work carried out

* any restrictions on site, such as working hours.

Policies

Policies are sets of principles or a programme of actions. The following are two good examples:

* environmental policy – how the business goes about protecting the environment

* safety policy – how the business deals with health and safety matters and who is responsible for monitoring and maintaining it.

You will normally find both policies and procedures in site rules. These are usually explained to each new employee when they first join the company. Sometimes there may be additional site rules, depending on the job and the location of the work.

Schedules

Schedules are cross-referenced to drawings that have been prepared by an architect. They will show specific design information. Usually they are prepared for jobs that will crop up regularly on site, such as:

* working on windows, doors, floors, walls or ceilings

* working on drainage, lintels or sanitary ware.

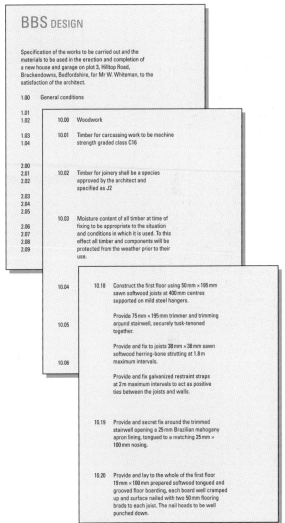

Figure 2.10 Extracts from a typical specification

A schedule can be seen in Fig 2.11.

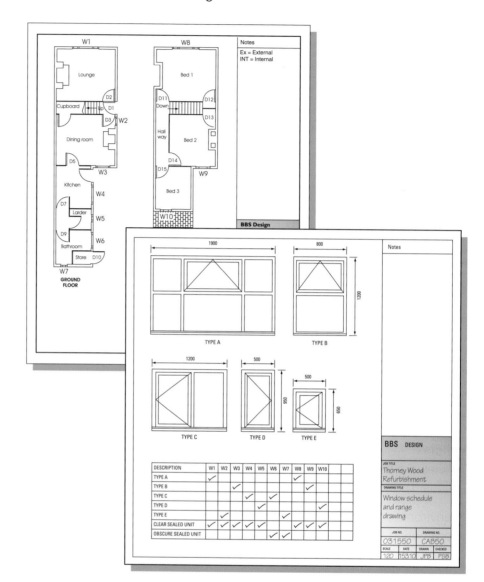

Figure 2.11 Typical windows schedule, range drawing and floor plans

The schedule is very useful for a number of reasons:

* working out the quantities of materials needed

* ordering materials and components and then checking them against deliveries

* locating where specific materials will be used.

Manufacturers' technical information

Almost everything that is bought to be used on site will come with a variety of information. The basic technical information provided will show what the equipment or material is intended to be used for, how it should be stored and any particular requirements it may have, such as handling or maintenance.

Technical information from the manufacturer can come from a variety of different sources:

* printed or downloadable data sheets

* printed or downloadable user instructions

* manufacturers' catalogues or brochures

* manufacturers' websites.

Organisational documentation
The potential list of organisational documentation and paperwork is massive. Examples are outlined in the following table.

Document	Purpose
Timesheet	Record of hours that you have worked and the jobs that you have carried out. They are used to help work out your wages and the total cost of the job.
Day worksheet	These detail work that has been carried out without providing an estimate beforehand. They usually include repairs or extra work and alterations.
Variation order	These are provided by the architect and given to the builder, showing any alterations, additions or omissions to the original job.
Confirmation notice	Provided by the architect to confirm any verbal instructions.
Daily report or site diary	Include things that might affect the project like detailed weather conditions, late deliveries or site visitors.
Orders and requisitions	These are order forms, requesting the delivery of materials.
Delivery notes	These are provided by the supplier of materials as a list of all materials being delivered. These need to be checked against materials actually delivered.
Delivery record	These are lists of all materials that have been delivered on site.
Memorandum	These are used for internal communications and are usually brief.
Letters	These are used for external communications, usually to customers or suppliers.
Fax	Even though email is commonly used, the industry still likes faxes, because they provide an exact copy of an original document.

Table 2.1

Training and development records
Training and development is an important part of any job, as it ensures that employees have all the skills and knowledge that they need to do their work. Most medium to large employers will have training policies that set out how they intend to do this.

To make sure that they are on track and to keep records they will have a range of different documents. These will record all the training that an employee has undertaken.

Training can take place in a number of different ways:

* induction
* toolbox talks

* in-house training
* specialist training

* training or education leading to formal qualifications.

Details required for floor plans

The floor plans shows the arrangement of the building, rather like a map. It is a cut through of the building, which shows openings, walls and other features usually at around 1 m above floor level.

The floor plan also includes elements of the building that can be seen below the 1 m level, such as the floor or part of the stairs. The drawing will show elements above the 1 m level as dotted lines. The floor plan is a vertical orthographic projection onto a horizontal plane. In effect the horizontal plane cuts through the building.

The floor plan will detail the following:

* Vertical and horizontal sections – these show the building cut along an axis to show the interior structure.

* Datum levels – these are taken from a nearby and convenient datum point. They show the building's levels in relation to the datum point.

* Wall constructions – this is revealed through the section or cross sections shown in the diagram. It details the wall construction methods and materials.

* Material codes – these will contain notes and links to specific materials and may also note particular parts of the Building Regulations that these construction materials comply with.

* Depth and height dimensions – these are drawn between the walls to show the room sizes and wall lengths. They are noted as width × depth.

* Schedules – these note repeated design information, such as types of door, windows and other features.

* Specifications – these outline the type, size and quality of materials, methods of fixing and quality of work and finish expected.

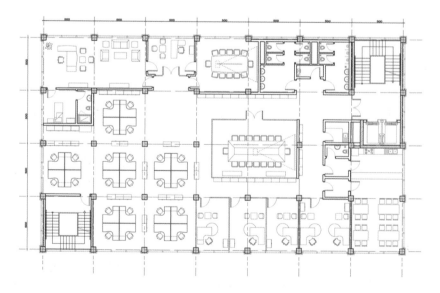

Figure 2.12 Example of a traditional floor plan

Details required for elevations

The details required for elevations in construction drawings are the same as those required for floor plans. An elevation is the view of the building as seen from one side. It can be used to show what the exterior of the building will look like. The elevation is labelled in relation to the compass direction. The elevation is a horizontal orthographic projection of the building onto a vertical plane. Usually the vertical plane is parallel to one side of the building (orthographic drawing).

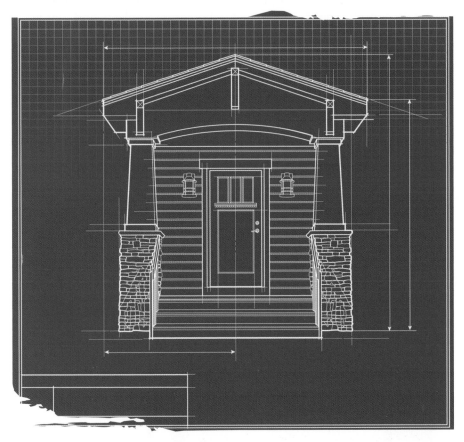

Figure 2.13. The details of the elevation of a building

Linking schedules to drawings

The schedule of work and the drawings create a single set of information. These documents need to be clear and comprehensive.

Before construction gets under way the specification schedule is the most important set of documents. It is used by the construction company to price up the job, work out how to tackle it, and then put in a bid for the work.

The construction company can look at each task in detail and see what materials are needed. This, along with all the construction information documents, will help them to make an estimate as to how long the task will take to complete and to what standard it should be completed.

During the construction period the most important documents are the drawings. Each piece of work is linked to those drawings and a schedule of work is set up. This might incorporate a Gantt chart or critical path analysis, showing expected dates and duration of on-site and off-site activities. This might need a good deal of cross-referencing. Obviously you cannot fit windows until the relevant cavity wall has been built and the opening formed.

It is important that the drawings and the specification schedules are closely linked. Reference numbers and headings that are on the drawings need to appear with exactly the same numbers and words on the schedule. This will avoid any confusion. It should be possible to look at the drawings, find a reference number or heading and then look through the schedule to find the details of that particular task. It also allows the drawings to be slightly clearer, as they won't need to have detailed information on them that can be found in the schedule.

Reasons for different projections in construction drawings

Designers will use a range of drawings in order to get across their requirements. Each is a 2D image. They show what the building will look like, along with the components or layout.

Orthographic projections

Orthographic projections are used to show the different elevations or views of an object. Each of the views is at right angles to the face.

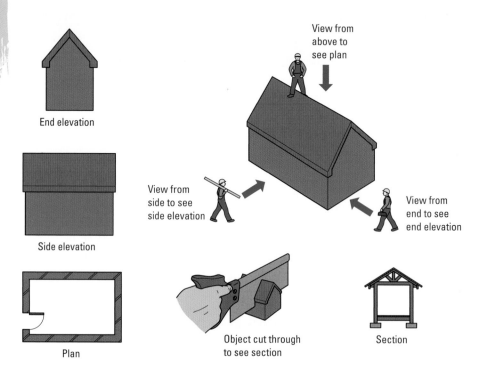

Figure 2.14 Plans, elevations and sections

Orthographic projection can be seen either as a first angle European projection or a third angle American projection. The following table shows the difference between these two views and there are examples in Figs 2.16 and 2.17, which relate to the shape shown in Fig 2.15.

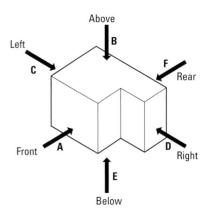

Figure 2.15 Isometric diagram showing the various views that can be portrayed in orthographic projection

Projection	Description
First angle	Everything is drawn in relation to the front view. The view from above is drawn below and the view from below is drawn from above. The view from the left is to the right and the right to the left. So all views, in effect, are reversed.
Third angle	This is often referred to as being an American projection. Everything again is in relation to the front elevation. The views from above and below are drawn in their correct position. Anything on the left is drawn to the left and the right to the right.

Table 2.2

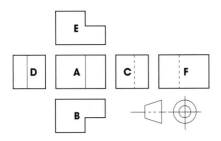

Figure 2.16 First angle projection

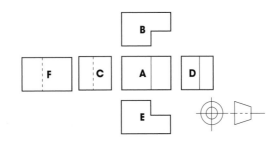

Figure 2.17 Third angle projection

Pictorial projections

Pictorial projections show objects in a 3D form. There are different ways of showing the view by varying the angles of the base line and the scale of any side projections. The most common is isometric. Vertical lines are drawn vertically, and horizontal lines are drawn at an angle of 30° to the horizontal. All of the other measurements are drawn to the same scale. This type of pictorial projection can be seen in Fig 2.18.

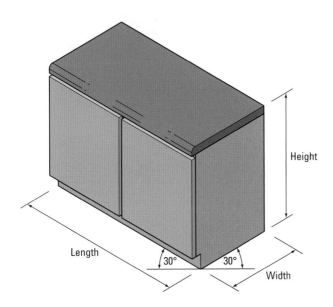

Figure 2.18 Isometric projection

There are four other different types of pictorial projection. These are not used as commonly as isometric projections.

Pictorial projection	Description
Planometric	Vertical lines are drawn vertically and horizontal lines on the front elevation of the object are drawn at 30°. The horizontal lines on the side elevation are drawn at 60° to horizontal.
Axonometric	The horizontal lines on all elevations are drawn at 45° to the horizontal. Otherwise the look is very similar to planometric.
Oblique	All of the vertical lines are drawn vertically. The horizontal lines on the front elevation are drawn horizontally but all the other horizontal lines are drawn at 45° to the horizontal.
Perspective	Horizontal lines are drawn so that they disappear into an imaginary horizon, known as a vanishing point. A one-point perspective drawing has all the sides disappearing to one vanishing point. An angular perspective, or two point perspective, has the elevations disappearing to two vanishing points.

Table 2.3

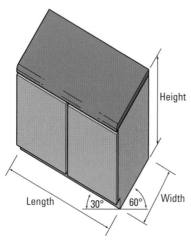

Figure 2.19 Planometric projection

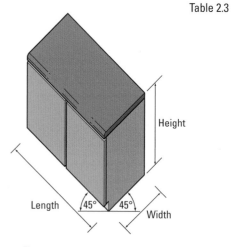

Figure 2.20 Axonometric projection

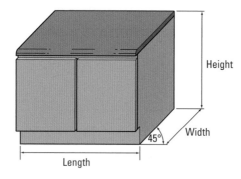

Figure 2.21 Oblique projection

VP = viewpoint

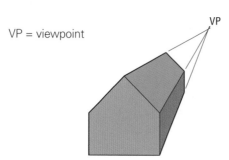

Figure 2.22 Parallel (one point) perspective projection

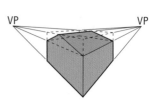

Figure 2.23 Angular (two point) perspective projection

Hatchings and symbols

Different materials and components are shown using symbols and hatchings. Abbreviations are also used. This makes the working drawings far less cluttered and easier to read.

Examples of symbols and abbreviations can be seen in Figs 2.24 and 2.25.

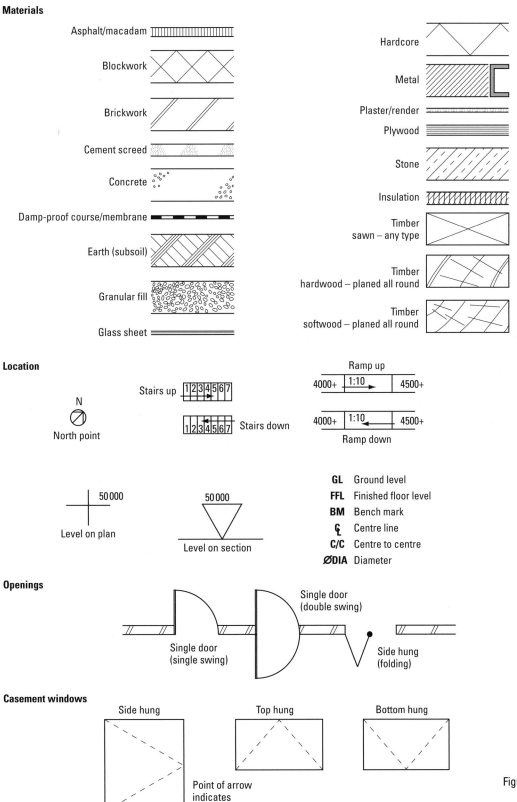

Figure 2.24 Symbols used on drawings

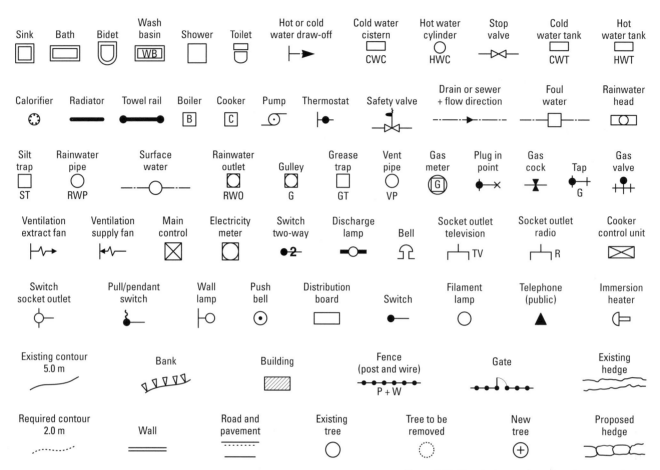

Figure 2.24 Symbols used on drawings *continued*

Aggregate	agg	BS tee	BST	Foundation	fdn	Polyvinyl acetate	PVA
Air brick	AB	Building	bldg	Fresh air inlet	FAI	Polyvinylchloride	PVC
Aluminium	al	Cast iron	CI	Glazed pipe	GP	Rainwater head	RWH
Asbestos	abs	Cement	ct	Granolithic	grano	Rainwater pipe	RWP
Asbestos cement	absct	Cleaning eye	CE	Hardcore	hc	Reinforced concrete	RC
Asphalt	asph	Column	col	Hardboard	hdbd	Rodding eye	RE
Bitumen	bit	Concrete	conc	Hardwood	hwd	Foul water sewer	FWS
Boarding	bdg	Copper	Copp cu	Inspection chamber	IC	Surface water sewer	SWS
Brickwork	bwk	Cupboard	cpd	Insulation	insul	Softwood	swd
BS* Beam	BSB	Damp-proof course	DPC	Invert	inv	Tongued and grooved	T&G
BS Universal beam	BSUB	Damp-proof membrane	DPM	Joist	jst	Unglazed pipe	UGP
BS Channel	BSC	Discharge pipe	DP	Mild steel	MS	Vent pipe	VP
BS equal angle	BSEA	Drawing	dwg	Pitch fibre	PF	Wrought iron	WI
BS unequal angle	BSUA	Expanding metal lathing	EML	Plasterboard	pbd		

Figure 2.25 Abbreviations commonly used on drawings

ESTIMATING QUANTITIES AND PRICING WORK FOR CONTRACTS

Working out the quantity and cost of resources that are needed to do a particular job can be difficult. In most cases you or the company you work for will be asked to provide a price for the work. It is generally accepted that there are three ways of doing this:

* Estimate – which is an approximate price, though estimation is a skill based on many factors.

* Quotation – which is a fixed price.

* Tender – which is a competitive quotation against other companies for a prescribed amount of work to a certain standard.

As we will see a little later in this section, these three ways of costing are very different and each of them has its own issues.

Resource requirements

As you become more experienced you will be able to estimate the amount of materials that will be needed on particular construction projects though this depends on the size and complexity of the job. This is also true of working out the best place to buy materials and how much the labour costs will be to get the job finished.

In order to work out how much a job will cost, you will need to know some basic information:

* What type of contract is agreed?

* What materials will be used?

* What are the costs of the materials?

Much of this information can be gained from the drawings, specification and other construction information for the proposed building.

To help work out the price of a job, many businesses use the *UK Building Blackbook,* which provides a construction cost guide. It breaks down all types of work and shows an average cost for each of them.

Computerised estimating packages are available, which will give a comprehensive detailed estimate that looks very professional. This will also help to estimate quantities and timescales.

Measurement

The standard unit for measurement is based on the metre (m). There are 100 centimetres (cm) and 1,000 millimetres (mm) in a metre. It is important to remember that drawings and plans have different scales, so these need to be converted to work out quantities of materials.

The most basic thing to work out is length, from which you can calculate perimeter, area and then volume, capacity, mass and weight, as can be seen in the following table.

Measurement	Explanation
Length	This is the distance from one end to the other. For most jobs metres will be sufficient, although for smaller work such as brick length or lengths of screws, millimetres are used.
Perimeter	This is the distance around a shape, such as the size of a room or a garden. It will help you estimate the length of a wall, for example. You just need to measure each side and then add them together.
Area	You can work out the area of a room, for example, by measuring its length and its width. Then you multiply the width by the length to give the number of square metres (m^2).
Volume and capacity	Volume shows how much space is taken up by an object, such as a room. Again this is simply worked out by multiplying the width of the room by its length and then by its height. This gives you the number of cubic metres (m^3).
	Capacity works in exactly the same way but instead of showing the figure as cubic metres you show it as litres. This is ideal if you are trying to work out the capacity of the water tank or a garden pond.
Mass or weight	Mass is measured usually in kilograms or in grams. Mass is the actual weight of a particular object, such as a brick.

Table 2.4

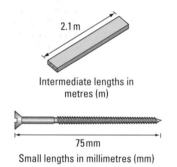

Figure 2.26 Length in metres and millimetres

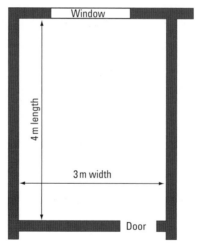

Figure 2.27 Measuring area and perimeter

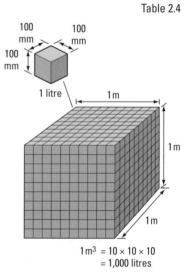

Figure 2.28 Relationship between volume and capacity

Formulae

These can appear to be complicated, but using formulae is essential for working out quantities of materials. Each formula is related to different shapes. In construction you will often have to work out quantities of materials needed for odd shaped areas.

Area

To work out the area of a triangular shape, you use the following formula:

$$\text{Area (A)} = \text{Base (B)} \times \text{Height (H)} \div 2$$

So if a triangle has a base of 4.5 and a height of 3.5 the calculation is:

$$4.5 \times 3.5 \div 2$$

Or $4.5 \times 3.5 = 15.75 \div 2 = 7.875\,m^2$

Height
If you want to work out the height of a triangle you switch the formulae around. To give us height = 2 × Area ÷ Base

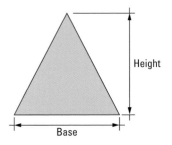

Figure 2.29 Triangle

Perimeter
To work out the perimeter of a rectangle use the formula:

$$\text{Perimeter} = 2 \times (\text{Length} + \text{Width})$$

It is important to remember this because you need to count the length and the width twice to ensure you have calculated the total distance around the object.

Circles
To work out the circumference or perimeter of a circle you use the formula:

$$\text{Circumference} = \pi\ (\text{pi}) \times \text{diameter}$$

π (pi) is always the same for all circles and is 3.142.

Diameter is the length of the widest part.

If you know the circumference and need to work out the diameter of the circle the formula is:

$$\text{Diameter} = \text{circumference} \div \pi\ (\text{pi})$$

For example if a circle has a circumference of 15.39 m then to work out the diameter:

$$15.39 \div 3.142 = 4.89\,m$$

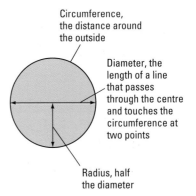

Circumference, the distance around the outside

Diameter, the length of a line that passes through the centre and touches the circumference at two points

Radius, half the diameter

Figure 2.30 Parts of a circle

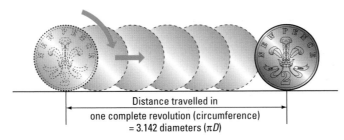

Distance travelled in one complete revolution (circumference) = 3.142 diameters (πD)

Figure 2.31 Relationship between circumference and diameter

Complex areas
Land, for example, is rarely square or rectangular. It is made up of odd shapes. Never be overwhelmed by complex areas, as all you need to do is to break them down into regular shapes.

By accurately measuring the perimeter you can then break down the shape into a series of triangles or rectangles. All you need to do then is to work out the area of each of the shapes within the overall shape and then add them together.

Shape		Area equals	Perimeter equals
Square 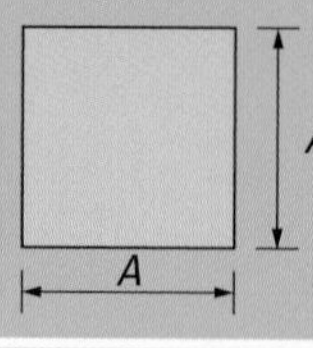		AA (or A multiplied by A)	4A (or A multiplied by 4)
Rectangle 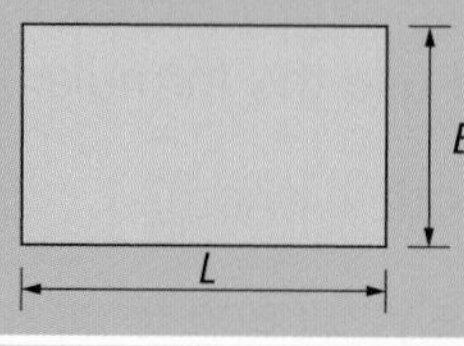		LB (or L multiplied by B)	2(L+B) (or L plus B multiplied by 2)
Trapezium 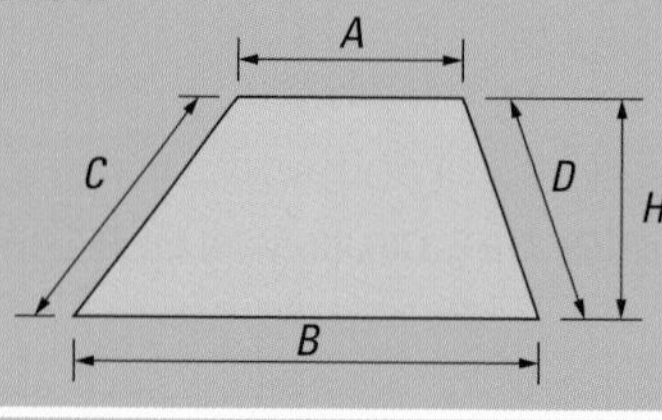		$\frac{(A+B)H}{2}$ (or A plus B multiplied by H and then divided by 2)	A+B+C+D
Triangle 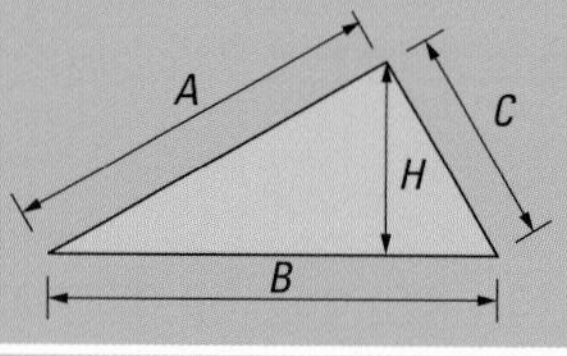		$\frac{BH}{2}$ (or B multiplied by H and then divided by 2)	A+B+C
Circle 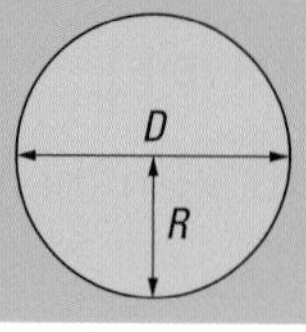		πR^2 (or R multiplied by itself and then multiplied by pi (3.142))	πD or $2\pi R$

Figure 2.32 Table of shapes and formulae

Volume

Sometimes it is necessary to work out the volume of an object, such as a cylinder or the amount of concrete needed. All that needs to be done is to work out the base area and then multiply that by the height.

For a concrete area, if a 1.2 m square needs 3 m of height then the calculation is:

$$1.2 \times 1.2 \times 3 = 4.32\,m^3$$

To work out the volume of a cylinder you need to know the base area × the height. The formula is:

$$\pi r^2 \times H$$

So if a cylinder has a radius (r) of 0.8 and a height of 3.5 m then the calculation is:

$$3.142 \times 0.8 \times 0.8 \times 3.5 = 7.038\,m^3$$

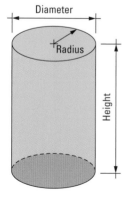

Figure 2.33 Cylinder

Pythagoras

Pythagoras' theorem is used to work out the length of the sides of right angled triangles. The theory states that:

In all right angled triangles the square of the longest side is equal to the sum of the squares of the other two sides (that is, the length of a side multiplied by itself).

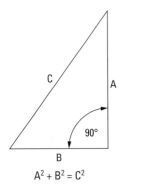

$$A^2 + B^2 = C^2$$

Figure 2.34 Pythagoras' theorem

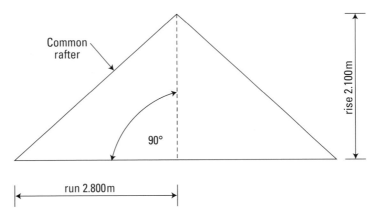

Figure 2.35 Section of a pitched roof

See Chapter 7 for more about geometry, trigonometry and Pythagoras.

Measuring materials

Using simple measurements and formulae can help you work out the amount of materials you will need. This is all summarised in the following table.

Material	Measurement
Timber	Can be sold by the cubic metre. To work out the length of material divide the cross section area of one section by the total cross section area of the material.
Flooring	To work out the amount of flooring for a particular area multiply the width of the floor by the length of the floor.
Stud walling	Measure the distance that the stud partition will cover then divide that distance by a specified spacing. This will give you the number of spaces between each stud.
Rafters and floor joists	Measure the distance between the adjacent walls then take into account that the first and last joist or rafter will be 50 mm away from the wall. Measure the total distance and then divide it by the specified spacing.
Fascias, barges and soffits	Measure the length and then add a little extra to take into account any necessary cutting and jointing.
Skirting	You need to work out the perimeter of the room and then subtract any doorways or other openings. This technique can be used to work out the necessary length of dado, picture rails and coving.
Bricks and mortar	Half-brick walls use 60 bricks per metre squared and one-brick walls use double that amount. You should add 5 per cent to take into account any cutting or damage. For mortar assume that you will need 1 kg for each brick.

Table 2.5

How to cost materials

Once you have found out the quantity of materials necessary you will need to find out the price of those materials. It is then simply a case of multiplying those prices by the amount of materials actually needed to find out approximately how much they will cost in total.

Materials and purchasing systems

Many builders and companies will have preferred suppliers of materials. Many of them will already have negotiated discounts based on their likely spending with that supplier over the course of a year. The supplier will be geared up to supply them at an agreed price.

In other cases builders may shop around to find the best price for the materials that match the specification. It is not always the case that the lowest price is necessarily the best. All materials need to be of a sufficient quality. The other key consideration is whether the materials are immediately available for delivery.

It is vital that suppliers are reliable and that they have sufficient materials in stock. Delays in deliveries can cause major setbacks on site. It is not always possible to warn suppliers that materials will be needed, but a well-run site should be able to anticipate the materials that are needed and put in the orders within good time.

Large quantities may be delivered direct from the manufacturer straight to site. This is preferable when dealing with items where consistency, for example of colour, is required.

Labour rates and costs

The cost of labour for particular jobs is based on the hourly charge-out rate for that individual or group of individuals multiplied by the time it would take to complete the job.

Labour rates can depend on the:

* expertise of the construction worker

* size of the business they work for

* part of the country in which the work is being carried out

* complexity of the work.

According to the International Construction Costs Survey 2012, the following were average costs per hour:

* Group 1 tradespeople – plumbers, electricians etc.: £30

* Group 2 tradespeople – carpenters, bricklayers etc.: £30

* Group 3 tradespeople – tillers, carpet layers and plasterers: £30

* general labourers: £18

* site supervisors: £46.

REED TIP

A great career path can start with an apprenticeship. 80 per cent of the staff at South Tyneside Homes started off as apprentices. Some have worked their way up to job roles such as team leaders, managers and heads of departments.

Quotes, estimated prices and tenders

As we have already seen, estimates, quotes and tenders are very different. We need to look at these in slightly more detail, as can be seen in the following table.

Type of costing	Explanation
Estimate	This needs to be a realistic and accurate calculation based on all the information available as to how much a job will cost. An estimate is not binding and the client needs to understand that the final cost might be more.
Quote	This is a fixed price based on a fixed specification. The final price may be different if the fixed specification changes; for example if the customer asks for additional work then the price will be higher.
Tender	This is a competitive process. The customer advertises the fact that they want a job done and invites tenders. The customer will specify the specifications and schedules and may even provide the drawings. The companies tendering then prepare their own documents and submit their price based on the information the customer has given them. All tenders are submitted to the customer by a particular date and are sealed. The customer then opens all tenders on a given date and awards the contract to the company of their choice. This process is particularly common among public sector customers such as local authorities.

Table 2.6

Inaccurate estimates

Larger companies will have an estimating team. Smaller businesses will have someone who has the job of being an estimator. Whenever they are pricing a job, whether it is a quote, an estimate or a tender, they will have to work out the costs of all materials, labour and other costs. They will also have to include a **mark-up.**

It is vital that all estimating is accurate. Everything needs to be measured and checked. All calculations need to be double-checked.

It can be disastrous if these figures are wrong because:

* if the figure is too high then the client is likely to reject the estimate and look elsewhere as some competitors could be cheaper

* if the figure is too low then the job may not provide the business with sufficient profit and it will be a struggle to make any money out of the job.

KEY TERMS

Mark-up

– a builder or building business, just like any other business, needs to make a profit. Mark-up is the difference between the total cost of the job and the price that the customer is asked to pay for the work.

DID YOU KNOW?

Many businesses fail as a result of not working out their costs properly. They may have plenty of work but they are making very little money.

CASE STUDY

South Tyneside Homes

South Tyneside Council's Housing Company

Bringing all your skills together to do a good job

Glen Campbell is a team leader at South Tyneside Homes.

'Your English and Maths skills really are important. As an apprentice, you have to be able to communicate properly – to get information and materials back and forth between tradespeople and yourself, to be able to sit and put a little drawing down, to label things up, to take information off drawings – especially on the capital works jobs. You're reading and writing stuff down all the time... even your timesheets because they have to be accurate.

When it comes to your maths skills, you're using measurement all the time. If you get measurements wrong, you're not making the money. For example, if you're using the wrong size timber for a roof – the drawing says you've got to use 200 x 50mm joists and then you go and use ones that are 150mm, it's either going to cost you more to go back and get it right, or it's not going to be able to take that stress load once the roof goes on. In the end it could even collapse.

Gary Kirsop, a Head of Property Services says:

'People seem to think that trades are all about your hands, but it's more than that. You're measuring complicated things – all the trades need to have about the same technical level for planning, calculation and writing reports. You need that level to get through your exams for the future too. When you have one day a week in college, but four days a week working with customers in the real world, without communications skills, it would all fall apart. You have to understand that people come from different backgrounds and that they have their own communication modes. Having good GCSEs will really help you get by in the trade.

Purchasing or hiring plant and equipment

Normally, if a piece of plant or equipment is going to be used on a regular basis then it is purchased by the company. By maximising the use of any plant or equipment, the business will save on the costs of repeatedly hiring and the transport of the item to and from the site.

It also does not make sense to leave plant and equipment on a site if it is no longer being used. It needs to be moved to a new site where it can be used.

Many smaller construction companies have no alternative other than to hire. This is because they cannot afford to have an enormous amount of money tied up in the plant or equipment, whether this comes from earned profits or from a loan or finance agreement. Loans and finance agreements have to be paid back over a period of time.

The decision as to whether to purchase or to hire is influenced by a number of factors:

* The working lives of the plant or equipment – how long will it last? This will usually depend on how much it is used and how well maintained it is.

* The use of the plant or equipment – is the company going to get good use out of it if they buy it? If they are hiring it then it should only be hired for the time it is actually needed. There is no point in having the plant or equipment on site and paying for its hire if it is not being used.

* Loss of value – just like buying a brand new car, the value of new plant or equipment takes an enormous drop the moment you take delivery of it. Even if it is hardly used it is considered second-hand and is not worth anything like its price when it was new. The biggest falls in value are in the first few years that the company owns it. It then reaches a value that it will sit at for some years until it is considered junk or scrap.

* Obsolescence – what might seem today to be the most advanced and technologically superior piece of plant or equipment may not be so tomorrow. Newer versions will come onto the market and may be more efficient or cost-effective. It is probable that the plant or equipment will be obsolete, or outdated, before it ends its useful working life.

* Cost of replacement – investing in plant or equipment today means that at some point in the future they will have to be replaced. The business will have to take account of this and arrange to have the necessary funds available for replacement in the future.

* Maintenance costs – if the construction business owns the plant or equipment they will have to pay for any routine maintenance, repairs and of course operators. Hired equipment, such as diggers or cranes, is the responsibility of the hiring company. They pay for all the maintenance and although they charge for the operator, the operator is on their wage bill.

* Insurance and licences – owning plant or equipment often means additional insurance payments and the company may also have to obtain licences that allow them to use that type of equipment in a particular area. Hired plant and equipment is already insured and should have the relevant licences.

* Financial costs – if the decision is to buy rather than hire, the money that would have otherwise been sitting in a bank account, earning interest, has been spent. If the company had to borrow the money to buy the plant or equipment then interest charges are payable on loans and finance agreements.

PRACTICAL TIP

Many construction companies that know they are going to be working on a project for a long period of time will actually buy plant and equipment for that contract. Once the contract has been completed they will sell on the plant and equipment.

Planning the sequence of materials and labour requirements

One of the most important jobs when organising work that will need to be carried out on site is to calculate when, where and how much materials and labour will be needed at any one time. This is organised in a number of different ways. The following headings cover the main documents or processes that are involved.

Bill of quantities

BILL OF QUANTITIES					
Contract			DWG No.		
DESCRIPTION	QUANTITY	UNIT	RATE	AMOUNT	

Figure 2.36 Bill of quantities form

This is used by building contractors when they quote for work on larger projects. It is usually prepared by a quantity surveyor. Fig 2.36 shows you what a bill of quantities looks like.

The form is completed using information from the working drawings, specification and schedule (this is called the take off). It describes each particular job and how many times that job needs to be carried out. It sets the number of units of material or labour, the rate at which they are charged and the total amount.

Programmes of work

A programme of work is also an important document, as it looks at the length of time and the sequence of jobs that will be needed to complete the construction. It has three main sections:

* A master programme that shows the start and finish dates. It shows the duration, sequence and any relationships between jobs across the whole contract.

* A stage programme – this is the next level down and it covers particular stages of the contract. A good example would be the foundation work or the process of making the building weather-tight. Alternatively it might look at a period of up to two months' worth of work in detail.

* A weekly programme – there will be several of these, which aim to predict where and when work will take place across the whole of the site. These are very important as they need to be compared against actual progress. The normal process is to review and update these weekly programmes and then update the stage and master programmes if delays have been encountered.

Stock systems and lead times

One of the greatest sources of delays in construction is not having the right materials and equipment available when it is needed. This means that someone has to work out not only what is needed and how many, but when. It is a balancing act because there are dangers in having the stock on site too early. If all the materials needed for a construction job arrived in the first week then this would cause problems and it is unlikely that there would be anywhere to store them. Materials need to be ordered to ensure that they are on site just before they are needed.

One of the problems is lead times. There is no guarantee that the supplier will have sufficient stock available when you need it. They need to be warned that you will need a certain amount of material at a certain time in advance. This will allow them to either manufacture the stock or get it from their supplier. Specialist materials have longer lead times. These may have to be specially manufactured, or perhaps imported from abroad. All of this takes time.

Once the quantities of materials have been calculated and the sequence of work decided, comparing that to the duration of the project and the schedule, it should be possible to predict when materials will be needed. You will need to liaise with your suppliers as soon as possible to find out the lead times they need to get the materials delivered to the site. This might mean that you will have to order materials out of sequence to the work schedule because some materials need longer lead times than others.

Planning and scheduling using charts

To plan the sequence of materials and labour requirements it is often a good idea to put the information in a format that can be easily read and understood. This is why many companies use charts, graphs and other types of illustrated diagram.

The most common is probably the Gantt chart. This is a series of horizontal bars. Each different task or operation involved in a project is shown on the left-hand side of the chart. Along the top are days, weeks or months. The planner marks the start day, week or month and the projected end day, week or month with a horizontal bar. It shows when tasks start and when they end. It will also be useful in showing when labour will be needed. It will also show which jobs have to be completed before another job can begin. An example of a Gantt chart can be seen in Fig 2.37.

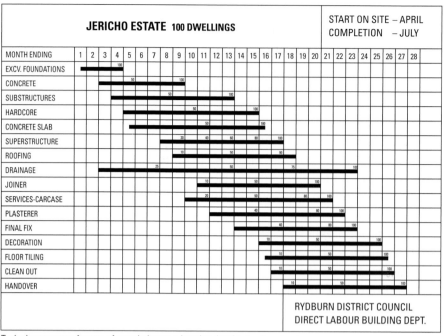

Typical programme for rate of completion on a housing development contract

Figure 2.37 Gantt chart

There are other types of bar chart that can be used to plan and monitor work on the construction site. It is important to remember that each chart relates to the plan of work:

* A single bar – this focuses in on a sequence of tasks and the bar is filled in to show progress.

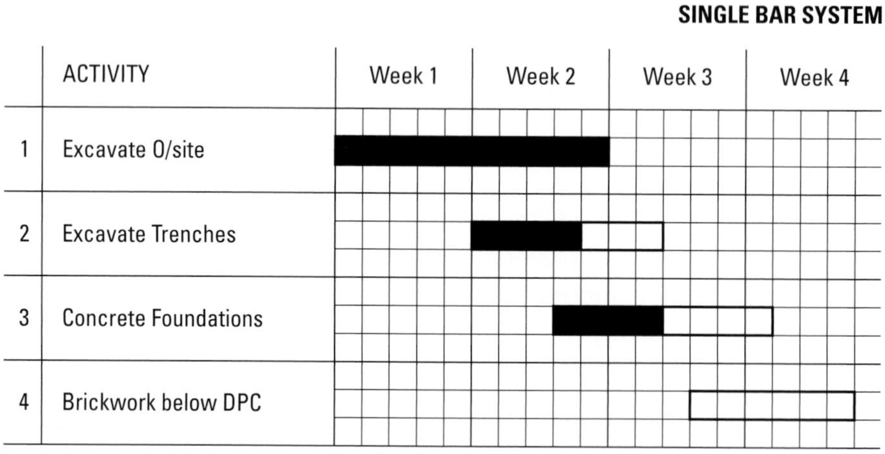

SINGLE BAR SYSTEM

	ACTIVITY	Week 1	Week 2	Week 3	Week 4
1	Excavate O/site				
2	Excavate Trenches				
3	Concrete Foundations				
4	Brickwork below DPC				

Figure 2.38 Single bar chart

- A two-bar – this tracks the amount of work that has been carried out against the planned amount of work that should have been carried out. In other words it shows the percentage of work that has been completed. It is there to alert the site manager that work may be falling behind and extra resources are needed.

TWO BAR SYSTEM
ACTIVITY
Week 1
Week 2
Week 3
Week 4
1
Excavate O/site
Percentage Completed
Planned Activity
2
Excavate Trenches
3
Concrete Foundations
4
Brickwork below DPC

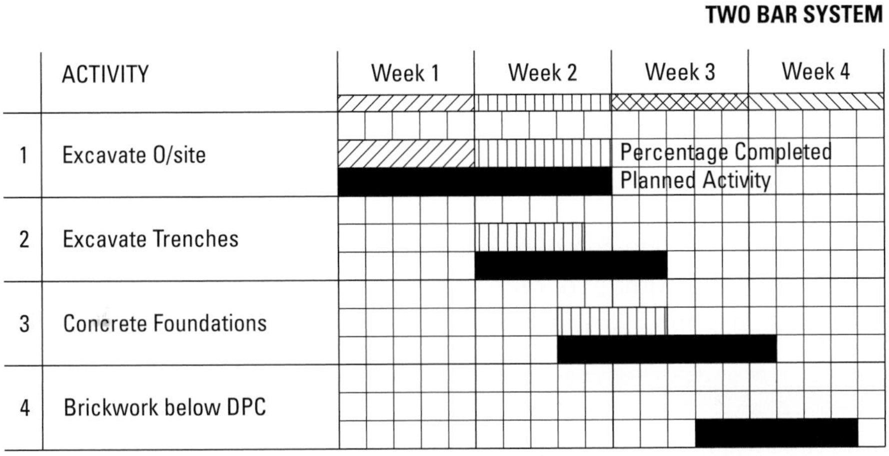

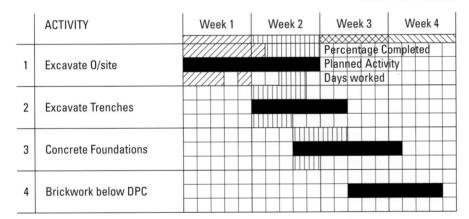

Figure 2.39 Two-bar system

- A three-bar – this shows the planned duration of the activity, the actual days that have seen work being done on that activity and the percentage of the activity that has been completed. This gives a snapshot view of how work has progressed over the course of a period of time.

THREE BAR SYSTEM
ACTIVITY
Week 1
Week 2
Week 3
Week 4
1
Excavate O/site
Percentage Completed
Planned Activity
Days worked
2
Excavate Trenches
3
Concrete Foundations
4
Brickwork below DPC

Figure 2.40 Three-bar system

Calculating hours required

We have already seen that different types of construction workers attract different hourly rates of pay. The simple solution in order to work out the cost to complete particular work is to look at the programmes of work and the estimated time required to complete it. The next stage is to estimate how many workers will be needed to carry out that activity and then multiply that by the estimated labour cost per hour.

Added costs

When a construction company estimates the costs of work they have to incorporate a number of other different costs. A summary of these can be seen in the following table.

Added cost	Explanation
National Insurance contributions	Companies employing workers have to pay National Insurance contributions to the government for each employee.
Value Added Tax (VAT)	For businesses that are registered for VAT they have to charge a sales tax on any services that they provide. They collect this money on behalf of the government. The VAT is added to the final cost of the work.
Pay As You Earn (PAYE)	PAYE, or income tax, has to be paid on the income of all workers straight to the government.
Travel expenses	This is particularly relevant if workers on site have to travel a considerable distance in order to do their work. This can reasonably be passed on to the client.
Profit and loss	Many businesses will make the mistake of trying to estimate the costs of their work in the knowledge that they are competing with other businesses, trimming their estimates if they can. As we will see when we look at profitability, a business does need to make money from contracts otherwise it will not have sufficient funds to continue to operate.
Suppliers' terms and conditions	Suppliers will often have set payment terms, such as 30, 60 or 90 days. The construction company needs to have sufficient funds to pay their suppliers on the due date stated on the invoice. If they fail to do this then they could run into difficulties as the supplier may decide not to give them any more credit until outstanding invoices have been paid.
Wastage	It is rarely possible to buy materials and components that are an exact fit. Blocks and bricks, for example, will have a percentage damaged or unusable on each pallet. Materials can also be mis-cut, damaged or otherwise wasted on site. It is sensible for the construction company to factor in a wastage rate of at least 5 per cent. This is often required to allow for cutting and fitting when using stock lengths.
Penalty clauses	Many projects are time sensitive and need to be completed by specified dates. The contracts will state whether there are any penalties to be made if critical dates are missed. Penalty clauses are rather like fines that the construction company pays if they fail to meet deadlines.

Table 2.7

Total estimated prices

As we have seen, the total estimated price needs to incorporate all of the added costs. But there are two other issues that should not be forgotten:

* The cost of any plant and equipment hire – the length of time that these are necessary will have to be calculated together with an additional period in case of delays.

* Contingencies – it is not always possible to determine exact prices, especially in groundworks, and, in any case, not all construction jobs will run smoothly. It is therefore sensible to set aside funds should additional work be needed. This may be particularly true if additional work needs to be done to secure the foundations or if workers and equipment are on site yet it is not possible to work due to poor weather conditions.

Profitability

Setting an initial price for a business's services is, perhaps, one of the most difficult tasks. It needs to take account of the costs that are incurred by the business. It also needs to consider the prices charged by key competitors, as the optimum price that a business wishes to charge may not be possible if competitors are charging considerably lower prices.

It is difficult for a new business to set prices, because its services may not be well known. Its costs may be comparatively higher because it will not have the advantages of providing services on a large scale. Equally, it cannot charge high prices because neither the company nor its services are established in the market.

The process of calculating revenue is a relatively simple task. Sales revenue or income is equal to the services sold, multiplied by the average selling price. In other words, all a business needs to know is how many services have been sold, or might sell, and the price they will charge.

We have already seen that a business incurs costs that must be paid. Clearly these have a direct impact on the profitability of a business.

We can already see that there is a direct relationship between costs and profit. Costs cut into the revenue generated by the business and reduce its overall profitability.

Gross profit is the difference between a company's revenue and its costs. Businesses will also calculate their operating profit. The operating profit is the business's gross profit minus its **overheads.**

A business may also calculate its pre-tax profits, which are its profits before it pays its taxes. It may have one-off costs, such as the replacement of a piece of plant or equipment. These costs are deducted from the operating profit to give the pre-tax profit.

KEY TERMS

Overheads

– these are expenses that need to be paid by the business regardless of how much work they have on at any one time, such as the rent of builders' yard.

The business will then pay tax on the remainder of its profit. This will leave them their net profit. This is the amount of money that they have actually made over the course of a year or on a particular job.

Profits are an important measure of the success of a business. Like other businesses construction companies do borrow money, but profit is the source of around 60 per cent of the funds that businesses use to help them grow.

Businesses can look for ways to gradually increase their profit. They can look at each type of job they do and work out the most efficient way of doing it. This might mean looking for a particular mix of employees, or buying or hiring particular plant and equipment that will speed up the work.

GOOD WORKING PRACTICES

Like any business, construction relies on a number of factors to make sure that everything runs smoothly and that a company's reputation is maintained.

There needs to be a good working relationship between those who work for the construction company, and other individuals or companies that they regularly deal with, such as the local authority, and professionals such as architects and clients.

This is achieved by making sure that these individuals and organisations continue to have trust and confidence in the company. Any promises or guarantees that are made must be kept.

In the normal course of events communication needs to be clear and straightforward. When there are problems accurate and honest communication can often deal with many of them. It can set aside the possibility of misunderstandings.

Good working relationships

Each construction job will require the services of a team of professionals. They will need to be able to work and communicate effectively with one another. Each has different roles and responsibilities.

Although you probably won't be working with exactly the same people all the time you are on site, you will be working with on-site colleagues every day. These may be people doing the same job as you, as well as people with other roles and responsibilities who you need to work with to ensure that the project runs smoothly.

Working with unskilled operatives

It's important to remember that everyone will have different levels of skill and experience. You, as a skilled or trade operative, are qualified in your trade, or working towards your qualification. Some people will be less experienced than you; for example, unskilled operatives (manual workers) are entry level operatives without any formal training. They may, however, be experienced on sites and will take instructions from the supervisor or site manager. You should be patient with colleagues who are less experienced or skilled than you – after all, everyone has to learn. However, if you see them carrying out unsafe practices, you should tell your supervisor or charge-hand straight away.

Working with skilled employees

You'll also work with people who are more experienced than you. It's a good idea to watch how they work and learn from their example. Show them respect and don't expect to know as much as they do if they have been working for much longer. However, if you see them ignoring safety rules, don't copy them; speak to your supervisor.

Working with professional technicians

You might also work with professional technicians, such as civil engineers or architectural technicians. They will have extensive knowledge in their field but may not know as much as you about bricklaying or carpentry. For your relationship to run smoothly, you should respect each other's knowledge, share your thoughts on any issues, and listen to what each other has to say.

Working with supervisors

Supervisors organise the day-to-day running of the site or a team. Charge-hands supervise a specific trade, such as bricklayers or carpenters. They will be your immediate boss, and you must listen to their instructions and obey any rules they set out. These rules enable the site to be run smoothly and safely so it is in your interest to do what your supervisor says.

Working with the site manager

The site manager or site agent runs the construction site, makes plans to avoid problems and meet deadlines, and ensures all processes are carried out safely. They communicate directly with the client. They are ultimately responsible for everything that goes on at the construction site. Even if you don't communicate with them directly, you should follow the guidance and rules that they have put in place. It's in your interest to do your bit to keep the site safe and efficient.

Working with other professionals

You may also need to work with or communicate with other professionals. For example, a clerk of works is employed by the architect on behalf of a client. They oversee the construction work and ensure that it represents the interests of the client and follows agreed specifications and designs. A contracts manager agrees prices and delivery dates. These professionals will expect you to do the job that has been specified and to draw their attention to anything that will change the plans they are responsible for.

Hierarchical charts

A hierarchy describes the different levels of responsibility, authority and power in a business or organisation. The larger the business the more levels of management it will have. The higher up the management structure the more responsibility each person will have.

Decisions are made at the top and instructions are passed down the hierarchy. It is best to imagine most organisations as like a pyramid. The directors or owners of the business are at the top of that pyramid. A site manager may be part-way down and at the bottom of the pyramid are all the workers who are on site.

Trust and confidence

The trust of colleagues develops as a result of showing that the company is reliable, cooperative and committed to the success or goals of the colleague or client. Trust does not happen automatically but has to be earned through actions. An important part of this is building a positive relationship with colleagues. Over time, trust will develop into confidence. Colleagues will have confidence in the company being able to deliver their promises.

The reputation of a construction company is very important. Criticisms of the company will always do far more damage than the positive benefits of a successfully completed contract. This shows how important it is to get things right the first time and every time.

In an industry where there is so much competition, trust and confidence can mean the difference between getting the contract and being rejected before your bid has even been considered.

As the construction company becomes established they will build up a network of colleagues. If these colleagues have trust and confidence in the business they will recommend the business to others.

Ultimately, earning trust and confidence relies on the business being able to solve any problems with the minimum of fuss and delay. Fair solutions need to be identified. These solutions should not be against the interests of anyone involved.

Accurate communication

Effective communication in all types of work is essential. It needs to be clear and to the point, as well as accurate. Above all it needs to be a two-way process. This means that any communication that you have with anyone must be understood.

In construction work it is essential to keep to deadlines and follow strict instructions and specifications. Failing to communicate will always cause confusion, extra cost and delays. In an industry such as this it is unacceptable and very easy to avoid. Negative communication or poor communication can damage the confidence that others have in you to do your job.

It is important to have a good working relationship with colleagues at work. An important part of this is to communicate in a clear way with them. This helps everyone understand what is going on, what decisions have been made. It also means being clear. Most communication with colleagues will be verbal (spoken). Good communication results in:

* cutting out mistakes and stoppages (saving money)

* avoiding delays

* making sure that the job is done right the first time and every time.

The more complex a contract, the more likely it is that changes and alterations will be needed. The longer the contract runs for, the more likely it is that changes will happen. Examples are as follows:

* Alterations to drawings – this can happen as a result of several different factors. The architect or the client may decide at a fairly late stage that changes need to be made to the design of the project. This will require all documents that rely on information from the drawings to be amended. This could mean changes to the schedule, specification and work programmes and the need for materials and labour at particular times.

* Variation to contracts – although the construction company may have agreed with the client to carry out work based on particular drawings and specifications, changes to design and to the requirements may happen. It may be necessary to put in new estimates for additional work and to inform the client of any likely delays.

* Changes to risk assessments – it is not always possible to predict exactly what hazards will be encountered during a project. Neither is it possible to predict whether new legislation will come into force that requires extra risk assessments.

* Work restrictions – although the site will have been surveyed for access and cleared of obstacles such as low trees, problems may arise during the work. Local residents, for example, may complain about lighting and noise. This could reduce working hours on site. This could all have an impact on the schedule of work.

* Change in circumstances – this could cover a wide variety of different problems. Key suppliers may not be able to deliver materials or components on time. Tried and trusted sub-contractors may not be available. The client may run out of money or a problem may be unearthed during excavation and preparation of the site.

REED TIP

Open and frank communication means being able to say no if something is not possible. It's OK to say that something can't be done, rather than saying 'yes, yes, yes' and then being unable to complete a task.

DID YOU KNOW?

During the construction of the Olympic basketball site in London the whole site had to be evacuated when a Second World War bomb was found. It had to be removed by specialists before work could continue.

TEST YOURSELF

1. What is the system that is gradually taking over from CAD as the main way to produce construction drawings?

   a. CTIBM

   b. CIM

   c. BIM

   d. SIM

2. What does a block plan show?

   a. The construction site and its surrounding area

   b. Local boundaries and roads

   c. Elements and components

   d. Constructional details

3. Who might give you a delivery note?

   a. A postal worker

   b. An architect

   c. A contractor

   d. A supplier

4. Which type of construction drawings show the different faces or views of an object?

   a. Orthographic

   b. Section

   c. Elevation

   d. Plan

5. How many different types of pictorial projection are there?

   a. 3

   b. 4

   c. 5

   d. 6

6. Which of the following is usually a bid for a fixed amount of work in competition with other companies?

   a. Estimate

   b. Quotation

   c. Tender

   d. Invoice

7. To calculate the area of a room, which two measurements are needed?

   a. Length and height

   b. Height and width

   c. Length and width

   d. Length and circumference

8. If you had 5 workmen being paid £25 per hour and they were working for 4 hours, what would be the total labour cost?

   a. £125

   b. £250

   c. £500

   d. £600

9. Some contracts state that if a deadline is missed a fine has to be paid. What are these called?

   a. Terms and conditions

   b. Wastage

   c. Penalty clause

   d. Critical date payment

10. A business's operating profit is its gross profit minus which of the following?

    a. Tax

    b. Overheads

    c. Net profit

    d. Labour costs

Chapter 3

Unit CSA–L3Core08
ANALYSING THE CONSTRUCTION INDUSTRY AND BUILT ENVIRONMENT

LEARNING OUTCOMES

LO1: Understand the different activities undertaken within the construction industry and built environment

LO2: Understand the different roles and responsibilities undertaken within the construction industry and built environment

LO3: Understand the physical and environmental factors when undertaking a construction project

LO4: Understand how construction projects can benefit the built environment

LO5: Understand the principles of sustainability within the construction industry and built environment

INTRODUCTION

The aim of this unit is to:

* help you understand more about the construction industry and its place in society.

CONSTRUCTION INDUSTRY AND BUILT ENVIRONMENT ACTIVITIES

Half of all the non-renewable resources used across the globe are consumed by construction. Construction and the built environment are also linked with the pollution of drinking water, the production of waste and poor air quality.

Nevertherless, buildings create wealth. In the UK, buildings represent three-quarters of all wealth. Buildings are long-term assets. Today it is recognised that buildings should have the ability to satisfy user needs for extended periods of time. They must be able to cope with any changing environmental conditions. They also need to be capable of being adapted over time as designs and demands change.

There is an increasing move towards naturally lit and well-ventilated buildings. There is also a move towards buildings that use alternative energy sources.

The first part of this chapter looks at the type of work that has developed around the broader construction industry and built environment. It looks at the work that is undertaken and the different types of clients who use the construction industry.

Range of activities

The construction industry and the broader built environment is a highly complex network of different activities. While there are a great many small businesses that focus on one particular aspect of construction, they need to be seen as part of a far larger industry. Increasingly it is a global industry, with major business organisations operating not just in the UK but also in a wide variety of locations around the world. Their skills and expertise are in great demand wherever there is construction. The following table outlines some of the activities that are undertaken by the construction industry and the broader built environment.

Activity	Description
Building	This is the accepted and traditional activity of the construction industry. It involves building homes and other structures, from garden walls to entire housing estates or even Olympic villages.
Finishing	Finishing refers to a part of the industry that focuses on decorative work, such as painting and decorating. Once buildings are completed, in order to make them ready for habitation a broad range of professions are needed. Plumbers will install water and sanitation. Electricians will connect electrical services and equipment. Interior designers will create the desired look for the building.
Architecture	Architects and technicians design buildings for clients. The structures are designed to meet the needs of the client while ensuring that they conform to Building Regulations, local planning laws and decisions, as well as other legislation such as CDM Regulations and ensure they are sustainable.
Town planning	Town planning involves organising the broader built environment in a particular area. Town planners need to examine each planning application and see how it fits into the overall long-term future of the area. They need to ensure that the area meets the needs of future generations.
Surveying	This involves measuring and examining land on which building or other external work will take place. It can involve setting out the building. Surveyors use drawings by an architect to correctly position the building. They will be able to work out the area of the building and any volumes. Building surveyors check that the building is structurally sound, while quantity surveyors look after costs.
Civil engineering	Civil engineers are usually involved in major projects, such as road and railway building, the construction of dams, reservoirs and other projects that are not usually buildings. They are involved in what is known as infrastructure projects, such as transport links, networks and hubs.
Repair and maintenance	All buildings need professionals who are able to repair and maintain a broad range of features. From the foundations to the roof, carpenters, builders, electricians, plumbers and more specialist companies, such as pest control, can all be considered to be part of the repair and maintenance side of the industry. Pre-1919 buildings also have particular requirements and are maintained and repaired in a way that suits their construction and to avoid further damage or inappropriate work that will look out of place. This requires people who have specialist heritage skills.
Building engineering services	When buildings are occupied they need to be continually supported in terms of a rigorous checking and maintenance programme. This part of the industry can deal with lifts and escalators, lighting and heating, fire alarms and other inbuilt systems.
Facilities management	For larger commercial buildings or hospitals, schools, colleges and universities, systems need to be in place to replace parts of the building if they wear out or are damaged. This includes cleaning, air conditioning companies, painting and decorating, replacement of doors, windows and a host of other activities.
Construction site management	Construction sites can be complex and demanding places and someone needs to organise them and to monitor progress. Construction site management involves organising the delivery of materials, security, safety, the management of the workforce and contractors.
Plant maintenance and operation	Just as commercial buildings and dwellings need constant maintenance, so too do factories and other sites where products are made or processes are carried out. These individuals can be involved in the energy industry, at gas, oil and nuclear plants, or be responsible for maintaining factories that produce vehicles or food.
Demolition	Demolition experts are responsible for levelling sites in a safe and controlled way. They may have to demolish buildings that could contain asbestos or they may have to use controlled explosions.

Table 3.1

Types of work

There is also a wide range of work that is undertaken in different sectors. Some of this is very specialised work. Some companies will focus purely on that type of work, gaining a reputation and expertise in that area. The following table outlines the types of work that is undertaken within the construction industry.

Type of work	Description
Residential	This is any work connected with domestic housing or dwellings. It can include the building of new homes, extensions or renovations on existing homes and the construction of affordable accommodation for organisations such as housing associations.
Commercial	This is work related to any buildings used by businesses. It can include factories, office blocks, production units, industrial units or private hospitals.
Industrial	This is more specialist work, as it can involve construction, including civil engineering, of heavy industrial factories, such as oil refineries or plants for car manufacturing.
Retail	This can include building or refurbishing shops in high streets or the construction of out-of-town retail parks.
Recreational and leisure	Many of these projects are designed for use by communities, such as sports facilities, fitness clubs, leisure centres, swimming pools and other community sports projects. In the past decade the construction industry was involved in the various London 2012 Olympic facilities.
Health	This includes specialist building services to create hospitals and other health facilities, such as doctors' surgeries and care homes.
Transport infrastructure	This is another broad area of work that includes roads, motorways, bridges, railways, underground trains and tram systems, as well as airports, bus routes and cycle paths.
Public buildings	This is the building and maintenance of large buildings for local and central government. It can include offices, town halls, art galleries, museums and libraries.
Heritage	Heritage involves work on listed properties of historical importance. This is a specialist area, as Building Regulations, planning laws and Listed Status require any work to be carried out in sympathy with the original design of the building.
Conservation	This is an increasingly important area of work, as it involves the protection of natural habitats. It would involve work in National Parks, Areas of Outstanding Natural Beauty, animal sanctuaries and could also include construction work related to coastal erosion and flood defences.
Educational	This is the construction of schools, colleges, universities and other buildings used for educational purposes.
Utilities and services	This is work that is related to the installation, maintenance and repair of the key utilities, which include gas, electricity and water.

Table 3.2

Types of client

As we have seen, there is a huge range of activities and types of work in the broader construction industry and built environment areas. This means that there is a huge range of different potential types of client. Some are private individuals but at the other end of the scale they might be huge companies or government departments. The following table outlines the range of different types of client.

Type of client	Description
Private	These are usually individual owners of homes or buildings. They may be people who want work done on their own homes, or on their own business premises, such as a small shop. Many of the individual shop or business owners may be sole traders. These are individuals who run and own a small business.
Corporate	Corporate is a term that is used to describe larger companies or businesses. They can be individuals that run factories, larger shops, industrial units or some kind of service-based organisation, including banks, insurance companies and estate agents. Some construction companies have long-term contracts with corporate businesses, which have many branches around the country. There is a rolling programme of maintenance, upgrading and repair. The companies can be public limited companies (PLC), who are owned by shareholders with their shares traded on the Stock Exchange.
Government	The government can be a client on a local, regional or national basis. This part of the industry has become more complicated, as there are multiple levels of government across the UK. There is also a Scottish Parliament and a Welsh Assembly, in addition to the UK Parliament based in London. Local councils will be responsible for maintaining a wide range of services and they will also be involved in construction. This includes schools, roads, the maintenance of social housing and parks and leisure facilities. In addition to this there are government departments based in London with regional offices, such as the Ministry of Defence, which is responsible for facilities related to the armed forces, and the National Health Service, which is responsible for hospitals and other health provision. The government (including local authorities and non-departmental public bodies) must comply with strict procurement (buying) rules, which often involve tenders. They also have limited budgets, which could affect the building project's schedule.

Table 3.3

CONSTRUCTION INDUSTRY AND BUILT ENVIRONMENT ROLES AND RESPONSIBILITIES

As we have discussed, the construction industry and the built environment is a complex network of different activities. As the industry has developed over time it has become important for individuals to specialise and take on specific roles and responsibilities.

Roles and responsibilities of the construction workforce

The following tables show the broad range of different roles and briefly outline their responsibilities within the construction industry.

From the design and planning phase onwards

Role	Responsibilities
Client	The client, such as a local authority, commissions the job. They define the scope of the work and agree on the timescale and schedule of payments.
Customer	For domestic dwellings, the customer may be the same as the client, but for larger projects a customer may be the end user of the building, such as a tenant renting local authority housing or a business renting an office. These individuals are most affected by any work on site. They should be considered and informed with a view to them suffering as little disruption as possible.
Architect	They are involved in designing new buildings, extensions and alterations. They work closely with clients and customers to ensure the designs match their needs. They also work closely with other construction professionals, such as surveyors and engineers.
Estimator	Estimators calculate detailed cost breakdowns of work based on specifications provided by the architect and main contractor. They work out the quantity and costs of all building materials, plant required and labour costs.
Planner	Consultant planners such as civil engineers work with clients to plan, manage, design or supervise construction projects. There are many different types of consultant, all with particular specialisms.
Buyer	This individual works closely with the quantity surveyor. It is the buyer's job to source suitable materials as specified by the architect. They will negotiate prices and delivery dates with a range of suppliers.

Table 3.4

Surveying

Role	Responsibilities
Land agent	This is an individual who is authorised to act as an agent in the sale of land or buildings by the owner. Basically they are estate agents that sell plots of land.
Land surveyor	A land surveyor measures, records and then produces a drawing of the landscape. The data that they produce is used to plan out construction work.
Building surveyor	A building surveyor is responsible for making sure that both old and new buildings are structurally sound. They are involved in the design, maintenance, repair, alteration and refurbishment of buildings.
Quantity surveyor	Quantity surveyors are concerned with building costs. They balance maintaining standards and quality against minimising the costs of any project. They need to make choices in line with Building Regulations. They may work either for the client or for the contractor.

Table 3.5

Engineering

Role	Responsibilities
Building services engineers	They are involved in the design, installation and maintenance of heating, water, electrics, lighting, gas and communications. They work either for the main contractor or the architect and give instruction to building services operatives.
Structural engineer	Structural engineers are involved in ensuring that construction work is strong enough to deal with its use and the external environment. So they will be involved in the shape, design and the materials used. They will not only deal with new construction work but also advise on older buildings or buildings that have been damaged.
Consulting/building engineer	These individuals are involved in site investigation, building inspection and surveys. They get involved in a wide range of construction and maintenance projects.
Plant engineer	A plant engineer is responsible for maintaining and repairing a variety of machinery and equipment. They will also install and modify machinery and equipment in factories as part of an industrial or manufacturing process.
Site engineer	A site engineer is involved in setting out the plans for sewers, drains, roads and other services.
Specialist engineer	A good example of a specialist engineer is one that deals entirely with insulation. They will advise and install a range of energy conservation materials and equipment. A geotechnical engineer is another example. They carry out investigations into below foundation level and look at rock, soil and water.
Mechanical engineer	Mechanical engineers are primarily involved in installing and maintaining machinery and tools. It is a wide ranging profession but they will have overall responsibility for their particular area of work.
Demolition engineer	These engineers perform the task of tearing down old structures or levelling ground to make way for new buildings.
Infrastructure engineer	These engineers deal with the planning, construction and management of roads, bridges and similar structures.

Table 3.6

REED
TIP
•••

Any work experience is relevant to your job applications.
It doesn't have to be paid work – e.g. volunteering to help
run Scout and Guide activities shows your sense of responsibility.
Think of the times when others have had to rely on you.

CASE STUDY

South Tyneside Homes

South Tyneside Council's
Housing Company

Your apprenticeship is just the start

Gary Kirsop, Head of Property Services, started at South Tyneside Homes as an apprentice 24 years ago.

'After becoming qualified, I had two options. I could have stayed working on the sites and become a site manager or technical assistant. I qualified as a building surveyor, doing my advanced craft at Sunderland College. After that, I went to Newcastle College to do my ONC and CHND, and eventually went on to finish a degree at Newcastle.

When I was a technical assistant I worked on education and public buildings, and spent a year in housing. As a technical assistant I was working on drawing (CAD), estimating small jobs to large jobs. Then an opportunity for Assistant Contracts Manager on capital works came up. Since then, I've also worked in disrepair and litigation, as well as two years with the empty homes department, and I've worked as a Construction Services Manager, responsible for the capital side, new homes, decent homes, and the gas team.

Four years ago, the Head of Property Services job came up and it's been a fantastic opportunity – my team has been one of the best in the country for performance. My department is responsible for repairs and maintenance, capital works, empty homes, and management of the operational side. We do responsive repairs for emergency situations, planned repairs, work for the "Decent Homes" programme where we bring properties up to standard, and we've recently built four new bungalows. Anything in construction, we have the skills and labour to do it in property services.

The full management team here in property services all started as apprentices, like me. It really helps that we understand the whole process from beginning to end.

So you can see that doing your apprenticeship is not only great in itself, but it also gives you skills for life and ongoing opportunities for education, training and your career.'

PHYSICAL AND ENVIRONMENTAL FACTORS AND CONSTRUCTION PROJECTS

Increasingly, people working in construction and the built environment are being asked to ensure that they minimise physical and environmental impacts when carrying out construction work. Construction has an enormous impact on the environment. Environmental measures will depend on the nature of the work and the site. For example, excavations that result in changes in the levels of land can cause problems with water quality and soil erosion. Many of these negative impacts can be reduced during the planning stage.

Physical and environmental factors

Physical factors relate to the impact that any new construction project will have on any existing structures and their occupants. Any new construction project is going to have a negative impact on home owners and businesses. There will be increased traffic on roads and a host of other considerations.

Once the construction has been completed there may be longer term impacts. A prime example would be building a new housing development in an area that lacks good roads, sufficient schools or access to health facilities. During the planning and development stage these factors will be looked at to see what the knock-on effects might be in the short and long term.

Environmental factors concern the impact that a construction project has on the natural environment. This would include any possible impacts on trees and vegetation, wildlife and habitats. It can also have an impact on the air quality or noise levels in the area.

Physical factors and the planning process

There is a wide variety of different physical factors that have to be taken into consideration during the planning process. These are outlined in the following table.

Physical factor	Explanation
Planning requirements	The majority of new developments or changes to existing buildings do require consent or planning permission. The local planning authority will make a decision whether any such construction will go ahead. Each authority has a development framework that outlines how planning is managed. This includes the change of use of a building or a piece of land.
Building Regulations	There are 14 technical parts of the Building Regulations covering everything from structural safety to electrical safety. They also outline standards of quality of work and materials used. All new developments and major changes to existing buildings must comply with Building Regulations.
Development or land restrictions	This is a complicated area, as there are often many restrictions on building and the use of land. One of the most complex is restrictive covenants, which are created in order to protect the interests of neighbours. They might restrict the use of the land and the amount of building work that can take place.
Building design and footprint	The footprint is the physical amount of space or area that the proposed development takes up on a given plot of land. There may be limits as to the size of this footprint. In terms of building design, certain areas may have restrictions as the local authority may not approve the construction of a building that is out of character, or that would adversely affect the overall look of the area.
Use of building or structure	Each building or structure will have a Use Class, such as 'residential', 'shops' or 'businesses'. Redeveloping an existing building and not changing the use to which it is put, for example renovating a building from a butcher to a chemist, does not usually require planning permission. However, changing from a bank to a bar would require planning permission. Certain uses, due to their unique nature, do not fall into any particular Use Class and planning permission is always required. A good example would be a nightclub or a casino.

Physical factor	Explanation
Impact on local amenities	During the construction phase it is likely that roads or access may have to be blocked, which could impact on local businesses. In the longer term additional traffic and the need for parking may have an impact on local amenities, as will the demand for their use.
Impact on existing services and utilities	Any new development or major change in use of an existing structure may put extra strain on services and utilities in the area. A new housing development, for example, would require power cables to be run to the site. It would also need excavation work to connect it to the sewers and underground pipes run onto the site for potable water. All of this is potentially disruptive and may require considerable investment by the utility or service provider.
Impact on transportation infrastructure	Major new developments will have a huge impact on the roads and public transport in an area. Permission for major developments often comes with the requirement to improve access routes, build new roads and the requirement to make a contribution to improvements in the infrastructure. New developments can radically change the flow of traffic in an area and may have a knock-on effect in terms of maintenance and repair in the longer term.
Topography of the proposed development site	The term topography refers to the location of the site and how dominant it will be in the local landscape. Obviously a development that is situated on a hill or ridge is far more obvious and will have a longer lasting impact on the local area. If the development is considered to be too obtrusive or visible then it may be deemed as inappropriate to situate the development on that site.
Greenfield or brownfield site	A greenfield site is an area of land that has never been used for non-agricultural purposes. A brownfield site is usually former industrial land, or land that has been used for some other purpose and is no longer in use. There is more information on greenfield and brownfield sites in the next section of this chapter.

Table 3.7

Environmental factors and the planning process

Just as there are physical factors, there are also different environmental factors that need to be considered. Some of the major ones are detailed in the following table.

Environmental factor	Explanation
Topography of the development site	As mentioned in the previous table, the topography of the development site can have a marked impact on the local environment. It may dominate what is otherwise a predominantly natural environment, perhaps with woodland or rolling hills.
Existing trees and vegetation	Sites may have to be cleared in order to provide the necessary space for the footprint of the structure. It may be prohibited to remove or otherwise interfere with certain trees and vegetation, as they may be protected. The normal course of events is to minimise the impact on existing plant life and to have a replanting phase after the site has been developed.
Impact on existing wildlife and habitats	Any potential impact on wildlife and plants that are under threat could mean that the site would not receive the go ahead. An environmental impact study will identify whether there are any specific dangers that will affect the natural habitat of the area, or endanger any local species of wildlife.
Size of land and building footprint	There is a formula that determines the usually permitted footprint of a piece of land compared to the actual size of the plot of land. For example, a 4-bedroom house on an average housing estate would take up approximately 1/12th of an acre (11.5 m × 29 m).

Environmental factor	Explanation
Access to the building or structure	It is not only the building plot that needs to be considered in terms of its environmental impact. Access to the site is another concern. Existing roads may have to be widened, perhaps a roundabout installed. Alternatively new roads may have to be built across other plots of land. For pedestrian traffic footpaths may also be necessary. These can either be alongside existing roads or built alongside new roads, requiring even more space. There may be existing footpaths and this could mean that access needs to be provided through the site or the footpaths diverted.
Supply of services to the building or structure	Running above ground services and utilities to the site may also present a problem as far as its impact on the environment is concerned. It may not be possible to allow features such as pylons or street lights to dominate the landscape.
Natural water resources	New developments can affect the biodiversity of an area by impacting on natural waterways. Local wildlife and plants rely on this resource. In addition to this, construction could either pollute or affect the quality of the local water.
Land restrictions	There may be land restrictions that limit either the use or the size of any development. Developments will not be allowed to adversely affect surrounding properties and owners. There are conservation areas, scheduled monuments, archaeological sites and scheduled or listed buildings. These are all protected and construction on or near them is either prohibited or severely limited.
Future development and expansion	Although the intention may be to restrict the environmental impact of the site in the first phase of development, in the future this might not be possible. Major housing development is often carried out in phases and the size of the development will gradually increase as demand increases. It is therefore important when permission is initially given that the likelihood of future development and expansion is taken into account.

Table 3.8

Figure 3.1 Trees on a proposed site may need to be protected during construction work

DID YOU KNOW?

In some cases, Tree Preservation Orders are put in place by the local planning authority. These prevent the removal of trees or work on them without permission. Some land, due to its natural beauty, importance to local wildlife and plants or special geological features, can also be protected, making it impossible for any development to take place on the site.

HOW CONSTRUCTION PROJECTS BENEFIT THE BUILT ENVIRONMENT

The construction industry is one of the UK's largest employers. It is a hugely diverse industry. Construction projects can have a massive impact on the built environment. They can rejuvenate whole areas; improve the housing stock, amenities and the general life and well-being of the local population. The built environment describes the overall look and layout of a specific area. Each new construction project and its architectural design will have an impact on that built environment and the broader, natural environment. If it is carefully and sympathetically planned and organised it can have a positive impact on the way people live, work and interact with one another.

Each new development has enormous environmental, social and economic consequences. Increasingly it has a role to play in ensuring that our built environment has a strong and sustainable future.

Land types available for development and their advantages and disadvantages

In March 2012 the National Planning Policy Framework was published, which aims to review planning guidance across the UK. The idea was to encourage the building of domestic dwellings. It stated that there would be a policy to try to use as many brownfield sites as possible, but that greenfield sites in rural areas would no longer be protected at any cost. Where development was necessary it would take place, as there was a huge demand for homes, shops and workplaces.

The first targets for development would be sites that had been used in the past for other purposes.

Greenfield land or sites

Greenfield sites are usually either agricultural or amenity land. Given the fact that there is a housing crisis in the UK and that land needs to be allocated to build millions of new homes, greenfield sites are very much under consideration.

The problem in doing this is that there is huge resistance, particularly in rural areas, to losing greenfield sites for the following reasons:

* Once a greenfield site has been developed it is extremely unlikely that it will ever return to agricultural use. Any loss of agricultural land means a reduction in the amount of food that can be produced in the UK. There might also be a drop in employment in the local area as fewer farm workers are needed.

* Natural habitats of wildlife and plants are destroyed forever.

* Greenfield or amenity land, if lost, means that the land can no longer be used for leisure and recreation.

- Developments on greenfield sites can have a negative impact on the local transport infrastructure and will increase the amount of energy used because things are further away from town centres.

- The loss of green belts of agricultural land around cities, towns and villages means that each separate area loses its identity and in effect becomes a suburb of a larger town or city.

Figure 3.2 Building on greenfield and greenbelt land is a controversial issue

Brownfield land or sites

Brownfield sites are pieces of land that have been previously developed. They were probably used for either industrial or commercial purposes, but are now derelict and abandoned.

Figure 3.3 Brownfield sites have already been built on

Brownfield sites can be found in areas where there is a high demand for new homes. It has been estimated that there are more than 66,000 hectares of brownfield sites in England alone. At least a third of this land can be found in the southeast of England, where there is the highest demand for housing. Around 60 per cent of new housing is being built on brownfield sites. This is a trend that is likely to accelerate over the next 10 years.

Brownfield sites are not just used for housing projects but are also sites for commercial buildings, as well as recreational sites and newly planted woodland.

Reclaimed land

There are areas, particularly around the coast and in estuaries, which for many years have been bogs or salt marshes. These damp grasslands can be gradually drained of water and eventually provide agricultural land or, in some cases, land suitable for housing developments. With global warming and climate change threatening to permanently flood huge areas of the UK, it may seem strange to consider humans reversing the process.

The area is converted by digging flood relief channels and drainage ditches to encourage the water to flow out and away from the land. To protect the land during this process banks are built to keep out river and seawater. It is a long and involved process but can provide possible land for redevelopment. This process has been successful in many different parts of the world, notably in the Fens in East Anglia, on the Netherlands coast, where pumping stations reclaim land from the sea, and in the Middle and Far East where huge projects have reclaimed vast areas of land.

Figure 3.4 Reclaiming land enables it to be put other uses

Contaminated land

Many brownfield sites, particularly those once used for industrial purposes, are contaminated with varying levels of hazardous waste and pollutants. Before any development can take place an environmental consultant will organise the analysis of soil, ground water and surface water to identify any risks.

Special licences are required to reclaim brownfield sites and this can be a very expensive process for developers. The main way of dealing with brownfield sites is a process known as remediation. This involves the removal of any known contaminants to a level that will not affect the health of anyone living or working on the site both during construction and after building is complete.

Not all brownfield sites are, therefore, suitable or cost-effective. In some cases the cost of removing the contaminants exceeds the value of the land after it has been developed. There are new ways of dealing with contaminants:

* Bioremediation – this uses bacteria, plants, fungi and micro-organisms to destroy or neutralise contaminants.

* Phytoremediation – plants are encouraged to grow on the site and the contaminants are taken up into the plant and stored in their leaves and stems.

* Chemical oxidation – this involves injecting oxygen or oxidants into contaminated soil and water to destroy contaminants.

DID YOU KNOW?

Brownfield redevelopment has huge advantages as it not only deals with environmental health hazards, but also regenerates areas. It can provide affordable housing, jobs and conservation.

Figure 3.5 Contaminated land must be cleaned before use

Social benefits of construction development

The construction industry and the built environment do provide a range of potential benefits, particularly to local areas. These are examined in the following table.

Social benefit	Explanation
Regeneration of brownfield sites	Disused land, usually former industrial sites, and have been developed for new housing and commercial sites. In London, virtually the whole of the 2012 Olympic village was built on brownfield sites.
Local employment	Construction sites need the skills of local construction workers and offer opportunities for small businesses. Long-term projects offer long-term employment for local people.
Improved housing	New developments and refurbishment of older properties provide greener and more energy efficient dwellings. This has a long-term positive impact for the environment and the reduction in the use of non-renewable resources.
Improvements to local infrastructure	A new development of any size often comes with the requirement for the developers to contribute towards the building of new roads and other infrastructure projects for the area. New developments, in order to work, need access roads, transport and other facilities.
Improvements to local amenities	Modern housing developments and commercial properties need to have amenities near them in order to make them viable in the longer term. This means the building of schools, hospitals, health centres and shops.

Table 3.9

Figure 3.6 Sustainable developments aim to be pleasant places to live

SUSTAINABILITY

Carbon is present in all fossil fuels, such as coal or natural gas. Burning fossil fuels releases carbon dioxide, which is a greenhouse gas linked to climate change.

Energy conservation aims to reduce the amount of carbon dioxide in the atmosphere. The idea is to do this by making buildings better insulated and, at the same time, making heating appliances more efficient. It also means attempting to generate energy using renewable and/or low or zero carbon methods.

According to the government's Environment Agency, sustainable construction is all about using resources in the most efficient way. It also means cutting down on waste on site and reducing the amount of materials that have to be disposed of and put into **landfill.**

In order to achieve sustainable construction the Environment Agency recommends:

* reducing construction, demolition and excavation waste that needs to go to landfill

* cutting back on carbon emissions from construction transport and machinery

* responsibly sourcing materials

* cutting back on the amount of water that is wasted

* making sure construction does not have an impact on **biodiversity.**

What is meant by sustainability?

In the past buildings have been constructed as quickly as possible and at the lowest cost. More recently the idea of sustainable construction has focused on ensuring that the building is not only of good quality and that it is affordable, but that it is also energy efficient.

Sustainable construction also means having the least negative environmental impact. So this means minimising the use of raw materials, energy, land and water. This is not only during the build period but also for the lifetime of the building.

Figure 3.7 Eco houses are becoming more common

KEY TERMS

Landfill

– 170 million tonnes of waste from homes and businesses are generated in England and Wales each year. Much of this has to be taken to a site to be buried.

Biodiversity

– wherever there is construction there is a danger that the wildlife and plants could be disturbed or destroyed. Protecting biodiversity ensures that at risk species are conserved.

Construction and the environment

In 2010, construction, demolition and excavation produced 20 million tonnes of waste that had to go into landfill. The construction industry is also responsible for most illegal fly tipping (illegally dumping waste). In any year there are at least 350 serious pollution incidents caused as a result of construction.

Figure 3.8 Always dispose of waste responsibly

Regardless of the size of the construction job, everyone in construction is responsible for the impact they have on the environment. Good site layout, planning and management can help reduce this impact.

Sustainable construction helps to encourage this because it means managing resources in a more efficient way, reducing waste and reducing your **carbon footprint**.

Finite and renewable resources

We all know that resources such as coal and oil will eventually run out. These are examples of finite resources.

Oil is not just used as fuel – it is used in plastic, dyes, lubricants and textiles. All of these are used in the construction process.

Renewable resources are those that can be produced by moving water, the sun or the wind. Materials that come from plants, such as biodiesel, or the oils used to make some pressure-sensitive adhesives, are examples of renewable resources.

The construction process itself is only part of the problem. It is also the longer term impact and demands that the building will have on the environment. This is why there has been a drive towards sustainable homes and there is a Code for Sustainable Homes, which is a certification of sustainability for new build housing.

The future

Sustainability also means ensuring that future generations do not suffer from the ill-considered activities of today's generation. The following table outlines some of the present dangers and concerns.

Present or future concern	Explanation
Global shortages	Many naturally found resources will eventually run out and they will have to be replaced with alternatives. Acting now to discover, develop or use alternatives will delay this. Construction is at the forefront of finding alternatives and looking at different construction materials and methods.
Needs of future generations	Buildings constructed today must to be useful and affordable for future generations. At the same time, materials and construction methods should not leave a bad legacy that future generations have to deal with.
Global warming	The construction industry has been criticised over its contribution to global warming. A lack of co-ordination between different parts of the industry has produced poor quality, energy-inefficient buildings. The government is keen to ensure that the industry trains people about the principles of sustainable design and efficient technologies. These steps need to be put in place to inform decisions at the design stage of a building.
Climate change	Construction projects need to take into account the effects of climate change and consider ways to reduce the project's impact on the environment. This means minimising carbon emissions, using sustainable (or renewable) energy and reducing water consumption.
Extinction of species and vegetation	Global warming and climate change has an impact on animals and plants. On a local level, this is also a problem as construction can destroy natural habitats. Increasingly, this is closely monitored and environmental impact studies are used to prevent this from happening.
Destruction of natural resources	There are strict planning laws that aim to prevent the industry from destroying or harming natural habitats. Ancient woodland, sites of scientific importance and other sites of interest are all protected. It is also the case that development in areas that are likely to flood or cause flooding are prohibited or controlled.

Table 3.10

KEY TERMS

Global warming

– a rise in temperature of the earth's atmosphere. The planet is naturally warmed by rays, some being reflected back out into space. The atmosphere is made up of gases (some are called greenhouse gases) which are mainly natural and form a kind of thermal blanket. The human-made gases are believed to make this blanket thicker, so less of the heat escapes back into space. Over the past 100 years, our climate has seen some rapid changes. This is believed to be linked to changes in the makeup of the atmosphere and land use.

Climate change

– the burning of fossil fuels (coal, gas, wood, oil) has resulted in an increase in the amount of greenhouse gases. This has pushed up global temperatures. Across the world, millions do not have enough water, species are dying out and sea levels are rising. In the UK we see extreme events such as flooding, storms, sea level rise and droughts. We have wetter warmer winters and hotter drier summers.

Figure 3.9 Climate change may be a serious problem over the next decades

Social regeneration

Construction projects are often used to regenerate areas of the UK that have lacked investment in the past. As industry develops and changes over time, whole areas that would once have been extremely busy in the past now have empty industrial units and high unemployment levels. As the area loses jobs housing deteriorates, as does the local infrastructure, as there is no money in the local economy.

Redeveloping these waste sites is seen as a way in which a whole area can be regenerated or reborn. Construction projects bring jobs relating to the project but they also bring the promise of longer term jobs. These areas have relatively cheap land and lower rents. Also the workforce expects lower rates of pay. This attracts businesses to relocate to the new buildings created by construction developers. This brings work, improved housing, and improvements to the local infrastructure and amenities.

Sustainability and its benefits

Energy efficiency is all about using less energy to provide the same result. The plan is to try to cut the world's energy needs by 30 per cent before 2050. This means producing more energy efficient buildings. It also means using energy efficient methods to produce the materials and resources needed to construct buildings.

Alternative methods of building

The most common type of construction in the UK is brick and blockwork. However there are plenty of other options:

* timber frame – using pre-fabricated timber frames which are then clad

* insulated concrete formwork – where a polystyrene mould is filled with reinforced concrete

* structural insulated panels – where buildings are made up of rigid building boards rather like huge sandwiches

* modular construction – this uses similar materials and techniques to standard construction, but the units are built off site and transported ready-constructed to their location.

Figure 3.10 Insulated concrete formwork

Figure 3.11 Modular construction

There are alternatives to traditional flooring and roofing, all of which are greener and more sustainable. Green roofing (both living roofs and roofs made from recycled materials) has become an increasing trend in recent years. Metal roofs made of steel, aluminium and copper often use a high percentage of recycled material. They are also lightweight. Solar roof shingles, or solar roof laminates, while expensive, decrease the cost of electricity and heating for the dwelling. Some buildings even have a living roof which consists of a waterproof membrane, a drainage layer, a growing material and plants such as sedum. This provides additional insulation, absorbs air pollution, helps to collect and process rainwater and keeps the roof surface temperature down.

Just as roofs are becoming greener, so too are the options for flooring. The use of renewable resources such as bamboo, eucalyptus and cork is becoming more common. A new version of linoleum has been developed with **biodegradable**, **organic** ingredients. Some buildings are also using floorboards and joists made from non-timber materials that can be coloured, stained or patterned.

KEY TERMS

Biodegradable

– the material will more easily break down when it is no longer needed. This breaking down process is done by micro-organisms.

Organic

– natural substance, usually extracted from plants.

Figure 3.12 Solar roof tiles provide their own solar power

Figure 3.13 A stained concrete floor can be a striking feature

An increasing trend has been for what is known as off-site manufacture (OSM). European businesses, particularly those in Germany, have built over 100,000 houses. The entire house is manufactured in a factory and then assembled on site. Walls, floors, roofs, windows and doors with built-in electrics and plumbing all arrive on a lorry. Some manufacturers even offer completely finished dwellings, including carpets and curtains. Many of these modular buildings are designed to be far more energy efficient than traditional brick and block constructions. Many come ready fitted with heat pumps, solar panels and triple-glazed windows.

Figure 3.14 A timber-framed HUF haus is assembled off site

Architecture and design

The Code for Sustainable Homes Rating Scheme was introduced in 2007. Many local authorities have instructed their planning departments to encourage sustainable development. This begins with the work of the architect who designs the building.

Local authorities ask that architects and building designers:

* ensure the land is safe for development – that if it is contaminated this is dealt with first

* ensure access to and protection for the natural environment – this supports biodiversity and tries to create open spaces for local people

* reduce the negative impact on the local environment – buildings should keep noise, air, light and water pollution down to a minimum

* conserve natural resources and cut back carbon emissions – this covers energy, materials and water

* ensure comfort and security – good access, close to public transport, safe parking and protection against flooding.

Figure 3.15 Eco developments, like this one in London, are becoming more common

Using locally managed resources

The construction industry imports nearly 6 million cubic metres of sawn wood each year. Around 80 per cent of all the softwood used in construction comes from Scandinavia or Russia. Another 15 per cent comes from the rest of Europe, or even North America. The remaining 5 per cent comes from tropical countries, and is usually sourced from sustainable forests. However there is plenty of scope to use the many millions of cubic metres of timber produced in managed forests, particularly in Scotland.

Local timber can be used for a wide variety of different construction projects:

* Softwood – including pines, firs, larch and spruce – for panels, decking, fencing and internal flooring.

* Hardwood – including oak, chestnut, ash, beech and sycamore – for a wide variety of internal joinery.

Eco-friendly, sustainable manufactured products and environmentally resourced timber

There are now many suppliers that offer sustainable building materials as a green alternative. Tiles, for example, can be made from recycled plastic bottles and stone particles.

There is a National Green Specification database of all environmentally friendly building materials. This provides a checklist where it is possible to compare specifications of environmentally friendly materials to those of traditionally manufactured products, such as bricks.

Simple changes to construction, such as using timber or ethylene-based plastics instead of PVCU window frames is a good example.

Finding locally managed resources such as timber makes sense in terms of cost and in terms of protecting the environment.

PRACTICAL TIP

www.recycledproducts. org,uk has a long list of recycled surfacing products, such as tiles, recycled wood and paving and detials of local suppliers

DID YOU KNOW?

The Forest Stewardship Council has a system that verifies that wood comes from well-managed forests. The Programme for the Endorsement of Forest Certification Schemes promotes sustainable managed forests throughout the world. (www.fsc.org and www.pefc.co.uk)

The Timber Trade Federation produces a Timber Certification System. This ensures that wood products are labelled to show that they are produced in sustainable forests.

Building Regulations

In terms of energy conservation, the most important UK law is the Building Regulations 2010, particularly Part L. The Building Regulations:

- list the minimum efficiency requirements
- provide guidance on compliance, the main testing methods, installation and control
- cover both new dwellings and existing dwellings.

A key part of the regulations is the Standard Assessment Procedure (SAP), which measures or estimates the energy efficiency performance of buildings.

Local planning authorities also now require that all new developments generate at least 10 per cent of their energy from renewable sources. This means that each new project has to be assessed one at a time.

Energy conservation

By law, each local authority is required to reduce carbon dioxide emissions and to encourage the conservation of energy. This means that everyone has a responsibility in some way to conserve energy:

- Clients, along with building designers, are required to include energy efficient technology in the build.
- Contractors and sub-contractors have to follow these design guidelines. They also need to play a role in conserving energy and resources when actually working on site.
- Suppliers of products are required by law to provide information on energy consumption.

DID YOU KNOW?

The Energy Saving Trust has lots of information about construction. Its website is www.energysavingtrust.org.uk.

energy® saving trust

Figure 3.16 The Energy Saving Trust encourages builders to use less wasteful building techniques and more energy efficient construction

In addition, new energy efficiency schemes and building regulations cover the energy performance of buildings. Each new build is required to have an Energy Performance Certificate. This rates a building's energy efficiency from A (which is very efficient) to G (which is least efficient).

Some building designers have also begun to adopt other voluntary ways of attempting to protect the environment. These include: BREEAM (Building Research Establishment Environmental Assessment Method, a voluntary measurement rating for green buildings) and the Code for Sustainable Homes (a certification of sustainability for new builds).

High, low and zero carbon

When we look at energy sources, we consider their environmental impact in terms of how much carbon dioxide they release. Accordingly, energy sources can be split into three different groups:

* high carbon – those that release a lot of carbon dioxide

* low carbon – those that release some carbon dioxide

* zero carbon – those that do not release any carbon dioxide.

Some examples of high carbon, low carbon and zero carbon energy sources are given in the tables below.

High carbon energy source	Description
Natural gas or LPG	Piped natural gas or liquid petroleum gas stored in bottles
Fuel oils	Domestic fuel oil, such as diesel
Solid fuels	Coal, coke and peat
Electricity	Generated from non-renewable sources, such as coal-fired power stations

Table 3.11

Low carbon energy source	Description
Solar thermal	Panels used to capture energy from the sun to heat water
Solid fuel	Biomass such as logs, wood chips and pellets
Hydrogen fuel cells	Converts chemical energy into electrical energy
Heat pumps	Devices that convert low temperature heat into higher temperature heat
Combined heat and power (CHP)	Generates electricity as well as heat for water and space heating
Combined cooling, heat and power (CCHP)	A variation on CHP that also provides a basic air conditioning system

Table 3.12

Zero carbon energy	Description
Electricity/wind	Uses natural wind resources to generate electrical energy
Electricity/tidal	Uses wave power to generate electrical energy
Hydroelectric	Uses the natural flow of rivers and streams to generate electrical energy
Solar photovoltaic	Uses solar cells to convert light energy from the sun into electricity

Table 3.13

It is important to try to conserve non-renewable energy so that there will be sufficient fuel for the future. The idea is that the fuel should last as long as is necessary to completely replace it with renewable sources, such as wind or solar energy.

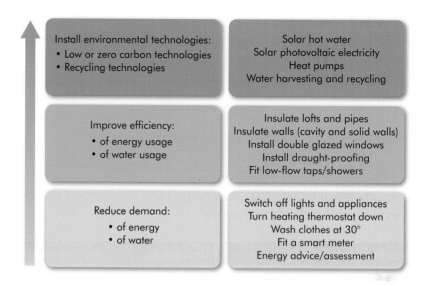

Figure 3.17 Working towards reducing carbon emissions

Alternative energy sources

There are several new ways in which we can harness the power of water, the sun and the wind to provide us with new heating sources. All of these systems are considered to be far more energy efficient than traditional heating systems, which rely on gas, oil, electricity or other fossil fuels.

Solar thermal

At the heart of this system is the solar collector, which is often referred to as a solar panel. The idea is that the collector absorbs the sun's energy, which is then converted into heat. This heat is then applied to the system's heat transfer fluid.

The system uses a differential temperature controller (DTC) that controls the system's circulating pump when solar energy is available and there is a demand for water to be heated.

In the UK, due to the lack of guaranteed solar energy, solar thermal hot water systems often have an auxiliary heat source, such as an immersion heater.

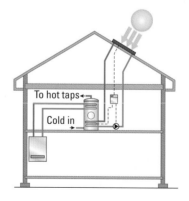

Figure 3.18 Solar thermal hot water system

Biomass (solid fuel)

Biomass stoves burn either pellets or logs. Some have integrated hoppers that transfer pellets to the burner. Biomass boilers are available for pellets, woodchips or logs. Most of them have automated systems to clean the heat exchanger surfaces. They can provide heat for domestic hot water and space heating.

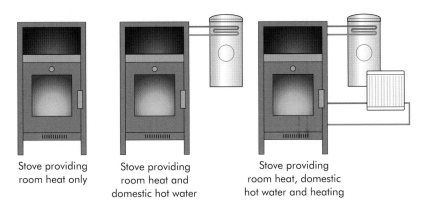

Stove providing room heat only

Stove providing room heat and domestic hot water

Stove providing room heat, domestic hot water and heating

Figure 3.19 Biomass stoves output options

Heat pumps

Heat pumps convert low temperature heat from air, ground or water sources to higher temperature heat. They can be used in ducted air or piped water **heat sink** systems.

There are different arrangements for each of the three main systems:

* Air source pumps operate at temperatures down to minus 20°C. They have units that receive incoming air through an inlet duct.

* Ground source pumps operate on **geothermal** ground heat. They use a sealed circuit collector loop, which is buried either vertically or horizontally underground.

* Water source pump systems can be used where there is a suitable water source, such as a pond or lake. Energy extracted from the water is used as heat

KEY TERMS

Heat sink

– this is a heat exchanger that transfers heat from one source into a fluid, such as in refrigeration, air conditioning or the radiator in a car.

Geothermal

– relating to the internal heat energy of the earth.

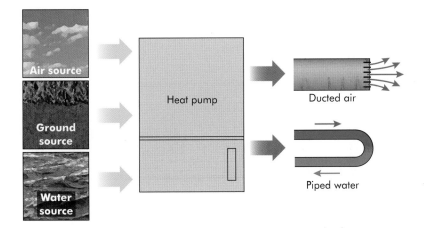

Figure 3.20 Heat pump input and output options

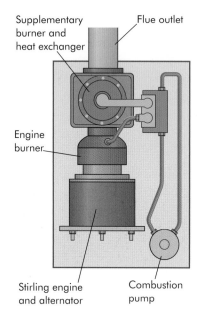

Supplementary burner and heat exchanger

Flue outlet

Engine burner

Stirling engine and alternator

Combustion pump

Figure 3.21 Example of a MCHP (micro combined heat and power) unit

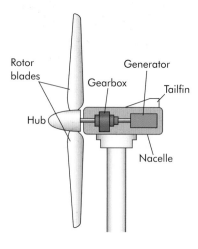

Rotor blades

Generator

Gearbox

Tailfin

Hub

Nacelle

Figure 3.22 A basic horizontal axis wind turbine

The heat pump system's efficiency relies on the temperature difference between the heat source and the heat sink. Special tank hot water cylinders are part of the system, giving a large surface-to-surface contact between the heating circuit water and the stored domestic hot water.

Combined heat and power (CHP) and combined cooling heat and power (CCHP) units

These are similar to heating system boilers, but they generate electricity as well as heat for hot water or space heating (or cooling). The heart of the system is an engine or gas turbine. The gas burner provides heat to the engine when there is a demand for heat. Electricity is generated along with sufficient energy to heat water and to provide space heating.

CCHP systems also incorporate the facility to cool spaces when necessary.

Wind turbines

Freestanding or building-mounted wind turbines capture the energy from wind to generate electrical energy. The wind passes across rotor blades of a turbine, which causes the hub to turn. The hub is connected by a shaft to a gearbox. This increases the speed of rotation. A high speed shaft is then connected to a generator that produces the electricity.

Solar photovoltaic systems

A solar photovoltaic system uses solar cells to convert light energy from the sun into electricity.

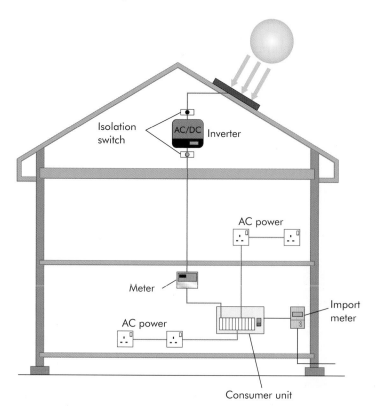

Isolation switch

AC/DC Inverter

AC power

Meter

Import meter

AC power

Consumer unit

Figure 3.23 A basic solar photovoltaic system

Energy ratings

Energy rating tables are used to measure the overall efficiency of a dwelling, with rating A being the most energy efficient and rating G the least energy efficient.

Alongside this, an environmental impact rating measures the dwelling's impact in terms of how much carbon dioxide it produces. Again, rating A is the highest, showing it has the least impact on the environment, and rating G is the lowest.

A Standard Assessment Procedure (SAP) is used to place the dwelling on the energy rating table. This will take into account:

* the date of construction, the type of construction and the location

* the heating system

* insulation (including cavity wall)

* double glazing.

The ratings are used by local authorities and other groups to assess the energy efficiency of new and old housing and must be provided when houses are sold.

Preventing heat loss

Most old buildings are under-insulated and will benefit from additional insulation, which can be for ceilings, walls or floors.

The measurement of heat loss in a building is known as the U Value. It measures how well parts of the building transfer heat. Low U Values represent high levels of insulation. U Values are becoming more important as they form the basis of energy and carbon reduction standards.

By 2016 all new housing is expected to be Net Zero Carbon. This means that the building should not be contributing to climate change.

Many of the guidelines are now part of Building Regulations (Part L). They cover:

* insulation requirements
* openings, such as doors and windows
* solar heating and other heating
* ventilation and air conditioning
* space heating controls
* lighting efficiency
* air tightness.

Building design

UK homes spend £2.4bn every year just on lighting. One of the ways of tackling this cost is to use energy saving lights, but also to maximise natural lighting. For the construction industry this means:

* increased window size

* orientating window angles to make the most of sunlight – south facing windows maximise sunlight in winter and limit overheating in the summer

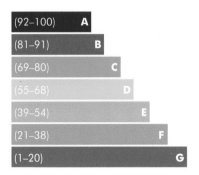

Figure 3.24 SAP energy efficiency rating table. The ranges in brackets show the percentage energy efficiency for each banding

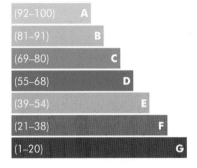

Figure 3.25 SAP environmental impact rating table

* window design – with a variety of different types of opening to allow ventilation.

Solar tubes are another way of increasing light. These are small domes on the roof, which collect sunlight and direct it through a tube (which is reflective). It is then directed through a diffuser in the ceiling to spread light into the room.

Waste water recycling

Water is a precious resource, so it is vital not to waste it. To meet the current demand for water in the UK, it is essential to reduce the amount of water used and to recycle water where possible.

The construction industry can contribute to water conservation by effective plumbing design and through the installation of water efficient appliances and fittings. These include low or dual flush WCs, and taps and fittings with flow regulators and restrictors. In addition, rainwater harvesting and waste water recycling should be incorporated into design and construction wherever possible.

Statutory legislation for water wastage and misuse

Water efficiency and conservation laws aim to help deal with the increasing demand for water. Just how this is approached will depend on the type of property:

* For new builds, the Code for Sustainable Homes and Part G of the Building Regulations set new water efficiency targets.

* For existing buildings, Part G of the Building Regulations applies to all refurbishment projects where there is a major change of use.

* For owners of non-domestic buildings, tax reduction schemes and grants are available for water efficiency projects.

In addition, the Water Supply (Water Fittings) Regulations 1999 set a series of efficiency improvements for fittings used in toilets, showers and washing machines, etc.

Reducing water wastage

There are many different ways in which water wastage can be reduced, as shown in the table below.

Method	Explanation
Flow reducing valves	Water pressure is often higher than necessary. By reducing the pressure, less water is wasted when taps are left running.
Spray taps	Fixing one of these inserts can reduce water consumption by as much as 70 per cent.
Low volume flush WC	These reduce water use from 13 litres per flush to 6 litres for a full flush and 4 litres for a reduced flush.
Maintenance of terminal fittings and float valves	Dripping taps or badly adjusted float valves can cause enormous water wastage. A dripping tap can waste 5,000 litres a year.
Promoting user awareness	Users who are on a meter will certainly see a difference if water efficiency is improved, and their energy bills will be reduced if they use less hot water.

Table 3.14

Captured and recycled water systems

There are two variations of captured and recycled water systems:

* Rainwater harvesting captures and stores rainwater for non-potable use (not for drinking).

* Greywater reuse systems capture and store waste water from baths, washbasins, showers, sinks and washing machines.

Rainwater harvesting

In this system, water is harvested usually from the roof and then distributed to a tank. Here it is filtered and then pumped into the dwelling for reuse. The recycled water is usually stored in a cistern at the top of the building.

Greywater reuse

The idea of this system is to reduce mains water consumption. The greywater is piped from points of use, such as sinks and showers, through a filter and into a storage tank. The greywater is then pumped into a cistern where it can be used for toilet flushing or for watering the garden.

Waste management

The expectation within the construction industry is increasingly that working practices conserve energy and protect the environment. Everyone can play a part in this. For example, you can contribute at home by turning off hose pipes when you have finished using water.

Simple things, such as keeping construction sites neat and orderly, can go a long way to conserving energy and protecting the environment. A good way to remember this is Sort, Set, Shine, Standardise:

Sort – sort and store items in your work area, eliminate clutter and manage deliveries.

Set – everything should have its own place and be clearly marked and easy to access. In other words, be neat!

Shine – clean your work area and you will be able to see potential problems far more easily.

Standardise – using standardised working practices you can keep organised, clean and safe.

Reducing material wastage

Reducing waste is all about good working practice. By reducing wastage disposal and recycling materials on site, you will benefit from savings on raw materials and lower transportation costs.

Let's start by looking at ways to reduce waste when buying and storing materials:

* Only order the amount of materials you actually need.

* Arrange regular deliveries so you can reduce storage and material losses.

* Think about using recycled materials, as they may be cheaper.

* Is all the packaging absolutely necessary? Can you reduce the amount of packaging?

* Reject damaged or incomplete deliveries.

* Make sure that storage areas are safe, secure and weatherproof.

* Store liquids away from drains to prevent pollution.

By planning ahead and accurately measuring and cutting materials, you will be able to reduce wastage.

Statutory legislation for waste management

By law, all construction sites should be kept in good order and clean. A vital part of this is the proper disposal of waste, which can range from low risk waste, such as metals, plastics, wood and cardboard, to hazardous waste, for example asbestos, electrical and electronic equipment and refrigerants.

Waste is anything that is thrown away because it is no longer useful or needed. However, you cannot simply discard it, as some waste can be recycled or reused while other waste will affect health or the quality of the environment.

Legislation aims not only to prevent waste from going into landfill but also to encourage people to recycle. For example, under the Environmental Protection Act (1990), the building services industry has the following duty of care with regard to waste disposal:

* All waste for disposal can only be passed over to a licensed operator.

* Waste must be stored safely and securely.

* Waste should not cause environmental pollution.

The main legislation covering the disposal of waste is outlined in the table below.

Legislation	Brief explanation
Environmental Protection Act (1990)	Defines waste and waste offences
Environmental Protection (Duty of Care) Regulations (1991)	Places the responsibility for disposal on the producer of the waste
Hazardous Waste Regulations (2005)	Defines hazardous waste and regulates the safe management of hazardous waste
Waste Electrical and Electronic Equipment (WEEE) Regulations (2006)	Requires those who produce electrical and electronic waste to pay for its collection, treatment and recovery
Waste Regulations (2011)	Introduces a system for waste carrier registration

Table 3.15

Safe methods of waste disposal

In order to dispose of waste materials legally, you must use the right method.

* **Waste transfer notes** are required for every load of waste that is passed on or accepted.

* **Licensed waste disposal** is carried out by operators of landfill sites or those that store other people's waste, treat it, carry out recycling or are involved in the final disposal of waste.

* **Waste carriers' licences** are required by any company that transports waste, not just waste contractors or skip operators. For example, electricians or plumbers that carry construction and demolition waste would need to have this licence, as would anyone involved in construction or demolition.

* **Recycling** of materials such as wood, glass, soil, paper, board or scrap metal is dealt with at materials reclamation facilities. They sort the material, which is then sent to reprocessing plants so it can be reused.

* **Specialist disposal** is used for waste such as asbestos. There are authorised asbestos disposal sites that specialise in dealing with this kind of waste.

Recycling metals

Scrap metal is divided into two different types:

* **Ferrous** scrap includes iron and steel, mainly from beams, cars and household appliances.

* **Non-ferrous** scrap is all other types of metals, including aluminium, lead, copper, zinc and nickel.

Recycling businesses will collect and store metals and then transport them to **foundries**. The operators will have a licence, permit or consent to store, handle, transport and treat the metal.

Recycling plastics

Different types of plastic are used for different things, so they will need to be recycled separately. Licensed collectors will pass on the plastics to recycling businesses that will then remould the plastics.

Recycling wood and cardboard

Building sites will often generate a wide variety of different wood waste, such as off-cuts, shavings, chippings and sawdust.

Paper and cardboard waste can be passed on to an authorised waste carrier.

Disposing of asbestos

Asbestos should only be disposed of by specialist contractors. It needs to be double wrapped in approved packaging, with a hazard sign and asbestos code information visible. You should also dispose of any contaminated PPE in this way. The standard practice is to use a

KEY TERMS

Ferrous – metals that contain iron.

Non-ferrous – metals that do not contain any iron.

Foundry – a place where metal is melted and poured into moulds.

PRACTICAL TIP

Before collection, plastics should be stored on hard, waterproof surfaces, undercover and away from water courses.

PRACTICAL TIP

Sites must only pass waste on to an authorised waste carrier, and it is important to keep records of all transfers.

red inner bag with the asbestos warning and a clear outer bag with a carriage of dangerous goods (CDG) sign.

Asbestos waste should be carried in a sealed skip or in a separate compartment to other waste. It should be transported by a registered waste carrier and disposed of at a licensed site. Documentation relating to the disposal of asbestos must be kept for three years.

Disposing of electrical and electronic equipment

The Waste Electrical and Electronic Equipment (WEEE) Regulations were first introduced in the UK in 2006. They were based on EU law – the WEEE Directive of 2003.

Normally, the costs of electrical and electronic waste collection and disposal fall on either the contractor or the client. Disposal of items such as this are part of Site Waste Management Plans, which apply to all construction projects in England worth more than £300,000.

* For equipment purchased after August 2005, it is the responsibility of the producer to collect and treat the waste.

* For equipment purchased before August 2005 that is being replaced, it is the responsibility of the supplier of the equipment to collect and dispose of the waste.

* For equipment purchased before August 2005 that is not being replaced, it is the responsibility of either the contractor or client to dispose of the waste.

Disposing of refrigerants

Refrigerators, freezer cabinets, dehumidifiers and air conditioners contain **fluorinated gases**, known as chloro-fluoro-carbons (CFCs). CFCs have been linked with damage to the Earth's **ozone layer**, so production of most CFCs ceased in 1995.

Refrigerants such as these have to be collected by a registered waste company, which will de-gas the equipment. During the de-gassing process, the coolant is removed so that it does not leak into the atmosphere.

Key benefits of using sustainable materials

In summary:

* Using locally sourced materials not only cuts down on the transportation costs but also the pollution and energy used in transporting that material. At the same time their use provides employment for local suppliers.

* In choosing sustainable materials rather than materials that have to go through complex production processes or be shipped in from other parts of the world, construction should be more efficient and have a lower general impact on the environment.

* The use of energy saving materials will have a long-term and lasting impact on the use of energy for the duration of the property's life.

KEY TERMS

Fluorinated gases

– powerful greenhouse gases that contribute to global warming.

Ozone layer

– thin layer of gas high in the Earth's atmosphere.

* Not only will the construction industry have a lower carbon footprint, but also everything they build will have been constructed using lower carbon technologies and materials.

* Protecting the local natural environment from damage by construction work or surrounding infrastructure is only part of the environmental consideration. In choosing sustainable materials to use in construction projects the natural environment is protected elsewhere, by reducing quarrying, tree-felling and the use of scarce resources

* Recycling as much construction waste as possible, particularly from demolition, means that the industry will make less contribution to landfill. Most materials except those that are toxic or hazardous can be repurposed.

TEST YOURSELF

1. What area of the construction and built environment industry would be involved in examining planning applications regarding the long-term future of an area?

   a. Town planners

   b. Surveyors

   c. Civil engineers

   d. Construction site managers

2. What is the term used to describe transport routes such as roads, motorways, bridges and railways?

   a. Services

   b. Infrastructure

   c. Commercial

   d. Utilities

3. Which of the following is an example of a corporate client?

   a. Small business owner

   b. Local authority

   c. Government department

   d. Insurance company

4. What is another term that can be used to describe a land agent?

   a. Land surveyor

   b. Quantity surveyor

   c. Estate agent

   d. Building inspector

5. Which job role involves overseeing construction work on behalf of an architect or client to represent their interests on site?

   a. Clerk of works

   b. Main contractor

   c. Sub-contractor

   d. Building control inspector

6. Which of the following is an example of a renewable energy resource?

   a. Plants

   b. Sun

   c. Wind

   d. All of these

7. What does the National Green Specification Database provide?

   a. Methods on how to recycle

   b. A list of all recycling sites

   c. A list of environmentally friendly building materials

   d. A list of components required for building jobs

8. Which part of the Building Regulations focuses on energy conservation?

   a. Part B

   b. Part G

   c. Part H

   d. Part L

9. Which of the following is an example of biomass?

   a. Coal

   b. Peat

   c. Coke

   d. Logs

10. In addition to providing heating, which of the following also provides cooling?

    a. CCHP

    b. CHP

    c. MCHP

    d. HPCP

Chapter 4

Unit CSA–L2Occ36
CARRY OUT FIRST FIXING OPERATIONS

LEARNING OUTCOMES

LO1/2: Know how to and be able to prepare for first fixing operations

LO3/4: Know how to and be able to install timber frames and linings

LO5/6: Know how to and be able to install timber floor coverings and flat roof decking

LO7/8: Know how to and be able to erect timber stud partitions

LO9/10: Know how to and be able to install straight flights of stairs and handrails

INTRODUCTION

The aims of this chapter are to:

* help you select resources and carry out the work

* help you to erect and fix first fixing components in accordance with the work specification.

FIRST FIXING OPERATIONS

The term first fix is common in the construction industry. It involves all operations that take a building from its foundations through to plastering.

For carpentry work this means involvement in the construction of walls, floors, ceilings and stairs, as well as many other activities. This chapter covers those activities required at Level 3:

* fixing frames and linings

* fitting and fixing floor coverings and flat roof decking

* erecting timber stud partitions

* assembling, erecting and fixing straight flights of stairs including handrails.

Working drawings, specifications and schedules

Drawings and their purpose are covered in detail in Chapter 2.

All drawings must follow the requirements of BS 1192:2007. This means that the drawings will have a common format and symbols. Building drawings use what is known as first angle orthographic projection. Drawings in this form will be identified by a special symbol.

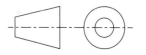

Figure 4.1 First angle projection symbol

Datum points

A site datum point is a fixed point against which all other levels on the site can be measured. It is usually located at the damp-proof course level. Site datums are now usually related to the Ordnance Survey national grid, a standard grid that applies across the country. It is at a known height above sea level. GPS may also be used. Less commonly, the site datum is related to another fixed point, such as:

- an **Ordnance Survey Benchmark (OSBM)** on public buildings or cut into walls, although these are not used as much these days because often they are not maintained

- curb edge

- maintenance/inspection chamber frame

- TBM (temporary benchmark), which could be any agreed item but may change as the site develops

- ABM (arbitrary benchmark), which could be a relatively permanent point, like the plinth of a building, with its level given an arbitrary height that may not be its actual height.

The site datum is marked on the site by a steel post or peg concreted into the ground, usually near the site office.

PPE

Refer to Chapter 1 for details about PPE required for work on site and elsewhere.

Tools and equipment

On site you will use a wide variety of different tools and equipment, depending on the job. You will need to be able to select the correct tool or piece of equipment for each of these jobs. They are detailed in Table 4.1.

Figure 4.2 The OSBM symbol

Tool or equipment	Use
Saws Figure 4.3 Cross-cut saw Figure 4.4 Panel saw Figure 4.5 Tenon saw	There is a wide variety of different saws. Some are modern hard point disposable saws but others are traditional hand saws that can last a lifetime. Saws include: • Cross-cut – for cutting timber across the grain • Panel – for fine cross-cutting, particularly plywood and hardboard. Cross-cut and panel saws are used at an angle of less than 45° to prevent tear out. Their teeth are sharpened at an angle • Tenon – a general purpose bench saw which provides a higher accuracy in cutting, due to its rigid spine along the top of the blade • Rip – for cutting along or with the grain. They are used at approximately 45° with teeth that cut like a chisel. They are sharpened on their front edge • Pull – used for ripping and cross-cutting • General or fine hard point panel saws– for most carpentry activities • Coping – for cutting out curved work and scribing on internal mouldings such as complex skirting profiles.

Tool or equipment	Use
Hammers  Figure 4.6 Claw hammer  Figure 4.7 Club or lump hammer	There are a number of different hammers used and on site these generally include: • Claw – a general all-purpose hammer, for nailing or for taking out nails. They are made of a variety of materials but mainly have a steel head with a steel, wood or fibreglass shaft • Mallet – can either be wedge or round-headed. The wedge shape is more common on site. A rubber mallet is most commonly used when carrying out bench joinery work • Warrington or cross pein – used for lighter work such as nailing glazing beads and mouldings • Lump hammers – used for heavier work such as chopping out masonry.
Chisels  Figure 4.8 Bevel-edged chisels	Split-proof handled chisels that have impact-resistant plastic handles are most favoured on site. Conventional wooden chisels are more likely to be used for bench work. Bevel-edged chisels sit tight into corners of trenches or housings. They are particularly useful when producing dovetail joints. Mortice chisels are used for dropping the mortice half of a mortice and tenon joint. They are very strong and are designed not to snap when chopping deep into the timber. They are rectangular in cross section.
Screwdrivers  Figure 4.9 A selection of screwdrivers	Pozidriv screwdrivers have star-shaped heads. Phillips screwdrivers have cross heads. Slotted screwdrivers are rectangular in section. All are available in different sizes to match screw heads and as stubby versions for use where there is limited access.
Spirit levels  Figure 4.10 Spirit levels	These are used for plumbing and levelling. They can be up to 2 m long. Generally though an 800 mm spirit level will work for most jobs. They are available as either box or beam; beam is the preferred and better quality type of level. Laser versions are available. Smaller levels are available for work in more restricted areas. Boat levels are used for levelling window boards and shorter levelling tasks with greater accuracy than using a longer spirit level.
Plumb bobs  Figure 4.11 Plumb bob	A plumb bob is a weight on the end of a string line used to find plumb. They are usually made of brass and often decoratively turned. They are available in different weights and provide a high level of accuracy over longer distance plumb levelling.

Tool or equipment	Use
Electric and cordless drills  Figure 4.12 Impact drill	Multipurpose drills can perform a variety of tasks. They fall into the following categories: • Rotary impact – these produce a hammer action, ideal for masonry and concrete • Rotary hammer – these go through masonry and concrete very quickly • Electro-pneumatic – much more powerful than normal hammer drills. There are also battery-powered versions. Drills can be slowed down for use as screwdrivers or they can incorporate impact or rotary hammer functions. Power tools on construction sites must operate at 110 V. Cordless drills are battery-powered.
Drill bits  Figure 4.13 Drill bits	HSS drill bits come in 1 mm to 12 mm sizes and can be used to drill wood or steel to a given diameter.
Powered nailer  Figure 4.14 Nail gun/powered nailer	Nail guns are widely used on site, particularly for new builds. There are three different types: • Pneumatic – with air hoses and portable compressors. • Cordless – with gas fuel cells, spark plugs and rechargeable batteries. • Cordless with rechargeable battery only. There are also nailing guns that will fix thin timber to hard surfaces, such as masonry, concrete or steel. Powered nailers are ballistic fixing tools and you must be certificated to use it.
Tape measure  Figure 4.15 Measures	Tape measures or rules can be lockable with return blades and belt clips. The metal versions are preferred as they are less likely to stretch. A carpenter's wooden ruler is known as a carpenter's rule. It is useful for measuring and marking smaller objects. Some are made from boxwood while others are in engineering plastic and are virtually unbreakable.
Laser level  Figure 4.16 Laser level	Laser levels have become very affordable. Originally they were expensive and only used by surveyors. They can be fixed to tripods and give very accurate levelling measurements. Another useful tool for setting out straight lines is the chalk line reel.

Tool or equipment	Use
Try square  Figure 4.17 Try square	It has a wood, plastic or metal stock and set at right angles to it is a ruled, metal straight edge blade. It is used for measuring and marking square work and for testing right angles. Similar to this is a combination square, which enables a 45° angle setting, and has an adjustable sliding blade.
Planes  Figure 4.18 Planes	All woodworking hand planes are numbered according to their width, length and or use. A No 4 (smoothing plane) is the most commonly used plane. A No 5 is a jack plane, a No 6 is a fore plane, a No 7 is a try plane and a No 8 is a jointer. There are also planes marked as ½, which denotes a plane that is wider than standard. Therefore a 4½ is the same length as a 4 but wider. Other planes that the carpenter/joiner should carry include a block plane, rebate plane and a carriage plane (badger) This is a small selection of the planes available.
Water level  Figure 4.19 Water level	This is a length of hose that has a transparent tube at each end. The hose is filled with water but must be clear of trapped air. It is an ideal resource for checking levels in distances of over 30 m. It is a simple device, as water will always find its own level. A great advantage is that you can take levels around corners or obstructions.
Sliding bevel  Figure 4.20 Sliding bevel	This is an adjustable gauge. The handle is made of either wood or plastic. Connected to the handle is a metal blade that is secured by a thumbscrew or a wing nut. The bevel is used to set and then to transfer angles. The blade pivots on the thumbscrew or wing nut so it can be locked at any angle required.
Spokeshave  Figure 4.21 Spokeshave	This is a very traditional tool, which has two handles and a central blade. It is used to cut down or shave timber to fit and to deal with uneven surfaces. The two handles allow the carpenter to apply differing amounts of pressure or to maintain a steady stroke with good control.
Circular saw  Figure 4.22 Circular saw	These are mainly for ripping and cross-cutting. Cordless circular saws are not usually powerful enough for constant use due to the limitations of their rechargeable batteries.

Tool or equipment	Use
Jig saw 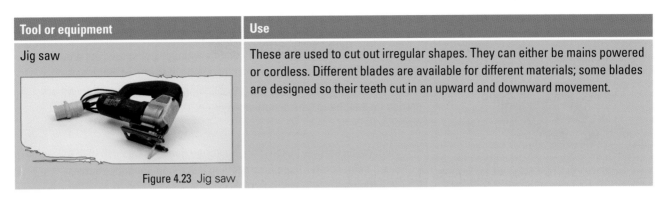 Figure 4.23 Jig saw	These are used to cut out irregular shapes. They can either be mains powered or cordless. Different blades are available for different materials; some blades are designed so their teeth cut in an upward and downward movement.

Table 4.1

Materials and fixings

Various materials are used for first fix. Many of these you will become very familiar with over time. Some are commonly used fixings while others have more specialist uses. These are detailed in Table 4.2.

Fixings	Uses
Plugs Figure 4.24 Plugs	Plastic wall plugs are screw fixing devices. They are usually made either from nylon or polythene. They are colour-coded to match screw gauge sizes.
Nails and pins Figure 4.25 Nails	There is a wide variety of different types of nails and pins, not only for different jobs but also in different sizes and shapes: • Round head wire – for first fixing, usually 75 mm × 3.75 mm or 100 mm × 4.5 mm are used. • Lost heads – generally 50 mm × 3 mm and 65 mm × 3.35 mm and are mainly used for fixing floorboards. • Ovals – mainly used for second fix on architraves and doorstops. • Cut clasp – made from mild steel and generally used for second fixings, particularly to fix directly into mortar joints, bricks or blocks. • Cut floor brads – mainly for fixing floorboards. • Annular ring shank – one of their many uses is for fixing wind bracing to trussed rafters or chipboard flooring. • Grooved shank – a reasonably new development, lightweight and with good grip. • Panel pins – mainly used for second fix carpentry such as fixing glazing beads. • Masonry nails – ideal for fixing into sand and cement rendering, mortar joints and blocks.

Fixings	Uses
Screws  Figure 4.26 Screws	As with nails there is a wide variety of different types of screw, not only in terms of gauge and length but also in the shape of the head. Each particular type of screw can also have a variety of driving slots or recess. Screws are graded by their head type, length and gauge. Their uses are countless but could include: • Countersunk screws used when the screw needs to be flush with the work. • Raised head screws used for attaching metal components, such as ironmongery. • Round head screws used for fixing sheet material to timber. • Mirror screws have a thread in the head, which can take a decorative dome. • Pan head screws are useful for fixing sheet material.
Joist hangers 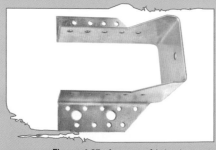 Figure 4.27 A type of joist hanger	These are U-shaped metal brackets that are used to support the ends of floor joists. They are attached with nails to a wall plate. They can also be walled or 'built in' to the brickwork. Types vary according to use; for example timber-to-timber, timber-to-masonry, etc.
Adhesives  Figure 4.28 Adhesives	Adhesives are used to bond materials together. There are two main classes: • Thermoplastic – sets when it cools and will soften if solvent is applied to the glue or it is reheated. • Thermosetting – sets and solidifies as a result of chemical reaction but this cannot be reversed. PVA adhesives bond through absorption, can be used internally and externally where specified and are a good general purpose adhesive suitable for hardwoods and softwoods, plywoods and other manufactured boards. Contact adhesives work through evaporation of solvent. This is a specific method of bonding as the adhesive is applied to both gluing surfaces, allowed to dry and then brought together so that the adhesive keys to itself. It is only used internally and is used for bonding plastic laminates. Synthetic and epoxy resins adhere through a chemical reaction when a hardener or catalyst is added to a resin in a specific quantity. They are used in laminating wooden beams, boat building and other external applications. This is just a small selection of different adhesives that you may see on site.

Materials	Uses
Timbers  Figure 4.29 Timbers	Some of the timber used during first fix will not be seen, so can be rough cut. Timber used in first fixing operations is usually but not always sawn. It is often stress-graded for uses such as floor joists and other structural work. More information about second fixing timbers can be found in Chapter 5.

Materials	Uses
Timber manufactured boards  Figure 4.30 Boards	These are wood products, such as plywood, fibreboards including the widely used medium density fibreboard **MDF** and chipboard. Wood layers or wood fibres are glued or pressured together in manufacture to create large sheets in various thicknesses. There are also other boards used that can be waterproof or water resistant. Sterling board, or orientated strand board (OSB), is made from softwood strands that have been compressed and glued together with a resin. This is suitable for exterior work and is water resistant. It is possible to prime sterling board and give it a top coat of oil-based timber paint. It is often seen as board protection over windows in empty buildings or construction site temporary hoardings.
Plasterboard  Figure 4.31 Plasterboard	This is a panel of gypsum plaster that has been pressed between two thick sheets of paper. One side of the plasterboard is used for **dry lining** and the other side for finishing (such as plastering). It is usual nowadays to apply board-finished plaster to the 'white' sides of plasterboards, so they tend to be fitted white-side-out.
Insulation  Figure 4.32 Insulation	This is material that is either inserted or pumped into cavity walling or in the void of a partition wall. It is also used in roofs. It can have thermal, acoustic or fire resistant properties or a combination of all three.

Table 4.2

Selection of materials

When selecting door frames and linings at the timber yard it is essential to get 'hands on' whenever possible. Five minutes spent checking frames and linings could save hours later, as leaving the choice to the supplier's staff is not always the best option. Remember that yard staff are generally not qualified tradespeople and, although they may have a good knowledge of the stock the yard carries, they may not understand what the carpenter or joiner would be looking for when selecting materials.

Materials delivered from suppliers

It is essential that all loads are secured when they are transported to site, for example bearers should be placed between frames to prevent damage to moulds. Where ropes or straps pass across the frames, protection should be provided: corrugated cardboard is ideal. In open-back trucks tarpaulins should be used in inclement weather.

KEY TERMS

MDF

– this is an artificial board made using sawdust. MDF stands for medium density fibreboard.

Dry lining

– plasterboard is bonded to wall surfaces using the 'dot and dab' technique. Dots of plasterboard adhesive are applied to the back of the plasterboard or the wall surface and then the board is pushed onto the wall.

PRACTICAL TIP

Timber from suppliers may have been stored in ideal and controlled conditions. When it is delivered to the site it should be given a period of acclimatisation. This means allowing the timber to react to the new conditions on site – temperature, moisture and light. This will reveal any problems with the timber in advance of installation.

When taking delivery of materials and components from suppliers:

* Operatives should briefly inspect the load before unloading begins, and any obvious damage should be brought to the attention of the driver immediately.

* While unloading, a further inspection should take place and any damaged items should be put to one side to return to the supplier. This should be recorded on the delivery note and signed by both parties.

* Count the items carefully.

* If the delivery driver disagrees with your assessment do not get involved. Instead report it to a supervisor immediately.

* If you have not had the opportunity to inspect a delivery, but you are still required to sign, mark the delivery note 'Uncounted and unchecked'.

Defects in timber

Timber is a natural product so is unlikely to be perfect. Usually there are two reasons for defects or imperfections in the wood:

* it may be naturally occurring, such as a knot

* it may be caused through poor handling or seasoning of the wood after it has been cut.

The main defects and how to rectify them are outlined in Table 4.3.

Defect	Explanation and ways of rectifying
Splits Figure 4.33	Wood may naturally contain splits, or it may dry out and shrink.
Waney edge Figure 4.34	A waney edge is a defect when the wood has been cut. Some bark is left on the board and this is still on the cut plank. This may happen through the process of converting and maximising materials to avoid undue waste. To rectify a waney edge, the bark that has been left on the board would have to be removed, and cut to give a square edge on the timber.. However, waney edge is often left intentionally as a decorative feature, such as on cladding on gable ends.

Defect	Explanation and ways of rectifying
Fungal attack  Figure 4.35	Timber that has got damp is at risk of fungal decay. For wet rot the damaged parts of the timber will need to be cut out as they will not be strong enough. For dry rot the wood needs to be sprayed with a biocide, which will kill off any strains or spores and then replaced with sound timber where necessary.
Damage caused in transit 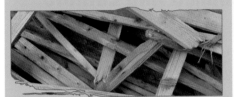 Figure 4.36	Damaged timber materials should have been rejected at the point of delivery. It is difficult to prove that the damage has not taken place on site if they have been accepted. This means that if you are responsible for signing off a delivery, you must always check timber for damage before accepting it. Your company should have a process in place for sending back damaged goods as this may impact schedules and budgets. The exact treatment of damaged timber will depend on the defect and whether it has affected the whole delivery.
Knots  Figure 4.37	Knots are fairly common and they occur when a branch has grown out of a trunk. Knots can mean that the timber is either weakened or more difficult to work with. There are two types of knot: Dead – generally black in colour, which means that the knot is not connected to the surrounding fibres and will probably fall out as soon as the board is machined or worked with tools Live – generally brown in colour. This is where the knot is still tight and connected to surrounding fibres. If sap is bleeding from the knot it has to be sealed with a knotting solution before surface decorations can be applied. The knotting prevents resin leeching through the paint finish. An arris knot is located at a corner between the face and the edge.
Shakes 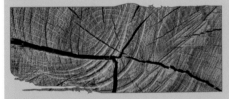 Figure 4.38	Shakes are usually found in uncut logs. There are a number of different types of shake, named after the shape in which they appear. The shakes are splits between the annual rings, or along the medullary rays, because tension has built in the tree while it was growing. If the wood is not seasoned properly and has dried out too quickly then a shake shape will appear. Shakes can also occur if the tree was allowed to fall onto a hard object when it was cut down. You cannot rectify a shake. It can be machined out at the conversion stage but is not always evident. The danger is that the timber will crack as it dries out. The wood should only ever be used where the timber is not likely to be subjected to bending.
Cupping  Figure 4.39	Cupping is a curvature across the width of a board. It is caused as a result of shrinkage occurring in relation to the growth rings.

Table 4.3

REED TIP

Everybody makes mistakes. As long as you learn from them and do not repeat them, your employer will accept this.

KEY TERMS

Profile

– this is a temporary frame.

Reveal

– a flat surface created by closing off the cavity at the opening of door and window frames.

Protecting the environment

In Chapter 3, we learned that it is important to ensure that all construction work has the least possible negative effect on the surrounding area. One of the ways of reducing its negative impacts is to keep it clean and dispose of waste in an environmentally friendly way. This means recycling as much waste as possible.

INSTALLING TIMBER FRAMES AND LININGS

There are many different types and styles of frames but there are essentially only two methods of fixing:

* Built-in frames are bedded in mortar propped level and plumb and walled in as the brickwork progresses.

* Fixed-in frames are fixed into pre-formed openings after the brickwork is complete at first fix.

The following section covers door frames, door linings, casement window frames and hatch linings.

Different types of door frames and door linings

Door frames and door linings are used for both internal and external purposes. The main difference is that the external ones are usually larger and more durable, as they have to cope with weather conditions.

The features of a door frame, regardless of whether it is internal or external, are largely the same. Door frames can either be fixed into a building as the brickwork is underway, or they can be fixed into an opening once the brickwork has been finished. It is common to use a temporary frame, known as a **profile**, if the opening is to be formed while the brickwork is underway. Once the brickwork has been finished the door frame will be permanently fixed to the brickwork.

Door linings tend to be used for internal doors. They are slightly different to door frames, as they cover the whole of the door **reveal.** These door linings are held in place with battens until the walls around them have been finished.

There are a number of different door frames and linings used in first fix operations. The following sections look at these different types in more detail.

Internal and external door casings

Interior door casings are the lining that will outline the dimension of the door. These tend to be made from softwood. Door casings can come in a variety of different widths to cope with different wall thicknesses. Internal door casings are lighter in construction than door frames. The jambs will take the weight of the door, so it is important when fixing the frame to consider the weight distribution. In other words, the jambs need to be sufficiently strong to cope with the weight and movement of the door that will be fitted into the opening.

External door casings are more robust. They also come in different sizes but are often made from hardwood. Each of the frames consists of:

* jambs – the upright components, also known as legs

* head – the top of the frame

* cill – the bottom piece of the frame (not always fitted)

* threshold – a batten fixed across a door opening that does not have a cill to prevent ingress of water and draughts.

Figure 4.40 External door on frame

Figure 4.41 Internal door and lining

Fire door casings

The British Woodworking Federation (BWF) states that all fire resistant doors should be purchased from a specialist manufacturer. They recommend:

* hardwood frames with a density of more than 650 kg/m³ for 60 minute fire doors

* softwood frames with a minimum density of 450 kg/m³ for 30 minute fire doors.

The frames or casings should always be built in brick or block, or with a timber stud or plasterboard partition that is capable of withstanding fire up to the rate of the door. Any voids need to be filled with mineral fibre or paste.

PRACTICAL TIP

All the heads of doors need to be set at the same height throughout the whole of the building. Use the site datum to achieve this. The legs of the frames or linings will extend to the floor in the case of wooden flooring but a gap needs to be left if concrete flooring has been used. Galvanised metal dowels are drilled into the bottom of the legs. These extend beyond the bottom of the leg and are concreted in when the finishing screed is applied to solid floors or beam and block flooring (or other similar construction types where there are screeds) to provide an additional fixing to the bottom of the frames' jambs or legs.

Double door casings

Fixing double door casings can be slightly more complex, and even more precise calculation is necessary. There are three gaps between the doors instead of two and the jamb on each side of the opening also needs to be taken into account. The height of the opening also needs to take into account a gap for any flooring beneath the door, as well as space for the gap between the head of the lining/casing and the top of the door.

Rebated linings

Rebated linings or casings have two rebated jambs and a rebated head. The rebate is actually wider than the width of the door. This means when the door is hung it will be flush with the edges of the lining. It will have a 1.5 mm clearance between the door and the stop and this will prevent it from binding.

Different types of window frames, linings and boards

Windows are designed to let in light to a building and they are also there to keep the weather out and the warmth in. There are, of course, various different types of window and each of these has particular characteristics. It is important to begin by understanding three key terms:

* Frame – this is the part of the window that supports the glass.

* Lining – this is the part of the window that fills the gap between the window and any surrounding masonry. New build windows may not have linings.

* Window board – this is at the bottom of the window and is an internal feature that caps off the top of the wall immediately below the window.

* Sash – this is a frame within the window frame that opens. It could be top hung, side hung or sliding.

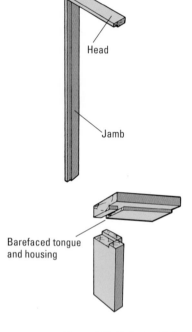

Figure 4.42 Rebated lining

Over time, a wide variety of different types of window have been developed for specific purposes. Some of them, such as dormers and skylights, tend only to feature in the roof space of a building. Other windows are more general and can be used throughout a building to contribute towards the overall style of the construction. Table 4.4 outlines some of the features of the most typical types of window.

Window type	Characteristics
Traditional	These types of window are rebated with the sash openings designed to be flush with the main frame. The joints are generally mortise and tenons.
Storm proof	These have two rebates. One of the rebates is around the main frame and the other around the casement. The main difference between these and traditional casements is that the rebates, along with other features, make them more weatherproof.
Sliding sash	There are two versions of the sliding sash window: Vertical – these have two sashes that slide up and down. They can be constructed with either boxed or solid frames. They are often referred to as being double hung sliding sash windows. Horizontal – these have windows that slide from side to side. The window is usually rectangular and the sashes slide either on a track or on hardwood runners that have been waxed.

Window type	Characteristics
Pivot	This type of window is designed so that both sides of the glass can be cleaned from the inside. In a traditional pivot window the frame and the pivoting sash are made using mortises and tenons. Storm-proof versions are also available.

Table 4.4

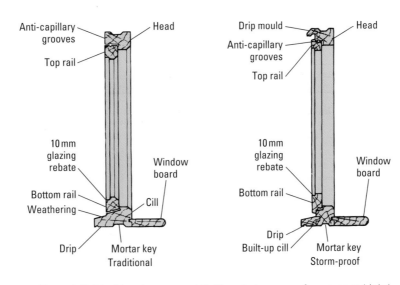

Figure 4.43 Traditional casement (left) and storm-proof casement (right)

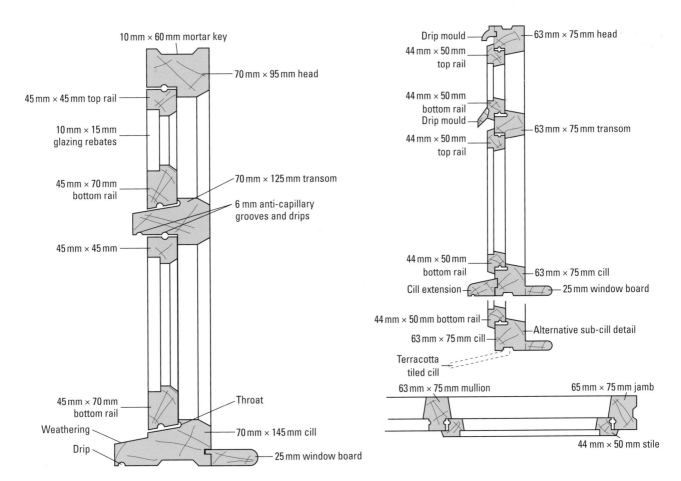

Figure 4.44 Traditional casement window (vertical section)

Figure 4.45 Storm-proof casement

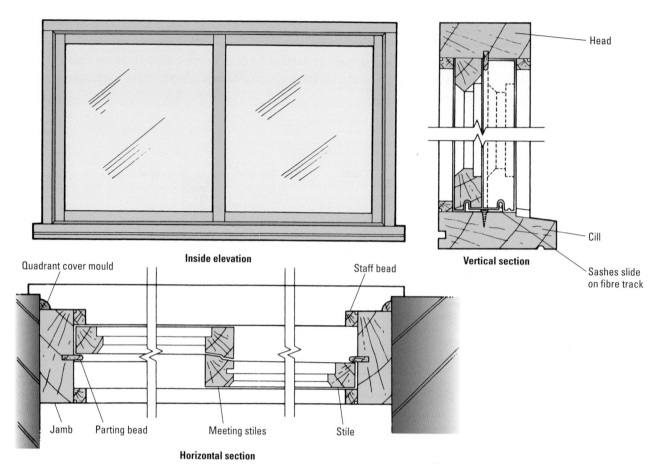

Inside elevation

Vertical section

Head

Cill

Sashes slide
on fibre track

Quadrant cover mould

Staff bead

Jamb

Parting bead

Meeting stiles

Stile

Horizontal section

Figure 4.46 Horizontal sliding sash window

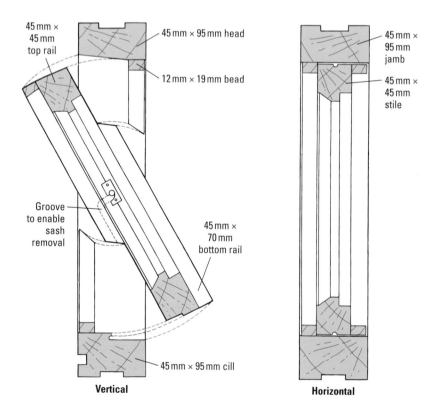

45 mm ×
45 mm
top rail

45 mm × 95 mm head

12 mm × 19 mm bead

45 mm ×
95 mm
jamb

45 mm ×
45 mm
stile

Groove
to enable
sash
removal

45 mm ×
70 mm
bottom rail

45 mm × 95 mm cill

Vertical

Horizontal

Figure 4.47 Traditional pivot window sections

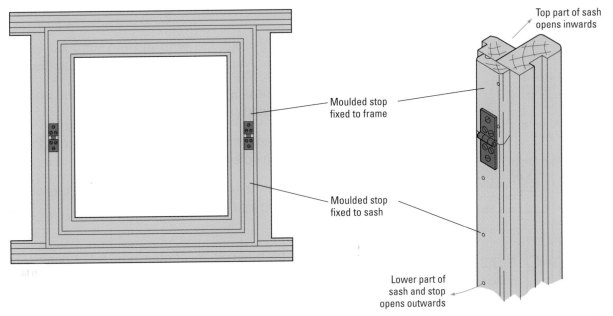

Figure 4.48 Storm-proof pivot window

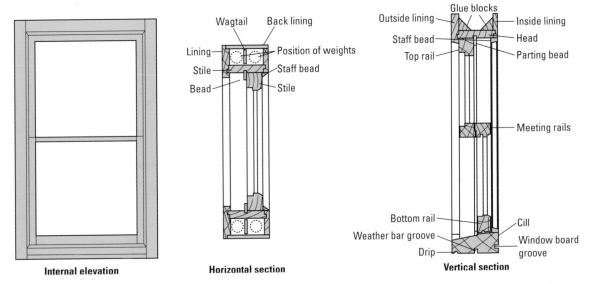

Figure 4.49 Boxed frame sliding sash window details

Methods of fixing door frames and linings in accordance with the given specification

Door frames and linings can either be built into the wall by bedding them into mortar and the surrounding wall, or they can be fixed into carefully measured openings. This happens at first fix, prior to the walls being plastered.

Fixed-in frames

Fixed-in frames are often more expensive. They are put into the openings after the bulk of the building work has been completed so that they are not damaged during that process. The lining is raised off the ground to avoid any moisture from the floor screed or any other wet products being absorbed by the wood. Any moisture that is being absorbed might make the screed dry out too quickly and this could cause cracking. Fig 4.50 shows the main ways in which the frames are fixed.

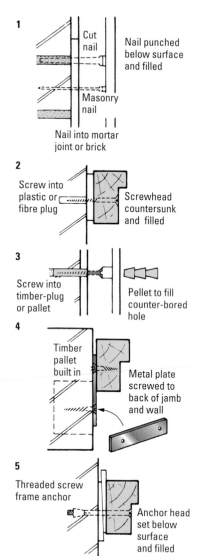

Figure 4.50 Methods of fixing frames

In the Fig 4.50 we can see that:

1 Cut nails can be driven through the jamb and into surrounding block or brick joints, or masonry nails can be driven straight into the brick.

2 and 3 Screws with plastic plugs can be driven through the jamb. Purpose made frame fixings are also available.

4 Metal plates can be attached to the jamb prior to fixing into the opening. These are then screwed into the brick or block reveal.

5 Anchors made of either metal or plastic can be fixed to the jamb and reveal and then screwed into position.

Built-in frames

This technique is used for the majority of openings. A temporary strut is put into position during wall construction. The frame can then be supported and plumbed. As the brickwork is formed around the frame, frame cramps are screwed into the jambs and then incorporated into the brickwork. The horns are cut back and treated.

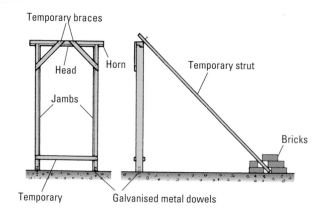

Figure 4.51 Building in a frame

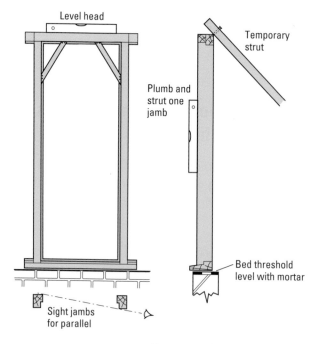

Figure 4.52 Building in a frame with threshold

PRACTICAL TIP

When using screws in softwood frames these should be countersunk. For hardwood frames the screw heads can be hidden by counter boring and pelleting (hiding the screw head with a plastic or wooden plug).

Adhesives and fixing foam

Two-part foam adhesives can also be used for the installation of frames and linings. These adhesives are often used to fix polyurethane doors. The product is mixed and activated when it is extruded using a standard silicone gun. The foam hardens quickly, it does not shrink and it expands into the gap.

It loses its stickiness in less than two minutes. It can be cut after about five minutes and becomes load bearing in half an hour. The adhesive usually hardens off between five and eight hours.

Installing timber frames and linings

There are several terms that will appear in any practical work related to installing timber frames and linings. It is important to understand these terms before you can attempt the installation of frames and linings.

Term	Internal	External
Internal or external position	If the door is inside the building, then we refer to **door linings**. An internal fire door has a frame rather than a lining.	If the door is external then it is a **door frame**.
Size	Linings for internal doors are lighter and can be up to 38 mm thick and up to 138 mm wide.	The frames for external doors are generally larger because they need to be strong and secure (50 mm to 95 mm thick).
Profile (or cross section)	Internal door linings have either planted on rebates or machined rebates.	External door frames have a rebated section with a solid stop. This makes them stronger and more weather resistant.
Proofing	Internal doors do not need to be weatherproof but they are normally draught proof.	External door frames need to have protection, particularly from rainwater. They need to be designed in such a way that rainwater will drip away from the building. They may also be fitted with a compression seal.
Construction	Door linings tend to be assembled on site.	Most external door frames will be delivered on site ready-made.
Installing	Internal linings are fit flush with the facing wall. Joints between the lining and the wall are covered by an architrave.	Most external door frames are not fitted flush with the facing brickwork. The joints between the frame and the brickwork are sealed with mastic and an architrave is sometimes put around the frame of an external door to cover the joint internally.
Wood	Linings for internal doors tend to be made from softwood.	Frames for external doors can be made from softwood but hardwood is preferable, particularly for the threshold. A hardwood cill is preferable, usually made from keruing or iroko.

Table 4.5

Frames

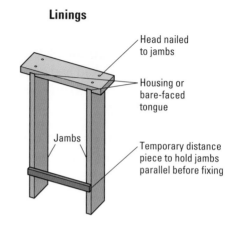

Head

Mortise and tenon

Jambs

Cill or threshold on external frames

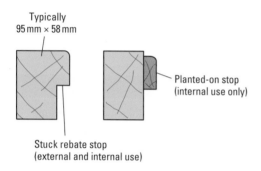

Typically 95 mm × 58 mm

Planted-on stop (internal use only)

Stuck rebate stop (external and internal use)

Linings

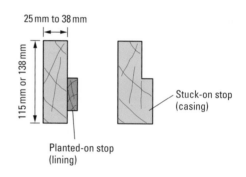

Head nailed to jambs

Housing or bare-faced tongue

Jambs

Temporary distance piece to hold jambs parallel before fixing

25 mm to 38 mm

115 mm or 138 mm

Stuck-on stop (casing)

Planted-on stop (lining)

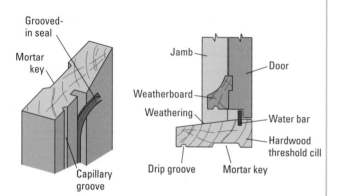

Grooved-in seal

Mortar key

Capillary groove

Jamb

Door

Weatherboard

Weathering

Water bar

Hardwood threshold cill

Drip groove

Mortar key

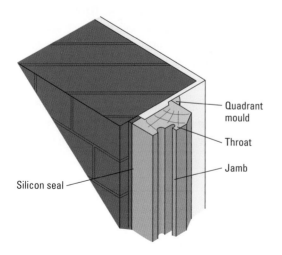

Quadrant mould

Throat

Jamb

Silicon seal

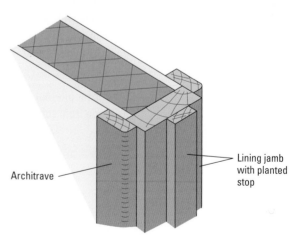

Architrave

Lining jamb with planted stop

Figure 4.53 Door frames and linings

FIT DOOR AND WINDOW FRAMES AND LININGS

The following practical tasks will cover door frames, door linings, casement window frames and hatch linings.

MATERIALS

Types of fixings are determined by the background material to which the frame or lining is to be secured. This could include the following:

Pressed and round wire nails

Slotted, Phillips or Pozidriv screws and plastic plugs

Anchor bolts

Hollow wall fixings

Expanding foam

Galvanised frame cramps

Open door frames (softwood or hardwood)

Closed door frames (softwood or hardwood)

Plain linings (planted on rebate)

Rebated linings

Traditional casement window frame

Storm proof window frame

Boxed frame (sliding sashes) window frame

Pivot hung window frame

Direct glazed window frame

TOOLS AND EQUIPMENT

Hand tools	Nail punch
Panel saw	Seaming /plugging chisel
Tenon saw	Bolster chisel
Bevel edged chisels	Lump hammer
Screwdrivers	Claw hammer

Large and small spirit level, 600 and 1200

Smoothing or Jack plane

Tape measure or four fold rule

Try square and/or combination square

Carpenter's pencil

Power tools:

Cordless drill/screwdriver and assorted bits

Assorted sizes of drill bits

Countersink

Other equipment:

2 x saw horses

Scaffold boards

1. FIT FIXED-IN FRAMES

OBJECTIVE

To fit a fixed-in frame after the walls and openings are formed.

Often this will require the carpenter/joiner to construct profiles for the bricklayer. These are simple braced frames nailed together to form a template for the bricklayer to build around. This method of construction reduces damage to window and door frames as they are fitted later in the build.

PPE

Ensure you select PPE appropriate to the job and site where you are working. Refer to the PPE section in Chapter 1.

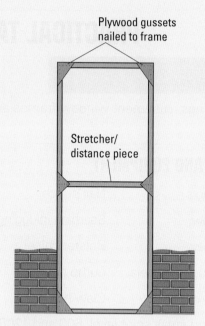

Plywood gussets nailed to frame

Stretcher/ distance piece

Figure 4.54 Example of a temporary wooden frame or profile

STEP 2 Lay the frame on two bearers and or saw horses and cut the horns, using the square, pencil and panel saw.

STEP 3 Establish reference datum point and, if possible, finished floor level (FFL).

STEP 4 Site the frame in the correct position, making sure the horizontal and vertical damp-proof course is in place. Using a long spirit level, plumb one of the jambs in both directions, sight-in the other jamb or repeat the process for the first jamb and check the head is level with a short spirit level.

STEP 1 Look at the drawing to determine the position of the frame. Consider whether the door or window opens outwards or inwards. By bearing in mind the specification and drawing the background material can be identified and the appropriate fixings selected.

PRACTICAL TIP

Pack the frame against the masonry with folding wedges, pre-cut plywood packings or proprietary plastic packings. Remember to allow for plastering on faces of frames and linings that finish flush.

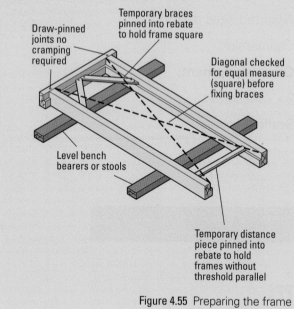

Draw-pinned joints no cramping required

Temporary braces pinned into rebate to hold frame square

Diagonal checked for equal measure (square) before fixing braces

Level bench bearers or stools

Temporary distance piece pinned into rebate to hold frames without threshold parallel

Figure 4.55 Preparing the frame

STEP 5 Eight fixings may be required for each jamb. These should be equally spaced using a square to keep them in line.

PRACTICAL TIP

A good tradesperson will hide some of the fixings behind the hinges, particularly with high class work.

PRACTICAL TIP

If the jambs are not parallel they are said to be 'out of wind'.

The fixings should go through the packings. If folding wedges are used, put the fixing below them, drive a nail through the frame and then both wedges will hold them in place. The two jambs should be checked for wind.

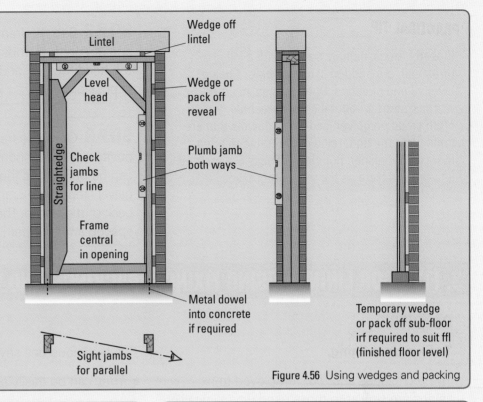

Figure 4.56 Using wedges and packing

STEP 6 After marking out, drill clearance holes using the correct sized drill bit for the gauge of screw. These should be countersunk to accommodate the head just below the surface of the frame. Using a hammer drill and masonry bit, drill through the frame into the background material.

STEP 7 Place the appropriate sized plastic plug into the hole and, using a hammer, tap it in almost flush. Place the screw into the plug and give it a slight turn to ensure it is centred then tap the screw and plug through the frame until the plug locates in the background. Tighten the screw using a hand or cordless screwdriver.

PRACTICAL TIP

Countersinking will reduce the risk of tearing up the surface with the masonry bit and will allow the screw to be extracted if necessary without breaking the surface of the timber. It also enables the effective filling over of the screwhead to allow for decoration.

2. FIT BUILT-IN FRAMES

OBJECTIVE

To fit a built-in frame before the walls and openings are formed.

This method is often used on small works where it is easier to limit damage to the frames/linings. The need for profiles is eliminated, which saves on labour and materials, but care has to be taken to ensure the frames are accurately positioned and set up, especially in the absence of finished floor levels.

STEP 1 Follow Steps 1 to 3 for *Fitting fixed-in frames* above.

PRACTICAL TIP

Closed frames, namely frames with a cill or threshold, are bedded in mortar before being levelled and plumbed. Open frames, in other words frames without a cill or threshold, are often stood on galvanised metal dowels that are drilled into the underside of the frame to bring them up to finished floor level. These are grouted into the concrete as the work progresses.

STEP 2 Site the frame in the correct position and plumb the jambs in both directions, check the head for level and temporarily strut to hold in position.

STEP 3 Once the frame is held in its final position with temporary struts the frame can be built in. As the bricklaying proceeds, galvanised frame cramps are screwed to the back of the frame. These should be evenly spaced and four per jamb is the norm.

3. FIX DOOR LININGS USING FIXINGS, PACKINGS AND WEDGES

OBJECTIVE

To fix a door lining.

The techniques and tools employed to fix linings are similar to those used when installing window and door frames. However, window and door frames are normally assembled in a workshop rather than on site, while door linings are usually delivered to site in sets and have to be assembled by the carpenter/joiner.

This technique has several advantages:

* They can be easily stored on site.

* Specific linings do not have to be ordered for different sized doors.

* Ease of manual handling.

* Low cost.

STEP 1 From the drawing and door schedule determine the size of the door.

STEP 2 Measure the structural opening to ensure the lining will fit, allowing sufficient clearance to plumb and level the lining.

STEP 3 Make or assemble the lining to suit. Allow clearance when calculating the width of the lining. The lining should be glued and nailed or screwed, and the fixings should be angled in a dovetail pattern.

PRACTICAL TIP

Some linings will be pre-housed for standard-sized doors while others will require the carpenter to form the housings to locate the jambs. This can be in the form of a full housing or tongue and groove.

STEP 4 Cut battens straps to the external width of the lining. These should be fixed parallel to the head close to the bottom of the lining, front and back ensuring there is no twist in the lining jambs.

Figure 4.57 Fixing the spacing straps

STEP 5 Square the head of the lining to the jambs and temporary nail top braces.

Figure 4.58 Squaring the lining

STEP 6 Measure the width at the top of the opening, deduct the overall width of the lining and divide by two. This will give the size of the horns to be left on either side of the lining head.

STEP 7 Place the lining in opening. The two horns will centralise the lining in the opening. Now follow Steps 5 to 7 for *Fitting fixed – in frames*. Remember to allow for plastering on faces of frames and linings that finish flush.

Figure 4.59 Screwing in the lining

Figure 4.60 Fixing wedges

PRACTICAL TIP

Alternative methods of fixing linings can be adopted. The method used will be governed by both the background materials and the particulars of the construction project. For example, fixing it into timber stud partitions will adopt the same procedure as fixing linings, above; however, the lining could be nailed through packers or folding wedges into the studwork. Alternatively, if care is taken to ensure the opening is accurately constructed the use of packings can be eliminated.

Figure 4.61 The fixed lining

4. FIX DOOR LINING TO TIMBER PROPELLER WEDGES OR PLUGS

OBJECTIVE

To fix a door lining by nailing it to timber propeller wedges or plugs.

STEP 1 Assemble the lining by following Steps 1 to 4 of *Fix door linings*.

STEP 2 Rake out the brickwork seams or joints using a plugging chisel. Allocate four plugs per jamb, and if possible, choose the same level seam on both sides of the opening.

STEP 3 Cut timber plugs (propellers) and drive them into brickwork joints. Leave them long.

STEP 4 Measure the door lining and the top of the opening. Deduct the lining size from the opening and divide by two. Mark this amount on one of the top plugs (either side will do).

STEP 5 Plumb down the face of the remaining three plugs on that side and square a line across the top of each plug. This should be square to the face of the brickwork.

STEP 6 Cut the plugs and check across all four with a level to ensure they are plumb.

STEP 7 Measure the external width of the lining from each cut plug to the plug opposite, then mark as before and cut to length. Check across all four with a level as before – because they are parallel to the previous plugs they should be plumb.

STEP 8 Place the lining in the opening and check the head for level. Use packings to lift the jamb on the low side until it is level and then reduce the opposite jamb by the height of packing. Use folding wedges to pack the head tight to finished floor level. Pack off the sub-floor to finished floor level if required.

STEP 9 Fix lining to plugs using first fix brads, screws or oval nails. Remember to allow for plastering on faces of frames and linings that finish flush.

INSTALLING TIMBER FLOOR COVERINGS AND FLAT ROOF DECKING

Boards — Square-edged

Tongue & groove (T&G)

Sheets — Chipboard or OSB — Plywood

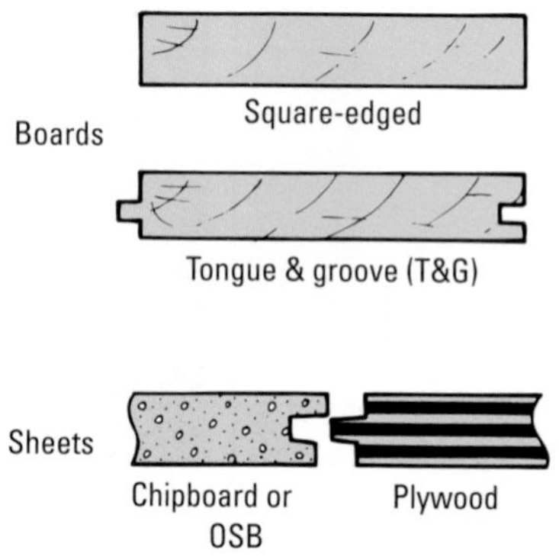

Figure 4.62 Floor coverings

Floor coverings and flat roof decking are also known as floor boarding or tongue and groove (T&G) sheet flooring. As can be seen in Fig 4.62, there are some key types of materials that are used to achieve this.

Floor coverings are normally laid:

* after any plumbing or electrical under-floor work has been carried out

* after the windows have been glazed

* after the roof tiling has been completed.

The last two points are important because this means that the building is comparatively weatherproof and any floor covering will not be exposed to the weather.

Different types and sizes of timber and manufactured board joist coverings

The main materials used include the following:

* PTG (planed tongued and grooved) timber floorboards

* square edged floorboards in older buildings

* tongue and grooved flooring grade particle board

* square edged chipboard

* orientated strand board (OSB)

* flooring grade plywood.

Boards are laid at right angles to the joists. On a floor there is a 10 mm gap left from the wall to help prevent damp from being absorbed into the floorboards as a result of contact with the wall. The gap also means that the floorboards have room to expand. The gap will be hidden by the skirting.

Softwoods can be used, including red deal, whitewood and Douglas fir, in the form of tongue and groove floorboards. Chipboard and plywood are classed as manufactured types of board.

The other alternative is what has become known as engineered wood flooring, laid on top of the existing floor (not directly onto the joists). These are made from materials such as oak, walnut or maple. There are three basic types of engineered floor:

* cross-ply birch with a plywood back

* sandwich board with each part made from the same species of tree

* double layer of poplar or similar wood.

The engineered wood flooring is usually between 20 and 21 mm thick. Solid boards tend to be 18 mm thick. Engineered wood floors consist of a top layer of hardwood, which is bonded to plywood using an adhesive.

* The plywood is made up of 2 mm slices of hardwood veneers.

* The top of the board is bonded to the plywood under high pressure.

* The adhesive is then cured and the board is put into a drying chamber to reduce the moisture content.

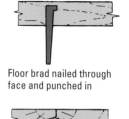

Floor brad nailed through
face and punched in

Lost heads used to secret
nail through tongue

Figure 4.63 Fixing softwood flooring

Methods of fixing joist coverings

Standard softwood flooring has a tongue and groove, which is offset from the face of the board. These boards are fixed by hammering in lost head nails or floor brads through the surface. Lost head nails are nailed through the tongue when secret nailing.

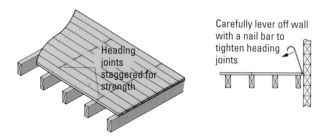

Figure 4.64 Positioning of heading joints

Heading joints are used wherever floorboards are jointed in length. The joint should always be made on a joist centre. In some cases they make use of offcuts of board and are staggered across the floor.

When boards are laid, taking into account the 10 mm gap from the outside wall, the boards are fitted, usually four to six at a time. They are pulled together using floorboard cramps. If floorboard cramps are not available, two other methods are used:

* Folding – two boards are fixed 10 mm less than the actual width of a total of five boards. The five boards are then placed into the gap and a short board is laid across them. Pressure is then applied, usually by standing on them, to press the boards into position.

* Wedging – the boards are cramped, usually between four and six boards at a time, using a fixed batten to the joist and folding wedges, as can be seen in Fig 4.66.

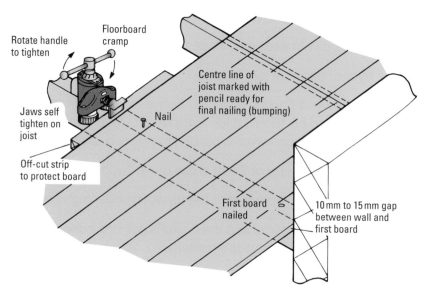

Figure 4.65 Use of a floorboard cramp

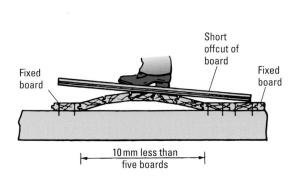

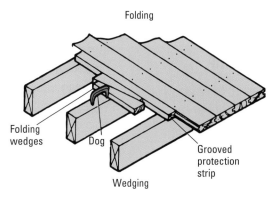

Figure 4.66 Tightening floorboards, folding and wedging

Flooring grade board is now a common material used for decking. Boards come supplied either with square edges or with tongue and grooved edges. Normally the square edged versions are laid lengthways over a joist. It is important to ensure that **noggins** are put between the joists to support the sheets.

Tongue and groove sheets have their lengths at right angles to the joists, with the short edges joining over the joists. When using tongue and grooved chipboard sheets, the shortest length permissible would be across at least two joist widths. There is no requirement for joining on a joist when 22 mm thickness is used and is glued on all edges. Where noggins are used is on the perimeter of the floor between the joist ends, and they provide a fixing for the plasterboard edges. Solid strutting prevents the joists from twisting.

It is normal practice to ensure that the joists have been specifically spaced out to match the size of the sheets. The most common spacing is 400 mm centres.

Plywood, OSB and chipboard sheets are fixed into place with nails. As with timber boards, a 10 mm gap is left along the wall for expansion and to prevent possible bridging of dampness from the external walls.

In the case of tongue and groove sheets, it is also common practice to run a line of PVA adhesive into the groove. This ensures that the floor is stiffened and there is less movement in the joints between the boards.

KEY TERMS

Noggin

– this is a short, horizontal beam timber that sits between the joists. It is used to carry sheet edges, either on the flooring when square-edged boarding is used, or the ceiling beneath the floor, and to stop the joist from twisting.

PRACTICAL TIP

Straight edge sheets of flooring grade chipboard are usually 1,220 mm × 2,440 mm. Tongue and groove sheets are usually 600 mm × 2,440 mm.

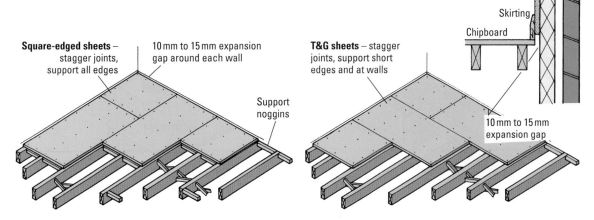

Figure 4.67 Layout of chipboard floors

Forming openings to services under floors

In many cases services may have to be run under or within the flooring. This means that any cables or pipes risk having nails driven into them. This can cause short circuits or flooding if it is not carefully managed. Where possible, services should be run through the centre of joists. This is called the neutral axis and is the optimum position, as the joist is weakened as little as possible as the forces of compression and tension are equal at this point. This also allows all flooring materials to be fully fixed, although maintenance traps should be formed routinely.

Areas where there are pipes and cables should have a board section that clearly states 'no fixing'. It is also good practice to build in access points so that these cables and pipes can be reached at a later date if there is a problem.

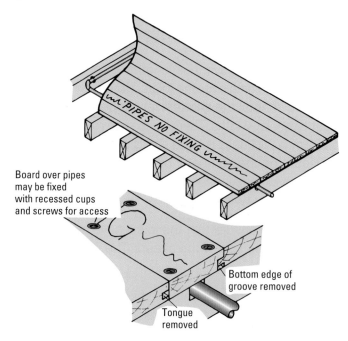

Board over pipes may be fixed with recessed cups and screws for access

Bottom edge of groove removed

Tongue removed

Figure 4.68 Marking position of services

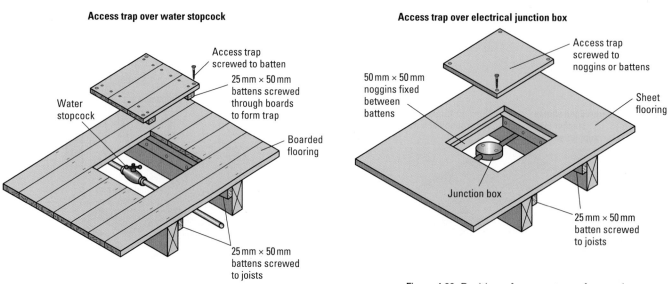

Access trap over water stopcock

Access trap screwed to batten

25 mm × 50 mm battens screwed through boards to form trap

Water stopcock

Boarded flooring

25 mm × 50 mm battens screwed to joists

Access trap over electrical junction box

Access trap screwed to noggins or battens

50 mm × 50 mm noggins fixed between battens

Sheet flooring

Junction box

25 mm × 50 mm batten screwed to joists

Figure 4.69 Position of access traps for services

Installing timber floor coverings and flat roof decking

Hardwood strip flooring is a decorative feature. It is visible in the finished building and not covered. This has also become the case with engineered woods, which are designed for decorative purposes.

Most other types of conventional flooring, particularly sheet flooring, is covered by another material for the final finish.

Materials that cover flat roof decking will be covered by a weatherproof material to insulate the property and it is likely that the decking itself will have insulation either below or above it as additional protection.

To create a functional floor, or deck, it is essential to cover the supporting joists using either manufactured sheet materials or floorboards (either softwood or hardwood). The fitting and fixing techniques for these materials are different for each and this will affect the tools required to complete the project.

Tongued and grooved particleboard sheets

These sheets are graded specifically for flooring applications and can be purchased in different thicknesses and sheet sizes: 2,400 mm × 600 mm is the most commonly used, usually in chipboard. Square-edged sheets are sometimes used and these can be formed from chipboard or manufactured boards.

Timber floorboards

Timber floorboards are planed, tongued and grooved (PTG) and are available in both softwood and hardwood. Softwood is more common. Square-edged random width boards are often encountered in older buildings.

Flooring grade plywood

This can be obtained in various grades such as water boil proof (WBP) and marine, which is preferable when covering joists in an area that may be subject to high moisture, such as bathrooms and kitchens.

Flat roof decking

Softwood timber boards are rarely used in modern-day construction but, if they are to be used, they should be laid on cross battens, the length of the boards corresponding to the fall of the roof. Alternatively they can be laid diagonally to prevent water holding on the boards as they cup.

Sheet materials are more commonly used in modern construction, and bitumen impregnated boards are often used. They are laid in much the same way as for floors. They should be screwed or nailed using annular ring shank nails.

The following practical task describes how to fix and fit a tongue and groove floor.

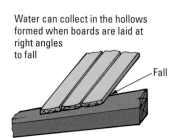

Water can collect in the hollows formed when boards are laid at right angles to fall

Fall

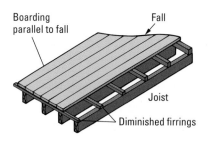

Boarding parallel to fall

Fall

Joist

Diminished firrings

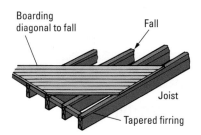

Boarding diagonal to fall

Fall

Joist

Tapered firring

Figure 4.70 Timber boarding for flat roofs

FIT AND FIX TYPES OF FLOORING

The following practical tasks will cover tongue and groove chipboard floor, softwood floorboards, and fitting access traps into both.

PPE

Ensure you select PPE appropriate to the job and site where you are working. Refer to the PPE section in Chapter 1.

TOOLS AND EQUIPMENT

Cross-cut hand saw	Nail bar
Portable circular saw	Floorboard cramps
Jig saw	Claw hammer
Tape	Flat bits
Pencil	Punch

Cordless screwdriver, nail gun or manual floor nailer

5. FIT AND FIX A TONGUE AND GROOVE CHIPBOARD FLOOR

OBJECTIVE

To learn how to fit and fix a tongue and groove chipboard floor.

STEP 1 Stack the sheets in a convenient area of the room near where they are to be fitted but away from your starting point to avoid double handling. It is good practice to do this a couple of days before work starts to allow the sheets to condition. However, in the real world this is not always possible!

STEP 2 Measure the room's width and length. (For the purposes of this example the length of the room is in line with the joists but this is not always the case.)

Divide the length of the room by the width of one sheet. This will give the number of full sheets and the remainder will be a part sheet (or ripping). If the ripping is too narrow it loses its structural stability and may break very easily. While making the calculation it is essential to allow for the 10 mm gap at both ends of the room.

PRACTICAL TIP

Example
The length of the room is 4,246 mm.
Deduct 2 × 10 mm gaps and divide this figure by the width of one sheet (600 mm). This gives a requirement for 7 sheets with a ripping of 26 mm.
Length of room = 4,246 mm
Deduct 2 × 10 mm gap = 4,226 mm
Divide by 600 = 7.043 = 7 sheets
7 sheets @ 600 = 4,200 mm
4,226 mm − 4,200 mm = 26 mm
Having calculated the ripping and found that it is too narrow, simply divide the ripping by 2 (26 mm ÷ 2 = 13) and add this to half a sheet width (300 mm) = 313. The first and last sheets will now be of equal width.

STEP 3 Divide the width of the room by the length of a sheet (2,400 mm). It will be rare that this will work out exactly; unlike the length of the room the joist spacing governs the way sheets are laid across the width. It is always good practice to have a joint on a joist; however, manufacturers now allow joints to be between joists, if all joints are glued. Assuming that our example is not to be glued, any cut board should be supported on at least two joists in its length.

Chipboard flooring should be staggered (stretcher bond). Start with a cut as close to a half sheet as possible that will leave a cut at the other side of the room that is at least the width of two 400 mm-spaced joists.

STEP 4 After you have cut the first sheet to length and width, lay it and the rest of the first row loose – do not fix at this stage. The sheets should be square to the joists; do not be tempted to push the sheets parallel to the wall.

STEP 5 There should be a gap of approximately 10 mm between the sheets and the wall along the full length of the first row. If this is not the case, for example if the wall is uneven or not square – then you will need to cut this first row of boards accordingly. Do this by setting a pair of compasses to the widest gap along the wall, then running the point of the compasses along the wall. The pencil will then mark the line to be cut along the face of the sheets. This is called scribing.

PRACTICAL TIP

A block of wood cut to the widest gap could be used as an alternative to compasses. Make the cut with a hand saw or jig saw.

STEP 6 Having made the cut, lay the sheets with a 10 mm gap, ensuring that they are square to the joists, then fix using lost head nails, annular ring shank nails or screws.

STEP 7 Start with a full sheet on the next row and continue staggering the joints on each subsequent row until you have laid the penultimate (second-last) row.

STEP 8 Measure the gap between the wall and the penultimate row. If it is consistent along its length, simply deduct 10 mm and cut the sheets to size. If the gap is not consistent then the last row of sheets will need to be scribed.

STEP 9 If scribing the last sheet, lay the sheet to be scribed parallel over the penultimate row and measure the overlap. Add the clearance gap of 10 mm to this measurement, set compasses to this figure, and temporarily nail the sheet to avoid it moving while scribing.

STEP 10 Extract any temporary nails and fix the last sheets, use a nail bar between the wall and the last sheet to ensure the joint slides home fully.

6. FIT AND FIX SOFTWOOD TONGUE AND GROOVE FLOORBOARDS

OBJECTIVE

To learn how to fit and fix a tongue and groove softwood floor.

STEP 1 Stack the sheets in a convenient area of the room near to where they are to be fitted but away from your starting point to avoid double handling. They should be stacked face up. Floorboards have a tongue and groove that is offset – this identifies the upper face.

STEP 2 Measure the width of the room and deduct the clearance from this measurement at approximately 10 mm on all walls.

STEP 3 Lay the first row square to the joists, not parallel to the wall. It may be necessary to scribe the first row as for sheet flooring.

PRACTICAL TIP

It may also be necessary to join the boards in length. This is referred to as a heading joint and should be made over a joist.

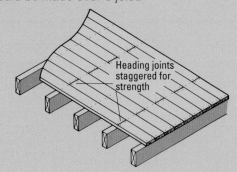

Figure 4.71 Positioning of heading joints

STEP 4 Lay a further five to six rows without fixing. These boards can then be cramped using a pair of floorboard cramps; a sacrificial board (a piece of waste wood) should be placed between the cramps and the last board. Alternatively the boards can be tightened using either of the methods shown below.

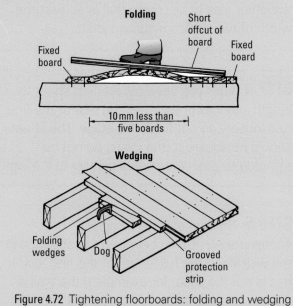

Figure 4.72 Tightening floorboards: folding and wedging

STEP 5 Nail the cramped boards using 65 mm lost head nails.

STEP 6 Continue cutting, fitting, cramping and nailing until the boarding is within one board of the wall.

STEP 7 The last board may require scribing to the wall and should have a 10 mm gap as for all other edges.

STEP 8 Using a nail bar, lever the last board off the wall to tighten the joint and fix using lost head nails.

7. FORM AN ACCESS TRAP INTO THE FLOOR

OBJECTIVE

To learn how to form access traps into floors to provide a means to install services and repair utilities, such as water, gas and electrics.

STEP 1 Determine the size and position of the trap.

STEP 2 Cut through the flooring between the joists.

STEP 3 Cut returns at 90° the first cuts to form a square or rectangular opening.

STEP 4 Screw 50 mm × 25 mm timber battens to the sides of the joists, extending past the length of the opening.

STEP 5 Fix 50 mm × 50 mm noggins between the battens; these should sit under the ends of the opening by 25 mm.

STEP 6 Screw the trap in position; ensure that the screws are below the surface and that the trap sits flush with the surrounding floor.

Figure 4.73 Dropping the trap into position

Figure 4.74 A finished trap

8. FORM AN ACCESS TRAP INTO TONGUED AND GROOVED FLOOR BOARDING

OBJECTIVE

To form an access trap into tongue and groove boarding.

STEP 1 Determine the position and size of the trap.

STEP 2 Cut through the floorboards between the joists.

Figure 4.75 Cutting through the floorboards

STEP 3 Cut through the tongue of a floorboard along the length of the board between the first two cuts.

STEP 4 Lift the floorboards out of the opening.

STEP 5 Fix 50 mm × 25 mm battens on to the sides of the joists. These should extend beyond the edges of the opening under the floor at both sides.

Figure 4.76 Fixing battens on to the joists

STEP 6 Screw 50 mm × 25 mm bearers to the underside of the floorboards to join them together.

STEP 7 Screw the ready-made access panel into position, ensuring that the boards are flush with the surrounding floor.

CASE STUDY

South
Tyneside *Homes*

South Tyneside Council's
Housing Company

Getting the first fix right

Michael Gaffney is a joiner in the final year of his apprenticeship at South Tyneside Homes.

'I mostly work on kitchens, going into people's houses and updating their units, worktops and floor coverings. We sometimes do adaptations for people with disabilities, for example, converting a bathroom so it has a walk-in shower. I also work on empty homes, where if a tenant were to move property or pass away, the property has to be brought back up to certain standards, a reasonable standard of living. I also get to do some bench joinery in the shop, making doors and a set of stairs recently.

I fitted my first staircase a few weeks ago; though we'd rarely get to do that because a lot of the new build work we do is bungalows. So when you get opportunity to build one, you should take it.

First fixing is the stuff I like the most because you're working from the ground up. You see things start to take shape, which is satisfying. You can more easily see that's your own work, rather than a little bit of work in the corner. You've actually built something that's substantial. First fixing progresses the job most quickly, and you see a big difference. I think it takes a little bit more skill as well because everything's got to be in the right place on the first fix. Everything that's done after that falls back onto how well the first fix has been done. Also, it's important to get it right in case it's not you who's doing the second fix, for example, when you might think you'll come back to something later at that stage. This would have a knock on effect, so it's vital to get it right and finished at the first fix.'

ERECTING TIMBER STUD PARTITIONS

A partition is a wall that divides up a large space into smaller spaces. There are two main types of partition wall: load-bearing and non-load-bearing. In modern construction, partition walling is rarely load-bearing; however, when carrying out renovation and restoration work, always investigate before removing walls in case they are load-bearing. This could be checked with a structural engineer if necessary.

There are two main types of partition wall construction:

* pre-fabricated
* in situ.

Timber stud partitions are the usual way in which a building can be divided up into separate areas. There are some key terms that need to be understood:

* Stud partition – this is a lightweight, non-load-bearing, timber-framed wall.

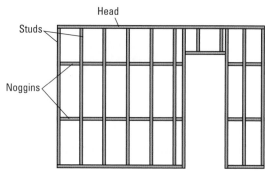

Figure 4.77 Components of a partition wall

* Stud – these are the vertical or upright members in a timber stud partition.
* Noggins – these are horizontal members that hold the studs parallel to maintain centres and to provide a fixing for the plasterboards.
* Head – this is the horizontal member that is fixed to the ceiling and forms the top of the partition.
* Sole – this is the horizontal member that is fixed to the floor and forms the bottom of the partition.

Some stud partitions are actually delivered on site ready-made. This is a perfectly workable arrangement, assuming that the spaces into which the partitions need to fit are both plumb and square. It can only be done as the storey levels are constructed and before the floors go in.

Types and sizes of timber used to construct partition walls

All the parts of the partition are usually made from sawn timber, which is either 100 mm × 50 mm or 75 mm × 50 mm. Most of the partitions are made on site.

Properties of materials required to cover partition walls

Table 4.6 outlines the main properties of materials that are used to cover partition walls.

PRACTICAL TIP

Pre-fabricated timber stud partitions are usually made in the rooms where they are to be fixed and are slightly smaller than required to allow them to be stood up and positioned. In situ refers to a stud partition that is built piece by piece in its final position.

Materials	Properties or uses
Framing brackets	These are also known as framing anchors. They are used to reinforce butt joints. In reality they are quite rarely used, as partition wall building specifications rarely require them.
Nails	Nails are not only used to fix the partition wall frame together, but also clout nails can be used to fix plasterboard to the partition walling frame.
Plugs	These are used when fixing the partition frame into brick or blockwork.
Screws	Screws could be used as an alternative to nails in fixing the partition walling together, or as a method of fixing the partition walling to brick or blockwork, along with the use of wall plugs.
Insulation	Should normally be fitted as standard in partition walling. The insulation may need to have additional properties, such as acoustic, fire or thermal resistance.
Horizontal cladding	The first length needs to be fixed perfectly level.
Vertical cladding	The cladding is fixed plumb at one end of the wall and pushed up tightly at the ceiling. Gaps at the bottom will be covered by the skirting. Nails are driven through into the battening of the partition wall.
Plasterboard	2,400 mm × 1,200 mm, 1,200 mm × 900 mm and 1,800 mm × 1,200 mm sheets are the most commonly used. However, 2,700 mm × 1,200 mm and 3,000 mm × 1,200 mm are also available to order. Sheet thicknesses increase as the sheets get larger. Generally either a 9.5 mm or 12.5 mm thickness of plasterboard is used.
Plywood	Plywood, or fibreboard, can be used for interior partition walling. The joints are usually covered later with mouldings. Plywood can be easily painted or plastered.

Table 4.6

Partition walls can perform other useful functions:

* The insulated material inside the partition wall can provide acoustic cushioning and cut down on noise that would otherwise easily be heard through thin partition walling.

* The insulation material can be fire resistant. This is not only valuable for dwellings but also important if partition walling is sectioning off offices from larger areas in commercial buildings.

* Thermal – in energy efficient dwellings it is important to retain the heat in selected rooms, which are being occupied. Thermal insulation in partition walling can help achieve this.

These functions are all recognised and often required by UK Building Regulations.

Methods of fixing services within partition walls

Partition walling can also hide otherwise unsightly services such as cables and pipes. These need to be supported in some way. When possible, studwork should be drilled for services rather than cutting notches into the studs; notching should only be adopted when there is no alternative. There are ways in which this weakness can be reduced, as can be seen in Fig 4.78.

Vertical studs should not be notched: all pipes and cables should be drilled through the centre of the vertical and horizontal members.

Holes in studs should be positioned away from the top and the bottom of the stud. Any additional holes into the stud should be at least three times their diameter away from any other hole.

Notches can be put in closer to the ends of the studs. But it is important to ensure that any cables or pipes are not routed through parts of the partition that will run the risk of being punctured. This means that considerable care has to be taken to make sure that any holes bored into the partition wall to hold cupboards, skirting boards or dado rails are not likely to compromise hidden cables or pipes. As a precaution, notches and holes can have a metal plate fitted over them on the wall facing.

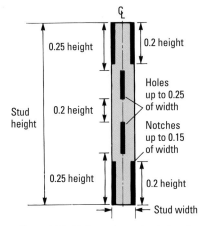

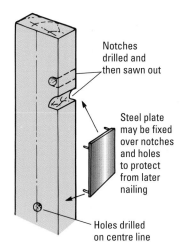

Figure 4.78 Hole and notched details and positioning

Fixing partition walls (in situ)

The timber sole plate is cut to size and placed in position. The head is then fixed to the ceiling directly above (using a plumb line). The studs can then be fitted into place. The exact distance between the studs will depend on which type of material is going to be used to cover the walls.

The noggins are added in last to hold the vertical studs parallel and provide rigidity.

The joints in a partition wall are fixed either with **framing anchors**, **nailed butt joints** or **skew nailing**.

Fixing partition walls (pre-fabricated)

Erecting timber stud partitions

As we have seen, partition walls are usually non-load-bearing and non-structural. This is very true of more modern housing. In older buildings partitions can be load-bearing.

This practical takes you through the process of forming a stud work frame. However, before work begins, a thorough survey of the location should be carried out to include:

* position of the partition: this could be from architect's drawings or direct discussion with customer

* position of any services

* position of doors and windows (both existing and proposed)

* position of any stairs

* shape of room (for example, are the walls square to one another?)

* background materials, walls, floor and ceiling

* direction of joist, floor and ceiling, if applicable.

As a result, a detailed inspection of the drawings and specification should be carried out to determine the position of the partition, the materials required and other details such as openings, coverings, trims, etc.

PRACTICAL TASK

9. ERECT TIMBER STUD PARTITIONS

OBJECTIVE

To erect a timber stud partition wall.

TOOLS AND EQUIPMENT

Hand tools:

Panel saw	Claw hammer
Tenon saw	Carpenter's pencil
Screwdrivers	Chalk line/laser
Tape measure	String line

Large and small spirit level, 600 mm and 1,200 mm

Smoothing or Jack plane

Try square and or combination square

Power tools:

Chop saw	Hammer drill
Cordless screwdriver	Nail gun

PPE

Ensure you select PPE appropriate to the job and site where you are working. Refer to the PPE section in Chapter 1.

PRE-FABRICATED METHOD

STEP 1 Mark the line of one side of the partition on the floor. Determine the square by using a large building square, the 3:4:5 method or a laser level, as many incorporate a 90° facility.

PRACTICAL TIP

Do not assume that walls are square to each other – measuring a parallel line off one wall may not give a square to another wall.

STEP 2 Take multiple measurements across the opening, both vertically and horizontally. The overall size of the frame will be the two shortest measurements, less a small allowance for clearance; this will ensure that the frame will fit the space and not become trapped by being 'long cornered'.

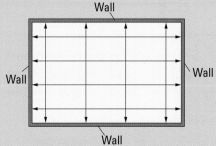

Figure 4.79 Taking multiple measurements of the room both vertically and horizontally

STEP 3 Select the straightest lengths of timber and cut the head and sole plate, remembering to allow clearance.

STEP 4 Mark out the position of the vertical studs on the head and sole plate (mark them as a pair by laying them next to one another) at 400 mm centres, allowing for any openings. 400 mm centres should be maintained above door openings and above and below window openings.

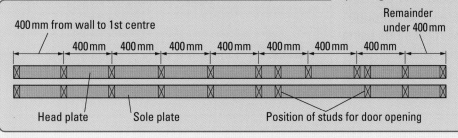

Figure 4.80 Head and sole marked out as a pair with 400 mm centre clearance maintained over door opening

STEP 5 Measure and cut the vertical studs. Remember to deduct the combined thickness of the head and sole plate from the measurement, and allow clearance.

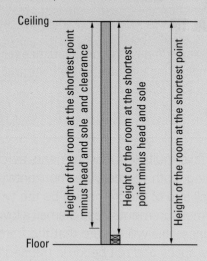

Figure 4.81 Measuring vertical studs (1)

STEP 6 Set out any horizontal members such as door heads on the vertical studs of any openings, such as for doors and windows.

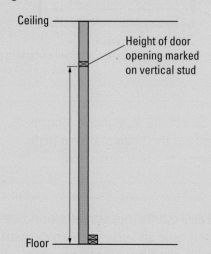

Height of door opening marked on vertical stud

Figure 4.82 Measuring vertical studs (2)

STEP 7 The stud partition should now be assembled on the floor. Dovetail a nail through the head and sole plate into vertical studs using 100 mm round-headed wire-cut nails or 90 mm first fix brads (using a nail gun). Ensure that the butt joints are flush.

STEP 8 Ensure the frame is square by checking the diagonal measurements. If necessary pull it square and attach a temporary brace across the face of the studs to make sure it stays square. Measure and cut horizontal members for doors and windows, and fix as in Step 7.

STEP 9 Mark out for noggins by measuring at 900 mm centres (assuming that the plasterboard is 1,200 mm × 900 mm) from the bottom of the frame and nail in as you did in Steps 7 and 8. It may not be possible to nail in all noggins at this stage because of the temporary brace; however the noggins can be fitted once the frame is in position and the brace has been removed. When using 2,400 mm × 1,200 mm sheets, noggins should be fixed at 1,200 mm centres to allow sheets to be fixed either horizontally or vertically and still be centred.

STEP 10 Stand the partition in position, ensuring sufficient operatives are employed for safety and to prevent the frame twisting and damaging the joints.

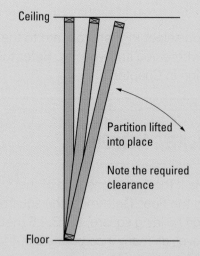

Partition lifted into place

Note the required clearance

Figure 4.83 Lifting the partition into place

STEP 11 Plumb the vertical studs at both ends of the frame and fix them to the background material.

STEP 12 The sole plate of the frame can now be pulled or pushed to the line previously marked on the floor in Step 1, and fixed to the floor at approximately 800 mm centres between the studs.

PRACTICAL TIP

An alternative to Steps 12 and 13 is to use packers and a traveller with a string line, sometimes known as string line and dollies.

STEP 13 Working from one end of the partition, plumb the studs and fix them to the ceiling as required. The partition wall is now fixed at both top and bottom.

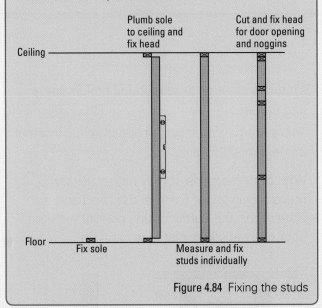

Figure 4.84 Fixing the studs

IN-SITU METHOD

STEP 1 Set out as pre-fabricated method by following Step 1 above.

STEP 2 Cut and fix a sole plate. Provision can be made for door openings at this stage; however, it is also perfectly acceptable to cut doorways out after the rest of the partition wall has been completed. This should be taken into account when placing fixings into the floor.

STEP 3 Mark out the sole plate at 400 mm centres and mark any door openings.

STEP 4 Measure and cut a head plate.

STEP 5 Take a short offcut and place it on top of the sole plate, then take a couple of measurements to the ceiling and cut two temporary props. These should be tight enough to hold the head plate to the ceiling when it is tapped in with a claw hammer. To avoid damaging the ceiling these should not be over-tightened.

STEP 6 Plumb a line up at both ends of the sole plate and transfer marks on to the ceiling. Connect these marks using a chalk line.

STEP 7 Lift head into position and hold it in place using temporary props. Starting from one end, fix the head plate to ceiling, pulling it straight to the chalk line while working across the length of the head. Remove temporary props.

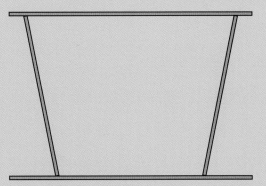

Figure 4.85 Temporary props holding head in position prior to fixing

STEP 8 Measure the distance of each vertical stud individually and proceed along the length of the partition fixing with 100 mm round headed wire cut nails or 90 mm first fix brads, stitch nailed into the head and sole plate.

PRACTICAL TIP

Stitch, or skew, nailing is a method of nailing diagonally through the side of the timber to fasten it to the adjoining timber.

STEP 9 Measure for horizontal members such as over-door and window openings, and then fix them in position, ensuring they are level. Fix shortened studs where required to maintain 400 mm centres.

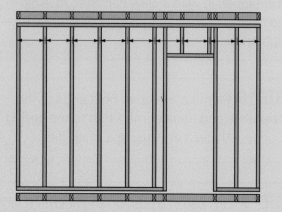

Figure 4.86 Fix all studs and then horizontal members on any openings

STEP 10 Measure and fix noggins at 900 mm centres (assuming 1,200 mm × 900 mm plasterboard) measured from the floor up. When using 2,400 mm × 1,200 mm sheets, noggins should be fixed at 1,200 mm centres to allow sheets to be fixed either horizontally or vertically and still be on centre.

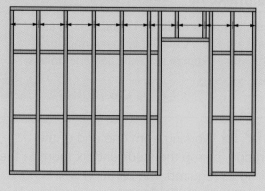

Figure 4.87 Fix all noggins

Methods of fixing to suspended timber floors and ceilings

There are two methods of constructing internal corners in stud walls.

With both methods, it may be necessary to make provision for fixing at the head and sole plate when the partition runs parallel with the floor and or ceiling joist (see Fig 4.88).

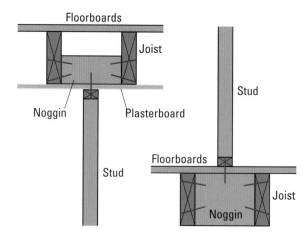

Figure 4.88 Fixing stud partitions that run parallel to joists

First erect stud partition as described using either pre-fabricated or in-situ method of construction.

METHOD 1: CORNER TRAPPING PLASTERBOARD

STEP 1 At the proposed site of the internal corner fix horizontal noggins at 400 mm centres. Alternatively fix an extra stud at the centre of the proposed corner.

STEP 2 Fix the plasterboard to the first partition.

STEP 3 Fix the last stud of partition number two through the plasterboards into noggins or stud of partition number one.

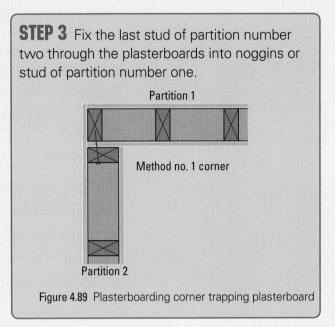

Figure 4.89 Plasterboarding corner trapping plasterboard

METHOD 2: CORNER PLASTERBOARDED AFTER STUD WORK IS COMPLETE

STEP 1 Fix partition number one, attaching a double stud where the corner is to be formed.

STEP 2 Fix partition number two to the double studs.

STEP 3 Fix the plasterboards. The double stud provides a fixing for plasterboard edges.

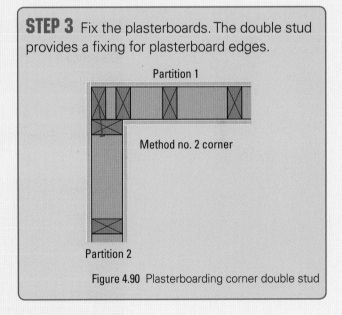

Figure 4.90 Plasterboarding corner double stud

Cladding

It is important to understand that not all studwork is clad using plasterboard. The studwork is a skeleton from which to hang the cladding, and the centres should reflect the materials that have been used. This could result in narrower or wider centres on studs, extra noggins, double head and sole pieces and so on.

Example:
9 mm boards use a maximum centre of 400 mm.
12 mm boards use a maximum centre of 600 mm.

Door and window openings

Door and window openings in stud partitions are formed from the same material as the surrounding studwork. Only the straightest timbers should be used for both vertical and horizontal members. It is common practice to allow clearance on openings; however, if planed square edge (PSE) timber is used, and care is taken, it is perfectly acceptable to construct openings to fine tolerances, so frames and linings slide in without the use of packings. The following example is for a typical door opening in a stud partition.

Door opening:

1. Measure the door width.

2. Add clearance × 2.

3. Add the thickness of two linings measured from the rebate, if the lining is rebated.

4. Measure the door height.

5. Add clearance top and bottom.

6. Add the thickness of one lining measured from rebate, if the lining is rebated.

Example:

Door width	762 mm
Clearance	6 mm allowing 2 × 3 mm
Lining thickness	36 mm allowing 2 × 18 mm
Tolerance	2 to 3 mm
Total width of opening	807 mm

Door height	1,981 mm
Clearance	3 mm top of door
Clearance	12 mm bottom of door
Lining	18 mm
Tolerance	1 to 2 mm
Total height of opening	2,016 mm

This method of construction is best adopted when the same operatives are completing both first and second fix. When adopting the more common practice of packing around openings, use calculations as above, changing the tolerance accordingly by allowing 12 to 18 mm maximum clearance. This would allow for packings between the opening and the door lining of between 6 to 9 mm on each side. Both common sizes of plywood are ideal for this.

INSTALLING STRAIGHT FLIGHTS OF STAIRS AND HANDRAILS

Most timber stairs are made off site and, in many cases, arrive on site partly assembled. On site the stairs are assembled and fixed as soon as the building is watertight.

There are various different types of staircase, but all of them have common features:

* They consist of steps, each of which has a tread and a riser.

* Each set of steps is known as a flight.

* Long flights are often broken up by landings.

* The landings are often designed so that a change of direction of the staircase can be made.

In Fig 4.91 we can see three different versions of straight flight stairs. The first shows a flight that has walls either side of it. The handrails are usually fixed directly onto the wall.

The second variation is one that is attached to a single wall and has an open side. The outer side is supported at either end by newel posts. There is a balustrade on the open side. On flights like this, with a width greater than 1 m, a handrail on the wall side is also fitted.

The final version is freestanding. It will have newel posts at the top and the bottom on each side, and a balustrade either side.

Staircases must comply with Part K of the Building Regulations.

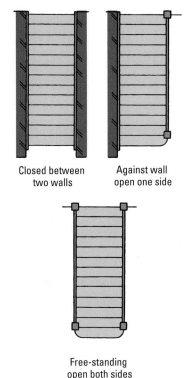

Closed between two walls   Against wall open one side

Free-standing open both sides

Figure 4.91 Straight flight stairs

Different components required to form a staircase and balustrades

It is important to use the correct terms when talking about staircases. Regional variances aside, some of the terms have changed over the years.

For example, strictly speaking a staircase is the space that surrounds a flight of stairs; however, this space is now referred to as the stairwell, and staircase has become the generic term for the entire structure.

The term spindle is now commonly used but is more correctly known as a baluster with the banister (handrail) and the baluster making the collective balustrade or balustrading.

The most important thing here is that everyone involved uses the same terms. If the customer is calling balusters spindles then do the same – don't alienate the customer to prove a point!

Stair terminology

Component	Description and purpose
Baluster	Sometimes referred to as a spindle outside the trade. The upright piece of timber, like a small pillar or column, which fills in the gap between the bottom of the handrail and the top of the string. The gap between each baluster should not allow a sphere of 100 mm to pass through. It can be either shaped or plain.
Balustrade	The collective name for the entire assembly, which includes the handrail, newel posts, balusters, baserails and cappings.
Banister	A handrail.
Bullnose step	A quartered circle design that usually features at the bottom of a stair. It could be on one or both sides of the stair.
Capping	Capping is the process of fixing hardwood stair covers that fit or cap over the tread and riser of the stairs.
Closed string	A string that has its treads and risers housed or trenched into the inside face of the string. It is sometimes used to describe what is more accurately called the wall string.
Continuous handrail	A continuous run of handrail without interruptions, such as newel post turnings or separations. It can be straight or curved.
Curtail step	A shaped step that accommodates the volute and volute newel at the bottom of a staircase. This would be found on a stair with a continuous handrail or banister.
Cut or open string	A string that is cut to the shape of the treads and risers, to allow the tread to sit on top of the string. A return bullnose is usual on the face of the string.
Glue blocks	These are blocks of wood that are fixed to the underside of the stair. They are fixed where the riser and tread meet. The purpose of the blocks is not only to fix the risers and treads together, but to cut down on creaking and movement of the stairs.
Going	The total going is the horizontal measurement from the face of the first riser to the face of the last riser. The individual going is the horizontal measurement from the face of one riser to the face of the next riser. Part K of the Building Regulations states that for domestic use this should be a minimum of 220 mm.
Handrail	This is a protective component. It is designed to stop people from falling into an open stairwell. The rail forms the upper edge of the balustrade and follows the pitch or angle of the staircase.
Margin	The distance between the top string and the pitch line, which is measured at 90° to the pitch line.
Newel	Provides a means of supporting the strings, handrail and treads and risers of the stair.
Nosing	The part of the tread that extends past the individual going line. It is usually semi-circular and provides additional tread width, a finish for carpeting to curve around and a decorative finish if left uncovered.
Pitch	Also known as rake and refers to the angle at which the staircase rises to the horizontal. The pitch line is a line which connects the nosings of all the treads on a flight of stairs.
Pitch line	A notional line connecting the point where each individual going and individual riser meets in a flight of stairs.
Rake	*See* pitch above.
Rise	The total rise of a flight is the vertical distance between one finished floor level and another. The individual rise is the vertical measurement from top of one tread to the top of the next tread.

Component	Description and purpose
Riser	A member that forms the vertical face of the step. This could be solid timber or a composite material such as MDF. Part K of the Building Regulations states that for domestic use that this should be a maximum of 220 mm.
Staircase	The collective name for the entire structure.
Stairway/stairwell	The footprint and the space above it that accommodates the staircase.
Step	The collective name for one riser and tread.
String	This is the board where the treads and risers are fixed or cut. They can be known as wall, outer, close, cut or wreathed.
String margin	The distance, which is measured parallel to the pitch line to the top of the string.
Tread	The horizontal surface of a step. It can have a number of different shapes, such as parallel, alternating or tapered.
Wall string	The string on a staircase that sits against the wall.
Wedges	These are tapered blocks of wood. They are glued into position and used to drive the treads and risers tightly into the string of the staircase.
Winders	Steps that are used to change direction in restricted going staircases. They are narrower at one end and radiate outwards, and are often referred to as kites because of their distinctive shape.

Table 4.7

Building Regulations Part K

This part of the Building Regulations covers staircases. Part K relates to private dwellings, commercial buildings and other types of building. It also covers staircases leading to loft conversions. For these purposes we only need to concern ourselves with the domestic staircase.

Assembling staircases

There are many types of stair configuration such as straight, open riser, dog leg and geometric stairs. In order to construct a straight flight staircase the carpenter must have a good knowledge of carpentry and joinery in the first instance. The practical exercise on pages 164–166 assumes that students will have some experience.

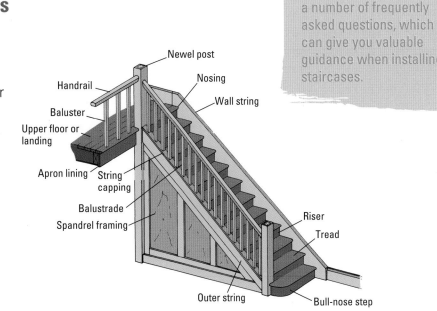

Figure 4.92 Stair construction and terminology

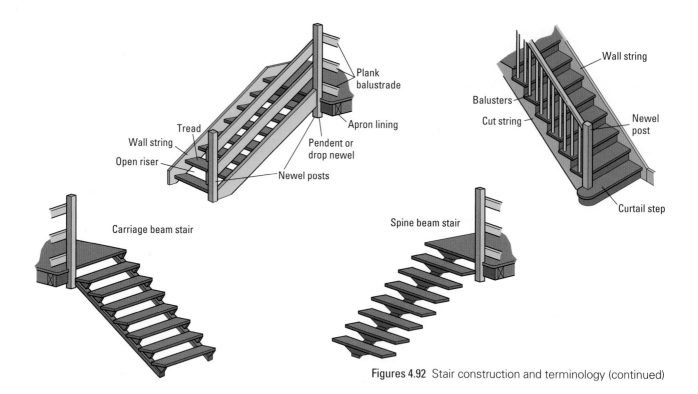

Plank balustrade

Tread

Wall string

Open riser

Apron lining

Pendent or drop newel

Newel posts

Wall string

Balusters

Cut string

Newel post

Curtail step

Carriage beam stair

Spine beam stair

Figures 4.92 Stair construction and terminology (continued)

CASE STUDY

Coco Chanel's apartment

Below is a photo of the famous faceted mirrored spiral staircase that the fashion designer Coco Chanel (1883–1971) designed for her apartment at 31 Rue Cambon in Paris. It connected all four levels of her apartment and made it possible for her to stand in one spot and see what was happening on every floor. The staircase has a continuous string that was formed around a drum in the workshop. The balusters are arranged in clusters with large spaces between each cluster on the turns. The staircase has a very contemporary feel and allows a clearer view to each floor. However, it would be illegal under current Building Regulations in the UK.

Figure 4.93 Coco Chanel's mirrored spiral staircase

Erecting and levelling staircases

Taking site measurements

Before a staircase can be manufactured it is essential that certain crucial site measurements are taken. These measurements can be found in Part K of the Building Regulations.

Vertical section through stairwell

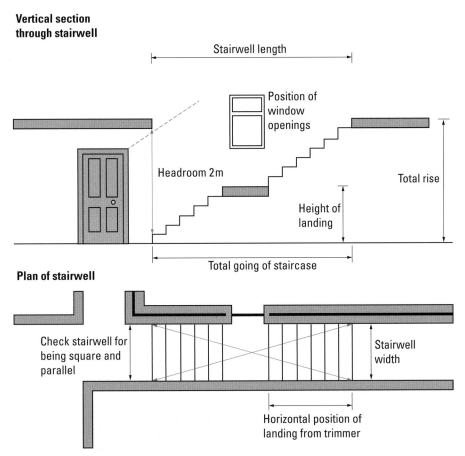

Plan of stairwell

Figure 4.94 Vertical and horizontal plan of a stairwell

The maximum pitch of a domestic staircase is 42°. For a commercial application, the pitch is 38°.

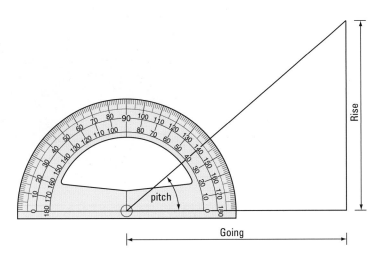

Figure 4.95 The maximum pitch of a staircase

10. ASSEMBLE A STRAIGHT FLIGHT STAIRCASE

OBJECTIVE

To assemble a straight flight staircase.

PPE

Ensure you select PPE appropriate to the job and site where you are working. Refer to the PPE section in Chapter 1.

TOOLS AND EQUIPMENT

Pencil	Wedges
Tape measure	Glue blocks
Combination square	Glue
Compass dividers	Sash cramps
Portable electric router with cutter	
Stair template	
Framing square with stair gauges	

SETTING OUT

STEP 1 Using the working drawing provided start by considering the total rise and total going. Check this with the site survey. Establish the individual riser and going dimensions and check they conform to the Building Regulations Part K.

STEP 2 Start by marking out the strings as a pair with face sides and edges

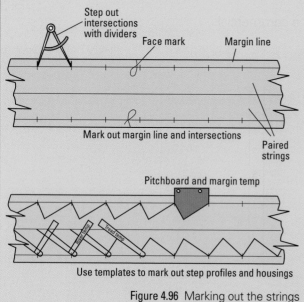

Figure 4.96 Marking out the strings

STEP 3 From the drawing, establish the margin dimension and set the combination square to this. Draw this margin on the face sides using the face edge, a pencil and the combination square.

Set the framing square to the riser and going measurements using the stair gauges.

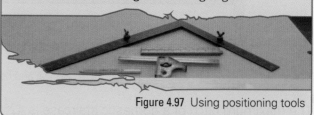

Figure 4.97 Using positioning tools

STEP 4 From the face edge, mark one riser and going dimension onto the strings. It is usual to establish the FFL (finished floor level) at the start.

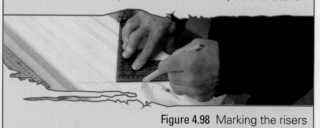

Figure 4.98 Marking the risers

STEP 5 Now set a pair of dividers to the hypotenuse (longest side) of the riser and going and step this out along the string. Square these points onto the edge of the string.

STEP 6 Bring the two strings together and square the lines across and down to the margin line on the opposite string. This will keep the riser and going accurate and will avoid multiplicity of errors (creeping dimensions).

STEP 7 Use the framing square to mark out the treads and risers on both strings.

Figure 4.99 Marking out the treads and risers

STEP 8 Mark out the position of the newel post mortise and tenon joint onto the string at the top and bottom.

STEP 9 Making sure that the string is firmly secured, position the stair template. Making allowance for the router guide in front of the riser and above the going, cramp the jig in position.

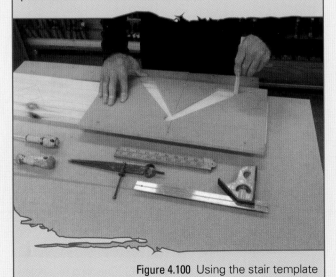

Figure 4.100 Using the stair template

STEP 10 Set the router to the correct depth and router out the tread housings on both strings.

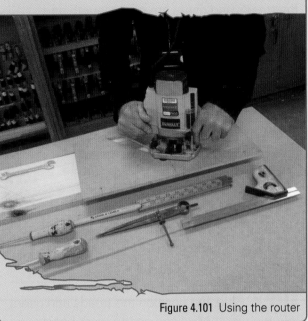

Figure 4.101 Using the router

STEP 11 Mark the mortices onto the newel posts.

STEP 12 Now mark and cut the tenons at both ends of the string.

STEP 13 Mortise the newel posts by machine or by hand.

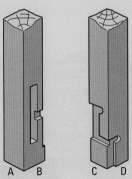

A   B   C   D

Figure 4.102 The mortise and the housing positions on the newel

ASSEMBLY

STEP 1 To assemble the staircase, make sure the treads and risers are cut to length and square, and that you have sufficient wedges, glue blocks, glue and sash cramps.

PRACTICAL TIP

Always make sure the stair is assembled dry, including the newel posts, to check the fit. Newel posts are usually fitted on site. This helps with transportation, prevents them from being damaged and allows the carpenter to make any site adjustments.

STEP 2 Glue and position the treads and risers into the string housings on the work bench.

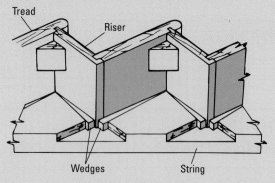

Figure 4.103 Fixing of steps onto string

STEP 3 Now cramp the strings together with sash cramps.

Figure 4.104 Cramping the strings together

STEP 4 Tap the treads into the front nosing positions and the risers into the grooves in the underside of the tread.

STEP 5 Glue and hammer wedges into position below the tread and behind the risers.

Figure 4.105 Fixing wedges under the stairs

STEP 6 Glue the triangular glue blocks in position under the tread and up to the risers.

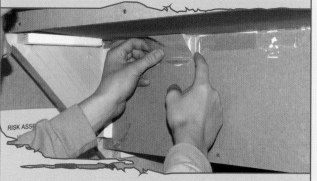

Figure 4.106 Gluing in the glue blocks

STEP 7 Check the diagonal measurement on the back of the stair. If it is square, leave the glue to set. If not, adjust the cramps to pull the stair into square and leave the glue to set.

Figure 4.107 Checking for square

PRACTICAL TIP

To work out if a staircase will be permissible, use the formula:

2 Rise + 1 Going = not less than 550 mm, not more than 700 mm.

Example calculation for a stairway for a private house

If we assume a FFL to FFL of 2.420 m and a total going of 2.880, and a figure below the maximum rise level of 220 mm, say 200 mm, we would get:

2420 ÷ 200 = 12.1 risers or 12 risers

2420 ÷ 12 = 201.66

If we chose a going above the minimum of 220 mm, say 240 mm, we would get:

11 goings (remember you need one less going than a riser)

Total going = 2.880 m

2.880 ÷ 11 = 261.8

If this fits in the available plan space we can then check:

$(2 \times 201.66) + (1 \times 261.8) = 665.12$ mm

It therefore falls within 2R + 1G = 550 to 700.

Logistics

The staircase will have been fully assembled during the manufacturing process and needs to be reassembled on site.

In most situations a staircase cannot be transported to its final location fully assembled. Usually, to allow access through doorways, the balustrade and newel posts are removed, along with the top riser board, landing nosings and, if applicable, the apron linings.

Fixing considerations

Fixing a staircase is regarded as a first fix operation because it occurs prior to plastering and creates easy access to the upper floors for the workforce. It also allows the surface treatment of the wall to sufficiently reduce the amount of wood that is visible on the top edge of the wall string – this should be equal to the top edge of the abutting skirting board. If the wall string is to be fixed, it should be done at this point.

There is an argument to suggest that wall strings do not require fixing to the wall. There is sound logic to support this theory, as the string is exactly the same thickness beside the wall as it is on the open side of the stair. In addition, the stair will move and if one string can move more than the other, then the resulting forces can pull the staircase apart.

Installing straight flights of stairs and handrails

You should first check the finished floor level (FFL). Stairs are often fitted prior to the FFL being finalised; if this is the case you must establish what allowance must be made for the surface covering, which could be a concrete screed, parquet or solid wood flooring.

REED TIP

Good communication is vital to getting a job done correctly. Imagine a surveyor measuring up and passing on information to your team leader, who then passes it on to you – if there's any miscommunication along the line, you'll end up building the wrong thing.

Packing blocks will have to be used to maintain this allowance under the bottom step.

Carpets are assumed to be covering the stairs as well as the floors and no allowance need be made for them.

When installing stairs, there are several stages you need to follow.

1 Having established the FFL, the wall string must be prepared to sit on that level. Cut the string parallel to the first tread, measured down by the depth of one rise – simply measure the rise between two subsequent treads (top of tread to top of tread). Cut from the face so that any tear out is against the wall.

2 Now the plumb cut can be marked and cut. This cut forms the abutment between the wall string and skirting so it should equal the depth of skirting. Measure up from FFL and mark a 90° cut, then once again cut from the face of the string and dress it up with a block plane.

3 At the top of the wall string, there are several things to consider when marking out and cutting over the trimmer or trimming joist. The first cut is a plumb cut made in line with the back of the riser; this should meet with a square cut that is level with the underside of the flooring on the upper floor.

4 Two further cuts now have to be made: a plumb cut made from somewhere in line with the centre of the trimmer and a horizontal cut made at the top of the string the height of the skirting. This will be parallel to the upper floor. These last two cuts should be planed to ensure a good fit to the skirting abutment and a suitable finish for paint or other decoration on the horizontal cut.

5 Check the stairs for level by offering the staircase into position, packing where necessary and checking the level front to back on several treads. Ensure the stair finishes flush with the upper floor. If all is well then proceed; if not, check with your supervisor or manufacturer.

PRACTICAL TIP

Draw bore pins or dowels should be tapered at one end. The pin is driven through taper first until it has cleared the other side of the newel post.

Draw boring is a method of tightening a shoulder on a sloping tenon without the use of cramps. Offset holes between the tenon and the outside of the newel pull the shoulder in. Remember, the holes in the tenon need to be fractionally closer to the shoulder than those in the newel.

PRACTICAL TIP

The same result can be obtained by placing the newel post on the bottom string tenon, ensuring the shoulder is tight and checking for plumb with a spirit level.

6 Now the top newel can be offered up and notched around the trimmer. It can then be fitted to the upper end of the string. Glue the tenon and shoulder. The draw bore holes should already be pre-drilled using the appropriate sized dowels so apply glue and drive through the newel post.

Preparing the bottom newel post

The bottom newel post can now be fitted in the same way as the top; however, there are several things to consider.

* Is the handrail mortised and tenoned into the newels in the traditional manner? If so, it will need to be fixed simultaneously with the bottom newel.

* If the handrail is to be fixed with a proprietary fixing system then both newels can be fitted in advance of the handrail.

These operations are carried out with the staircase on its side if there is sufficient room. If space is restricted, it may be necessary to lift the staircase steeper than its finished pitch and rest it on the upper floor or landing. Struts (temporary kickers) will need to be fixed to the floor at the bottom riser to prevent the staircase slipping.

If the FFL does not yet exist, the newel may sit on the sub-floor or over-site concrete. The bottom of the newel will either need to be suitably sealed with a preservative or wrapped in building polythene sheet if it is to be screeded in.

An alternative is to cut the newel to finished floor level and to drill into the end grain. A galvanised bar or pipe can then be inserted into the hole and allowed to protrude to the sub-floor, and it can then be screeded in. This is usually done with a stronger mix than the rest of the sand and cement screed.

Fixing the newel

If the staircase sits on the FFL then, depending on the floor finish, there are numerous ways of fixing the newel. These include skew nailing or screwing, housing and skew nailing. On traditional suspended timber floors, the newel can be allowed to sit into the space between the floor joist (a trap is formed first). Noggins are fixed either side of the newel and the newel can then be bolted or screwed through. With a bit of forward planning this can be achieved before FFL and makes an incredibly strong fixing.

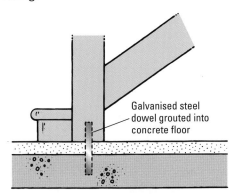

Galvanised steel dowel grouted into concrete floor

Figure 4.108 Fixing the newel to a solid floor

Fitting the top riser and nosing

The top riser and nosing can now be fitted into the staircase. The riser should be glued and screwed into the back of the last tread and the riser should be glued and pocket-screwed from the back into the nosing. If there is any difference in thickness between the upper FFL and the nosing then the nosing should be rebated from the underside before being fitted.

Checking the staircase

The staircase should now be dry fitted to check that everything is level square and plumb. While in this position mark the back of the bottom riser onto the floor if the stair is sitting on finished floor level. Lift the staircase back into its temporary position and screw a permanent kicker to the floor. This should be cut to fit between the string and the bottom newel.

Fixing staircases

Lift the staircase into its final position and fix the bottom newel as previously described. The top newel should be fixed into the trimmer, by pocket screwing or skew nailing using suitable length oval nails.

If a kicker is fitted the bottom riser can now be fixed through the face using screws and pellets or nails, depending on finish.

If the wall string is to be fixed, and if access to the underside is available, fix it with plugs and screws, cut clasp nails or hammer fixings, depending on wall construction.

Fixing balusters (spindles)

The design of balusters can vary greatly and there are many different types on the market. In older properties the range of designs is countless, as many would have been bespoke items.

Originally balusters would have been mortised and tenoned into the top of the string and the bottom of the handrail, but these days the handrail incorporates a wide groove in its underside that corresponds with the thickness of the balusters. A capping piece with the same groove is fixed to the top of the string. The space between the balusters is then taken up with infill pieces that are cut to the rake of the staircase.

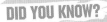

DID YOU KNOW?

Bespoke means custom-made or made especially to the customer's requirements.

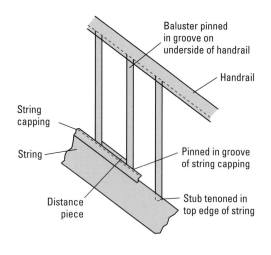

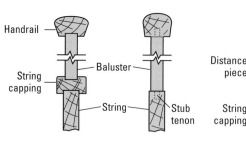

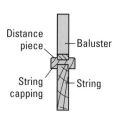

Figure 4.109 Balusters

The building regulations state that the balusters should be spaced with a gap between them that does not allow a 100 mm sphere to pass through; this sets the maximum gap at 99 mm.

The number of balusters required is dependent on the above regulation. A rough estimation can be made by taking an approximate length horizontally and dividing it up.

The balusters can be cut top and bottom at the required angles to the required length and placed in the grooves and then allowed to sit against the bottom newel. A spacer can then be temporarily fixed at the top to keep them in place. Measure the remaining distance horizontally, and divide the remaining space by one more than the number of balusters. If the gap is under 100 mm, fixing can commence; if not, add more balusters and repeat the process.

A far more accurate calculation is along the pitch/rake of the capping piece on top of the string.

PRACTICAL TIP

If the length along the capping between the newels is 3.202 m and the thickness of one baluster is 38 mm and the gap required is 99 mm, adopt the following method:

Hold a spindle in position with the required maximum spacing measured horizontally and measure the space plus the thickness of the spindle along the pitch/rake of the capping. This will give a total measurement.

Assume for the purpose of the example that this is 172 mm: 50 mm across the baluster and 122 mm across the gap.

Take the total length of the capping measured between newels and add the thickness of one baluster:

3202 + 38 = 3230

Therefore:

3230 ÷ 172 = 18.78

= 18 spaces with 0.78 mm remaining

This is not a round number so we need to try again with 170:

3230 ÷ 170 = 19 spaces

The difference between our two attempts is 2 mm. Deduct this from our original gap (122 mm) to give us a spacer of 120 mm.

122 − 2 = 120

If there are 19 spaces then we have one less for balusters. Therefore **18** would be required to complete the balustrade.

TEST YOURSELF

1. What is an OSBM?

   a. Ordnance Survey Benchmark

   b. Ordinary Site Benchmark

   c. Ordinary Site Bench work

   d. Ordnance Site Benchmark

2. Which of the following is an example of a collective protective measure on a building site?

   a. Hard hat

   b. Goggles

   c. Scaffold

   d. Gloves

3. Which of the following materials is commonly used to make the shaft of claw hammers?

   a. Steel

   b. Fibreglass

   c. Wood

   d. All of these

4. Which of the following types of powered nailer uses air hoses and portable compressors?

   a. Cordless with gas fuel cells

   b. Mains

   c. Pneumatic

   d. Cordless with rechargeable battery

5. What method is used to easily identify the right plug to match a screw gauge size?

   a. The shape

   b. The markings

   c. The colour

   d. The length

6. What type of adhesive sets and solidifies through chemical reaction?

   a. Thermoplastic

   b. Thermosetting

   c. Thermal

   d. None of these

7. If a piece of timber has bark left on it, what type of defect does it have?

   a. Knots

   b. Shakes

   c. Waney edge

   d. Fungal attack

8. What is the top of a door frame called?

   a. Head

   b. Post

   c. Jamb

   d. Threshold

9. In joist coverings what does PTG mean?

   a. Part Treated Groundwork

   b. Planed Tongued and Grooved

   c. Plain Timber Groups

   d. Planed Timber Groups

10. Where would you find a glue block on a staircase?

    a. On the balustrade

    b. On top of the tread

    c. On the underside of where the riser and tread meet

    d. At the edge of a tread

Chapter 5

Unit CSA–L2Occ37
CARRY OUT SECOND FIXING OPERATIONS

LEARNING OUTCOMES

LO1/2: Know how to and be able to prepare for second fixing operations

LO3/4: Know how to and be able to install service encasements and cladding

LO5/6: Know how to and be able to install wall units, floor units and fitments

LO7/8: Know how to and be able to install side hung doors and associated ironmongery

LO9/10: Know how to and be able to install timber mouldings

INTRODUCTION

The aims of this chapter are to:

* help you select resources and carry out the tasks

* show you how to erect and fix second fixing components in accordance with the given specification.

SECOND FIXING OPERATIONS

First fix operations refer to carpentry work that is carried out before the building is plastered. This includes roofing members, door frames, joists and partition walling.

The second fix carpentry tasks usually take place after the plastering has been completed. This will mean working on skirting and architraves. It has become common practice to separate the two parts of a carpenter's job. Once the first fix operations are over, other trades, such as electricians and plumbers, come in to do their work. The carpenters then come back for the second fix work.

It is at second fix stage where carpenters take on a different role, finishing off rooms and decorative features in the building. This means they could be working in bathrooms, kitchens and around the building on internal doors, architraves and skirting. They will also be finishing off the stairs by fixing handrails and balustrades. One of the other jobs will be to fix door furniture.

Additional relevant tools and equipment

At second fix some additional tools and equipment are used on site. These are outlined below.

Marking gauge
This tool is usually made from beech and has a clear, yellow plastic thumbscrew. The gauge is held with the thumb behind the pin and with the forefinger on the round surface of the stock.

Holding devices
These are cramps, such as G-cramps, sash cramps, quick release cramps (one-handed operation) that can hold pieces of timber together, or against another object. They can be used to free both of your hands so that you can fix the work more accurately.

Figure 5.1 Marking gauge

Electric mitre saw

These are often referred to as chop saws. This is because the rotating saw is brought down onto the timber. Because they speed up the operation and give consistent accuracy, many carpenters prefer to use these rather than traditional hand saws and mitre boxes.

Mitre saws are precision instruments. They can mitre cut, cross cut and cut compound bevels. They can also cut a variety of materials other than wood, including fibreglass, providing a suitable blade is fitted.

Electric router

This is another portable piece of equipment that is widely used for second fixing. Typically it will be used for:

* cutting out pockets for door hinges

* cutting out openings for letter plates

* cutting out mortices for locks and latches on doors

* jointing of laminate worktops

* cutting out the holes for handrail bolts connectors for stair handrails

* cutting apertures for sinks and hobs and cutting out slots for connecting bolts on worktops

* forming a variety of mouldings.

For some of the heavier jobs plunge routers need to be around 1300W.

Figure 5.2 Electric plunge router

Additional materials

Hanging doors, fitting kitchens and wardrobes have a priority of function over form and in actual fact skirting boards, architraves, dado rails and picture rails all have specific purposes before their aesthetics are considered. For example, dado rails are sometimes referred to as chair rails because they are fixed at a height that would prevent damage to the plasterwork or wallpaper finishes by being scraped by chair backs.

Ironmongery

This term describes door furniture. Some is decorative, like the frame or plate that goes around a letterbox, although this also protects the door aperture. Other pieces of ironmongery are to do with the function of the door, such as hinges, locks and latches. Other items are security devices and include sliding bolts and dead bolts.

Usually ironmongery is chosen to perform a particular task or to add particular detail to a door. A good example would be installing **finger plates** to an internal door.

Encasing services in bathrooms and kitchens can be problematic if the room is going to be tiled. Boxing would need to be constructed at just over 150 mm for a full tile or 75 mm for a half tile. This makes for quite large boxing considering the fact that the actual services and area that you might want to conceal is only 20 mm away from the wall. This means that the client would not necessarily want the carpenter to build an oversize box. It therefore falls to the skills and expertise of the tiler to deal with these small encased areas by cutting the tiles to fit.

KEY TERMS

MRMDF

– moisture-resistant medium density fibreboard.

INSTALLING SERVICE ENCASEMENTS AND CLADDING

To cover unsightly services such as electrics, water and gas and to provide an easily decorated surface, pipework needs to be encased or boxed with the overall size kept to a minimum. Access may be necessary to the pipe or cable work to provide for maintenance of the service. For example, plumbers may need to access stopcocks, pipework and valves, or electrical connections might have to be tested and repaired.

Methods of encasing services

Encasing services should be tackled in a careful way. You do not want the casing to cause unnecessary problems, particularly with the final finish of a room. The following points should be taken into consideration:

* Always try to use standard measurements of timber – if this means making the casing slightly larger than is necessary you should do so. This will make all other measurement and preparation of the room easier.

* Casing in bathrooms and kitchens that are going to be tiled should ideally be in multiples of a whole tile or half a tile; this gives a more pleasing result and makes tiling easier.

* Remember that access points may be needed. Whenever there is a junction or valve the casing needs to have a removable face board.

* Make sure you use the correct materials – for example, in kitchens and bathrooms **MRMDF**, marine plywoods and external MDF boards such as medite are commonly used.

Types and sizes of cladding

There are various different types and sizes of cladding. These are outlined in Table 5.1:

Type of cladding	Size and description
Solid panel	This is made from slow-grown, softwood timber, such as spruce. It is used for a variety of internal cladding jobs. It is V-jointed and can be installed horizontally, vertically or diagonally. It has a finished size of 8 mm × 94 mm with a coverage of 88 mm. Sizes available are usually up to 3 m.
Manufactured boards	These are either PVC or polypropylene sheet systems. Each of the sheets is joined to the next using a joining strip and an edge piece. The joints and edges are screwed to the wall. The sheets are 3 mm deep, up to 3 m long and 1.5 m wide. These include MDF, plywood, plasterboard and hardboard.
Tongue and groove boarding	This has a finished size of around 8 mm × 94 mm with a coverage of 88 mm per board. It can be used as either vertical or horizontal cladding. Usually it is available in lengths of 1.8 m, 2.4 m and 3 m.
Horizontal and vertical boarding	This type of boarding is softwood and V-jointed. It has a finished size of around 14 mm × 94 mm with a coverage of 87 mm per board. It is usually available in 1.8 m and 2.4 m lengths.

Table 5.1

Insulation

All materials have an insulation value measured in terms of the amount of thermal loss through the material. This is known as a U-value rating. The lower the U-value the better the thermal insulation properties. The insulation of properties should be carefully planned as insulation placed in the wrong sequence can cause internal problems such as condensation.

Internal walls can also benefit from insulation. Rather than make standard partition stud walling, stud wall insulation can be used. This uses rigid insulation boards. These can be fitted over existing walling. One widely used insulation material is made from a foamed plastic that is between 60 and 100 mm thick.

In the case of stud walls a metal or wooden framework is built and then filled with mineral wool fibre. The mineral wool insulation is not as effective as rigid insulation boards and this means that the filling has to be thicker.

To provide additional insulation a standard stud wall framework is built and rather than covering the framework with plasterboard it is covered with rigid insulation boards.

Soundproofing

Soundproofing, or sound insulation, is designed to cut down on the impact of sound from one part of the building to another. This is also known as acoustic separation.

Different materials have different sound insulation properties.

Soundproofing panels can be fitted on walls, ceilings, onto roof panels (to cut out rain noise) and they can also be fixed to the outside of a building. They are usually around 50 to 60 mm thick. A series of steel studs hold them in place and it is usual to have a second protective layer, or architectural wall panel, fitted over them.

Fixing timber grounds plumb and level

All panelling, whether it is a small box that encases pipes or cables or a larger piece of panelling, must be straight level horizontally and plumb vertically. The walls onto which the panelling will be fixed have to be battened. A ground is a timber batten that is fixed to masonry walls to provide a fixing. They should be fixed either vertically or horizontally depending on their application but are fixed to the structure before panelling.

As you can see in Fig 5.3 there are three types of grounds: framed grounds, separate grounds and counter-battening.

Grounds provide a fixing for surface materials that disguise very uneven wall surfaces. Using a level and a straight edge it is possible to identify surface irregularities. The grounds can then be packed out to meet the line. This will ensure the wall is plumb and in line.

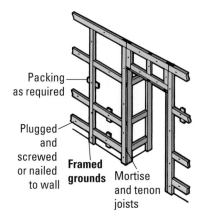

Packing as required

Plugged and screwed or nailed to wall

Framed grounds

Mortise and tenon joists

Framed using pre-fabricated mortise and tenon frame

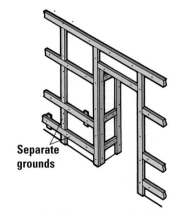

Separate grounds

Individual grounds fixed on centres

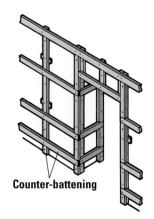

Counter-battening

Corner battered horizontally

Figure 5.3 Types of ground

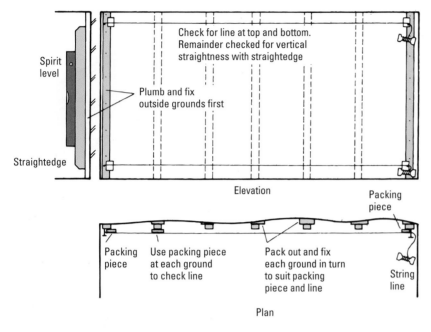

Figure 5.4 Plumbing and lining grounds

Framed grounds tend to be made off site, and are generally packed off the surface in the same way as the separate timber grounds noted above. The process of plumbing and lining grounds can be seen in Fig 5.4.

Methods of fixing cladding (internal panelling)

When you fix panels to grounds the actual fixings sometimes have to be concealed. There are various ways of achieving this, as can be seen in Fig 5.5.

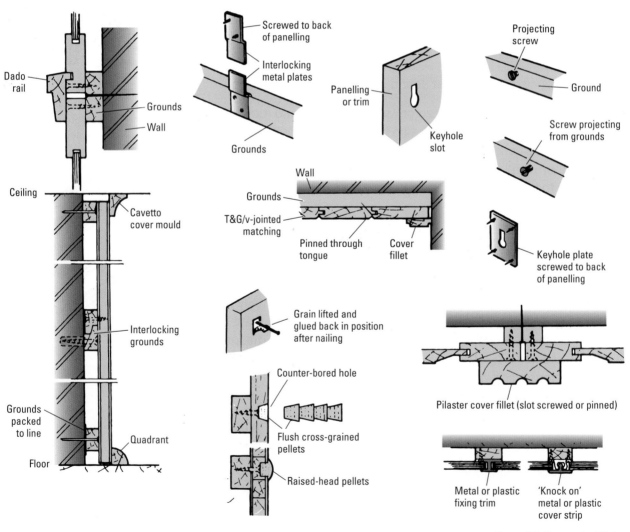

Figure 5.5 Concealed fixings

There are various ways of fixing cladding and these can be concealed or surface fixed. These are listed and described in Table 5.2.

Fixing	Use and fitting
Interlocking grounds	This technique uses either splayed or rebated grounds. These are fixed to the back of the panelling and to the wall. The panel is lowered and then hooked into position.
Slot screwing	These are keyhole shaped slots that are on the back of the panelling. The slots are drilled and prepared so that they match the countersunk head screws that have been driven into the grounds. The panel is manoeuvred into position so that the slots are over the head of the screws. The panel is then tapped into position.
Slotted and interlocking metal plates	Keyhole slotted metal plates are fixed into recesses on the back of the panels. In every other respect they work on the same basis as interlocking grounds (in the case of interlocking metal plates) and slot screws (in the case of slotted metal plates).
Pellets	Holes are bored into the panelling and then pellets or plugs are inserted into the holes and glued into place. The pellets, which are cross grained, are virtually invisible once they have been installed.
Cover fillets	The panels are simply screwed directly into the grounds. Where the surface screws are still visible, a fillet, or moulded feature, is then pinned to cover the screws. In practice these could be cornices, skirting, dado rails or coving.
Nails	This involves driving a nail through the panelling and into the ground. The nail head can be hidden using hard wax or exterior filler. In some cases a tiny piece of the grain can be lifted with a chisel or grain lifter. The nail is then driven in. The grain is then replaced and glued to cover the nail head.
Trim	These are raised and very obvious, so they are features of the panelling. They can be made of either metal or plastic.

Table 5.2

Figure 5.6 shows how internal and external angles can be handled.

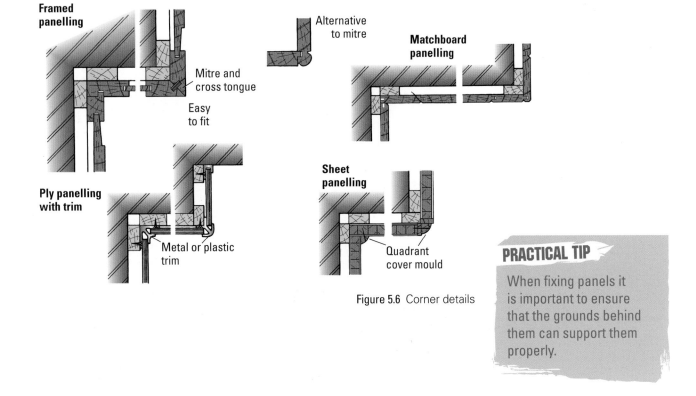

Figure 5.6 Corner details

PRACTICAL TIP

When fixing panels it is important to ensure that the grounds behind them can support them properly.

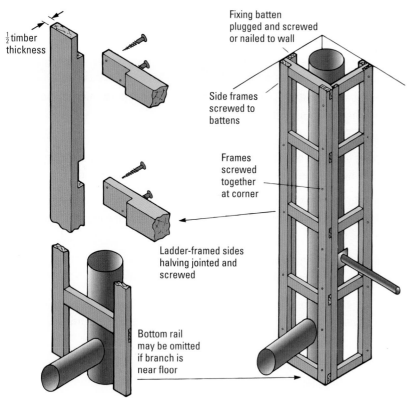

½ timber thickness

Fixing batten plugged and screwed or nailed to wall

Side frames screwed to battens

Frames screwed together at corner

Ladder-framed sides halving jointed and screwed

Bottom rail may be omitted if branch is near floor

Figure 5.7 Use of ladder frame for pipe casing

Pipe casing

For vertical pipes one of the common casing techniques is to use ladder frames. Battens are fixed to the wall and then softwood is fixed to the battens to provide a solid ladder-framed box. This can be seen in Fig 5.7.

There are issues when constructing L-shaped, U-shaped casings or where the wall surface is uneven.

L-shaped casings are used to cover services in internal corners. Begin by using a spirit level and a straight edge to mark plumb lines on the wall. The battens then have to be fixed to the wall. The sides of the case and finally the front can be fixed. It is also possible to use a ladder frame. A notch should be created where a pipe branches off. If the pipe is small then it is possible to simply drill a hole and saw the side. But for larger pipes the technique to cover this is usually by scribing and having a two-part split face, as can be seen in the diagram.

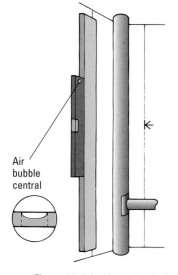

Air bubble central

Figure 5.8 Marking plumb line on wall

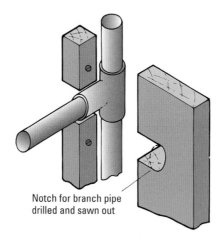

Notch for branch pipe drilled and sawn out

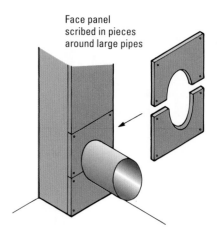

Face panel scribed in pieces around large pipes

Figure 5.9 Cutting around branch pipes

U-shaped casings are used to cover services in the middle of a wall. The plumb lines are again marked before fixing battens using the same procedures as for L-shaped casings.

For uneven walls scribing is usually required. Put the side piece of external cladding against the wall and then mark down the piece of timber using either a pencil for a small scribe or use a compass set to the maximum space identified to mark a line. You will then need to plane or cut the cladding to the line. This can be seen in Fig 5.10.

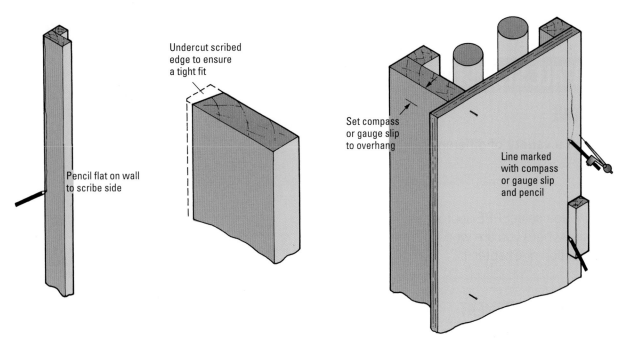

Pencil flat on wall to scribe side

Undercut scribed edge to ensure a tight fit

Set compass or gauge slip to overhang

Line marked with compass or gauge slip and pencil

Figure 5.10 Scribing and cutting to fit an uneven wall

Covering horizontal pipes can be achieved in exactly the same way as for vertical pipes. In some cases it may be desirable to cover the facing with skirting board or to fix an overhang on the top. This would effectively provide a shelf. The two alternatives for horizontal pipe casings can be seen in Fig 5.11.

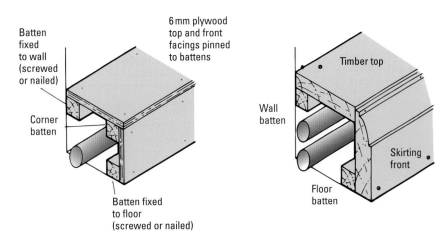

Batten fixed to wall (screwed or nailed)

6 mm plywood top and front facings pinned to battens

Corner batten

Batten fixed to floor (screwed or nailed)

Timber top

Wall batten

Skirting front

Floor batten

Figure 5.11 Horizontal pipe casings

PRACTICAL TASK

1. INSTALL SERVICE ENCASEMENT AND CLADDING

OBJECTIVE

To install a variety of different casings.

PPE

Ensure you select PPE appropriate to the job and site where you are working. Refer to the PPE section of Chapter 1.

TOOLS AND EQUIPMENT

Hand tools:

Tape measure	Claw hammer
Pencil	Screwdrivers
Spirit level	Drill bits
Straightedge	Countersink
Hand saw, panel and or tenon	

Power tools:

Cordless screwdriver

Drill bits, for wood and masonry

Chop saw	Hammer drill
Jig saw	110V transformer

U-SHAPED CASINGS

STEP 1 Mark a plumb line either side of the pipework, allowing enough room to accommodate the chuck of the drill during Step 2. This is to avoid damaging the pipework or services.

STEP 2 Fix battens to the lines marked on the walls.

STEP 3 Fix the side panels to the battens.

STEP 4 Fix the front panel to the sides.

PRACTICAL TIP

When using thin sheet material it may be necessary to fix front fillets to the sides, to allow a fixing for the front panel.

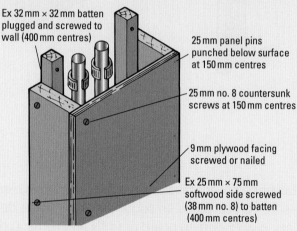

Ex 32 mm × 32 mm batten plugged and screwed to wall (400 mm centres)

25 mm panel pins punched below surface at 150 mm centres

25 mm no. 8 countersunk screws at 150 mm centres

9 mm plywood facing screwed or nailed

Ex 25 mm × 75 mm softwood side screwed (38 mm no. 8) to batten (400 mm centres)

Figure 5.12 U-shaped pipe casings

L-SHAPED CASINGS

STEP 1 Mark plumb lines on the walls using a spirit level and a straight edge, ensuring there is room for the chuck of the drill.

STEP 2 Fix battens to lines using appropriate fixings for the background material.

STEP 3 Fix the side panel to the batten.

STEP 4 Fix the front panel to the side panel and wall batten.

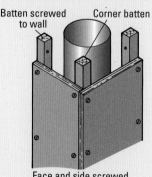

Batten screwed to wall   Corner batten

Face and side screwed to battens

Figure 5.13 L-shaped pipe casings

LADDER FRAMES

Ladder frames are often constructed off or on site to carry the finishing material for the encasement of services. They consist of simple lightweight frames, which, once fixed and clad, become extremely strong.

STEP 1 Measure up for the frames. For L-shaped casings two frames will be required. For U-shaped casings three frames will be required.

STEP 2 Cut the timber to the required lengths and widths and half lap or mortice and tenon the frames together (the latter would usually be manufactured in a workshop).

STEP 3 Screw the frames together on the front corners.

STEP 4 Mark plumb lines in the corners and fix using appropriate fixings.

STEP 5 Clad with finishing material.

SCRIBING COVER PANEL TO UNEVEN SURFACES

In many cases the sides and faces of casings will need to be scribed to fit uneven wall or floor surfaces.

STEP 1 Position the panel to be scribed against the framework or in its position. Ensure it is plumb or level depending whether it is a horizontal or vertical pipe box, and temporarily nail it in place.

STEP 2 Set a pair of compasses to the overhang and mark a line down the face of the panel.

STEP 3 Cut the panel, slightly undercutting to ensure a tight fit. It may be necessary to dress in with a block plane to obtain the required finish.

STEP 4 Fix the panel.

STEP 5 Repeat for other faces as required.

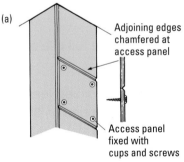

(a) Adjoining edges chamfered at access panel

Access panel fixed with cups and screws

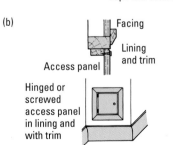

(b) Facing

Lining and trim

Access panel

Hinged or screwed access panel in lining and with trim

Figure 5.14 Access panels

Access panels

We already know that access panels may be necessary to allow other trades such as electricians or plumbers to access cables and pipes. Usually this is achieved by creating a removable panel that is fixed into position with brass cups and screws. Sometimes a hinged door is more suitable.

Access panels often have chamfered edges. The reason for this is that the edges of the access panels are often prone to damage each time they are removed or fixed back into position. It also means that when the panelling has been painted the joints are easy to cut open with a knife, as they will have only a thin film of paint.

The framework is constructed in the normal way but the panels will have to be joined where access is required.

Options for access panels can be seen in Fig 5.14.

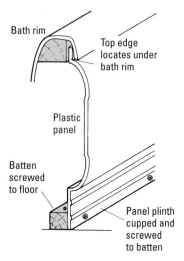

Figure 5.15 Fixing standard bath panel

Bath panels

Some baths will come as kits with standard plastic bath panels. All that is necessary is to position a floor batten. The bottom of the bath panel is fixed to the batten after the top has been located into position under the bath rim.

In other cases it is necessary to create a batten framework for the panel. Usually this is made from 25 mm × 50 mm softwood. It is usually planed all round, halved and then screwed into position.

Regardless of the type of panel material chosen, the sheet material needs to be moisture resistant. In many cases hardboard that has been faced with melamine or MRMDF can be used. In other cases match boarding is used.

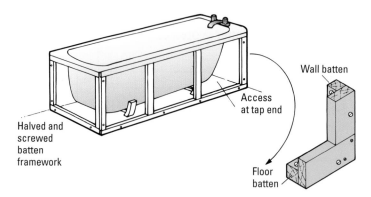

Figure 5.16 Batten framework for a bath panel

INSTALLING WALL UNITS, FLOOR UNITS AND FITMENTS

In most dwellings, kitchens are laid out to a plan to make full use of the available space.

The usual rule of thumb is that there is a triangular pattern between the sink, cooker and fridge. The distance and spacing will depend on the client's preferences. The cooker is not usually next to the sink due to the fact that the cooker will usually require an electricity supply and the sink will need water. Several other factors also need to be considered:

* The need for a food preparation area between the sink and the cooker.

* There needs to be a work surface over or near the fridge.

* The cooker should not be too far from the sink.

* The need to make good use of natural light. It is common for the sink to be underneath the window.

Many units come in standard sizes. These can be bought off the shelf from a variety of suppliers. Kitchens may also have purpose-built units, and in most kitchens each work surface or worktop will have to be specifically cut to fit. This will involve taking into account the layout of the room.

Detecting and protecting electric cables and gas and water pipes

It is a sensible and necessary precaution to disconnect any electrical wiring. It is also a good idea to cap off hot and cold water supplies. The gas supply should be turned off and disconnected. When this is required you must use qualified and competent relevant trades.

Electricity

A kitchen will have a ring main or ring circuit. This will provide a number of double socket outlets above the worktops. There will also be electric sockets to provide power for washing machines, fridges and dishwashers. These are sometimes wired directly into a fused box – if so, a qualified electrician should always be consulted. A separate circuit may be necessary if the cooker or hob is electric, depending on the load of the appliance.

All electrical work needs to be carried out by a competent electrician. However a non-specialist can create the channels to conceal the cables providing no connections are made.

Tracing hidden electrical wiring can be tricky. Voltage detectors are only helpful once you have found the wire. They will tell you whether the wire is live or not. The best practice is to use all-in-one wire tracers to detect wires behind walls but extreme care must be taken when fixing units.

Many professionals will use multiwall scanners and detectors. These are able to find cables, pipes, girders, frames and even small metal objects like nails and screws.

Figure 5.17 Using a multiwall scanner

Gas

Pipes can be detected in a similar way to electrical cables. Once their routes have been identified they should be marked 'Pipes No Fixing' to ensure that no screws or nails are driven into these areas. It is highly likely that gas pipes will be concealed within stud partitions.

Water

Water pipes are another example of hidden or buried services. Pipes that are buried in walls can be difficult to find but the position of sockets, gas outlets and taps offer clues to the possible direction of hidden services. Alternatively, water services can be detected using a scanner. These should also be marked to prevent nails or screws being driven into the danger areas.

Methods of fixing wall and floor (base) units

The ways of assembling and installing standard flat pack units will vary. You should always read the supplier's instructions.

Usually there are three stages involved:

1. Assemble the units if they are not pre-assembled. Make sure that you check the contents as you unpack them. Only open one pack at a time so that you can identify which parts belong to each unit and whether there are any missing parts.

2. Carry out the installation starting from the highest point within the room. Usually you will start with a corner base unit and work outwards. After the base units are installed a corner wall unit is fitted and then you work outwards from that.

3. Once the units are in place they need to be finished. Worktops should be installed first, then cornice and lighting pelmets and finally doors and drawers, as there is a chance of damaging the doors or drawers if they are installed too early in the process. This should always be one of the last tasks, leaving only the fitting of the handles.

Floor (base) units

Each base unit needs to be level and plumb. Packing or, more commonly, legs can be adjusted to allow for any uneven floors. Each of the units needs to be flush with each other. This means making sure the top edges and the fronts are in line. Each unit is then secured to its neighbour with screws or purpose made joining bolts supplied with the kitchen.

Once this has been done the base units can then be fixed to the walls. Brackets are usually provided. You then drill and plug before screwing the units to the walls.

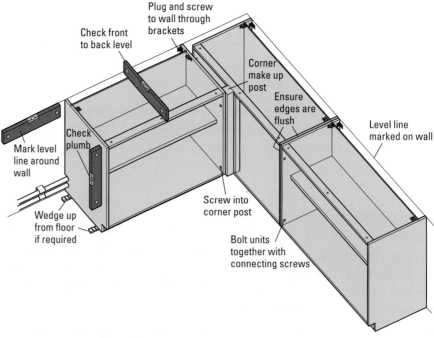

Figure 5.18 Fixing base units

Wall units

Wall units can be a mix of tall units, which are basically large cupboards, or standard wall units. In most kitchens the tops of all these wall units are level. In order to achieve this, a horizontal datum line is drawn onto the wall to mark the top of each of the units. A second line is then drawn to mark the depth of the unit below this line.

You now have the upper side and underside fixing positions marked.

Fig 5.19 shows how wall units are fixed. It is necessary to mark the wall through the fixing holes provided. These holes will then have to be drilled and plugged before the unit can be screwed to the wall. You can use the hanging brackets provided or you might need to fix packing behind the wall unit if the surface of the wall is uneven.

Once the wall units are flush they can be secured together with either screws, plugs or the connecting bolts provided with the kitchen.

PRACTICAL TIP

It is usual practice to have a gap of around 450mm from the underside of a wall unit to the top of a work surface.

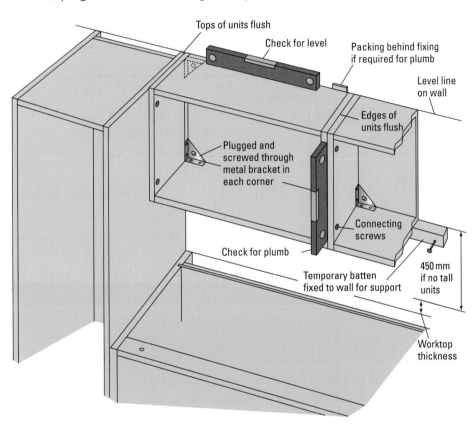

Figure 5.19 Fixing wall units

Jointing post-formed and timber worktops

Just as the styles of base units and wall units have changed over time, so too have preferences about worktops. Not all worktops are made from timber. Metal, marble, stone and other solid sheet material may need equipment and cutters that are not part of the standard kit of a carpenter, so specialist fitters may be required.

There are various different types of timber worktops, which can be seen in Fig 5.20.

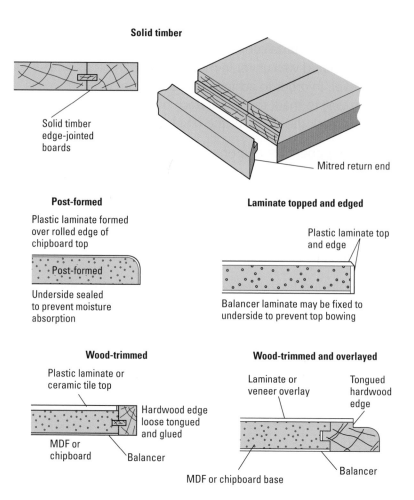

Figure 5.20 Worktop details

The features and uses of each of these different types of worktop are outlined in Table 5.3.

Worktop type	Features and uses
Solid timber	These are made from jointed boards. They are prone to movement as a result of moisture so this needs to be taken into account when they are fitted. These are generally untreated and must be sealed after fitting.
Post-formed	This is the most common type of kitchen worktop surface. They comprise of either MDF or chipboard covered in a plastic laminate. Apart from cutting at the wall side and for fitting appliances such as hobs and sinks they are essentially ready for installation.
Laminated in situ worktops	These are also either chipboard or MDF and they can be covered with plastic laminate, wood veneer or melamine. Once these have been fitted into place a matching sheet material is then applied to the edging. This can then be sealed, as can the underside, with varnish or adhesive. Note that edged sheet is rarely used in modern kitchen fitting as it is labour intensive, does not give as good a finish when complete and is overly dependent on the skills of the carpenter/joiner to achieve the quality demanded.
Wood trimmed	This is another chipboard and MDF material. It also has a wood veneer, plastic laminate or melamine covering. A hardwood edging is fixed using glue and screws or it can be rebated.
Wood trimmed and overlaid	This has either a chipboard or MDF base. It has a hardwood edge, with either a laminate or wood veneer overlay.

Table 5.3

There are several different ways in which worktops can be jointed. Fig 5.21 explains how post-formed worktops are fixed and jointed.

Once the worktops have been measured and cut to fit there are a number of options available. Post-formed worktops can either be jointed using grouted butt and mitre joints or metal jointing strips. When forming routed joints the worktop will require the use of connecting bolts to ensure a tight joint. Square-edged worktops can be butted directly but they will still require bolting. Then the worktop can be screwed into place.

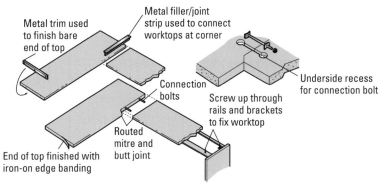

Figure 5.21 Fixing post-formed worktops

PRACTICAL TASK

2. INSTALL KITCHEN WALL AND FLOOR UNITS

OBJECTIVE

To install a range of kitchen wall and floor units according to specification.

PPE

When undertaking this task, and those that follow, ensure you select PPE appropriate to the job and site where you are working. Refer to the PPE section of Chapter 1.

PRACTICAL TIP

The majority of kitchen fitting work is completed using power tools. This is to speed up the process and also to provide a degree of accuracy and quality that only accomplished carpenters and joiners could achieve using hand tools.

TOOLS AND EQUIPMENT

Hand tools:

Tenon, panel, coping and hack saws

Claw hammer	Spirit levels
Various chisels	Smoothing plane
Screwdrivers	Block plane

Marking gauge

Try and/or combination square

G-cramps or quick release cramps (nylon faced)

Power tools:

Circular saw	HSS drill bits
Cordless drill/driver	Spur bits
Router 12 mm collet	Jig saw
Planer	110V transformer
Chop or mitre saw	Extension lead
Masonry bits	

Additional equipment:

2 × saw horses	Worktop jig
Workmate-style bench	

STEP 1 Using the manufacturer's check sheet, ensure that all items have been delivered to site and that no components are damaged.

STEP 2 Spend some time studying all the floor plans, details and accompanying notes.

STEP 3 Carefully mark a horizontal datum line around the room at a height that will be visible throughout the build. This should be above the worktop height and below wall units.

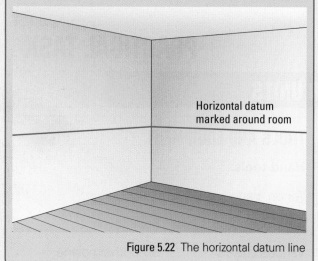

Figure 5.22 The horizontal datum line

STEP 4 Measure down from datum to establish the highest point on the floor. Make a rod (a piece of 50 mm × 25 mm timber is ideal for the purpose) and stand it on the highest point on the floor and transfer the datum line onto the rod.

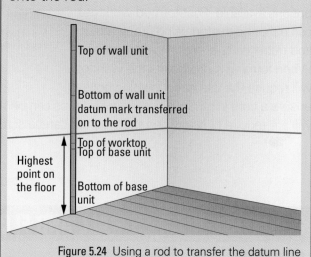

Figure 5.24 Using a rod to transfer the datum line

STEP 5 Place a mark on the rod, measured down from the datum mark to the required height of the worktop. Then add marks for the top and bottom of the base unit and the top and bottom of the wall unit on the rod.

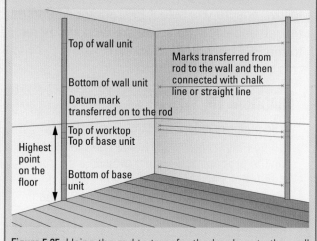

Figure 5.25 Using the rod to transfer the levels onto the wall

PRACTICAL TIP

When using a level to mark a horizontal line around a room, mark one end of the level with a piece of tape or a marker pen and switch the level end for end as you proceed around the room. This reduces multiplication of error in the level.

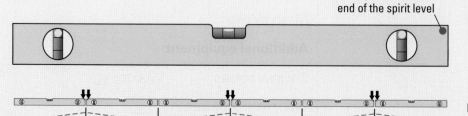

Figure 5.23 When levelling around a room, alternate the level from end to end to reduce accumulative errors

STEP 6 Transfer the marks from the rod to the walls, where required, around the room and connect them using a straight edge or chalk line. This reduces the risk of multiplying errors when marking multiple level lines around a room.

PRACTICAL TIP

You could fasten a 45 mm × 25 mm softwood batten around the wall to the level of the underside of the worktop. This was common practice when worktops were very thin (25 mm to 30 mm), but is less common when using 40 mm plus worktops.

If you are using rigid kitchen units proceed to Step 8.

STEP 7 Carefully open the base unit packs and assemble them in accordance with the manufacturer's instructions. Avoid the temptation to open them with a utility knife as this could damage the units. Often a suggested tool list will be included with the assembly instructions.

PRACTICAL TIP

It is helpful to reuse the flat pack packaging by opening it out on the floor to protect the units during assembly.

STEP 8 Start in a corner with a base unit. Raise or lower the legs until the top is in line with the corresponding marks on the wall. The benefits of the marks for the bottom will now be clear as the unit can be levelled without you having to constantly check the top.

PRACTICAL TIP

Some systems use a corner base unit and other systems incorporate standard base units with the use of a corner post to space the units, providing the clearance for the doors or drawers.

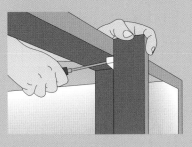

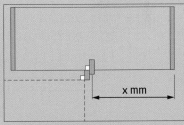

x = 400 mm for a 800 mm wide base unit
x = 500 mm for a 1,000 mm wide base unit

Figure 5.26 Fixing different types of base unit

STEP 9 With the unit located, check the measurement from the wall to the front of the unit to ensure that the worktop can cover this distance plus the thickness of a door or drawer plus the recommended overhang. If not, the units will require scribing back to the wall.

Measure from wall to the front of the unit to ensure the worktop can cover the drawer or door plus overhang

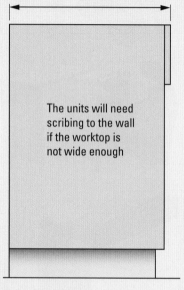

The units will need scribing to the wall if the worktop is not wide enough

Figure 5.27 Checking the measurements from the wall

STEP 10 With the corner unit positioned and levelled, it can be fixed in position using the brackets provided. This will be fixed onto the timber batten if one has been used.

PRACTICAL TIP

It will be necessary to notch the base units to allow them to sit around the battens, where used.

STEP 11 Continue fixing base units, levelling and fixing as before, scribing back to the wall as required. Subsequent units should be fixed to each other using the fixings provided. Units should be held flush with cramps to ensure a tight joint.

STEP 12 Measure carefully when leaving spaces between units for appliances allowing sufficient space for free-standing appliances to be removed, usually +15mm.

STEP 13 If a continuous batten has not been used, fix battens to the wall between appliance spaces.

STEP 14 Fix any tall units such as larder units or fridge freezer housings; this will set the top of the wall units.

STEP 15 Carefully open the packages of the wall units and assemble them as for base units.

STEP 16 Wall units are supplied with two-part wall brackets. Fix the first part to the wall following the manufacturer's instructions. Often a template is provided.

STEP 17 Hang the wall units on to the brackets and adjust the two screws found on the brackets that are located in the top internal corners of the unit. One screw adjusts the height and the other secures the unit back to the wall.

STEP 18 Continue fixing wall units as in Step 17 and fix the wall units to each other using fixings supplied.

STEP 19 Ensure all base and wall units are level, plumb and fixed before moving on to the worktops.

PRACTICAL TASK

3. INSTALL KITCHEN WORKTOPS

OBJECTIVE

To fix laminated post-formed worktops using a butt and mitred joint.

This practical task takes you through the preferred method for quality work, but remember that jointing strips offer a cheaper alternative.

✴ Refer to the practical task *Install kitchen and wall units* for details of the tools and equipment you will need for this exercise.

Worktop A

| Left-hand female joint | Right-hand female joint |
| Left-hand male joint | Right-hand male joint |

Worktop B   Worktop C

Figure 5.28 A typical kitchen layout with 90° corners

STEP 1 Cut worktop A to length. When fitting a worktop between two walls it may require scribing on three sides. Allow some clearance to ease removal when forming the joints.

STEP 2 To form the left-hand female joint, put worktop A face down and place the worktop jig on the post-formed edge using the pegs provided to locate the jig in position.

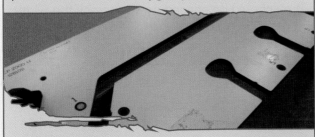

Figure 5.29 Worktop jig in position with worktop face down

STEP 3 Secure the worktop to prevent movement. Using a router with a ½ shank fitted with a guide bush, plunge the router to a depth of 10 mm to 15 mm and move it from left to right in the jig to make the cut. This is called a pass.

Figure 5.30 Plunge the router and make a pass from left to right across the worktop

STEP 4 Make several more passes from left to right until the cut is made.

Figure 5.31 The completed cut and worktop face up

STEP 5 To form the left-hand male joint, start with worktop B face up, and position the worktop jig using the pegs.

Figure 5.32 Make several passes until the left-hand male cut is made

STEP 6 Secure the worktop.

STEP 7 Make several passes with the router from left to right in the jig until the cut is made.

Figure 5.33 Left-hand male cut complete

STEP 8 With worktop B face down, reposition the jig to form the bolt slots. Again make several passes to achieve the required depth. (This will be about two-thirds of the depth of the worktop.)

Figure 5.34 Reposition the jig to form worktop connector bolt slots

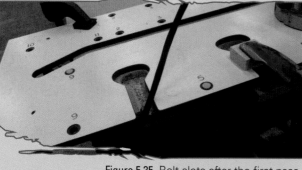

Figure 5.35 Bolt slots after the first pass

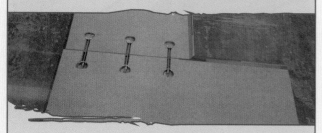

Figure 5.36 Worktop connectors in place

STEP 9 With worktop A placed face down, position the jig to form the bolt slots and make the cuts.

STEP 10 Repeat Steps 2 to 9 for worktop C. However, worktop A will be face up to form the right-hand female joint and worktop C will be face down. This allows the router to be moved from left to right to make each cut, preventing any breakout on the post-formed edge.

STEP 11 Position worktop A and fix it to the base units.

STEP 12 Dry-fit worktops B and C and ensure there is a tight fit on the joints. Check that the front edge is parallel to the face of the base units.

STEP 13 Using a biscuit jointer, form slots for biscuit joints. These are set into the edge of the worktop to keep the upper surface perfectly in line. Three is sufficient for a 600 mm worktop. They should be spaced evenly across the width of the worktop.

STEP 14 Apply silicone sealant to the joints before final positioning and tightening of the bolts. Do not try to clean excess silicone while it is still wet – allow it to cure then peel it off.

PRACTICAL TIP

Sealants are available that match the colour of the worktops, making the joint almost invisible when complete.

PRACTICAL TIP

The biscuits prevent the worktop joint from slipping vertically as the bolts are tightened.

PRACTICAL TASK

4. INSTALL KITCHEN WORKTOPS TO HOUSE HOBS AND SINKS

OBJECTIVE

To fix laminated post-formed worktops to house hobs and sinks.

Worktops will need to be cut to house hobs and sinks. Templates are often provided with the product and these should be used when available. When laying out the shape on the worktop, use masking tape to provide a surface on which to mark the lines. The procedure is the same for both sinks and hobs. These housings need to be sealed to prevent the ingress of moisture.

Refer to the practical exercise *Install kitchen and wall units* for details of the tools and equipment you will need for this exercise.

STEP 1 Place the worktop on two saw horses.

STEP 2 Lay out the shape of the cut onto the face of the worktop. Mask it using decorators' masking tape.

STEP 3 Drill holes on all four corners of the cut-out. These should be large enough to allow a jig saw blade to pass through.

STEP 4 Mask the bottom of the metal base using tape; this prevents the base from scratching the surface of the worktop. Fit the jig saw with a down-cutting blade.

STEP 5 Cut between the holes, supporting the cut-out throughout to prevent waste material dropping and breaking the face.

PRACTICAL TASK

5. FIT PLINTHS TO KITCHEN BASE UNITS

OBJECTIVE

To fit plinths to the legs of the base units.

Refer to the practical exercise *Install kitchen and wall units* for details of the tools and equipment you will need for this exercise.

PRACTICAL TIP

U-shaped brackets are screwed to the back of the plinth and they snap-fit onto the legs.

STEP 1 Measure the plinth length.

STEP 2 The plinth may need scribing if the floor is uneven or out of level.

STEP 3 Lay the plinth in front of the base units, ensuring that the end is line with its final position. Mark the centres of the brackets and screw them in place.

STEP 4 Push the plinth onto the base unit legs, ensuring they snap into place.

STEP 5 Repeat process around rest of the base units.

PRACTICAL TIP

When two plinths meet on an internal corner a spring clip is used to join the two plinths together; alternatively the corner secould be fixed together using connector blocks, when the corner would then have to be installed as one piece.

6. FIT A CORNICE TO WALL UNITS

OBJECTIVE

To fit a cornice to a wall unit for a decorative finish.

A cornice and pelmet or a lighting rail provides a decorative finish to the top and bottom of the wall units. They also tie the units together, giving them continuity. The fixing procedure is similar for both.

Refer to the practical exercise *Install kitchen and wall units* for details of the tools and equipment you will need for this exercise.

PRACTICAL TIP

The cornice steps out over the edge of the wall units to clear the doors. This distance will be specified in the kitchen manufacturer's instructions or is sometimes indicated by a line or groove on the cornice. This will set the distance to the back of the cornice on the top of the unit. This is known as a margin.

PRACTICAL TIP

The cornice can be fixed to the units as individual pieces or glued at the mitres and offered up in sections. Mitres should be held with Mitre Mate or similar wood glue.

STEP 1 Mark the margin on to the top of the wall units. Where the margin lines cross will denote the short point of all external mitres and the long point of internal mitres.

STEP 2 Measure the first length of cornice then cut the mitre using a chop saw. Cut from the face to avoid breakout.

STEP 3 Cut the second piece of cornice and test the fit of the mitre.

STEP 4 Fix the cornice to the top of the wall units, holding the back edge to the margin using the screws specified in the installation instructions.

7. FIT DOORS TO KITCHEN UNITS

OBJECTIVE

To fit doors onto complete kitchen units.

Refer to the practical exercise *Install kitchen and wall units* for details of the tools and equipment you will need for this exercise.

STEP 1 The unit doors should be carefully unpacked.

STEP 2 Fit the hinges. This is best carried out with a hand screwdriver as the screws are very short and can easily strip their pilot holes. If a cordless screwdriver must be used, ensure the torque setting is correctly adjusted.

STEP 3 Fit the hinge mounting to the inside front edge of each unit.

STEP 4 Hang the door and adjust height, alignment, clearance and closing action with the screws on the inside of the hinge. Consult the manufacturer's instructions to ensure a good fit.

CASE STUDY

South
Tyneside *Homes*

South Tyneside Council's
Housing Company

Learning on the job

Glen Campbell is a team leader at South Tyneside Homes:

'When I came out of school, I had 8 or 9 GCSEs at A to C. But something my father said always stuck with me: "If you've got a trade behind you, you've always got something to fall back on." So I started applying for apprenticeships before I got my results, and applied to the South Tyneside Council (as South Tyneside Homes used to be). As part of the apprenticeship, I completed my NVQ Levels 2 and 3 over the three-year period.

For my day-to-day work as apprentice, I was based at the maintenance depot. I would undertake anything from replacing a door handle, fixing a window, putting a new kitchen in, hanging doors, putting down new floors… all aspects really. In my first year, it was basically repairs and learning my hand skills.

Colleagues would show you how to do new things, and as long as you were receptive, you'd learn. A lot of young lads these days come in and say "I know it all already". But the reality is that they haven't done it on a live site yet.

After my first year, I was lucky enough to be chosen to come onto the capital or major works, where you're on new sites, building bungalows and new roofs from scratch, all the way through the process.'

INSTALLING SIDE HUNG DOORS AND ASSOCIATED IRONMONGERY

Door hanging makes up a large part of the carpenter and joiner's second fix work. Different types of door have different functions. There are two distinct door types:

* internal   * external.

The design and detail of each door is in addition to its basic function.

All doors need to be easy to open and to be durable. But they may need to perform other functions, such as the following:

* Security – these may need to be solid, reinforced and have ironmongery fittings, such as security latches and bolts.

* Weatherproofing – they need to be able to provide at least the same amount of weather protection as the outside of the house. Openings are always a weak point, so their construction and fitting is very important.

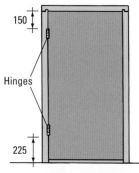

150

Hinges

225

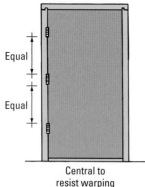

Equal

Equal

Central to
resist warping

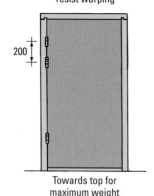

200

Towards top for
maximum weight
capacity

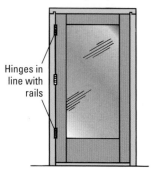

Hinges in
line with
rails

Figure 5.37 Hinge positioning

* Fire resistance – these may need to be able to separate parts of a building. They also need to provide an easy way to escape from the building. Some of these doors may be shut for most of the time, if not all of the time, and only used in an emergency.

* Sound or thermal insulation – these doors need to separate parts of the building. They can contribute to cutting out noise and commonly help to prevent draughts and loss of heat.

* Privacy – inside a normal domestic dwelling, doors are there to ensure privacy even if they are partly open. This means that most internal doors should cover the room.

* Ease of use – the weight and the ironmongery of a door is important. The door needs to match the traffic that will pass through it.

* Durable – most doors will be opened and closed on numerous occasions each day. They may be misused and slammed. The door and its ironmongery should be fit for purpose.

Different types of side hung door

Internal doors tend to be hung on one-and-a-half pairs (three) of 75 mm hinges. These doors are relatively lightweight. Sometimes a pair will be specified (see the top diagram in Fig 5.37).

External doors are fixed on three 100 mm hinges. This is also the case for one-hour fire doors. Half-hour fire doors are also usually fixed with 3 × 100 mm hinges. Architects will usually state in the specification the number of hinges to be used in each situation.

The diagram shows the typical hinge positions for different types of doors.

Types of ironmongery

Ironmongery includes a wide variety of different types of door furniture. Some of these are common to all types of door, such as hinges, locks, latches and handles. Other doors will have different types of ironmongery, such as bolts or letter plates.

Hinges

The hinge secures the door to the frame and enables it to be opened and closed. Fig 5.38 shows the wide range of different hinges for doors.

Figure 5.38 Range of hinges for doors

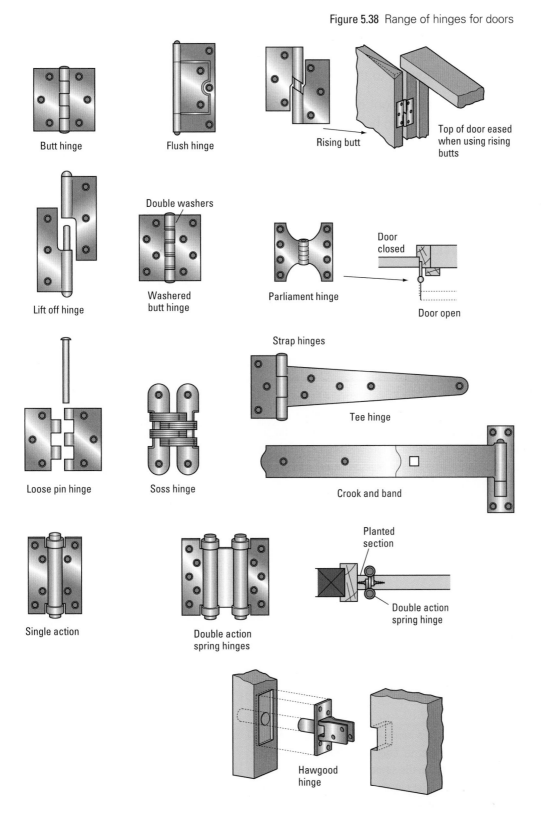

As far as hinges are concerned, there are three different options in terms of their material:

* Internal doors tend to have pressed, mild steel hinges. These are comparatively cheap and can be plated or finished in a variety of different ways. They are known in the trade as self-colour.

* Hardwood and external doors will usually have mild steel hinges although for high quality work, they may have stainless steel or solid brass hinges. It is not usual practice to put steel hinges on external doors due to the fact that they may rust and stain the timber.

* Heavyweight doors need strong, cast iron hinges. However cast iron hinges can be brittle.

There are several ways of fitting hinges, including half-and-half, feathering, knuckle-half in or out, etc.

Note that door size, width, height, location and weight dictate the number and sizes of hinges.

Locks and latches

Locks and latches are used to secure the door. Just how the door is secured will depend on where it is positioned and whether it is internal or external.

Table 5.4 outlines the different types of locks and latches.

Type of lock or latch	Description	
Cylinder rim night latch	These allow the door to be opened from the outside using a key or from the inside by turning a handle. Double locking versions are available and tend to be used for glazed doors. This is a security feature as the handle will not turn if the glazed pane is broken and someone tries to open it from the outside.	Figure 5.39
Mortise deadlock	These are key-operated. The more levers the more secure the lock. They are often added to doors where there is an existing cylinder rim latch.	Figure 5.40
Mortise latch	These are internal latches and do not lock. They simply hold the door in a closed position. The door is opened by using the handle.	Figure 5.41
Horizontal mortise lock or latch	This is a combination of a mortise deadlock and latch. This lock is used on external doors. It usually has 5 levers and is insurance-rated in the same way as a vertical mortice lock latch. It differs in that it is designed to be used with door knobs instead of lever handles and it gives enough clearance for fingers against the door frame. Horizontal latches are relatively rare because of their length.	Figure 5.42

Vertical mortise lock or latch	These are also known as narrow style locks or latches. They are a useful general purpose lock or latch used on external doors.	 Figure 5.43
Rebated mortise lock or latch	These are used for double doors with rebated styles.	 Figure 5.44
Rim deadlock	These are surface-fixed locks. They are still used in refurbishment of period buildings and heritage-type work.	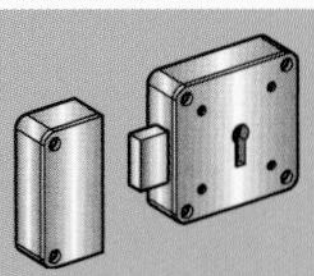 Figure 5.45
Rim lock or latch	These tend to be used either for garden sheds, gates or refurbishment works. Knobs or handles operate the latch and they are surface-fixed.	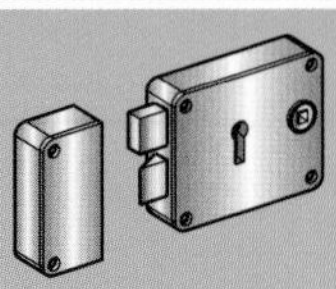 Figure 5.46

Table 5.4

With each different type of lock there are a number of key accessories that add to the range of ironmongery:

* Knob sets – these are mortise latches and a pair of knob handles that can be locked with a key.

* Escutcheons – these are designed to give a neat finish to a keyhole.

* Lever furniture – most lever handles consist of a simple pair of matching handles that use the principle of leverage to turn the spindle (as an alternative to knob-style handles, which require a twisting action).

* Padlocks, hasps and staples – these are usually used on sheds and gates. The hasp is fixed to the door; the staple to the frame. When the door is closed the padlock secures the door.

Cylinders

Fig 5.47 shows how a cylinder rim night latch is fitted.

The manufacturer will tend to supply a template showing the recommended height and position of the centre of the cylinder hole. The cylinder hole needs to be drilled out and then the cylinder is passed through the hole and secured to a mounting plate.

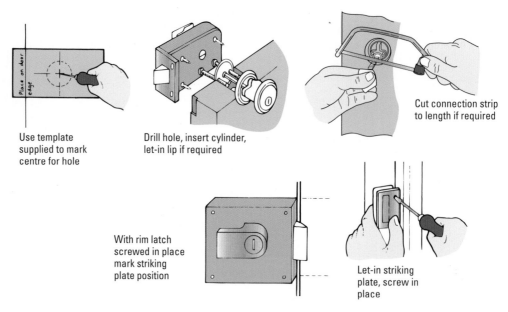

Use template supplied to mark centre for hole

Drill hole, insert cylinder, let-in lip if required

Cut connection strip to length if required

With rim latch screwed in place mark striking plate position

Let-in striking plate, screw in place

Figure 5.47 Fixing a cylinder rim night latch

Most of the latches are designed to fit doors of varying thicknesses and it is necessary to use a hack saw to trim the flat connection strip to fit. The case is then fixed over the mounting plate and marked out. It can then be secured and checked for smooth operation.

The cylinder rim latch case will show where the striking plate needs to be positioned when the door is closed. This will need to be chiselled out of the door frame and then the striking plate can be secured in place with wood screws.

Bolts and chains

Bolts and chains are additional security devices. There are a number of different types, which are covered in Table 5.5.

Types of bolt or chain	Description and use
Barrel and tower bolts	These are used on external doors and gates, with one bolt at the top and one at the bottom.
Flush bolts	These are recessed into the wood and can be used for external doors, particularly double doors and French windows. There is usually one at the top and one at the bottom.
Mortise bolts	These are key operated dead bolts that are fixed into the edge of the door at the top and the bottom.
Panic bolts	These have push bars that disengage the bolts. They tend to be used for emergency exit doors.
Hinge bolts	These are designed to stop doors from being forced off their hinges. They tend to be used on doors that open inwards to prevent the hinge side being crow-barred out against the rebate.
Door holders	These are foot operated stops that keep doors in an open position.
Security chains	These have slides fixed to the doors and chains fixed to the frames. When they are in operation the door can only be opened a limited amount.

Table 5.5

The position of locks, latches, bolts and chains can be seen in Fig 5.48.

Letter plates

Letter plates can be fairly straightforward designs and are essentially a framed opening in the door with or without a hinged cover. Some may have integral draught-proofing in the form of plastic fibre strands.

The position of letter plates is largely dependent on the design of the door. They can be fitted into the middle or bottom rail, and vertically into some styles of door. In fact letter plates can be purchased with a pre-drilled hole for a cylinder rim latch. This has to be fitted to accommodate the lock. Doors hung in wing lights or porch frames will often have the letter plate mounted in the frame rather than the door. This has the advantage of not weakening the door.

Letter plates differ in their manufacture in terms of overlap and spring positions. Templates are often provided and should be used to ensure a good fit. If numerous letter plates of the same design are to be fitted, for instance on a housing development, it is a good idea to make a template for use with a router to get a consistently good finish and to speed up installation.

Mortise locks and latches

990 mm lever furniture

Cylinder rim latch and letter plate

760 mm to 1,450 mm letter plate

1,200 mm to 1,500 mm cylinder rim latch

Typical external door ironmongery

Barrel or rack bolt
Hinge bolt
Hinge bolt
Barrel or rack bolt

$\frac{1}{3}$ height

$\frac{1}{3}$ height rim latch

$\frac{1}{2}$ height security chain

$\frac{1}{3}$ height dead lock

Plates and signs

Sign
Push plate
Kicking plate

1,200 mm
1,500 mm

Figure 5.48 Fixing heights of locks, latches, bolts and chains

Door closers

These are not so common in domestic dwellings, but are used widely in commercial properties. They tend to be fitted to heavy doors to provide a self-closing action. They will also allow the door to be held open.

The door closer can be adjusted to determine how fast the door closes. Others are fitted with temperature sensors, which will automatically close the door if there is a fire. Other door closers have a delayed closing action; some will snap shut when nearly closed to ensure that the latch is engaged; others will have a safety mechanism to prevent them from slamming against walls when opened.

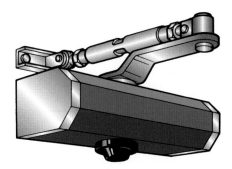

Figure 5.49 Overhead door closer

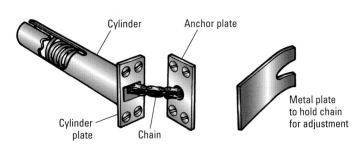

Cylinder
Anchor plate
Cylinder plate
Chain
Metal plate to hold chain for adjustment

Figure 5.50 Concealed door closer

Figure 5.51 Ensure the grain is facing in the right direction

Fixing side hung doors

These practical tasks show how to hang a variety of doors to a given specification, and install associated ironmongery.

The method of fitting a side hung door can be applied to most types of doors; however, special regulations govern the installation and fixing of fire doors.

Fire doors are best fitted into their frames in a workshop environment, installing the intumescent strips and the smoke seal after fitting is complete. They can then be delivered to site in a set to be fitted into pre-prepared openings.

It is possible to fit and hang doors with hand tools but it is now more common to use a mixture of hand and power tools where appropriate, as listed in the practical task below.

You need to fully examine the door to determine its best face, which needs to be where the surface of the door is seen on the most occasions. If the door is faced with a timber surface, examine the grain and ensure that any pointed grain faces upwards.

PRACTICAL TASK

8. FIT A SIDE HUNG DOOR

OBJECTIVE

To fit a door into a door frame.

This list applies to all the practical tasks that follow.

PPE

Ensure you select PPE appropriate to the job and site where you are working. Refer to the PPE section of Chapter 1.

TOOLS AND EQUIPMENT

Hand tools:

Claw hammer	Bradawl
Mallet	Combination square
Screwdriver	Marking gauge or butt gauge
Jack or fore plane	Panel saw
Smoothing plane	Tape measure or rule
Chisels	Utility knife
Carpenters brace with various size auger bits	

Power tools:

Cordless drill/driver with bits

Portable powered plane

Portable powered circular saw

Jig saw

Portable powered router with an assortment of cutters

Transformer   Extension lead

In addition to the tool list the following may be advantageous:

2 × saw horses/stools   Proprietary hinge, letter plate or mortise lock templates

STEP 1 Whenever drawings and door schedules are available check them to confirm size, type, style, position and hang of the door.

PRACTICAL TIP

If drawings or schedules are not available, the door should be hung, whenever possible, in a manner that gives maximum privacy to the largest part of the room. This is known as 'covering the room'. However, in modern construction this is not always possible, as the position of light switches and sockets would obviously affect the hanging side, and with ever-decreasing room space, the area needs to be maximised.

STEP 2 Check the overall size of the door before doing any cutting. Many doors are supplied with lugs or horns from the manufacturing process left on for protection. If they are still on the door you are fitting, place the door onto two saw horses, mark a square face and edge across each of the horns of the door with a try or combination square and a sharp pencil, then remove the horns using a panel saw, keeping the angle of the saw low to minimise break out on the underside.

Figure 5.52 Removing the horns

STEP 3 Once the horns are removed, shoot (plane) the edges and the ends of the door, removing the minimum amount of material to allow the door to sit inside the frame.

Figure 5.53 Remove just enough to allow the door to fit in the frame

STEP 4 Using a jack plane, shoot the hanging side of the door to fit the jamb.

Figure 5.54 Shooting the hanging side

STEP 5 Shoot the top edge of the door to fit the head if required.

STEP 6 Wedge the door tight to the head of the frame and deduct top and bottom clearance from the bottom of the door. This should be around 2 to 3 mm at the top. The clearance at the bottom will depend on floor coverings, the use of storm guard cills and anything else that takes up space beneath the door.

Figure 5.55 Setting clearance at the bottom of the door

Figure 5.56 Setting clearance at the top of the door

PRACTICAL TIP

When hanging doors in frames with water bars they will require a rebate forming at the bottom of the door.

STEP 7 Shoot the closing stile or edge of the door until it is parallel and the gap is twice the required clearance. This should be done with the door wedged tight in the frame to the hinge side and the head.

STEP 8 Shoot a slight leading edge on the hinge and closing stiles; this should be minimal to avoid problems when fitting the lock. Remove the arris (sharp edge of the timber) from all edges of the door with a smoothing, block plane or glass paper.

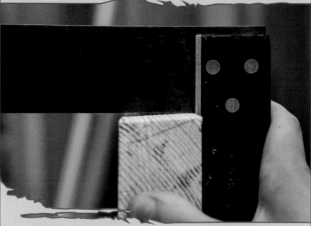

Figure 5.57 Checking the leading edge with a square

Figure 5.58 Plane at an angle

PRACTICAL TIP

Shooting a leading edge on the hinge side of the door ensures that the hinge never fully closes, reducing the chance of the door being hinge-bound. This is where there is insufficient clearance for the hinges or the door against the frame or lining. Hinge-bound is a term that describes the effect of the hinge side of the door springing against either the screw heads or the back of the rebate. It is a result of poor workmanship, often because the hinges have been cut too deep.

STEP 9 Place the door back in the opening. Put a suitable spacer (such as the blade from a combination square) between the head of the door and the frame; wedge the door tight to the hinge side and the spacer at the head. Mark the positions of the top of the hinges on both the door and the frame.

PRACTICAL TASK

9. FIT HINGES TO A DOOR

OBJECTIVE

To prepare the hinge pockets of a door.

PRACTICAL TIP

Take the position of the hinges from the door schedule, if there is one. Often there is not one and in these circumstances the industry-accepted standard for the UK is 150 mm down from the top of the door and 225 mm from the bottom, with the third hinge in the centre of the two. Hinges are normally described as being in pairs, which simply means that there are two matching hinges.

3 × (1½ pairs of) 100 mm butt hinges are needed for external doors

3 × (1½ pairs of) 75 mm butt hinges are needed for internal doors

STEP 2 Set a marking gauge or butt gauge to the hinge leaf width. Gauge leaf width along the door edge between the marks.

Figure 5.60 Gauging the leaf width

STEP 1 Having marked the top of all three hinges (Step 9 in the task above) square these lines onto the edge of the door. Offer a hinge up to the marks and place a pencil mark for the bottom of the hinge on the edge of the door. Do not draw around the hinge. Square these marks across the door edge and back onto the face.

Figure 5.59 Marking the position of the hinges

PRACTICAL TIP

It is good practice to use cut lines to provide an accurate position for paring the hinge.

STEP 3 Set a marking or butt gauge to the hinge leaf thickness and mark between the lines on the face of the door.

Figure 5.61 Gauging the leaf depth

STEP 4 Mark the hinge leaf height onto the frame or lining in the same way.

STEP 5 While the gauge is set for leaf thickness, gauge between the marks on the face of the frame or lining.

STEP 6 Chop the ends of the hinge pockets.

Figure 5.62 Chopping the ends of the hinge pockets

STEP 7 Feather across the grain to the required depth.

Figure 5.63 Feathering to the required depth

STEP 8 Lightly chop the back edge of the hinge pocket with a wide chisel.

Figure 5.64 Using a chisel to chop the back edge

STEP 9 Pare across the grain to the back of the hinge pocket and then work the holes for the hinge with a bradawl, using the hinge as a guide.

Figure 5.65 Paring out the waste

Figure 5.66 The hinge pockets ready for installation

STEP 10 Repeat Steps 6 to 9 for hinge pockets on the frame or lining.

Figure 5.67 Using the bradawl to mark the holes

PRACTICAL TASK

10. PREPARE A DOOR'S HINGE POCKETS

OBJECTIVE

To prepare the hinge pockets on the door frame.

STEP 1 Mark the hinge leaf height onto the frame or lining in the same way as for the door at the end of Task 8.

STEP 2 While the gauge is set for leaf thickness, gauge between the marks on the face of the frame or lining.

STEP 3 Measure the distance from the back of the hinge pocket on the door to the back edge of the door. Add approximately 2 mm to this measurement and call this 'x'.

STEP 4 Measure out 'x' from the back of the rebate on the frame and mark with a pencil. Set a gauge from the face of the frame to this mark. Gauge between the hinge leaf height marks.

PRACTICAL TIP

Many carpenter/joiners modify marking gauges by shortening the end of the gauge so that it will fit into the rebate on a door frame. Butt gauges will do this job without modification; however they are not as commonly used these days.

STEP 5 Chop the ends of the hinge pockets.

Figure 5.68 Chopping the ends of the hinge pockets

STEP 6 Feather across the grain to the required depth.

STEP 7 Lightly chop the back edge of the hinge pocket with a wide chisel.

STEP 8 Pare across the grain to the back of the hinge pocket.

Figure 5.69 Paring across the grain to remove the waste

STEP 9 Repeat Steps 6 to 8 for hinge pockets on the frame or lining.

PRACTICAL TASK

11. HANG THE DOOR

OBJECTIVE

To fix a side hung door in position.

STEP 1 Using one of the hinges as a template, place it in each of the hinge pockets and drill a pilot hole through the lowest hole of the hinge.

STEP 2 Screw the hinges to the door.

STEP 3 Offer the door up to the frame, so that it is approximately 90° to the frame in the open position. The door should be angled back slightly to lift it, making it possible to locate the screw into the pilot hole for the top hinge. Partially drive this screw leaving the head clear of the hinge leaf.

Figure 5.70 The top pilot screw

PRACTICAL TIP

Make sure that the hinges are partially closed to ensure that the lower hinges do not get fouled behind the frame when the top hinge is located and fastened. Offset the screw to the back of the hole so that it pulls the hinge in tight to the back of the pocket.

KEY TERMS

Wind

– if something is said to be 'in wind' it is twisted. It is pronounced 'wined' as in 'wined and dined'.

STEP 4 Pull the door out to the bottom hinge pocket and secure with screws.

STEP 5 Locate the middle hinge, push the top of the door in towards the frame and drive the top screw fully home.

Figure 5.71 Fixing the bottom pilot screw to ensure the door is parallel

STEP 6 Drive one screw into the middle and swing the door into the closed position to test for fit. If they fit and clearance is good, fix all remaining screws.

Some fine tuning or secondary fitting may need to be carried out at this point.

Figure 5.72 The fitted door

TROUBLESHOOTING

Problem	Action
The door is binding against the back of the rebate.	1. Loosen each hinge in turn. 2. Ease hinge out towards front of frame. 3. Drill a new pilot hole in another hole. 4. Drive home screws.
The door is hinge-bound (it seems to be springing on the hinge side). Hinge pockets are too deep.	1. Cut suitable packings to establish an even clearance gap down the hinge side. This may not be necessary for all hinges. Veneers of a similar timber make the most suitable packings – try to avoid screw box lids, glass paper and cigarette packets. 2. Place the packing in dry and test fit. 3. If all is well, unscrew and remove the packing then apply a little PVA to the back of the packing. 4. Replace and re-fix.
The door has the correct clearance gap on all edges when closed but catches the rebate when opening and closing.	Leading edge is not sufficient; this may not be along the full length. Shoot edges where required, remembering to take the arris off. It may be necessary to remove the door.
The door is not sitting tight to the rebate on the lock side.	Either the door is in **wind** or the frame is in wind. If the gap is very small it can be solved by letting out a hinge diagonally from the gap; the centre hinge will also need letting out but by a lesser amount. This has the effect of halving the twist. If the gap is larger the rebate will need to be opened up with a rebate plane and finished into the corner with a sharp chisel.

Table 5.6

PRACTICAL TASK

12. FIT MORTICE LOCKS AND LATCHES

OBJECTIVE

To fit a mortice lock and latch into a door.

STEP 1 Wedge the door open.

STEP 2 Mark the spindle height on the edge of the door. This will be approximately 990 mm; however, if the handle has to match existing furniture, take a site measurement.

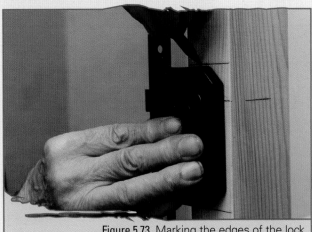

Figure 5.73 Marking the edges of the lock

STEP 3 Line the spindle hole up with the mark on the door, then mark the top and bottom edges of the lock on the edge of the door.

STEP 4 Set a marking gauge to half the thickness of the door and gauge a line between the two marks.

STEP 5 Drill a series of overlapping holes to the depth of the lock, along the centre line, using an auger that is slightly more than the thickness of the lock. The diameter of the bit should be checked after measuring the actual lock to be fitted. Locks include full fitting instructions but if these are not available, the holes should be just wider than the lock case.

Figure 5.74 Drilling overlapping holes with an auger

Figure 5.75 Drilling overlapping holes with a drill

STEP 6 Pare the sides with a firmer or bevel-edged chisel to form the sides of the mortise.

STEP 7 Square the top and bottom edges with a firmer or mortise chisel.

STEP 8 Clean debris out of the mortise. Avoid blowing in the hole as dust can often end up in your eye.

Figure 5.76 Preparing the mortise

STEP 9 Push the body of the lock into the mortise. Do not force the lock in – if it does not fit, you can remove more material from any high spots within the mortise.

Figure 5.77 The mortice with the lock

PRACTICAL TIP

With the lock sitting in the mortise, the back of the face plate should sit tight against the door edge. Some locks have a separate face plate; ensure that this is on the front of the lock.

STEP 10 You now need to form a recess that will leave the lock face plate flush with the edge of the door. There are a couple of options:

Option A Draw around the lock, feather with a chisel and remove the timber within the lines.

Figure 5.78 Feathering to the required depth

Option B Use two small screws to fasten the face plate and lock in position, then carefully cut around the face plate with a utility knife, angling the blade in slightly to keep the edge as tight as possible. Remove screws and lock, then form recess as above.

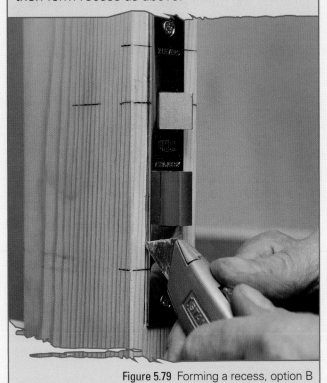

Figure 5.79 Forming a recess, option B

STEP 11 Hold the lock against the face of the door, line it up with the face plate housing on the edge of the door and, using a bradawl, mark the centres of the spindle and the keyhole. Square these marks onto the opposite face and measure the same distance in from the edge of the door, remembering to make the allowance for the leading edge.

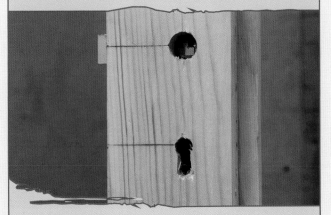

Figure 5.80 Marking the position of the spindle and keyhole

STEP 12 Drill a 16mm hole for the spindle. Make sure you drill from both sides to avoid breakout.

STEP 13 Drill a 10mm hole for the keyhole. Then form the keyhole by cutting down with a pad saw and finishing it off with a chisel, again working from both sides of the door. Alternatively, drill a second hole (6mm in diameter) just below the first and clean out with a sharp bevel edged chisel.

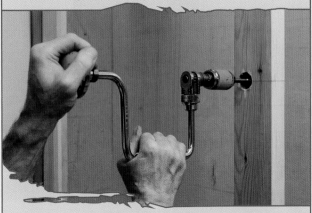

Figure 5.81 Making a hole with an auger

Figure 5.82 Making a hole with a drill

PRACTICAL TIP

Never drill one large hole for the keyhole. The hole should be formed as described in Step 13 to provide a guide for the key, and to maximise the hole's strength by retaining as much material as possible next to the lock.

STEP 14 Insert the lock along with the face plate. Check that the spindle hole and the keyhole line up when the face plate is flush. Check the operation of the key in the lock. Fix using the screws provided.

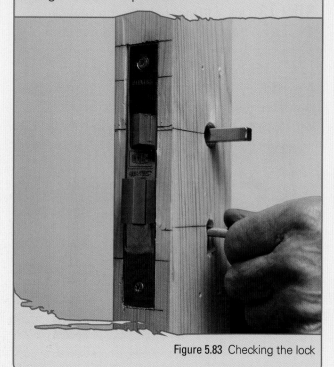

Figure 5.83 Checking the lock

STEP 15 With the dead bolt out, close the door against the frame and mark the positions of the bolt and latch. Use a combination square to mark lines on to the face of the frame.

STEP 16 Measure the distance from the outside of the door to the square face of the latch. Now measure out this distance from the back of the rebate, adding 2 mm, and mark between the latch marks on the frame.

STEP 17 Hold the striking plate in position, lining up the front edge of the latch mortice with the mark on the frame. Ensure that the mortises line up with the corresponding marks for the height of latch and dead bolt. Screw the face plate in position and cut around it using a utility knife. Mark the mortises using a pencil.

STEP 18 Using a sharp chisel, chop out the mortises for the bolt and latch, and then chisel out the recess to the striking plate depth. The striking plate has a lead in to the mortises, and to allow this to sit flush, the corner must be taken off the frame across its width. Fix using the screws provided.

Figure 5.84 Positioning the striking plate

STEP 19 Fit the specified lever handle set or door furniture.

STEP 20 Check that the latch engages smoothly and that the dead bolt can be locked easily from inside and outside with all the keys provided. Check that the door does not rattle in the frame.

Figure 5.85 Door with the latch and handle fitted

PRACTICAL TASK

13. FIT CYLINDER RIM LOCKS

OBJECTIVE

To fit a cylinder rim lock into a door.

STEP 1 Wedge the door open.

STEP 2 Read the instructions supplied with the lock. Mark the centre of the cylinder hole at the required height, using the paper template supplied as part of the instructions.

STEP 3 Drill a 32 mm diameter hole with a suitable drill bit such as a spade bit or auger. Drill from both sides to avoid breakout and to keep the hole square to the edge of the door.

STEP 4 Place the cylinder in the hole from the outside of the door and secure it using the mounting plate and the two long machine screws provided.

Figure 5.86 The secured cylinder

STEP 5 Place the key in the cylinder and keep the key slot vertical as the screws are tightened. These screws may need shortening with a hack saw. Take care as the strength of the lock is reduced if these machine screws are only just long enough. Cutting points into the screw are incorporated into better quality versions to avoid cross threading.

STEP 6 When the cylinder is suitably aligned by checking the operating parts of the lock, secure the mounting plate to the back of the door using the wood screws provided.

STEP 7 The flat strip that connects the cylinder to the lock case will need shortening – it should project past the backplate by about 16 mm. Check the installation instructions to confirm this projection.

STEP 8 Line up the arrow on the backplate of the lock casing with the slot in the thimble.

PRACTICAL TIP

Some models of cylinder lock require letting in to the edge of the door.

STEP 9 Offer the lock case over the mounting plate, making sure the connecting strip is engaged in the slot.

Figure 5.87 Ensuring the connecting strip is engaged

STEP 10 Secure the lock case to the door. Some models are secured with two machine screws into the mounting plate while others are fixed directly to the surface of the door with wood screws.

STEP 11 Check that the key and lever handle both operate the latch and that the latch can be locked off.

STEP 12 Close the door and use the lock casing to mark out the position of the keep or striking plate onto the door frame.

STEP 13 Offer the keep onto the frame between the marks. Mark the shape of the fixing plate onto the frame and let-in using a sharp chisel.

STEP 14 Fix the keep using the screws provided.

STEP 15 Check that the lock operates smoothly from both sides of the door.

Figure 5.88 The finished door

PRACTICAL TASK

14. FIT LETTER PLATES

OBJECTIVE

To fit a letter plate into a door.

STEP 1 Remove the door and place it on a pair of saw horses.

STEP 2 Mark the centre line of the plate on the face of the door. Centralise the letter plate on the centre line and draw around the outer edge.

STEP 3 Measure the size of the flap and mark this on the door, adding 2–5 mm for clearance.

STEP 4 Mark the bolt holes.

> **PRACTICAL TIP**
>
> Letter plates can be installed with the door on; however, fitting is made easier with the door off and it is worth the extra effort of doing this.

STEP 5 Drill holes for the fixing bolts. To avoid breakout, alternately drill from both sides of the door. Drill a fine pilot hole through the door before drilling the clearance hole from both sides or clamp a sacrificial piece of wood to the back of the door.

STEP 6 Drill holes at each corner of the flap cut out to aid the use of a jig saw if you are using one. If you are using a purpose-made letterbox jig and a router, this stage is unnecessary.

STEP 7 Use a jig saw to cut between the holes, scoring across the cross grain with a utility knife to minimise breakout on the upper face.

STEP 8 Clean up the inside of the opening with glass paper and remove the arris.

STEP 9 Secure the letter plate with the bolts provided, and ensure that the plate is parallel to the rail in which it is housed.

STEP 10 Check operation and adjust if necessary.

Fire doors are fitted in much the same way as any other side hung door, with a number of additional considerations. All fire doors are fire-rated and this can be found in one of two places on the door – either a label on the top or on a plug in the edge, which is colour-coded, denoting its particular fire rating.

Fire doors are best fitted into their frames in a workshop environment, installing the intumescent strips and the smoke seal after fitting is complete. They can then be delivered to site in a set to be fitted into pre-prepared openings.

PRACTICAL TASK

15. FIT FIRE DOORS

OBJECTIVE

To fit a fire door.

Consult the specification, door schedule and drawings before starting work.

STEP 1 Remove the intumescent strip from the door.

STEP 2 Fit the door in the normal way, taking particular care with clearance gaps. These should be within the parameters of the specification to allow the correct functioning of intumescent strips and smoke seals.

STEP 3 Using a router, re-house the strips or seals back to their original depth.

STEP 4 In some instances the frame will require routing out to take the strip. This can also be done in situ using a router for the bulk of the work, and finishing to the corners and the bottom of the casing legs with a sharp chisel.

STEP 5 Hang the door in the normal way. Do not remove the label or plug from the door that states its fire rating as this needs to be visible for fire regulation inspections.

PRACTICAL TIP

Some frames have double intumescent strips that are parallel to each other in the frame. This ensures that there is a continuous seal when the hinge is chopped through the first strip.

INSTALLING INTERNAL TIMBER MOULDINGS

Timber mouldings are ornamental contours and shapes that are used for decorative purposes, named after their profile, as can be seen in Fig 5.89. Timber internal mouldings use geometric shapes based on Grecian or Roman designs. Grecian designs are based on elliptical shapes and Roman on circles. They are used to finish off openings where the plaster meets the frames or floors.

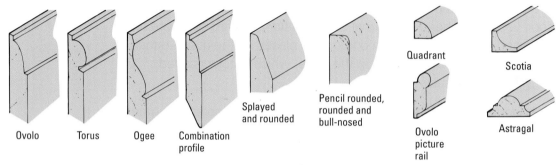

Ovolo   Torus   Ogee   Combination profile   Splayed and rounded   Pencil rounded, rounded and bull-nosed   Quadrant   Scotia   Ovolo picture rail   Astragal

Figure 5.89 Mouldings

Mouldings such as these can be fitted in a variety of different places. They are installed at second fix stage and are mainly for internal use. In a typical room timber mouldings can be used for the skirting board or architrave and for additional decorative features such as dado or picture rails.

Cornice
Architrave
Picture rail
Dado rail
Plinth block
Skirting board

Figure 5.90 Types of trim

Types and sizes of mouldings

The different types of mouldings are shaped and sized for particular uses, as can be seen in Fig 5.90.

Each of these different types of trim has a particular purpose, as can be seen in Fig 5.91. Most of these functions are to cover up gaps or to protect plaster work.

(These drawings are not in proportion.)

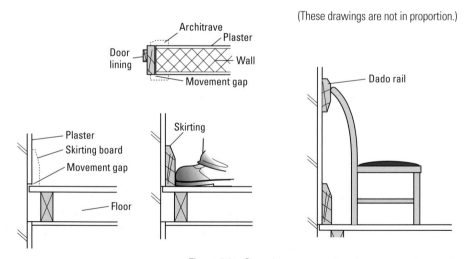

Architrave
Plaster
Door lining
Wall
Movement gap

Dado rail

Plaster
Skirting board
Movement gap
Floor

Skirting

Figure 5.91 Covering gaps and protecting plaster work

The main types of timber mouldings or trim are outlined in Table 5.7.

Timber moulding or trim	Use and position
Skirting	This is fixed at the bottom of the wall. It covers the joint between the floor and the wall. It is there to also protect the plaster from kicks and scrapes.
Architrave	This is a timber moulding that is placed around either door or window openings. It serves a double purpose as it covers the joint between the wall and the timber and also hides any gaps due to shrinkage.
Dado rail	This is traditionally placed at a height of a tall chair back. This means it is usually around 1 m from the floor. Sometimes it is referred to as a chair rail.
Picture rail	This is usually positioned around 1.8 to 2.1 m from the floor. It has a special shape designed to allow clips to be hooked over it to hold picture frame wire.
Plinth block	This is fixed at the base of an architrave. It is usually wider and taller than the skirting that abuts it because on deeper section skirtings the thickness is increased, and is often thicker than the architrave it would usually sit against.
Cornice	These are mouldings positioned at the junction of the wall and ceiling. They can be made from timber but are usually made out of plaster or polystyrene.

Table 5.7

Skirting boards and architraves provide a finish to the edges of plastering where it meets the floor and around frames and linings, concealing any gaps caused through shrinkage and protecting the plaster from knocks and bumps.

Dado rails, sometimes known as chair rails, again provide protection for the plasterwork and split the height of the room in older properties, providing a finish for wallpapers or contrasting finishes above and below. Picture rails were installed in the past to provide a means of hanging pictures without damaging the walls.

The shape and size of the timber being used for these various purposes will depend on the specification and styling of the room. They can be made from hardwood, softwood or MDF. Most of them are supplied on site ready for installation.

Fixing, mitring and scribing mouldings

The following practical tasks show how to fix, mitre and scribe mouldings.

The process is shown for installing skirting boards but should be followed for installing dado and picture rails as well.

It is usual to deal with the architrave first. Once the architrave has been fitted along with a plinth block if this is being used, the skirting is then cut and fixed. After this any other decorative features are then measured up, cut and fixed.

16. INSTALL ARCHITRAVES

OBJECTIVE

To fix architraves around a door.

Architraves are fixed after the doors have been hung; this makes it easier by allowing a marking gauge to be run down the face of the frame or lining, to mark out the hinge pockets. Unless a plinth block is to be used, architraves should be at least as thick as the skirting board.

PPE

In this task, and those that follow, ensure you select PPE appropriate to the job and site where you are working. Refer to the PPE section of Chapter 1.

TOOLS AND EQUIPMENT

Hand tools:

Combination square	Mitre box
Tape measure	Pair of compasses
Pencil	Block plane
Tenon saw	Panel saw
Claw hammer	Coping saw
Nail punch	Screwdriver
Sliding bevel	

Power tools:

Hammer drill	Plug cutter
Cordless screwdriver	Chop saw
HSS bits	Nail gun
Countersink	110V transformer
Counter bore	Extension lead

These tools and equipment apply to all the practical tasks that follow.

STEP 1 Architraves should be fixed to a margin – a line around the frame or lining that is set back from the front edge by approximately 6mm. Use a combination square to transfer a pencil line onto both legs and the head; this line should meet in the corners.

PRACTICAL TIP

If you are right-handed, you will probably find it easier to work from left to right and vice versa if you are left-handed.

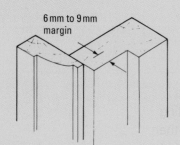

6mm to 9mm margin

Figure 5.92 Margin to architraves should be approx. 6mm

STEP 2 Cut a square end on a length of architrave. Stand this cut on the floor and offer the architrave up to the frame (you may need to tack this in place temporarily) with the thinnest edge touching the margin line. Mark the architrave where the vertical and horizontal margin lines meet.

STEP 3 The mark on the architrave represents the short point of the mitre joint. Place the architrave in a mitre box and cut it with a tenon saw or chop saw if available and if you have been sufficiently trained and are competent in its operation. Alternatively, mark a 45° line across the face of the architrave and cut it freehand, undercutting slightly to ensure a tight fit on the face.

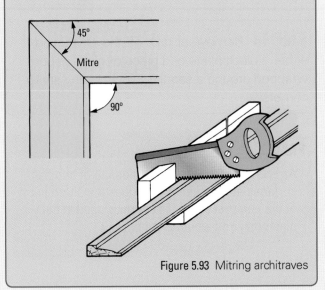

Figure 5.93 Mitring architraves

STEP 4 Place the architrave leg against the margin, check its length and temporarily fix it using oval nails. Do not use round-headed nails such as lost heads or pins as these do not close around the grain when punched below the surface. Try to disguise the fixings by nailing through quirks (deep penetrations already in the moulded surface) where possible.

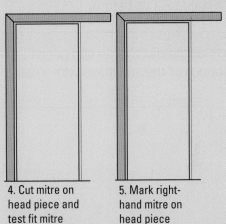

1. Mark margin approx 6 mm

2. Mark position of first mitre on left-hand leg

3. Cut mitre and fix leaving nails proud

4. Cut mitre on head piece and test fit mitre

5. Mark right-hand mitre on head piece

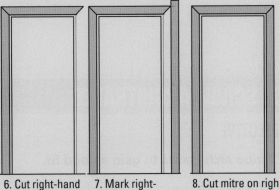

6. Cut right-hand mitre and fix leaving nails proud

7. Mark right-hand leg

8. Cut mitre on right-hand leg, test fit mitre and fix, drive all nails home and punch below the surface

Figure 5.94 Building up the architrave

STEP 5 Cut a 45° angle on the head piece and offer it up to the architrave that has already been fixed. Check the fit – if the joint is tight, mark the other end of the head piece at the intersection of the margin and cut a 45° angle. If there is a gap, the head piece will need planing with a block plane until the joint fits tightly, taking care to support the external edge.

STEP 6 Temporarily fix the head piece.

STEP 7 Cut a square end on the second leg and offer it up to the head piece, with the back of the leg facing outwards, and mark the long point from the head. Transfer this mark on to the face and cut as before.

STEP 8 Check the fit as in Step 5 and trim the leg to fit, and then fix it as before.

STEP 9 Drive all the nails home and punch below the surface of the architrave with a nail punch.

STEP 10 Check that the joints are flush on the face and pin the mitres through the head into the legs. A small amount of PVA adhesive can be applied to this mitre prior to pinning.

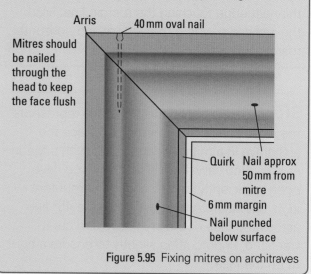

Figure 5.95 Fixing mitres on architraves

STEP 11 Remove or take off the arris using either a block plane or a piece of glass paper wrapped around a sanding block on any sharp corners.

PRACTICAL TIP

Arris is a trade term for the meeting of two flat surfaces at a corner. It describes the sharp point of the external angle. This term is used in both plastering and woodworking.

PRACTICAL TASK

17. SCRIBE ARCHITRAVES

OBJECTIVE

To scribe architraves to gain a good fit.

Architraves often need scribing where there is not enough room to accommodate the full width of the architrave in corners.

Scribing is a term used to describe the process of cutting materials to fit irregularly shaped walls or the profile of mouldings. In this instance the square edge of an architrave is scribed to a wall; we do not assume that plastering is completely flat. Scribes are also used on internal corners where two mouldings meet and one moulding is cut to fit over the other. This is because we only get single shrinkage on a scribe and double shrinkage on a mitre. On mouldings wherever possible you would use a scribe.

STEP 1 Temporarily nail the architrave to the door lining, allowing the architrave to overhang the edge. The overhang should be equal all the way down the leg.

STEP 2 Measure the overhang and add the width of the margin. Set a pair of compasses or cut a gauge block to this resulting size.

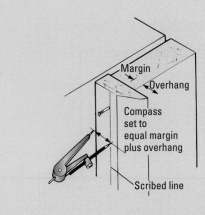

Figure 5.96 Scribing architraves

STEP 3 With the compass held against the wall, mark the line to be cut.

STEP 4 Using a panel, coping saw or a jig saw, cut along the line, undercutting slightly to ensure a tight fit on the face. Using a panel saw, remove any high points with a block plane until the required fit is obtained.

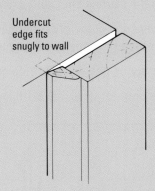

Figure 5.97 Scribing should fit snugly to the wall surface

PRACTICAL TASK

18. INSTALLING SKIRTING

OBJECTIVE

To fit and fix skirting around a room.

There are three joints used when fixing skirting:

* mitre (used on external corners)

* scribe (used on internal corners)

* heading joint (used to joint two pieces in length). It is good practice to mitre the section together to minimise the effects of shrinkage.

STEP 1 Look at the shape of the room and plan out which lengths to cut first. It is common practice to start with the longest walls; however, this is not always the most efficient method.

PRACTICAL TIP

Alcoves and bays are good starting points, as they are usually focal points in a room, and because the skirting is trapped between two walls. It is much easier to scribe out of a corner than to scribe both ends of a length of skirting.

Shrinkage on a scribe only shows in one direction so scribes facing into alcoves and bays will not be as obvious if the skirting shrinks.

Often the second piece of skirting to be fixed is also trapped between two walls. In this case scribe one end to sit over the first piece and continue around the room in the same way.

Check for water, gas and electrics before beginning fixing.

Check the floor for level: the skirting may need scribing level, always starting from the lowest point.

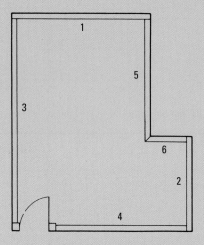

Figure 5.98 Order of fixing (trapped pieces first)

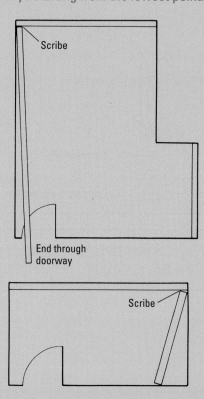

Figure 5.99 Extend through doorway to permit scribing of joint, or angle and scribe when both ends are trapped

STEP 2 Having decided on where to start, measure and cut the first pieces. These should be straight cuts with no joints if possible. Fix these lengths, unless they require scribing to the floor, in which case leave them loose at this stage.

STEP 3 Work out of the corners, scribing over skirting.

STEP 4 Mitre around external corners, checking the fit of each mitre before fixing.

PRACTICAL TIP

Try to avoid having lengths of skirting with scribes on both ends.

PRACTICAL TASK

19. MARK AND CUT AN EXTERNAL MITRE

OBJECTIVE

To fit and fix a mitre on a straight piece of skirting.

Skirting is mitred at external corners; a butt joint would expose end grain on one of the pieces which would look unsightly. Mitres are subject to double shrinkage, when both halves of the mitre shrink away from the corner.

STEP 1 Remove any build-up of plaster that may obstruct the joint or throw the skirting out of upright, as this will cause real difficulty when cutting joints and will look unsightly.

STEP 2 Place the piece of skirting in position and mark the top edge where it sits against the corner.

STEP 3 If you are using a purpose-made mitre box ensure you use the same saw you have made the original cut with when making your box. You can of course use a frame saw if the skirting is not too deep to enable this. Alternatively, use a chop saw, as long as you are trained and competent in its use.

Make the cut in a mitre box using a panel, frame or tenon saw, depending on the depth of cut. Alternatively mark and cut freehand or use a chop saw. Cut from the face so any breakout is on the back and will not show.

STEP 4 Repeat for the other half of the mitre.

STEP 5 Offer both pieces up to the corner and check the fit. Trim with a block plane if required until a good fit is achieved.

STEP 6 Complete any cuts that are required at the other end of the pieces and fix it back to the wall using the appropriate method for the background material.

STEP 7 Dovetail nail the mitre and punch all nails below the surface, adding a small amount of PVA adhesive to the join, if necessary.

20. CUT MITRING AROUND CORNERS THAT ARE UNDER OR OVER 90°

OBJECTIVE

To fit and fix a mitre on corner of skirting.

When cutting skirting around acute or obtuse corners, the angle can be determined by bisecting.

STEP 1 Place the skirting against the wall and mark the thickness on the floor for both halves of the joint. Where the lines meet, allow them to cross.

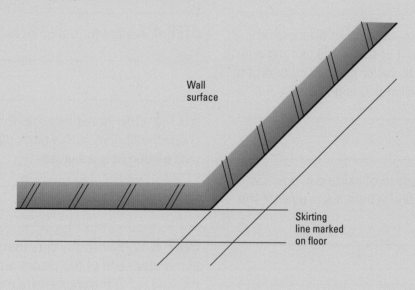

Wall surface

Skirting line marked on floor

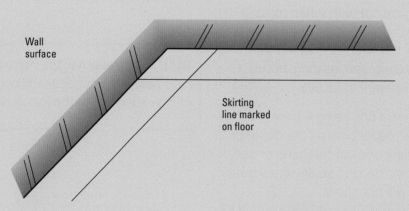

Wall surface

Skirting line marked on floor

Figure 5.100 Line of skirting for corners over 90°

STEP 2 Place the skirting in position and mark the top edge, front outside edge and back inside edge.

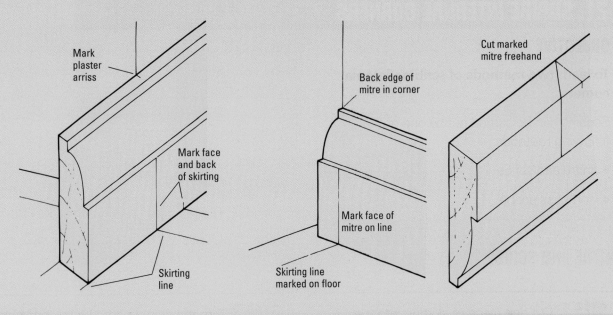

Mark plaster arriss

Mark face and back of skirting

Skirting line

Back edge of mitre in corner

Mark face of mitre on line

Skirting line marked on floor

Cut marked mitre freehand

Figure 5.101 Marking out external and internal corners over 90°

STEP 3 Mark a line across the front and back of the skirting with a try or combination square.

STEP 4 Set a sliding bevel to the required angle from the setting out on the floor and use this to set the required cut with your mitre box or chop saw.

STEP 5 Repeat the process for the other half of the joint.

STEP 6 Fit the joint with block plane if required.

STEP 7 Fix the skirting in position and nail the mitre as previously described.

21. SCRIBE INTERNAL CORNERS

OBJECTIVE

To learn two methods of scribing internal corners.

Scribing can be carried out by one of the following methods:

* mitre and scribe

* compass scribe.

MITRE AND SCRIBE

STEP 1 Cut one piece of skirting into the corner. This should be a square cut but if the wall is not plumb the piece should be cut to fit.

STEP 2 Cut an internal mitre on the other piece. This will make the profile of the skirting apparent, outlining the shape of the cut required.

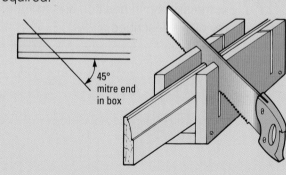

45°
mitre end
in box

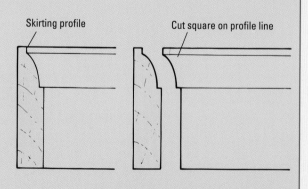

Skirting profile

Cut square on profile line

Figure 5.102 Cutting an internal scribe

STEP 3 Turn the skirting onto its top edge and cut the flat section of the profile with a tenon saw, slightly undercutting to ensure a tight fit.

STEP 4 Use a coping saw to follow the shape of the mould formed by the mitre on the top edge of the skirting, again slightly undercutting.

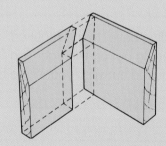

Figure 5.103 Scribing internal corners

STEP 5 Test the scribe against the skirting, making sure of a tight fit, and secure with appropriate fixings.

COMPASS SCRIBE

STEP 1 Cut one piece of skirting into the corner.

STEP 2 Offer the piece of skirting that is to be scribed against the first, set a compass and scribe to the face of the first piece of skirting.

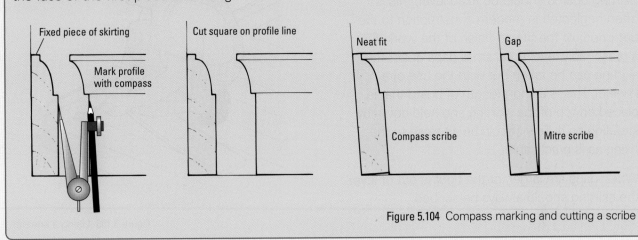

Figure 5.104 Compass marking and cutting a scribe

STEP 3 Cut to the shape of the scribe, following Steps 3 and 4 of the previous practical task.

Internal angles over 90° (obtuse)

The general rule with internal corners is to scribe due to single shrinkage; however, on obtuse angles the scribe becomes almost impossible to execute because of the clearance required behind the scribe. In these instances a bisected mitred joint should be used.

Heading joints

Jointing in length may be required when suitably long lengths of skirting are not available. Here you would use a heading joint. The skirting could be butted but this would result in an inferior finish and so it should always be mitred. The mitred heading joint makes any shrinkage in the skirting less obvious than would a butted joint.

The heading joint is simply two mitres placed on the ends of the skirting and jointed and fixed against the wall.

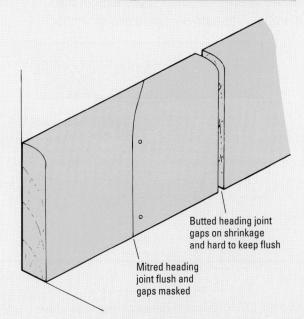

Figure 5.105 Mitres are preferred for heading joints

22. SCRIBING SKIRTING BOARD TO THE FLOOR

OBJECTIVE

To fit and fix a length of skirting to the floor.

Skirting boards should be fixed level; this is often neglected in modern construction to the detriment of the fit and finish of the work. On a reasonably level floor, small gaps under the skirting can be taken out with the use of a kneeler. This is a short length of board that is placed on top of the skirting and held down by kneeling on it. This should be as close to the fixing as is practicable.

When gaps are larger, or the floor is out of level, the skirting should always be scribed.

Figure 5.106 Using a kneeler

STEP 1 Holding the cut length of skirting in place, level and temporarily nail it in position, leaving the heads proud for removal.

STEP 3 Remove the skirting and using a hand saw or jig saw cut to the line, undercutting slightly for a tight fit on the front edge.

STEP 2 Set a pair of compasses to the widest gap under the skirting and mark a line parallel to the uneven floor along the face of the skirting. Alternatively, use a slip of timber.

STEP 4 Fix the skirting in position.

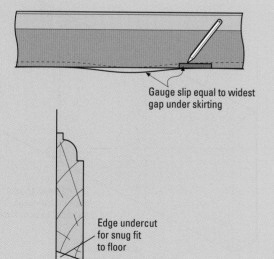

Gauge slip equal to widest gap under skirting

Edge undercut for snug fit to floor

Figure 5.107 Scribing and cutting skirting to an uneven floor surface

PRACTICAL TASK

23. INSTALL A PICTURE AND DADO RAIL

OBJECTIVE

To fix picture and dado rails to walls.

The methods for installing picture and dado rails are the same as for skirting; however, unlike skirting, a horizontal line is required around the room before installation can begin.

STEP 1 Mark a horizontal line around the room to a given height – this may be taken from the drawings, client instruction or governed by wall coverings such as wallpaper or panelling. This should represent the underside of the moulding.

If a datum is established on the site then the height will be directly related on the drawings.

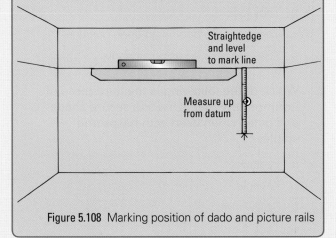

Figure 5.108 Marking position of dado and picture rails

STEP 2 When you are working alone, temporary nails should be knocked into the surface along the line to provide support for the moulding until it is fixed.

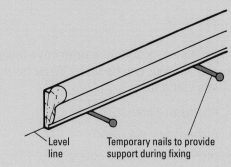

Figure 5.109 Temporary support for dado and picture rails during fixing

STEP 3 Follow the procedure for fixing skirting.

STEP 4 Nail all external mitres.

TEST YOURSELF

1. What is another name for a portable powered mitre saw?

   a. Chop saw

   b. Hack saw

   c. Precision saw

   d. Timber saw

2. When sound-proofing, a protective layer, known as AWP, can be fitted. What do these initials stand for?

   a. Anodised waterproofing

   b. Architectural wall panel

   c. Architectural warp proofing

   d. Architectural waterproofing

3. What feature is added to access panels to protect them from damage each time they are removed or fixed back into position?

   a. Metal plate

   b. Plastic veneer cover

   c. Chamfered edges

   d. A thicker coat of paint

4. What material is commonly used to make a batten framework for a bath panel?

   a. Softwood

   b. Hardwood

   c. MDF

   d. Plastic struts

5. What can be used to ensure that base units are level and plumb when dealing with an uneven floor?

   a. Relaying the floor

   b. Fixing the base units more securely to the wall

   c. Adjusting the legs or wedges

   d. Fixing pegs to the next unit

6. Which is the most common type of kitchen worktop surface used?

   a. Post-formed

   b. Solid timber

   c. Marble

   d. Granite

7. Which of the following is likely to be a function of an external door?

   a. Security

   b. Weatherproofing

   c. Durability

   d. All of these

8. Which of the following is a true statement about a mortise latch?

   a. They are external latches

   b. They lock

   c. They hold the door in an open position

   d. They are opened using a handle

9. Which of the following is the third piece of ironmongery that is used to secure sheds and gates when used with hasps and staples?

   a. Padlock

   b. Keyhole

   c. Screw slot

   d. Knob handle

10. Which of the following timber mouldings is most likely to be closest to the cornice on a wall?

    a. Plinth block

    b. Skirting

    c. Picture rail

    d. Dado rail

Chapter 6

Unit CSA–L2Occ40
SET UP AND OPERATE CUTTING AND SHAPING MACHINERY

LEARNING OUTCOMES

LO1/2: Know how to and be able to prepare for operating cutting and shaping machinery

LO3/4: Know how to and be able to set up cutting and shaping machinery

LO5/6: Know how to and be able to operate cutting and shaping machinery

INTRODUCTION

The aims of this chapter are to:

* help you to operate machinery to cut wood and wood-based products

* help you to maintain, use and change tooling on cutting machinery.

PREPARING FOR OPERATING CUTTING AND SHAPING MACHINERY

Cutting and shaping machinery is said to be the major cause of woodworking accidents. Many accidents can easily be avoided, but investigations by the Health and Safety Executive have shown that many circular saws, for example, are being used without adequate guards, or are even missing guards. To avoid accidents, you need to have a properly adjusted saw guard and use a push stick. Another hazard associated with using circular rip saws is 'kickback'. This can occur if the timber binds on the saw blade, causing the workpiece to be ejected at high speed towards the machine operator.

Never use cutting or shaping machinery unless you have had proper training.

Cutting and shaping machinery is either fixed or transportable. Their uses and hazards are different. This chapter covers both.

Potential hazards

There are many things to consider when using cutting and shaping machinery. All possible safeguards should be implemented to prevent injury. The following examples apply to cross cutting on circular saws:

* A fixed guard should enclose the non-cutting part of the blade as far as the spindle.

* The nose guard must be set as close as practicable to the workpiece to minimise the risk of the operator's hands coming into contact with the saw blade. This nose guard also stops you from touching the front of the blade while it is cutting. It should not be able to reach beyond the front of the saw table.

* A brake should be fitted, to stop the blade within 10 seconds.

* The timber being cut should be supported by a fence on either side of the cutting line. The gap should only be wide enough for the nose guard.

* A portion of the table, at least 300 mm on either side of the blade, should be cross-hatched and designated a 'hands free' area.

* When the circular saw is in operation, any off-cuts must be removed using a push stick or similar safety aid to ensure the operator's hands are kept out of the 'hands free' area at all times.

* For small pieces of wood, holders or jigs should be used.

* If the wood being cut is bowed then the bow should be on the table and wood should be packed to prevent it springing.

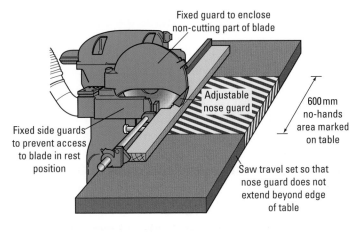

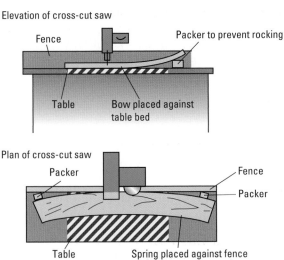

Figure 6.1 Safe use of manually operated cross-cut saws

Legislation and manufacturers' instructions

You should always read the risk assessment before starting work. This will help to identify any action that you might need to take, to ensure any hazards are eliminated or control measures are put in place to minimise any risk to the operator. There may be a safer way to carry out the operation and sometimes this might mean not using the piece of machinery at all.

It is vital to always use cutting machinery bearing a CE mark. Reputable manufacturers will always have this mark. The machinery will have been designed and built to meet British Standards as will accessories such as saw blades.

Both legislation and manufacturers recommend ways in which you should set up your cutting machinery. This extends to the work piece support that is an essential part of a bench. Legislation and manufacturers recommend that:

* large work pieces should be supported both at the in-feed and out-feed ends

* if there is a second operator then they should always be at the out-feed end and never reach forward towards the saw

* a rip fence or cross-cut fence should always be used to support the timber during cutting to prevent 'grabbing' or 'kickback' of the workpiece

* when you are making shallow or angled cuts, a normal fence needs to be replaced with a low fence and you must use a push stick.

Provision and use of Work Equipment Regulations 1998 (PUWER)

These regulations aim to make sure that any machine that is used is safe and that it is only used for the right job. You should be trained before you use the machine and you should only ever use it if it has suitable safety devices and push sticks are readily available.

The regulations cover nearly all types of equipment that you might use either in the workshop or on site. This means everything from hammers through to dumper trucks.

The most important thing to remember is that all equipment needs to be suitable for what you are using it for. It needs to be maintained and regularly inspected.

Health and Safety At Work Act (1974)

Cutting and shaping machinery is powered in different ways. Health and safety law tries to cover any potential problem. Obviously there are particular hazards if you are using machinery powered by mains electricity. But even battery powered machinery can be hazardous.

You should refer to Chapter 1 for general advice about safety in the workplace.

PPE

Each different machine and job may require a different type of PPE. In some cases the machines produce a great deal of noise, so ear defenders must be used. Any machine that produces dust or particles that could fly up into your eyes, nose or mouth could require you to wear some form of eye protection. Face screens are sometimes more appropriate for better protection rather than a simple pair of goggles.

To protect yourself against inhaling dust a suitable dust mask should always be used. For prolonged exposure to dust you may need to wear a respirator.

Some jobs, particularly when handling the machines, make it difficult to wear any kind of hand protection. But if you are assisting in, for example, holding or pushing timber into a machine then you should wear gloves.

PRACTICAL TIP

Gloves are not just worn to protect against splinters and other damage. They are vital as many tools cause vibration and gloves will help prevent any long-term damage.

Machines and components

The following table outlines most of the major sorts of machines used by carpenters.

Cutting and shaping machine	Description and use
Circular saw	This cutting machine is useful for a variety of different tasks, including rip sawing, bevelling, grooving, trenching, cross-cutting and cutting up sheet material. There are various different blades for various materials and tasks. Tungsten carbide tipped saw blades are extremely effective for a wide variety of these different materials.
Chop saw and mitre saw	These are down stroking saws. They have a rotating base plate and saw, so square or mitred cross-cuts can be made. The blade can also be set at an angle.
Bench saw	A portable bench saw, *with the correct blade*, can not only cut through timber products but also through bricks, blocks and tiles. Some will have blade assemblies that allow mitre cutting.
Jig saw	The blade cuts on the upward stroke on most machines, but more expensive versions have an action that moves the blade into the material on the upward stroke and away on the downward stroke. This minimises wear and tear on the blade. Again a number of different blades are available.
Drill	Drills are perhaps the most common type of portable power tool. Good quality drills can perform a variety of different actions and with the right bits, drills and other accessories they can reduce the effort needed and the time taken.
Mortiser	A mortiser is designed to replace the mortise chisel. It is ideal for cutting mortises in the construction of doors and windows.
Biscuit jointer	This is like a small circular saw for forming edge joints. Biscuit jointing involves fitting oval biscuits into saw slots cut by the jointer and then gluing them into position.
Planer	A planer is used for chamfering, rebating and edging. On site it is often used to trim the edges of sheet material and for door hanging.
Sander	These machines aim to take much of the effort out of finishing work. Each different type of sander leaves a more or less smooth surface, so it is important to use the right belt or paper for the job. Belt sanders are good for removing stubborn defects or old paint. Orbital sanders are good for fine finished work.
Router	Routers have a huge number of uses – from trimming and recessing to dovetailing, drilling, moulding, rebating and grooving. They have a router cutter that can be adjusted on a spring-loaded column.

Table 6.1

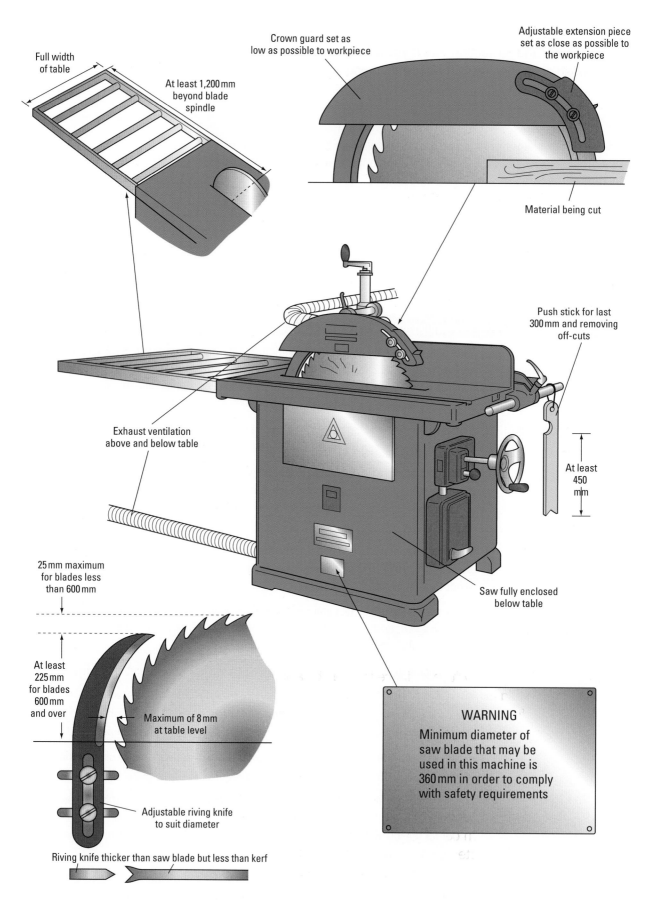

Full width of table

At least 1,200 mm beyond blade spindle

Crown guard set as low as possible to workpiece

Adjustable extension piece set as close as possible to the workpiece

Material being cut

Push stick for last 300 mm and removing off-cuts

Exhaust ventilation above and below table

At least 450 mm

Saw fully enclosed below table

25 mm maximum for blades less than 600 mm

At least 225 mm for blades 600 mm and over

Maximum of 8 mm at table level

Adjustable riving knife to suit diameter

Riving knife thicker than saw blade but less than kerf

WARNING
Minimum diameter of saw blade that may be used in this machine is 360 mm in order to comply with safety requirements

Figure 6.2 Safe working practices of circular saw benches

There are several key components in a range of different cutting and shaping machinery. Not all of the cutting machines and planers will necessarily have all of the following components, but as a carpenter you will come to know these components. You will not only need to be able to identify them, but also know their purpose and importance. The following set of headings describes their purpose in circular saws.

Guards

Circular saws have fixed or interlock bottom guards that aim to prevent contact with the moving parts of the mechanism and the blade. They also have either an adjustable or self-adjusting crown guard. This covers the saw blade above the table.

All guards should:

* be designed in such a way that you cannot access any moving parts, even after the power is turned off, until all movement stops

* be difficult to either disable or bypass

* not obstruct your view of the cutting

* restrict access, but allow you to be able to carry out any repairs, servicing, installation or normal maintenance. These operations should require you to use either a tool or key to remove the guard

* be easily adjustable and easy to maintain

* be rigid so they do not touch the blade when it is in motion and if they are knocked they are not bent out of shape

* cover the main moving parts, including the pulleys and shafts, motor and belts. The crown guard needs to be set as close to the timber that is being cut as possible.

Extraction points

The machine should be fitted to a dust extraction (LEV) system that must operate efficiently. The extraction system should be fitted both above and below the table.

Fences

The bench needs to be fitted with a rip fence that can be adjusted. The fence positioning should be possible without using a tool. The fence is usually made either from wood, plastic or a soft alloy. This is so that it will not damage the blade if contact occurs.

Riving knife

The riving knife is a thin plate that is mounted behind the saw. This is designed to reduce the chance of timber being ejected at high velocity. It should prevent the work piece from closing on the body of the saw blade and loose material from coming into contact with the blade. The knife is manufactured from steel and is a gauge thicker than the body plate of the saw blade, but slightly narrower than the saw kerf.

Bed

The bed is the working surface which the timber being cut is placed on. It is important that the bed is clean and flat, in order to cut accurately and reduce potential hazards.

Blade

Unlike most artificial sheet material, natural woods have directional fibres. Consider this when you are choosing to use either a coarse or fine blade. Usually you should pick a rip saw blade if you want to cut with the grain. Cross-cut blades are mandatory if you want to cut across the grain.

Steel blades are relatively cheap and are good for cutting softwood, but they will dull very quickly if cutting hardwood. The other two main choices are tungsten-carbide tipped (TCT), which will stay sharper for longer, or blades with polycrystalline diamond tips, which are consequently more expensive, but they will stay sharp for much longer.

Information plate

Manufacturers label their blades with information about the saw type and materials or how each one is designed to be used. Circular saw machines should also have an information plate that states the diameter of the smallest blade that can be used with the machine.

Faults and hazards

You should make other checks before the machine is regarded as safe. These are:

* damage to machinery – cracks, splits, missing parts

* DIY repair – gaffer or insulation tape or temporary repairs to the machine

* missing riving knife – the machine will kickback any timber without this

* poorly fitted or missing guards – this exposes you to the moving cutting part of the machine

* poor wiring – if the cable is frayed, damaged or poorly repaired you could get an electric shock

* lack of maintenance – broken, dirty and damaged machinery should not be used

* inadequate or blocked extraction – this may cause the machine to overheat which could cause a short circuit or fire, or jam due to insufficient removal of waste material (saw dust)

* unsafe work area – balancing cutting and shaping machinery on uneven surfaces or in wet conditions could be very hazardous.

Safety aids

There are several different safety aids that you can use to help to prevent or minimise accidents. A push stick is usually custom-made. It may get damaged or destroyed, but it saves your fingers and hands from being injured. Push sticks must always be used to feed the workpiece, to ensure that the operator's hands are kept a minimum of 300 mm away from the saw blade. A push stick must be used to feed the last 300 mm of the workpiece through the saw. The push stick has a 'birdsmouth' that helps to get a firm hold on the piece of wood being

REED TIP

Employers will want to know that you understand the importance of health and safety. Make sure you know the reasons for each safe working practice.

pushed. You should also use the push stick to remove any cut pieces between the saw blade and the fence.

Jigs

Bevelled pieces, angled pieces, tapered firrings and wedges can be produced on the circular rip saw, provided that a suitable and well-constructed jig or saddle is used to support and guide the work piece. It may not be necessary to use a saddle to support the cutting of bevelled pieces on saws with blades that are able to cant (tilt), such as dimension saws.

Wedges can be cut safely on the circular rip saw using an appropriate jig with the guards set correctly. The jig may be used with a push stick to hold the work piece in the jig and move the cut wedges away from the saw.

For tapered firrings, use the circular rip saw with a firring template. The firring piece template can be held securely to the work piece using nails that are long enough to penetrate the work piece but not so long as to be at risk of coming into contact with the saw during the cut, as the nails would damage the saw teeth.

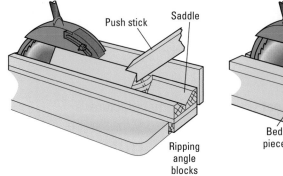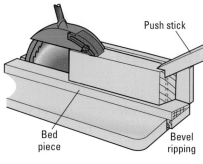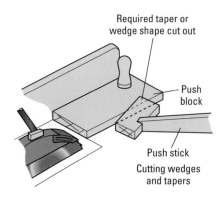

Figure 6.3 Bed pieces, saddles and jigs

Pre-operational checks

It is your responsibility to make sure that the machine, or what you are expecting it to do, will not injure you. You should always carry out the following before using any machine:

* Check the voltage – does the setting match the power using? This means checking whether any adaptors have been properly adjusted.

* Safety cut-offs – these will shut the machine down if, for example, the blade is jammed. You should not use a machine that does not have safety cut-offs or if they have been disabled.

* Circuit breakers – these safety devices cut off the power supply to the machine and isolate it from the main power system if you damage or accidentally cut through the cable. This will reduce the chance of you being electrocuted, as the electricity will flow through a cut cable.

CASE STUDY

Safety always comes first

Joshua Richardson is a third-year apprentice joiner at Laing O'Rourke.

'When you're on site, you're thinking about health and safety all the time. You've always got to wear your PPE on site. Every time you do a job, you've got to think about doing it safely. If someone gives you a job, you're thinking, "How am I going to get up there safely? Are they cutting over there?" and so on.

When it comes to the circular saw, it depends on what you're cutting and what it will be used for. But either way, you're always supervised. The main thing is to follow your line and keep your fingers away! You don't want to have to go back and cut twice, because you're using more wood. Not only is that more cost, but there's less of it, and there might not be a delivery for two weeks. The more precise you are, the less you'll waste.'

HOW TO SET UP CUTTING AND SHAPING MACHINERY

You should always ensure that you follow the manufacturer's instructions and use the correct blade or accessory for the job.

Changing blades and accessories

The diameter of the smallest blade that can be used for the machine will be marked on the machine. If you use a blade that is less than 60 per cent of the diameter of the largest blade for the machine then it will cut in an inefficient way and be more likely to kick back.

To minimise the risk of kickback, when you change a saw blade you must ensure that it is adjusted high enough above the machine table for the saw teeth at the gullet of the saw tooth to project above the surface of the workpiece. You should not set the blade higher than is needed. It is also important to make sure that you are using the correct saw blade designed for the type of work. For example, use a cross-cut or combination blade for cross-cutting and not a ripping blade.

Safe methods of changing saw blades

You should always make sure that the blade is of a type stipulated by the manufacturer. The blade selected must have a saw tooth configuration that is suitable for cutting the nature of materials to be processed.

You should make sure that the saw blade teeth have enough clearance to prevent burning. Saw blades with good vibration dampening qualities can significantly reduce the noise levels when cutting. Above all, the saw blade must be kept sharp as a blunt blade is very dangerous.

PRACTICAL TASK

1. PROCEDURE FOR CHANGING A CIRCULAR RIP SAW BLADE

STEP 1 Isolate the machine from the electrical supply. Remove or raise the guards/crown guard out of the way.

STEP 2 Remove finger plate and packing, if fitted (the saw spindle on some machines may require the machine table to be slid out of the way). If access is from under the table remove the appropriate cover to expose the saw spindle.

STEP 3 Using the correct tools undo the nut by slackening it off in the same direction as the saw rotates (left-hand thread). Remove the nut.

STEP 4 Wearing gloves, remove any collar or washers then carefully remove the saw blade.

STEP 5 Clean the saw spindle including the nut and collar/washer.

STEP 6 Ensure that the replacement blade is of the correct size and type for the machine and for the materials to be cut. Locate the replacement blade on the saw spindle (on the driving pin if one is fitted), making sure that the saw is in the correct running direction.

STEP 7 Refit the collar/washer and replace the nut ensuring it is tightened securely.

STEP 8 Check that the riving knife on the rip sawing machine is of the correct size and is set in the correct position in relation to the saw blade.

STEP 9 Replace any packings if fitted and ensure that any guards protecting the lower portion of the saw are replaced.

STEP 10 Reset the guards/crown guard and position them to suit the saw blade and thickness of the timber to be sawn. Some guards automatically adjust to the thickness of material being cut.

STEP 11 Rotate the saw by hand to ensure it does not come into contact with the guards or with the machine table.

STEP 12 Remove all tools from the machine table and store them in the appropriate place.

STEP 13 Switch the isolator back on and turn the machine on to check that it runs correctly. Perform a test cut.

243

KEY TERMS

Chamfered

– this is a bevelled edge

Kerf

– this is the width of the saw cut and not the width of the saw blade

Fitting the riving knife

A riving knife must be fitted to a circular saw to ensure the rear of the saw is guarded to prevent materials from being inadvertently pushed into the back of the saw. It also holds the saw cut open as the material is being cut to minimise the chance of kickback and avoid serious injury to the operator.

The riving knife must be made of a material that is robust and hardwearing. It must also be adjustable to suit the minimum and maximum size of saw that can be fitted to the machine. It has a **chamfered** leading edge. The thickness of the riving knife should be greater than the steel plate that the saw is made from but less than the saw **kerf**, to prevent the work piece from binding on it. The riving knife must be large enough to extend to a minimum of 225 mm above the saw table for saws of 600 mm and above in diameter, and to within 25 mm from the top of the saw blade for saws below 600 mm in diameter. The distance from the saw blade to the riving knife must be no more than 8 mm.

Machinery guards

At least 10 people die each year, and as many as 40,000 injuries occur, as a result of poorly maintained or missing guards on machinery.

You should always use the equipment's guards and any safety devices correctly and never remove them or restrict them so that they cannot operate. The guard is there to cover the cutting edge of a saw. Some machines and power tools have guards that automatically retract as the material is being cut and close on completion of the operation.

Guards are there to control the risk to the person using the machine. You should always follow the manufacturer's instructions and the 1998 PUWER regulatory requirements about using the guard and making sure that it works properly.

Maintaining and cleaning

Over time the blade can become contaminated with materials that cling to the teeth of the saw blade, and other parts of the blade body. These can be natural materials from the wood, such as resin or adhesive deposits from manufactured boards. The problems are:

* the contaminants will cause friction, which generates heat

* they also insulate the blade preventing heat that can build up during the cutting process, discharging from the saw blade

* as a result of both of these situations, friction and an excessive heating of the saw blade can mean the blade becomes blunt prematurely

* the blade is more likely to warp or distort causing it to run out of true, which in turn could result in kickback

* you might need to push the timber through the blade with much greater force. The feed rate will be far slower and you may even notice smoke.

Many serviceable blades are thrown away when all they actually need is to be cleaned.

Inspecting saw blades

Over time the blade will lose its effectiveness. It can burn the timber, overheat and will require extra pressure to cut through the timber. Circular saw blades should never be sharpened on the machine but should be removed and either hand-filed or sharpened using a saw sharpening machine.

If any resin or adhesive deposits are found on a saw blade, these should be first softened using a solution of oil and paraffin, and then the deposits should be removed using a scraper, ensuring the saw teeth are not damaged by the process.

Lubricants

Lubricants have a wide variety of different uses. There are a number of traditional types, such as oil or paraffin, but increasingly plant oil is used. The key benefits of using lubricants are:

* they are rust inhibitors (they stop rust)

* the blade is cleaner

* the times between having to sharpen the blades are longer

* the blade tension is retained for longer.

Specialised lubricants often act as cleaners as well and they will dissolve organic substances such as resin or oils. They are biodegradable and solvent-free.

Servicing and cleaning

You should always follow the instructions in the manufacturer's maintenance manual. This will ensure that the equipment is always kept effective and efficient. You should always check the dust extraction system at the same time.

PRACTICAL TIP

If you are having problems with a blade, before cleaning it have a look and see if it is pitted, bent or otherwise damaged. If it is then it is probably not worth cleaning and needs to be replaced.

The following general maintenance list should be carried out:

* Check the general area of the machine for woodworking debris and other materials that could get into the machine.

* Check the guards, fences and tables, making sure that they can all be adjusted without a problem.

* Check that the guards and other safety devices are in a safe condition. This includes braking devices.

* Check the saw blade and teeth to see if they are dull or defective in any way.

A maintenance schedule should be developed which stipulates what needs doing and the frequency at which it should be carried out. This should:

* include any changes to manufacturers' recommendations for the machine

* identify all regular maintenance requirements.

However, circular bench saws are quite low maintenance. Using a sharp blade will significantly improve the safe operation of the machine. The saw blades do need to be maintained, so they should be kept clean and sharp. Always have an additional saw blade ready, as this will avoid delays with work while a dull blade is being re-sharpened.

Routine maintenance, cleaning and lubrication will go a long way to ensuring that the saw works and that the safeguards are fully functional.

OPERATING CUTTING AND SHAPING MACHINERY

Having set up your cutting and shaping machinery, you now need to use it safely and efficiently. Wherever you are working, construction needs to be efficient and produce minimum amounts of waste and dust.

Cutting lists

When particular jobs have to be done either in the workshop or on site a document called a cutting list will be prepared. It will:

* state the job title, such as making rods for stairs or architrave for doors

* identify the materials that you will be using

* state the number of finished items that need to be produced

* describe the items to be produced and the finished size of each item.

The cutting list will aim to make sure that the maximum number of finished items is made from the minimum amount of original material, with the minimum amount of waste. This will be an important part of the original setting out procedure for a job.

Cutting list					
Rod no. 52		Date		Contract no. 5	
Job title		Casement window			
Item no.	Item	No. off	Finished size (mm)	Sawn size	Material
	Frame:				
1	Jambs	12	70 × 95 × 1000	75 × 100 × 1000	Redwood
2	Head	6	70 × 95 × 700	75 × 100 × 700	Redwood
3	Cill	6	70 × 120 × 700	75 × 125 × 700	Oak
	Casement:				
4	Stiles	12	45 × 45 × 500	50 × 50 × 500	Redwood
5	Top rail	6	45 × 45 × 900	50 × 50 × 900	Redwood
6	Bottom rail	6	45 ×70 × 500	50 × 75 × 500	Redwood

Figure 6.4 Detailed cutting list

Dust extraction

Efficient dust collection is vital for health reasons but also to comply with the law. Circular saw operators can suffer from allergic reactions which can affect the nose, eyes and skin. A build-up of dust can also pose a fire hazard. Larger particles that cling to surfaces can cause scoring and poor visibility can make accurate measurement and cuts impossible.

A simple dust collection system uses a duct system. This moves the dust from the saw to a collection device that is attached to the ducting. Metal ducting is usually thought to be better than plastic piping. This is for three reasons:

* There is a limited choice of suitable plastic pipe fittings that would meet the needs of the extraction.

* The elbows in plastic pipes tend to clog.

* Plastic piping is **non-conductive** – it builds up a static charge as the charge particles pass along it. This charge can shock and there is also the risk of explosion or fire.

Spiral, steel pipe with fittings that have a long radius are less likely to clog. They can also be fitted with sections that can unclip and be cleaned out. The pipe is **conductive** and is less likely to be a fire hazard.

Waste disposal

Nearly every cutting and shaping task will produce some waste, whether it is dust or small pieces of wood. A good cutting list will minimise the number of off-cuts.

The Building Act (1984) clearly states that it is construction's responsibility to prevent and control waste. It should also make sure that resources are not wasted unnecessarily.

KEY TERMS

Non-conductive

– this is a material that does not readily conduct electricity, and static electricity may build up in the material

Conductive

– this means that an electrical current can pass through the material and not build up in it

Building Regulations cover the problem of waste disposal. This is in Part H, which covers all types of building materials, including wood.

The drive towards sustainable and secure buildings also aims to control waste and to protect the environment. You could refer back to Chapter 3, to refresh your memory about sustainability.

In order to reduce the amount of waste the following table can be used as a guide.

Waste reduction and disposal method	Explanation
Elimination	Don't produce the waste in the first place. Regularly checking materials on site or in a workshop stops over-ordering. Using cutting lists means you can order the right lengths of materials and reduce the waste. Once the materials have arrived, if they are stored properly they will be in a good state for another job.
Reduction	Always keep materials in their protective packaging and try not to handle the material unless necessary as this will avoid damage. Always put materials back into storage. If you have large off-cuts set them aside as they might be useful later. Always use up opened stock before breaking into a new package.
Re-use	Use off-cuts for pegs, profile boards and repairs. Re-use timber off-cuts as many times as you can. They can be used for hoardings or form work.
Recycle	Most timber can be recycled. Some has a high value, such as reclaimed oak or pine for furniture. Most other timber, no matter how small the off-cut, can be used to produce chipboard or MDF. You should only throw wood into a skip as a last resort.

Table 6.2

PRACTICAL TASK

2. SETTING A CIRCULAR SAW UP FOR RIP SAWING TIMBER

OBJECTIVE

To practise setting up a circular saw.

PPE

In this and the tasks that follow, ensure you select PPE appropriate to the job and site where you are working. Refer to the PPE section of Chapter 1

STEP 1 Ensure the machine is switched off and cannot be accidently started. Check the blade is sharp and in good condition, and is of the correct type for the material to be cut.

STEP 2 Adjust the height of the saw blade to suit the thickness of timber to be sawn.

STEP 3 Set the guards as close as practicable to the work piece (some machines have guards that are self-adjusting). Set and lock the fence to the required dimension.

STEP 4 Ensure the machine table is clear of any off cuts or other debris and check that all safety aids (push sticks) are available and in place ready for the operation.

STEP 5 Turn the machine on. Ensure it gets up to running speed then make a trial cut and check that it is the correct size. Make any adjustment to the fence as necessary.

PRACTICAL TIP

If quantities are being cut stack safely and not in a position that might obstruct the safe use of the machine.

STEP 6 Feed the material through the machine using push sticks or push blocks.

STEP 7 On completion of the operation switch the machine off. Clear away any off-cuts and leave the machine tidy ready for the next operation.

PRACTICAL TASK

3. SETTING UP A CROSS CUT SAW FOR CUTTING BOARDS TO LENGTH

OBJECTIVE

To practise setting up a cross saw.

STEP 1 Ensure the machine is switched off and cannot be accidently started. Check the blade is sharp and in good condition with the correct hook angle (negative hook).

STEP 2 Set the stop or stops to the required positions.

STEP 3 Load the work piece onto the cross cut table. Trim the end of the work piece to check it is sound and to remove any foreign bodies that might damage the saw or the tooling on other machines if more operations are to be carried out on it. (This is known as fair ending.)

STEP 4 Push the end that has just been trimmed up to the stop, taking care not to hit the stop too hard as this may move it and make the timber oversize. Check that there is no debris trapped between the stop and the work piece as this may cause it to be cut undersize.

PRACTICAL TIP

Ensure the longest pieces required are cut first to minimise waste. If a quantity of pieces is required check the first piece to ensure it is the correct size.

STEP 5 On completion of the work, stop the machine. Ensure that the saw has come to a complete halt then remove any waste or other debris from the machine table and leave the area tidy for the next operation.

PRACTICAL TASK

4. SETTING UP A CHOP SAW FOR CUTTING MATERIALS TO LENGTH

OBJECTIVE

To practise setting up a chop saw.

STEP 1 Ensure that the machine is disconnected from the power supply then check that the blade is sharp and in good condition with the correct hook angle (negative). Check that the blade is set at 90° to the fence.

STEP 2 If long lengths are to be cut ensure the material is supported at each side of the machine using trestles or tables. Some machines have specially designed frames to support long work pieces. Where fitted, set length stops.

STEP 3 Load the material to be cut onto the table. If the material is bent ensure it is down on the table at the point that the saw makes contact. If the timber is bowed, the convex face of the board needs to be placed down on the machine table and the convex edge of the board needs to be pushed up to the fence.

STEP 4 Cramp the work piece to the machine bed – refer to manufacturers manual for how to do this.

STEP 5 Hold the timber, taking note of the 'no go areas' on the machine table. If the work piece is too short, hold it with the cramp and, if necessary, with a push stick.

STEP 6 Ensure there are no tools such as tape measures left on the machine bed.

STEP 7 Turn the power on. Activate the start switch and draw the saw down steadily until it has cut through the work piece. Release the start switch but do not let the saw back up until it has stopped. When the saw blade has stopped, return the saw back to the home position.

STEP 8 Unclamp the timber and check for size.

STEP 9 Repeat cycle until the job is completed.

STEP 10 When operations are complete, remove all waste and off-cuts from on and around the machine, leaving it in a safe condition ready for the next operation.

PRACTICAL TIP

When angled and/or compound angled work pieces have to be cut, more of the saw blade can be exposed. This means that you must take extra care when holding the timber and act with extreme caution at all times.

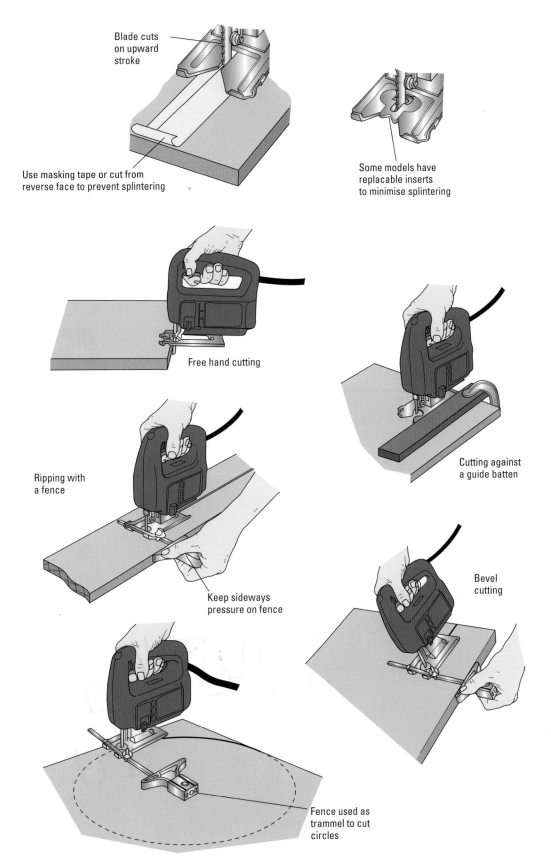

Blade cuts on upward stroke

Use masking tape or cut from reverse face to prevent splintering

Some models have replacable inserts to minimise splintering

Free hand cutting

Cutting against a guide batten

Ripping with a fence

Keep sideways pressure on fence

Bevel cutting

Fence used as trammel to cut circles

Figure 6.5 Operation of a jig saw

No gloves are worn in these pictures, in order to clearly show how to use hand tools. However, you should wear gloves and other PPE required by your college or employer.

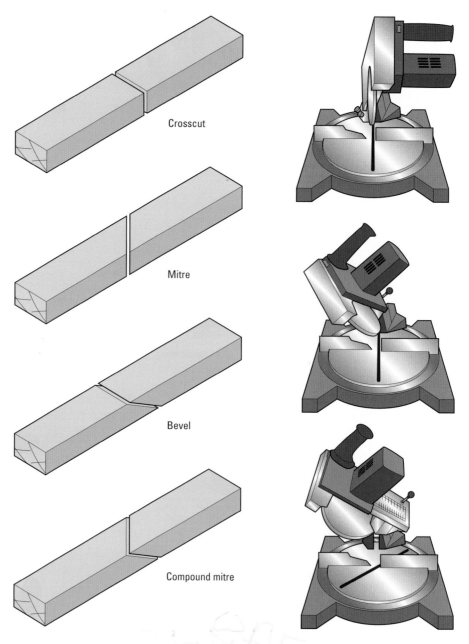

Crosscut

Mitre

Bevel

Compound mitre

Figure 6.6 Types of cut using a mitre saw

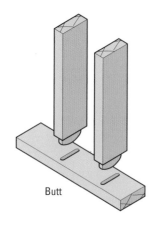

Butt

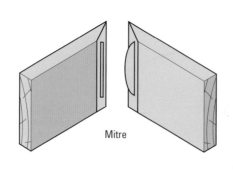

Mitre

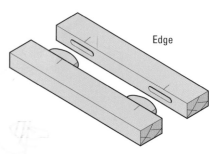

Edge

Figure 6.7 Use of biscuits for jointing

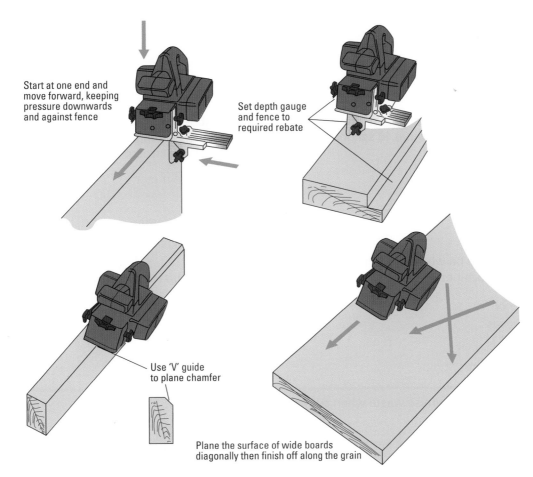

Start at one end and move forward, keeping pressure downwards and against fence

Set depth gauge and fence to required rebate

Use 'V' guide to plane chamfer

Plane the surface of wide boards diagonally then finish off along the grain

Figure 6.8 Using a planer

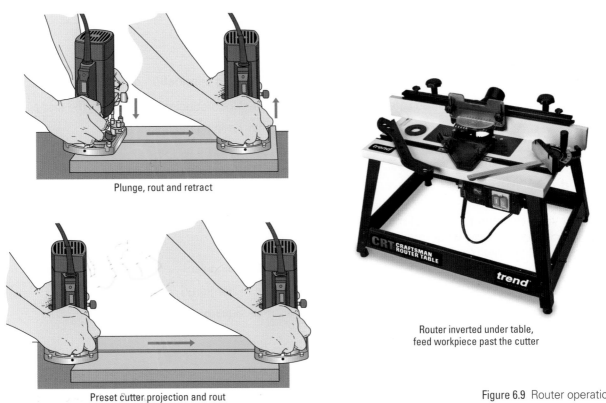

Plunge, rout and retract

Preset cutter projection and rout

Router inverted under table, feed workpiece past the cutter

Figure 6.9 Router operation

No gloves are worn in these pictures, in order to clearly show how to use hand tools. However, you should wear gloves and other PPE required by your college or employer.

TEST YOURSELF

1. What is the device called that should stop a circular saw blade within 10 seconds?

   a. Spring

   b. Jig

   c. Push stick

   d. Brake

2. What should be worn as a form of protection against machinery vibration?

   a. Goggles

   b. Gloves

   c. Face screen

   d. Respirator

3. How can you minimise waste when cutting boards to length?

   a. Cut the shortest pieces first

   b. Cut the longest pieces first

   c. Cut each piece to the same size and trim them afterwards

   d. Ensure there is debris between the stop and the work piece

4. Which of the following is true about guards?

   a. They should be easily adjustable and easy to maintain

   b. They should be rigid

   c. They should not obstruct your view

   d. All of these are true

5. If you are cutting a piece of material on a circular rip saw, what must you use to protect yourself?

   a. Push stick

   b. Jig

   c. Gloves

   d. Wedge

6. What device should be fitted to a mains powered cutting or shaping machine to prevent electrocution?

   a. Voltage meter

   b. Guard

   c. Circuit breaker

   d. Riving knife

7. What is the term used to describe a material that allows an electric current to pass through it and not build up in it?

   a. Magnetic

   b. Non-conductive

   c. Conductive

   d. Metallic

8. Which part of the Building Regulations covers waste disposal?

   a. A

   b. C

   c. H

   d. J

9. What is elimination of waste?

   a. Not producing the waste in the first place

   b. Keeping offcuts for later

   c. Reusing timber

   d. Disposing of waste carefully

10. What shape is the leading edge of a riving knife?

    a. Flat

    b. Triangular

    c. Chamfered

    d. Square

Chapter 7

Unit CSA–L3Occ1176
ERECT COMPLEX STRUCTURAL CARCASSING COMPONENTS

LEARNING OUTCOMES

LO1/2: Know how to and be able to prepare for erecting structural carcassing components

LO3/4: Know how to and be able to erect trussed rafter roofs

LO5/6: Know how to and be able to construct verge and eaves finishes

LO7/8: Know how to and be able to form dormer windows and roofs

LO9/10: Know how to and be able to construct traditional cut roofs with hips and valleys

INTRODUCTION

The aims of this chapter are to:

* help you to interpret relevant information

* help you to select resources to carry out the work

* help you to erect structural carcassing components in accordance with the work specification.

PREPARING TO ERECT STRUCTURAL CARCASSING COMPONENTS

Many of the necessary preparations are similar to those that are needed for first and second fix operations, which were looked at in Chapters 4 and 5. There are some particular elements that need to be looked at in more detail here.

Health and safety and potential hazards

Some structural work will almost certainly involve working at height, for example on roofs. This means that falls and potential injuries or fatalities from materials falling from height are a concern. Materials used are generally extremely heavy and will require you to be trained in manual or mechanical lifting operations, depending on the work.

It is the duty of the site manager to assess, eliminate and control the risks of anyone falling from height or lifting operations.

There is always the chance that the structure might collapse part-way through construction. You should note the following:

* Any area on the site that is at risk from falling materials needs to be clearly marked. It must include an exclusion zone and be strictly a hard hat area.

* Any walkways need to be covered.

* Where possible high-reach machines should be used and the machine cabs need to be reinforced. This is a specialist job and the operative must be fully competent and have the correct qualification for the category of lifting equipment used. In some cases a crane may be required.

* Anyone working on the site needs to be trained, fully qualified and properly supervised. This means that a full risk assessment relative to each task needs to be carried out and, where appropriate, further advice should be taken from the Health and Safety Executive.

Working drawings, schedules and specifications

When you are involved in erecting complex structural carcassing components you will need to refer to different types of drawings, but in particular you will also have to understand:

* abbreviations

* hatchings

* drawings produced, including scale drawings

* scales used.

See Chapter 2 for more information on drawings, schedules and specifications.

Details and assembly
Details can be drawn at 1:10, 1:5 or even 1:1. These are 100 mm or 200 mm to the metre, and in the case of 1:1 they are full size. Assembly drawings are at 1:20, 1:10 or 1:5, which means they are 50, 100 or 200 mm to 1 m.

Sectional
Sectional drawings are a way of showing details either vertically or horizontally. They represent a theoretical cut through the building. Section lines indicate the direction from which the section is being viewed – this could be up, down, left or right. Cross-sections are used to show every aspect of construction, for example to show how different components are sited in relation to each other. At ground floor level, a typical vertical cross-section would show the foundations, the ground level, the hardcore, the DPM, the oversite concrete and the wall details, including below and above DPC.

First angle orthographic projection
First angle projection should show a face elevation with a plan below. Left side elevation is drawn on the right and right side elevation is drawn on the left. Third angle projection is the term used in America (the difference is explained in Chapter 2).

Isometric projection
Isometric projection is a way of representing three-dimensional objects in two dimensions, as can also be seen in Fig 2.15.

PPE

See Chapter 1 for details about PPE.

Access equipment

It is important always to manage any work at height. The HSE uses a hierarchy of controls: before taking the responsibility of using any access equipment you should be fully trained and competent in its use.

* Avoid – this means looking at other options, such as being able to do the work safely on the ground rather than at height.

* Prevent – if work at height is necessary, what can be done to eliminate it or make it less likely that someone will hurt themselves? This may mean putting in fall restraints and using harnesses.

* Arrest – if the worst should happen and someone does fall, restraints, fall bags and safety netting should be in place. These are arresting devices that break the fall.

There are various ways in which safe access when working at height can be achieved. The following table outlines the main methods.

Types of access equipment	Description
Putlog scaffold	This is dependent on the building to remain erect. It is built into the brickwork as the work proceeds. It must be erected by a qualified, card-holding scaffolder.
Independent scaffold	This is tied to the building but is not dependent on it to remain erect. It must be erected by a qualified, card-holding scaffolder.
Stair tower and fixed or mobile scaffold towers	These are safer than ladders. They are usually made from aluminium components, although some are steel. The components are locked together to give considerable strength. They need to be properly secured and erected by a fully trained and competent operative.
Mobile access equipment	Many of these are referred to as mobile elevating work platforms (MEWP). A scissor lift will lift materials or objects vertically only. A telescopic boom is also known as a cherry picker. It lifts vertically and can also reach outwards. The final option is an articulating and telescopic boom, which is often mounted on a vehicle. These are all ideal for lifting objects while working at height. They should only be operated by trained and competent individuals who are qualified in the specific plant that is to be operated. Any other users should also have been trained.
Ladders	Ladders can be used if, after assessing the risks, the use of more suitable work equipment is not justified because of low risk and short duration (up to about 30 minutes). When ladders are used they must always have three points of contact by the user. Industrial grade ladders should always be used. They must be secure, tied at the top and bottom, in good condition and regularly inspected.
Roof access hatches	These are essentially covers for openings for roof access ladders on an access platform. They are designed to prevent people from falling through the holes. The best practice is to ensure that the roof hatches are always closed after use and only opened while workers or materials are being passed up or down through the hole.

Table 7.1

Protecting the work and surrounding area
See Chapter 3 for more about protecting work and sustainability.

ERECTING TRUSSED RAFTER ROOFS

The majority of modern domestic dwellings have factory-made roof units; these are manufactured as triangulated frames, which are called trussed rafters. Many of them have specific design names, such as 'fan' or 'fink'. The timber is prepared and stress graded. The joints are butt jointed and sandwiched between galvanised steel face fixing plates. These plates have spikes for machine pressing onto the joints. Once these trusses have been positioned to the correct specification they need to be braced following the plan normally provided by the manufacturer.

Roofs are normally constructed using a number of trussed rafters. These are spaced at centres between 400 mm and 600 mm. Each of the roof trusses is designed to sit on a wall plate. The rafters are then fixed into place using truss clips. Further support is given by galvanised wall straps or restraints.

Typically, the erection of truss rafters follows a set procedure:

* The position of each of the truss rafters is marked on the wall plate.

* Each of the rafters is then lifted into place.

* The rafters are stacked upright at one end of the roof. Note that they should not be leaned against the gable end, as the brickwork may not be strong enough to take the load.

* The first rafter is then lifted into position and secured with truss clips.

* The first rafter is plumbed and braced (temporarily) using diagonal braces and binders.

* Each of the remaining rafters is then put into position.

* Each of them is secured and temporarily braced.

* Once all of the rafters are in place the diagonal and longitudinal braces are then secured.

* Finally any necessary straps and restraints are secured.

Usually the gable end walls are either partially or fully completed before the truss rafter roof is erected. When this is the case a single trussed rafter frame or even a pair of common rafters is fixed and braced at each gable. This acts as a guide for the bricklayer to shape the top of the walls. If the building is to have gable ladders (which project over the face of the wall) the brickwork is only built up to the underside of the truss. The brickwork is then finished off once the gable ladder is in position.

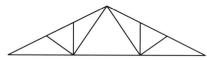

Figure 7.1 Fan trussed rafter

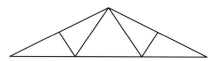

Figure 7.2 Fink trussed rafter

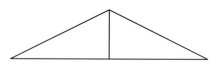

Figure 7.3 King post trussed rafter

Figure 7.4 Attic trussed rafter

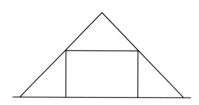

Figure 7.5 Queen post trussed rafter

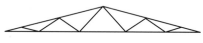

Figure 7.6 Double W trussed rafter

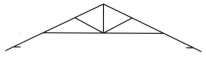

Figure 7.7 Raised tie trussed rafter

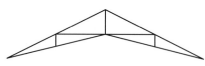

Figure 7.8 Scissor trussed rafter

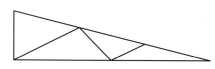

Figure 7.9 Mono trussed rafter

Types of trussed rafter roof

There are many different trussed rafter types, which are used for a wide range of different building types. As they are pre-fabricated a great deal of labour costs can be saved on site. Some are duo-pitched, which means that they are used to span the entire roof. Others are mono-pitched trussed rafters, which are used for example for hip ends, lean-to roofs or hip ends that span onto fire walls.

Fan
These tend to be used for commercial buildings or larger domestic dwellings. They have a span of up to 16 m.

Fink
This is often used if a water tank needs to be installed. They are suitable for spans of up to 11 m.

King post
These are used for domestic dwellings and garages, with a span of up to 4.5 m.

Attic
These provide a structural roof and a floor for the attic space in one section.

Queen post
These are used for domestic dwellings and have a span of up to 6 m.

Double W
These tend to be used either for domestic dwellings or commercial buildings and have a span of up to 16 m.

Raised tie
These types of roof not only provide additional headroom, but give more architectural detail to the interior of the room.

Scissor
These have a sloping bottom chord in order to give extra headroom. The pitch difference between the top and bottom is around 15°. There is also a modified scissor shape, which is broadly similar to the basic scissor truss shape. It has sloping chords to the side, but has a flat section to create a ceiling.

Mono
These are used for lean-to buildings, roofs that need to span onto fire walls or for hipped end roofs.

Hip
These are used when there is no gable end wall where two slopes on different elevations meet on a corner.

Figure 7.10 Hip trussed rafter

Lattice

These tend to be used to create attic sections around dormers and stairs, but they can also be used for flat roof structures.

Figure 7.11 Lattice trussed rafter

Components needed to erect trussed rafter roofs

The trussed rafter roof has several key components, which need to be understood in terms of their positioning and their purpose. These are outlined in the following table.

Component	Description
Hips	The trusses, girders and timbers that are needed to create a hip end are known as a hip set. A hip end is an alternative to a gable end. This defines two planes on a roof that meet at an external corner. The end wall finishes at the same height as the other walls. The roof inclines from the end wall, usually at the same pitch as the main trusses. A hip rafter is a term used to describe a timber that slopes from ridge to corner in the hip end construction.
Valleys	A valley is an area of roof that connects two different roof directions on an internal corner. The diminishing trusses that are used infill this area of roof.
Diminishing trusses	These are also known as valley jack trusses. They are used to infill the area of roof that forms a hip or valley.
Gable	This is the end wall, parallel to the trusses. It extends upwards vertically to the rafters.
Ladder	These are the components that are used to form an overhang at the gable end.
Eaves	This is the area that comprises the rafter feet, the soffit, the fascia board, and sometimes the sprocketing.
Soffits	These are boards that are fixed to the seat cut of the rafter ends underneath the eaves, along the length of the building. These conceal the timbers and will incorporate a ventilation strip of some description.
Verge	The verge is the line where trussed rafters meet the gable wall. They can either be finished with a bargeboard with an overhanging verge or flush, which sits tight to the brickwork, or where no bargeboard is to be used, the brickwork is topped with an undercloak and the tiles or slates are bedded in mortar, or verge tiles may be used.
Wall plate	This is a timber that is laid along the length of a load-bearing wall in order to support the trusses and provide a means of fixing common rafters. It is bedded in mortar at the top of the internal blockwork of a building and is secured with vertical restraining straps. The wall plate should be a minimum of 75 mm wide.
Straps	Both horizontal and vertical restraint straps are used. They are made from galvanised steel and have holes punched at regular intervals along their length. The horizontal straps are usually 30 × 5 mm in section. They can have a combination of different bends and angle twists. The vertical straps are usually 30 × 2.5 mm in section, as these have lighter loads.
Bracing	Bracing consists of different types. Stability bracing is the arrangement of the timbers that are fixed into the roof space to provide lateral support for the trusses. These are called binders or longitudinal braces. Temporary bracing is the use of internal and external diagonal, and external longitudinal, bracing during the erection of the roof. Sometimes these temporary bracings will be retained and become part of the stability bracing or provide additional bracing against wind. The third type of bracing is wind bracing. This is used to describe the arrangement of additional timbers or other structural parts. These are designed to transmit any strong wind to the load-bearing walls. The fourth type of bracing is chevron bracing. This is like diagonal bracing but the direction of the braces alternates as you proceed along the roof.
Truss clips	These are used to fix the timber trusses to the wall plates. They are used to avoid possible damage that can be caused by skew nailing.

Table 7.2

Constructing trussed rafter roofs at ground level

In order to speed up the building of dwellings, trussed rafters can be constructed at ground level. Their major advantages are safety and speed of construction.

They are pre-fabricated and then erected on site and braced, just like normal trussed rafters. A crane then lifts the entire structure into position.

Lateral restraint

Lateral restraint straps need to be provided at rafter level for gable walls to stabilise the trusses and the gable wall. Where there is a larger gable or separating walls additional restraints may be needed at ceiling level. The lateral restraint straps should have a cross section of 30 mm × 5 mm. The straps need to be of sufficient length to be fixed to three trusses. The alternative in trussed rafter roofs is to provide lateral restraint through gable ladders.

Lateral stability involves fixing binders at both ceiling and apex level. Added to this, diagonal rafter bracing is fixed to the underside of the rafters, as can be seen in the following diagram.

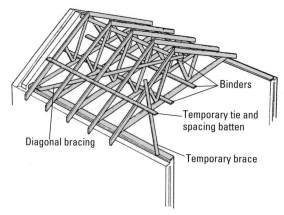

Figure 7.12 Bracing and binder details

Forming openings

There will almost certainly be a requirement to provide openings in a roof. This can be for a variety of different purposes:

* roof lights or dormer windows

* chimneys

* loft access hatches.

Openings will be included in the roof's design brief. This type of roof should never be modified when in place without consulting a design engineer.

In the case of chimneys, it is also important to ensure that there is a gap between the brickwork and any structural timbers. In practice this is 40 mm. The purpose of the gap is not only to provide ventilation, but also to reduce the exposure of the timber to hot brickwork in the chimney – preventing fire. The area around the chimney stack on the roof has to be waterproofed and this means fixing a framework to support any gutter or flashings.

Roof lights and dormer windows

Roof lights usually comprise either dormer windows or skylights. Both of these types of window have a trimmed opening in the slope of the roof. This is usually achieved by the use of double trusses on either side of the opening, together with the use of trimmers and trimmed rafters, according to the size of the opening and the number of trimmed rafters that need to be carried.

Dormer windows project vertically from the surface of the roof. Their position can be determined by a number of factors, such as the pitch of the principal roof, the FFL inside the roof space and type of roof covering. The triangular sides are called cheeks. They are made from sawn studs of a minimum of 100mm × 50mm. These are sheathed externally by diagonal boarding. The cheeks can also be prepared to take tile or slate cladding. In these cases they will need a breather membrane.

Chimney stacks

Where a chimney passes through a trussed rafter roof, the opening should not exceed twice the normal design spacing less the opening width; however, this can be exceeded by the use of double trusses.

The section of roof on either side of the chimney has to be constructed in situ. A trimmer is fixed between the two last trusses either side of the chimney and loose trimmed infill rafters are used to fill the space. Ceiling tiles should be treated in the same way. Short purlins should be incorporated midspan and binders should extend onto the adjacent trusses. The infill rafters are nailed to the side of the infill joists and the wall plate. They need to be 25mm deeper than the trussed rafters. This allows a **birdsmouth** to be created at the wall plate.

KEY TERMS

Birdsmouth

– this is a joint formed at the intersection of a plumb and seat cut. The two cuts are at 90° to each other. They form the seating for the rafter on the wallplate. As the name implies, it looks like the mouth of a bird.

PRACTICAL TIP

Building Regulations state that you should not have any combustible material within 200mm of the inside of a chimney flue and that there should be no combustible material within 40mm of the chimney itself.

CASE STUDY

South Tyneside Homes

South Tyneside Council's
Housing Company

Making the most of your apprenticeship

Glen Campbell is a team leader at South Tyneside Homes.

'Make sure you've got right size materials, and that you're following the specification. Always work from your drawing – even after you've set it out, always check it against your drawings. The specs are so important.

Don't try to cut corners – ever – especially when you're talking about roofs. Anything that's got to be structurally sound, you don't cut corners full stop. Once you've been doing the job for a while, you'll know where you can save a bit of time and save the company a bit of money here and there. But this is something that only comes with time and experience.

When you're talking commons, jack rafters, ridge boards, you're applying all your hand skills and the theory as well. Make sure you pick up your analytical methods at college because that's what you'll apply to the actual physical act of setting your bevels, cutting your birdsmouth, putting all your compound mitres in. You've got to be able to apply the theory to the physical, get the theory down, and understand where all your angles come from, where you're going to be cutting. I know it sounds basic, but make sure you have a decent saw, otherwise you're all over the shop and then you'll end up with compound bevels that don't sit flush.

Enjoy your apprenticeship – it seems to go by so fast. It's amazing how much you pick up in such a short time. At 16 you think that 3 years is ages and that you've got all the time in the world. Make the most of that time because you've got no pressure to perform, so use it to hone the skills that are being taught. And if you get any opportunity to do something out of the norm, do it, have a go at it.'

CONSTRUCTING VERGE AND EAVES FINISHES

The verge and eaves can be finished using a number of methods. Both can be open or closed, overhanging or flush.

When the gable end is finished with an overhang, a bargeboard is fixed to the side of the gable ladder. The space from the face of the masonry to the face of the bargeboard is known as the verge. The underside of the gable ladder is boarded in the same way as a soffit at the eaves. This is called a closed or boxed verge.

When the rafter feet extend past the masonry, the space from the face of masonry to the face of the facia board is called the eaves. The fascia board is fixed vertically to the ends of the rafters on the plumb cut and a soffit is fixed horizontally behind it, incorporating ventilation strips. This is called closed or boxed eaves.

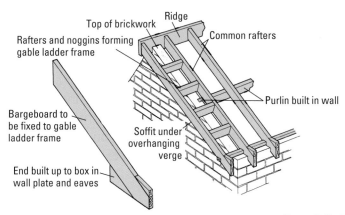

Figure 7.13 Gable end detail

This is not the only method that can be adopted. Where the verge and eaves meet, a triangular infill piece must be secured to the bottom edge of the bargeboard to close off the eaves. This is often shaped to produce a decorative finish.

In order to finish off the overhanging verge:

* the ridge and the wall plate are extended beyond the gable end wall

* noggins are fixed between the last pair of rafters, to create a gable ladder

* the gable ladder provides the fixing for the bargeboard, the soffit and the tile battens.

Assessing the roof space for ventilation and insulation requirements

Under the Building Regulations ventilation is required within the roof space. This is designed to prevent, or at least reduce, condensation. The roof needs to be cross ventilated at the level of the eaves by ensuring there are permanent vents. These vents must have an equivalent area that is equal to a continuous gap along both sides of the roof. This needs to be 10 mm or 25 mm if the roof pitch is less than 15°. This is also true if the insulation follows the pitch of the roof.

There are clear ventilation requirements and a number of different ways in which this can be achieved:

* A continuous ventilation strip can be fitted onto the back of the fascia.

* Soffit ventilators, which are circular in shape, can be fixed into the soffit.

* If the insulation follows the roof pitch there needs to be an air space of 50 mm between the underside of the roof and the insulation. There are manufactured ridge vents for this purpose.

* A gap can be left between the wall and the soffit – usually a wire mesh is inserted to prevent birds and other creatures from getting into the loft space.

Insulation is traditionally achieved by inserting sheets of rock wool or glass fibre between each of the ceiling joists. As a vapour check, foil-backed plasterboard can be fitted at ceiling level below the insulation. The insulation sits between the ceiling joists to prevent heat from the rooms below escaping into the roof space, where on contact with the cold air it would condense. The roof is ventilated to avoid dry rot, which thrives in warm, moist, poorly ventilated spaces.

Increasingly, additional insulation layers are required for new builds. This means that a second insulation layer of approximately 300 mm is installed over the ceiling joists. The insulation extends over the inner leaf of the cavity wall and into the eaves. The danger is that the insulation material could block the eaves and prevent the roof space from being properly ventilated. Eaves ventilators, or timber boards, can be nailed between the rafters, as can be seen in Fig 7.14:

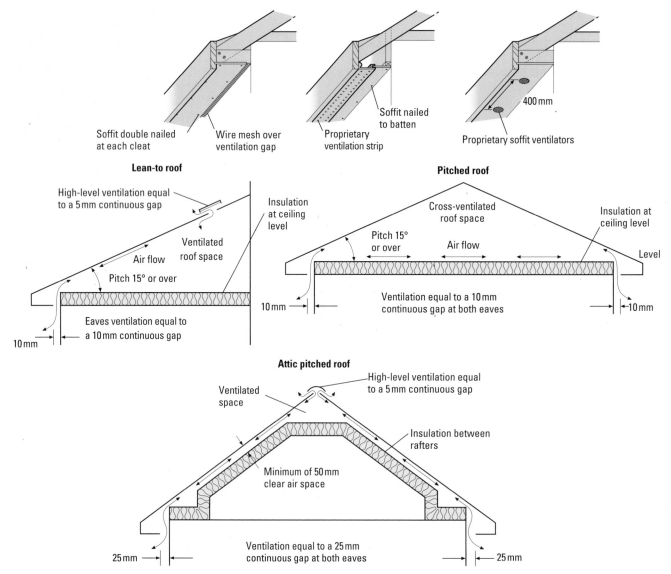

Figure 7.14 Pitch roof insulation between and over ceiling joists

Finishing verges

When the verge is finished using a bargeboard. There will be an angled joint to cut at the top, in line with the centre of the ridge. At the bottom, the eaves will often be closed or boxed in. Sometimes, especially for ornate work, the bargeboard is manufactured in a workshop to the exact shape of the eaves; however, most are produced in situ.

In order to work out the bevels at the top or apex of the bargeboard and the bottom or foot of the bargeboard one of two methods are used:

* The board can be marked in position – this is achieved by temporarily fixing it and then using a spirit level to mark the vertical plumb cut and the horizontal seat cut, as can be seen in the following diagram.

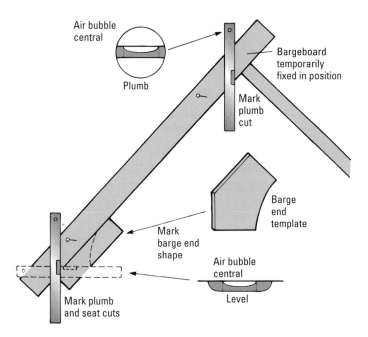

Figure 7.15 Marking out a bargeboard

* The alternative way of doing it is to use adjustable sliding bevels. These can be set to the correct angles using a roofing square. The plumb and seat cuts can then be marked. The angles in question are determined from the pitch of the roof. This will have already been established when setting out the roof. The seat cut will be the same as the pitch and plumb cut.

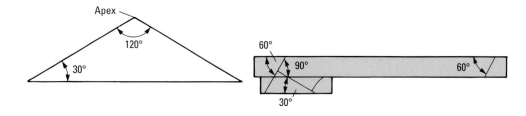

Figure 7.16 Determining angles for a bargeboard

For a high quality finish, the foot or bottom of the bargeboard is usually mitred to the fascia board. It can also be butted and finished flush, or as an alternative it can be extended so that it is slightly in front of the fascia board, as can be seen in the following diagram.

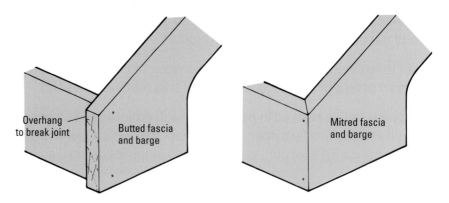

Figure 7.17 Jointing barge to fascia board

Most carpenters will work out the mitre angles for the bargeboard and fascia in position. They fix the bargeboard and fascia temporarily and then use a piece of timber that is of the same thickness to mark the pair of lines. The lines are marked across the edge of the board and then they join the opposite corners to create the mitre. The face angle is 90° for the fascia board and there is a plumb cut for the bargeboard.

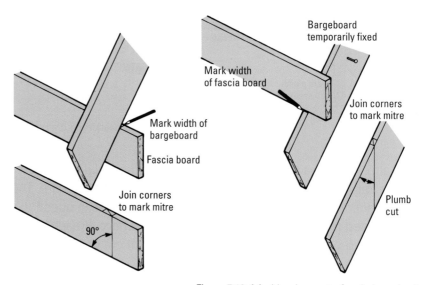

Figure 7.18 Marking barge to fascia board mitre

Once the bargeboard has been marked out, cut, mitred and fitted, it is then double nailed at intervals of 400 mm centres to the gable ladder. The nails need to be at least 2.5 times longer than the thickness of the bargeboard. Usually the nails are punched below the surface and the holes are then filled before painting.

UPVC for verges, eaves and soffits

Although timber is traditionally used for verges and eaves there is an increasing tendency to use extruded UPVC sections. They are often chosen as they require far less maintenance and do not require repainting. As can be seen in the following diagram, UPVC components can be used as an alternative for bargeboards, fascias and soffits.

The profiles are cut to length using a fine tooth panel saw. The fixing procedure involves using stainless steel pins or screws, with matching plastic dome heads.

Finishing eaves

The eaves are the lowest part of the pitched roof slope. This is where the rafters end. They will overhang the wall and be finished off with a fascia board and soffit. There are several different ways that this can be achieved, as can be seen in the following table.

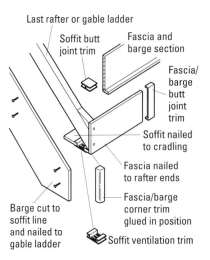

Figure 7.19 Use of UPVC profiles for eaves and verge finishing

Eaves finish	Description
Flush	The rafters are cut so that they end between 10 to 15mm beyond the brickwork face. The fascia board is then nailed straight onto them. The fascia board provides a fixing for the gutter. In order to achieve roof space ventilation there is a small gap at the back of the fascia board.
Open (overhanging)	These types of eaves extend past the face of the wall and provide the building with improved weather protection. The rafter ends need to be finished in accordance with the drawings. Often they are planed, shaped and treated with preservative or paint finish, as they will be in full view from ground level.
Closed (overhanging)	The eaves project over the wall in the same way as open eaves. The major difference is that the ends of the rafters are closed and hidden from view by a soffit. In order to support the soffit at the wall edge cradling brackets are nailed to the sides of the rafters. In modern construction, the soffit sits in a continuous vent strip fastened to the back of the fascia. Its opposite edge sits on top of the external masonry and is held in position by noggins cut and fixed between the rafter ends, or by timbers nailed or screwed vertically to the sides of the rafters.
Sprocketed	This method is used on roofs that have a steep pitch. If they were not used then rainwater flowing off the surface of the roof would miss the gutter. In effect the sprockets are designed to reduce the pitch and slow down the rainwater before it reaches the eaves. The sprockets are nailed to the side of each of the rafters or alternatively shaped pieces are nailed directly to the top edge of each rafter..

Table 7.3

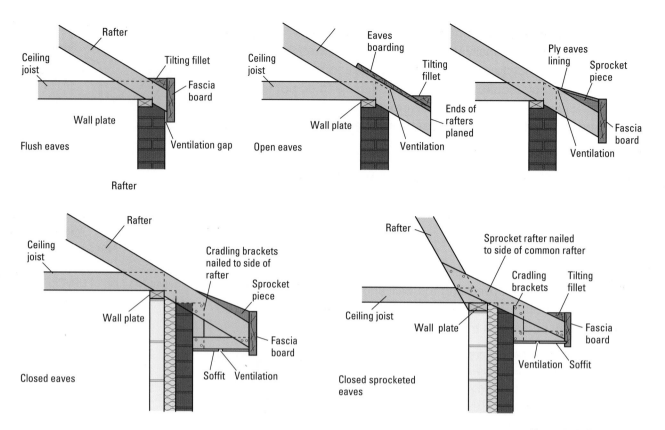

Figure 7.20 Eaves details

Fascia boards

Fascia boards are fixed to the end of rafters. They are usually softwood and fixed horizontally. Fascias also provide the fixing for the guttering. Before they can be fixed it is important to mark and cut the rafter feet plumb and in line with the other rafters. These are the ends of the rafters. This process can be seen in the following diagram.

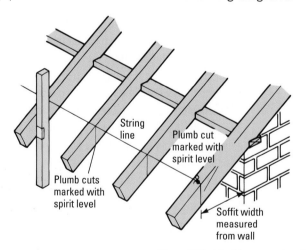

Figure 7.21 Marking out plumb cut at eaves

The process required has a number of steps:

* The first thing to do is to establish the width of the required soffit. This is achieved by measuring out from the brickwork at the point of the last rafter at either end of the roof.

* A plumb cut and seat cut are marked using a spirit level.

* A string line is then stretched between the two end rafters and over the top of the rest of the rafters that make up the roof.

* A spirit level is used to mark each individual plumb cut on each of the rafters.

* The plumb cuts are then made using either a portable circular saw or a hand saw.

* If a seat cut is needed the line is moved down to the seat cut on the end rafters and then a spirit level is used to mark each of the individual seat cuts.

In some cases it is not possible to complete the fascia using a single piece of board. In order to ensure that the fascia is properly secured all the joints should be positioned at a central point over a rafter end.

Where there are corners the fascia board is joined using a mitre joint at external corners and a butt joint at internal corners. The usual procedure is to nail the joints using 50 mm oval nails.

Oval nails can also be used to secure the fascia boards to each rafter, although some prefer to use cut nails, lost head nails or wire nails. Usually two nails are used. Nails of at least 2.5 times the thickness of the fascia should be used in order to secure the fascia. The normal procedure is to punch them in below the surface.

However, before committing to the final fixing of the fascia boards it is important to check that the fascia board is in line. The usual procedure for doing this can be seen in the following diagram.

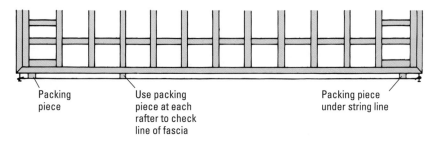

Figure 7.22 Checking fascia board for line

A nail is driven into the fascia at each end of the roof. A line is then stretched and secured to the nails. Three pieces of packing are then prepared. Two are placed at each end under the line and the third is placed systematically between the fascia and the string at each rafter position. Ideally the piece of packing should fit snugly between the fascia and line along the length of the roof. If this is not the case then it might be necessary to either saw a little off the end of a rafter or to fit packing at the end of a rafter.

Soffit boards

Soffit boards close the gap between the building's wall and the fascia. The soffit is usually plywood or a non-combustible sheet material. The soffits can either be fixed to the underside using L-shaped brackets fixed to the sides of each rafter, by the use of cleats or by wedging down on to the top of the external masonry with noggins secured to the rafter sides.

The soffit is secured using a pair of 25 mm galvanised wire nails at each bracket or cleat position.

FORMING DORMER WINDOWS AND ROOFS

Dormer windows project vertically from the eaves, or from the middle area of the roof. They have triangular sides, called cheeks, and are framed. They can be sheathed with diagonal boarding. The cheeks can also be constructed to take tile or slate cladding.

The windows can either be timber or UPVC. The roofs on dormers tend to be either flat or pitched.

There are other varieties of dormer roof, which are segmental or semi-circular. The pitched ones can either have gable ends or hipped ends and these are usually either tiled or slated to match the main roof.

Types of dormer windows and roofs

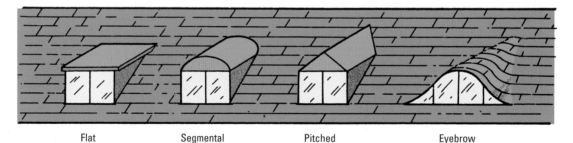

| Flat | Segmental | Pitched | Eyebrow |

Figure 7.23 Dormer roofs

The most common types of dormer window are the flat and pitched roof versions.

An eyebrow dormer is curved instead of having an angled pitch and perhaps the most complex to construct so is relatively rare.

A hipped dormer has three sloping roof planes. They are of a more conventional shape and easier to construct.

A gable dormer has two sloping roof panels. They can add as much as 30 per cent more floor space to a room.

Finally there is the moon-pitched or Beeston dormer, which has a single roof plane that slopes.

Constructing dormer roofs and windows

Fig 7.24 shows an isometric view of the framework construction, with twin rafters on either side of the opening. These rafters carry the increased load. The dormer window roof, when flat, uses 100mm × 50mm minimum joists, which are fitted to slope backwards towards the main roof. They can also be fitted to fall towards a front gutter and downpipe in the corner. The downpipe will discharge onto the main roof. The timbers used need to be treated with preservatives and the roof covering needs to be waterproof.

Figure 7.24 Flat roof dormer window

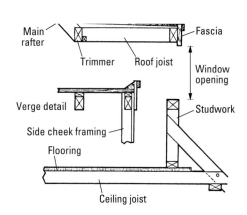

Figure 7.25 Dormer details

CONSTRUCTING TRADITIONAL CUT ROOFS WITH HIPS AND VALLEYS

Traditional roofing techniques have existed for centuries. Some historians think that the first roofs to use spars may have been overturned boats, such as Viking longboats taken out of the water for the winter. It does not take much imagination to visualise a modern roof as an upside down boat.

Traditional roofing is not as widely used today as it once was. However, a modern carpenter will still be required to use traditional techniques on projects such as extensions, one-off builds, restricted access sites, renovation work, complex shaped roofs and heritage work.

Traditional cut roofs are constructed on site using individual loose timber sections. They all use simple jointing methods. There are a large number of different types of traditional cut roof structures. They are chosen and classified according to their load, shape and span.

REED TIP

If you're having trouble completing a particular task and find yourself getting frustrated, take a step back, work on something else that needs doing, try to approach it from a different angle, or use a fresh set of eyes – someone else might be able to see where you're going wrong.

Types of traditional cut roof construction

As we have seen, there is a variety of different traditional framed cut roofs. They are constructed as single, double or triple roofs.

Single roofs

Single roof structures are used for spans of up to 5.5 m. They use rafters that span from the wall plate to the ridge. There are various different types of single roof structure, as can be seen in the following diagram.

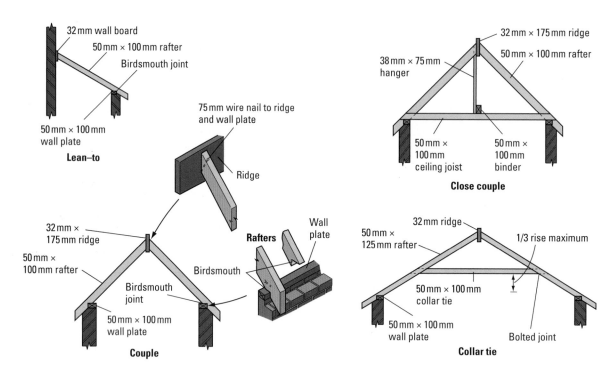

Figure 7.26 Single roof structures

A couple roof has a pair of rafters that are fixed at one end to the wall plates and at the other end to the ridge board. This has a restricted span because there is no tie to the feet or bottom of the rafter, meaning that the roof is exerting pressure on the walls and could force them outward.

A close couple roof is very similar, but allows the span to be increased by having the feet of the rafters closed with a tie. The tie serves another purpose, as it is also the ceiling joist. A central binder can be fixed to this ceiling joist. It is hung from the ridge at a spacing of every third or fourth rafter. In effect this binds the whole structure together and stops the ceiling joists from sagging.

A collar tie (collared) roof is very similar to a close couple roof. The main difference is that the span can be even greater because the tie is moved up the rafter to a maximum of a third of the rise. This creates more headroom if the space is to be used as a living area.

Double roofs

Double roofs need intermediate support by structural components known as purlins. Their position and purpose can be seen in Fig 7.27.

The inclusion of purlins means that the rafters used can be reduced in size. The roof also has struts, collars and hangers. These are spaced out along the roof on every third or fourth rafter. These provide additional support to the purlins. In many cases binders are also fixed to the ceiling joists. These are hung from the ridge or collar in order to bind the structure together and to prevent the ceiling joists from sagging.

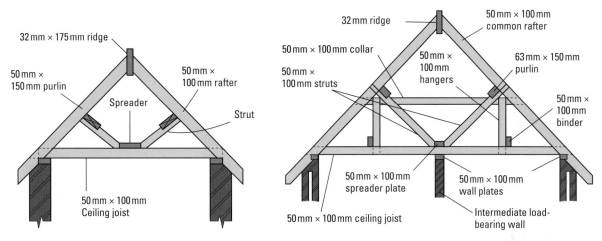

Figure 7.27 Double roofs

Triple roofs

Triple roofs often use pre-fabricated roof trusses. They are spaced out at intervals to give support to the purlins. The purlins are there to provide intermediate support for the common rafters. This form of construction does not tend to be used in new builds, but is fairly common in older dwellings. The structure of the roof can be seen in the following diagram.

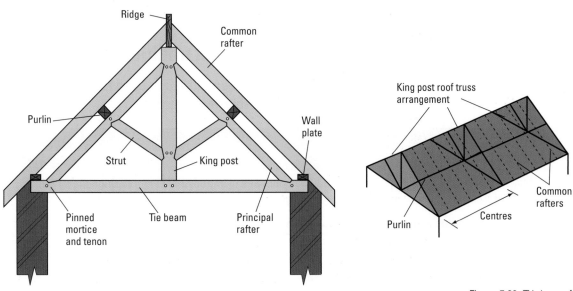

Figure 7.28 Triple roof

When you are carrying out maintenance work on roofs like this the trusses can be:

* mortised and tenoned together

* bolted together with simple overlapping joints.

Flat

The term flat roof is slightly misleading. A truly flat roof would not be able to cope with rainfall. Therefore, a flat roof has a slight pitch, usually around 10°. There are three ways of achieving this.

The first method is to lay the joists level, with the slope then being created by tapered pieces of timber, known as firring pieces. These are nailed to the upper edges of the joists. This is a common method because it provides a flat under-surface inside the building to fix the plasterboards for the ceiling.

The second alternative is to lay out the joists to the required slope without using firrings. This, however, means that the ceiling will be sloped.

The third alternative is to use a technique known as diminishing firrings. This is rarely used as it is expensive and labour-intensive. The joists are laid level but at right angles to the intended direction of the slope. The underside of the joists, being level, makes fixing plasterboard for the ceiling a simple task. To achieve the slope on the upper surface of the roof, angled sections of timber, which diminish in size from the top of the slope to the bottom of the slope, are nailed into place.

Hipped

A hipped roof is one of the more complex roof structures and requires a good understanding of geometry. The most common type of hipped roof is called a regular hipped roof – its hips are all 45° when viewed on plan, regardless of its pitch. This means that the ridge will be central.

This form of construction is covered in the practical task at the end of this section.

Components used to construct traditional roofs

There are several different components that are used to construct traditional roofs. The following table itemises them.

Component	Description
Wall plate	These are timber-bearing plates. They are laid flat and bedded in cement to the inner blockwork. They provide a means of fixing the rafters at the birdsmouth and distribute the weight through the length of the wall. They are anchored down with restraint straps.
Common rafters	Structural members that extend from the wall plate to the ridge.
Ridge	This is the point at which two sloping roof surfaces meet at their highest point, or the apex of the roof. Along the ridge is the ridge board. This is the spine of the roof structure. It usually runs horizontally and the rafters are fixed to it.

Component	Description
Hips	This is a timber that forms the intersection where the two sloping surfaces meet at an external angle.
Hip rafters	These are compound cut structural members that form an external corner on a roof. They extend from the ridge to the outside edge of the corner of the wall plate. They act as part of the spine of the roof and the heads of the jack rafters are fixed to them. They also carry the purlin in a ring purlin roof.
Jack rafters	These are structural members that extend from the wall plate to the hip. They are shortened common rafters as they are in the same plane. These have a compound bevel cut at their head and are fixed in diminishing pairs either side of the hip rafters.
Valleys	This is a timber that forms the intersection where two sloping surfaces meet at an internal angle.
Valley rafters	These are rather like hip rafters. They are designed to create an internal angle in the roof and extend from the ridge to the outside edge of the internal corner of the wall plate. They also provide the spine that allows cripple rafters to be fixed onto them. They also carry the purlin in a ring purlin roof.
Lay boards	These are non-structural valleys. They are laid flat and diagonally on the common rafters. They are designed to provide a seating and fixing for the compound cut of the cripple rafters being used to form a valley.
Cripple rafters	These are structural members that extend from the ridge to the valley and are shortened common rafters as they are in the same plane. They have a compound cut at their foot. They diminish in length across the length of the valley. They are fixed in pairs on either side of the valley.
Purlins	These are horizontal beams. They allow the common rafters to be reduced in size because they are designed to support the rafters midspan between the ridge and the wall plate if the rafters are more than 2.5 m long.
Restraint straps	These are fixed over the wall plates and down the inside face of the brick or blockwork. They are made from galvanised steel. Straps are also used to reinforce wall plate joints. They are used across ceiling joists and rafters in order to anchor gable end walls.
Gable ladder	A gable ladder is a framed assembly that is fixed to the last common rafter in the gable roof to span the brickwork and provide a fixing for the bargeboard and soffit at the verge.
Soffit	Soffits are waterproof exterior board, which fit in between the fascia board and the wall. They close the eaves and are fixed using cradling brackets. They can be plywood, plastic or softwood.
Fascias	A fascia is a board that runs along the ends of rafters at the eaves. It closes the eaves and provides a board for the fixing of guttering.
Verge	This is the finish to a gable-ended roof. It can be finished with cement-pointed slates or tiles, bargeboards with a closed or open verge, or proprietary verge closers.
Bargeboards	They are rather like fascia boards. They are fixed to the projecting end of a roof at the gable end verges. Usually a soffit board is fitted to their underside.

Table 7.4

Forming openings

It may be necessary to construct openings in the roofs in order to take in roof lights, chimney stacks, dormer windows or loft access hatches. This will mean that either the rafters or the ceiling joists will need to be trimmed to create the necessary opening space.

The following diagram shows how this is achieved either in the slope of a roof or in the ceiling.

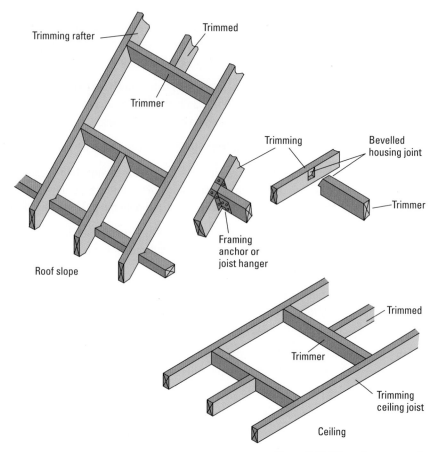

Figure 7.29 Trimming to openings

As the diagram illustrates, the opening needs to be large enough not only to accommodate the structure but also any window or hatch lining. In the case of openings on roof slopes and ceilings for chimneys an additional 40 mm gap must be incorporated to separate the structural timber and the brickwork. This is an important precaution and it serves two purposes:

● it allows ventilation in and around the chimney stack

● it reduces the chance that timber close to the brickwork of the chimney will catch fire if the brickwork is very hot.

The area around the chimney stack at roof level is weatherproofed. The process involves creating a framework on the upper slope and fixing lay boards to the lower slope and sides. These will then have lead or zinc-lined gutter and flashings fitted, as can be seen in Fig 7.30.

Building Regulations also state that it is not just the roof structural timbers but also any other structural timbers that should not be near sources of heat. This means separating them with a distance of no less than 200 mm. It also means there should not be any combustible material closer than 40 mm from the chimney. As can be seen in the following diagram, this is achieved by leaving an air gap of 50 mm between the structural timber and the brickwork, while at the same time making sure that the timber is 200 mm away from the actual lining of the flue.

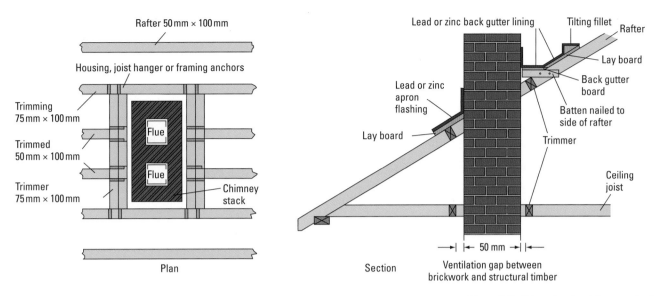

Figure 7.30 Trimming to chimney stack

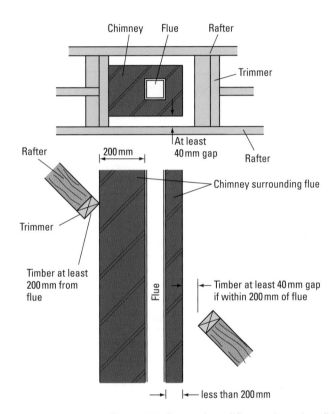

Figure 7.31 Separation of flue and combustible materials

Developing a roof using geometry

A variety of systems can be employed in the development of traditional roofing:

* geometry

* trigonometry

* the roofing or framing square (this combines the first two techniques).

Whichever system is used, some geometrical knowledge is required.

METHODS OF DETERMINING ANGLES AND LENGTHS OF TIMBERS IN A CUT ROOF

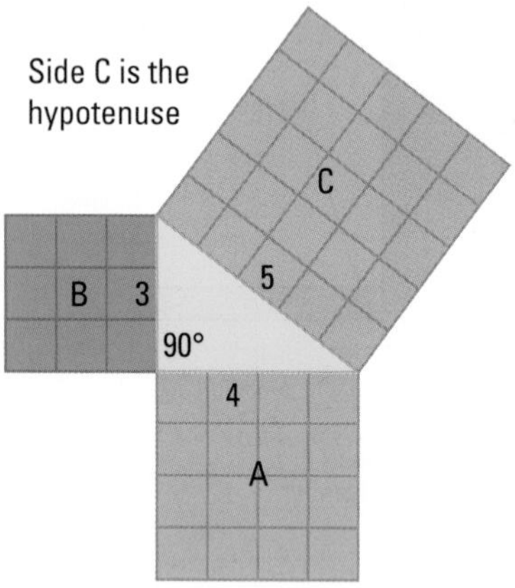

Side C is the hypotenuse

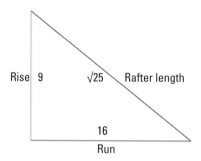

Figure 7.32 Pythagoras' theorem

Using trigonometry

Trigonometry is a method of finding the relevant bevels and lengths.

Pythagoras' theorem states that $A^2 + B^2 = C^2$.

In roofing terms this would relate to the triangle shown in Fig 7.33.

Rise 9   √25   Rafter length

16
Run

Figure 7.33 The right angle in relation to roofing terms

Carpenters describe roofs in terms of pitch or pitching. The following are common pitches used in the construction industry.

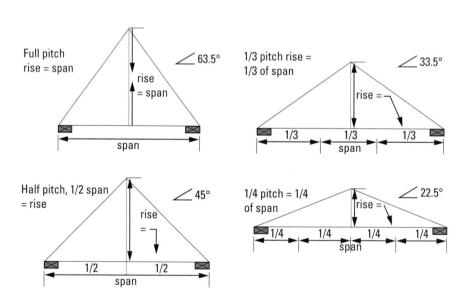

Figure 7.34 Half, quarter, third and full pitches

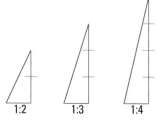

1:2   1:3   1:4

Figure 7.35 Ratios

The angles of these roofs will always be those given when these ratios are applied.

The following diagrams show the maths behind these terms, which will be useful when working with roof components.

You can use the acronym SOHCAHTOA as a way of remembering how to compute the sine, cosine, and tangent of an angle.

SOH means sine equals opposite divided by hypoteneuse.

CAH means cosine equals adjacent over hypoteneuse.

TOA means tangent equals opposite over adjacent.

SOHCAHTOA

$$\text{Sin } \theta = \frac{\text{opposite}}{\text{hypotenuse}}$$

$$\text{Cos } \theta = \frac{\text{adjacent}}{\text{hypotenuse}}$$

$$\text{Tan } \theta = \frac{\text{opposite}}{\text{adjacent}}$$

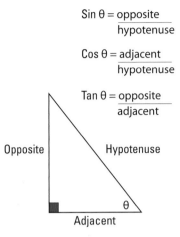

Figure 7.36 SOHCAHTOA

Finding the rise when you know the pitch and run

$$\text{Tan } \theta = \frac{\text{opposite}}{\text{adjacent}}$$

$$\text{Tan (pitch)} = \frac{\text{rise}}{\text{run}}$$

So
rise = run × tan (pitch)

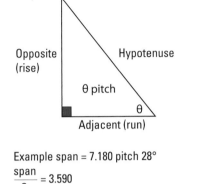

Example span = 7.180 pitch 28°

$$\frac{\text{span}}{2} = 3.590$$

Press tan 28 = 05317 × 3.590 = 1.908 m rise

Figure 7.37 Finding the rise when you know the pitch and run

Finding the rafter length when you know the rise and run
(hyp + adj means use Cos)

$$\text{Cos } \theta = \frac{\text{adjacent}}{\text{hypotenuse}}$$

$$\text{Cos (pitch)} = \frac{\text{run}}{\text{rafter}}$$

Cos pitch × rafter = run

$$\text{Rafter} = \frac{\text{run}}{\text{Cos pitch}}$$

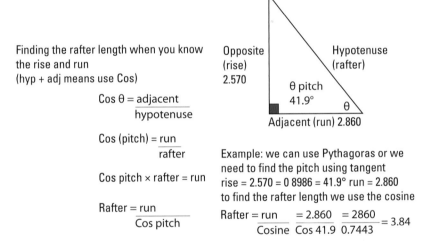

Example: we can use Pythagoras or we need to find the pitch using tangent
rise = 2.570 = 0 8986 = 41.9° run = 2.860
to find the rafter length we use the cosine

$$\text{Rafter} = \frac{\text{run}}{\text{Cosine}} = \frac{2.860}{\text{Cos } 41.9} = \frac{2860}{0.7443} = 3.84$$

Figure 7.38 Finding the pitch when you know the rise and run

Finding the pitch when you know the rise and run
(know opp + adj so use Tan)

$$\text{Tan } \theta = \frac{\text{opposite}}{\text{adjacent}}$$

$$\text{Tan (pitch)} = \frac{\text{rise}}{\text{run}}$$

$$\text{Pitch} = \text{Tan minus 1}\left(\frac{\text{rise}}{\text{run}}\right)$$

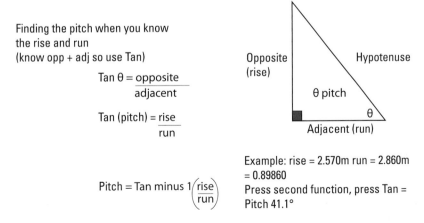

Example: rise = 2.570m run = 2.860m
= 0.89860
Press second function, press Tan =
Pitch 41.1°

Figure 7.39 Finding the rafter length when you know the pitch and run

The right-angled roofing square

The modern day square is also known as the steel square, carpenter's square, the rafter square and the framing square. They can be used for roofing, stair construction, arch construction, ellipses, octagons and to find the centre of a given arc. The modern day square has tables printed on it. They use the imperial system of measurement and work on the common rafter length, per foot run (12 inch), and hip valley, per foot run. Both imperial and metric squares work on similar right angled triangles.

The anatomy of the square (metric)

The square is a simple L-shaped piece of steel. The shorter side is the 'tongue' and the longer side is the 'blade'.

The tongue is 450 mm x 40 mm, while the blade is 620 mm x 50 mm. The square also has a face and a back. On both the tongue and the blade are a series of tables, measurements and pivot points. Unlike the imperial squares, the metric square uses the metric run rather than the foot run.

You should have good knowledge of trigonometry and geometry. Some carpenters think it is faster to set out using trigonometry and geometry, while others think it is faster using the square. Good site carpenters should be able to use all three.

The mechanics of the square

The square works on lengths per metre run. All lengths and bevels for regular plan roofing can be found in the square's instruction manual.

There are four pivot points on the tongue. Two are for pitches up to 66° and two are for pitched roofs from 66° to 85°.

The common rafter run pivot point is marked at 250 mm on the tongue, which is a quarter scale for pitches up to 66°. The hip and valley pivot point is at 353 mm for a pitch of 66°.

For pitches over 66°, the scale is 1:20. The common rafter pivot is marked at 50 mm on the tongue. The hip and valley is marked at 70 mm on the tongue.

Both the face and back of the blade are marked in degrees (°), mm and cm.

Two alternatives to the square are the Roof Master and the Constructor master pro calculator.

Although the practical task at the end of this section looks at how to calculate the angles of timber in constructing traditional roofs with hip and valley rafters, it is important to look at how this can be achieved using a steel square.

Roofing square tables

Remember, good roofing squares will have sets of tables marked on them. They will give you the rafter length per metre run for standard pitches.

Roofing square tables have been worked out in advance to save the carpenter from having to do this on site; however, sometimes it is necessary to use trigonometry.

This uses cosine for the common rafter and tangent and Pythagoras for the hip rafter.

Examples

Common rafter

Pitch = 40°   Run = 1m

The length of the common rafter = Run ÷ cos (pitch) = 1 ÷ cos 40 = 1.3054

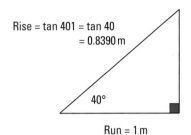

Rise = tan 401 = tan 40
= 0.8390 m

40°

Run = 1 m

Figure 7.40 Finding the rise of the roof

Hip rafter

To calculate the length of the hip rafter, remember that it will be lower than the common rafter so it makes a smaller angle with the horizontal than the common rafter.

First find the rise of the roof. Now find the distance between the corner of the roof and under the hip. This is the horizontal distance under the hip rafter.

A plan view shows that this point is the distance of the run (1 metre) from each of the walls.

This distance is the diagonal (hypotenuse) of a right angled triangle, with the length of the two short sides being 1 metre. Use Pythagoras to find the length of the diagonal.

$Diagonal^2 = 1^2 + 1^2 = 1 + 1 = 2$

Diagonal = 1.4142 m

Then combine the height of the rise and the horizontal distance under the hip rafter. Below is a side view of this.

Now you must use Pythagoras again.

$Hip\ rafter^2 = 0.8390^2 + 1.4142^2 = 0.7039 + 1.9999$

$Hip\ rafter = \sqrt{2.7038} = 1.6443\,m$

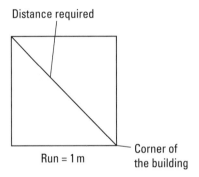

Distance required

Run = 1 m

Corner of the building

Figure 7.41 Finding the distance between the corner of the roof and under the hip

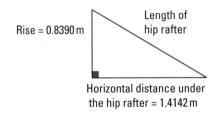

Rise = 0.8390 m

Length of hip rafter

Horizontal distance under the hip rafter = 1.4142 m

Figure 7.42 Plan of the right angle

PRACTICAL TASK

1. USING A ROOFING OR FRAMING SQUARE

SETTING OUT A COMMON RAFTER AT 40°

STEP 1 Consider the drawings for the pitch and take site measurements from the wall plate.

Example Span = 6.000 m   Pitch = 40°

STEP 2 Divide the span by 2 to obtain the run of the common rafter.

Example 6.000 m ÷ 2 = 3 m run   Pitch = 40°

STEP 3 Using the common rafter pivot point on the tongue for roofs up to 66°, place this point on to the rafter and swing the square around to 40°, found on the blade of the square. This will give a seat cut at 40°.

STEP 4 Using the figures on the blade or from the common rafter tables 40° =1.3054. Note this is a centre line and half the thickness of the ridge will need to be deducted parallel to the plumb cut from the measurement.

A 3m run × 1.3054 means that the length of the common rafter minus the deduction is 3.9162m.

STEP 5 Slide the square down to the foot of the rafter to the length of 3.9162m and mark the same plumb cut. The roofing square can be used to mark this plumb cut from the pitch line, or from the top edge, which is more common.

STEP 6 Using the tongue, mark the birdsmouth seat cut. This should be no more than one-third of the thickness of the rafter. Using the worked example below, the method described can be used to calculate the rafter overhang. The drawing indicates the overhang is 600mm.

Example 0.600m × 1.3054 = 0.783m overhang
This will be needed to be added to the common rafter length giving a total length of timber required (4.700m).

PRACTICAL TIP

The roofing square works on similar triangles.

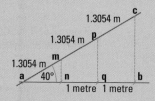

Figure 7.43 Total length of common rafter = 3.9162m

PRACTICAL TASK

2. CALCULATE THE HIP RAFTER LENGTHS AND ANGLES

The hip rafter can be marked out in one of two ways: with or without a backing bevel (dihedral). The method used is similar to that adopted for marking out the common rafter. The method in this task includes a backing bevel, which is used on quality work.

STEP 1 Calculate the hip lengths and bevels for the same pitch and span as previously. Place the tongue on to the hip/valley pivot point for up to 66° roof pitch. Swing the square around to 40° on the blade. Mark the plumb cut.

STEP 2 Use the previous method for the common rafter and from the tables or square.

For hip rafters = 1.6444m and using the common rafter run (3.000m).

Length of hip rafter = 3.000m × 1.6444 = 4.9332m

The hip rafter birdsmouth must be the same vertical height above the wall plate as for the common rafter.

STEP 3 The hip overhang is as before except now use 1.6444 × 0.600 m = 0.9866 (rounded up to 0.987). This is added to the length of the hip rafter.

Remember this is a centre line and half the diagonal thickness of the common rafter will need to be deducted from this measurement. (Note: if a saddle board is used then the full thickness measured diagonally will have to be deducted.)

Hip length = 4.933 + 0.987 = 5.920 m.

STEP 4 To determine the hip top cut or edge cut several methods can be used. The following method is a practical solution for regular plan roofs.

Using the hip rafter plumb cut, mark a 90° line on both sides of the hip. Mark half the hip rafter thickness on to the 90° lines on both sides of the hip and, using the same angle, mark a second plumb cut.

STEP 5 Square the two plumb cut marks across the top edge and mark the centre. Join the second plumb marks to the centre line to determine the hip rafter top or edge cut.

STEP 6 Now you need to calculate the backing angle. The hip rafter will need to be seated on to the corner of the wall plate. The wall plate will need to have a 45° corner cut off. This is the thickness of the hip.

STEP 7 Use the length shown in Step 1. Using the plumb, cut at the foot of the rafter. Measure down the depth of the common rafter birdsmouth. Using the square, mark the seat cut.

Then measure the reduction of the wall plate and draw a new plumb line on the inside. This will accommodate the reduction previously made.

PRACTICAL TIP

The height above the wall plate must be the same for all rafters.

PRACTICAL TASK

3. CALCULATE THE JACK RAFTER LENGTHS AND ANGLES

The jack rafter plumb cut and overhang are the same as for the common rafter. Using the previous common rafter steps for the length, calculate a reduction for the subsequent jack rafters. This is also known as the diminish.

STEP 1 Use the figure for the common rafter: 1.3054. Divide this figure by 10 = 0.13054. For traditional cut roofs the rafters are usually spaced at 400 mm. The rule is to multiply 0.13054 by 4. If the rafter centres were spaced at 600 centres the figure 0.13054 should be multiplied by 6.

Example 1
4 × 0.13054 = 0.522 m, this is the diminish

Example 2
6 × 0.13054 = 0.7832 m diminish

STEP 2 The process is repeated for the remaining jack rafters.

STEP 3 For a regular hip plan roof, the jack rafter top or edge cut is made using a site practical method. This is similar to that for the hip rafter, except only one angle is required.

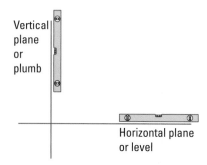

Vertical plane or plumb

Horizontal plane or level

Figure 7.44 The level and plumb planes

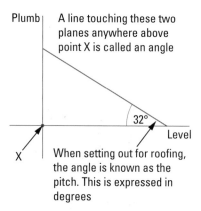

Plumb

A line touching these two planes anywhere above point X is called an angle

32°

Level

X

When setting out for roofing, the angle is known as the pitch. This is expressed in degrees

Figure 7.45 Angles and degrees

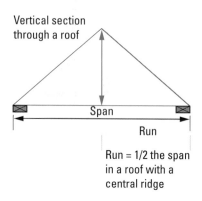

Vertical section through a roof

Span

Run

Run = 1/2 the span in a roof with a central ridge

Figure 7.46 Vertical section through a roof

In the following section we will be setting out a roof using geometrical solutions. We will start with the common rafter, the simplest of the components, and work through the various members, including hips, jacks, valleys, cripples and purlins.

Set out a common rafter using geometry

The first component to mark out is the common rafter. As its name suggests it is usually the most frequently occurring timber in a roof.

The line method of geometry is used in the development of lengths, angles and bevels of the various roofing components. Line geometry is based on laying down right-angled triangles on reference points or datum lines. The lengths, widths and thickness of the timber are then added.

Fig 7.44 shows the horizontal and vertical planes. To a carpenter these are known as level and plumb. Fig 7.45 shows a line added to the horizontal and vertical planes at an angle. This forms a right-angled triangle. The slope is known as the pitch. (Remember that the three angles of a triangle always add up to 180°.) Carpenters determine pitch through a given span and rise.

The span is the measurement from the outside edge of one wall plate to the outside edge of the opposite wall plate. Half the span is called the run in a roof with a central ridge.

The rise is a measurement taken from a datum line on the top edge of the wall plates to the apex formed by the pitch lines. The rise is not the height of the roof because the material depth plus coverings will need to be added.

The run gives us the base of our right-angled triangle. This is always measured on the horizontal plane (level). The rise is a vertical (plumb) line that is at 90° to the base. This forms a right angle. The pitch line is a sloping line that connects the two and forms the hypotenuse (the longest side) of the right-angled triangle.

Fig 7.48 shows how the plumb cut and seat cut are taken from the right-angled triangle. The plumb cut, as its name suggests, is a vertical cut, the seat cut therefore is a horizontal cut.

Now that the angles have been determined, we only require the length to mark out the common rafter. Note: The seat cut is at 90° to the plumb cut. The following task uses the geometry shown in Fig 7.49 as its basis.

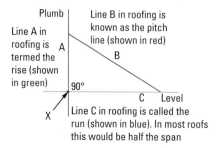

Plumb

Line A in roofing is termed the rise (shown in green)

A

Line B in roofing is known as the pitch line (shown in red)

B

90°

C   Level

X

Line C in roofing is called the run (shown in blue). In most roofs this would be half the span

Figure 7.47 The rise, pitch line and run

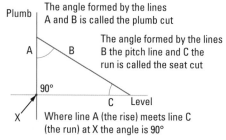

Plumb

The angle formed by the lines A and B is called the plumb cut

A

B

The angle formed by the lines B the pitch line and C the run is called the seat cut

90°

C   Level

X

Where line A (the rise) meets line C (the run) at X the angle is 90°

Figure 7.48 Taking the plumb cut and seat cut from the right-angled triangle

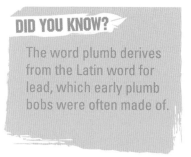

4. GEOMETRIC SOLUTION FOR HIP AND VALLEY ROOF

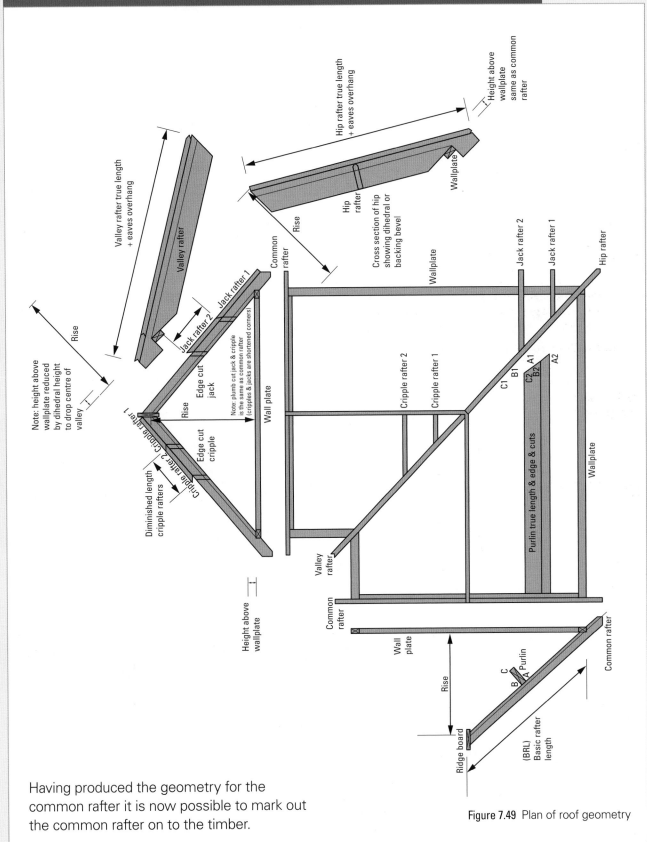

Having produced the geometry for the common rafter it is now possible to mark out the common rafter on to the timber.

Figure 7.49 Plan of roof geometry

SETTING OUT A COMMON RAFTER

PPE

In this and the tasks that follow, ensure you select PPE appropriate to the job and site where you are working. Refer to the PPE section of Chapter 1.

STEP 1 Select a straight piece of timber.

STEP 2 Set a sliding bevel to the plumb cut on your setting out.

Figure 7.52 Marking the true rafter length

STEP 3 Mark a plumb cut line on one end of the timber. You would normally use a pencil to do this but these photos show pen lines for clarity.

Figure 7.50 Marking a plumb cut line for the basic rafter length

STEP 4 From the plumb cut line measure down the length of the timber the basic rafter length and mark a second plumb cut (do not make any cuts at this stage).

STEP 5 Now deduct half the thickness of the ridge parallel to the first plumb line and mark a second plumb line. This will be the line where you make the plumb cut.

Figure 7.51 Deducting half the thickness of the ridge

STEP 6 Now the birdsmouth can be marked out. The general rule when establishing this cut is to remove no more than a third of the depth of the common rafter. Measure no more than a third in from the bottom of the rafter and mark a line that crosses the plumb cut parallel to the bottom of the rafter.

Figure 7.53 Marking out the birdsmouth

Figure 7.54 Measuring from the basic rafter length to the first plumb cut

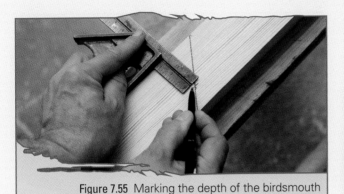

Figure 7.55 Marking the depth of the birdsmouth

STEP 7 Set up a bevel to the seat cut and mark from where the plumb line intersects the pitch line; this will always be 90° to the plumb.

Figure 7.56 Marking the seat cut

STEP 8 An allowance will have to be added to the rafter foot to enable the timber to clear the hidden and visible eaves projection.

Figure 7.57 The plumb cut at the eaves is marked in the same way

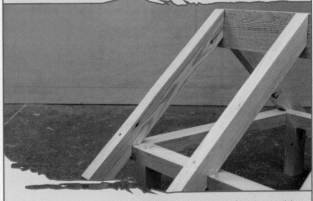

Figure 7.58 The common rafter in position

PRACTICAL TASK

5. MARK OUT, CUT AND FIX A HIP

STEP 1 From the setting out, set a sliding bevel to the hip plumb cut.

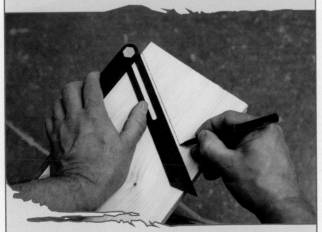

Figure 7.59 Setting the bevel to the hip plumb cut

STEP 2 From the setting out, set a sliding bevel to the hip seat cut.

STEP 3 With the timber crown up mark a plumb cut line on the hip rafter close to one end.

Figure 7.60 Setting the bevel to the plumb cut at the birdsmouth

STEP 4 Using the measurement from the setting out, measure the hip rafter length from the plumb cut along the hip and mark a second plumb cut.

STEP 5 Mark the height above plate on the second plumb cut line, using the bevel set to the seat cut hip mark a line to form the birdsmouth.

Figure 7.61 Marking the height above the plate

Figure 7.62 Marking the seat cut at the birdsmouth

STEP 6 To allow the birdsmouth to sit flat against the wall plate, the corner of the wall plate must be cut back at an angle. The flat should equal the thickness of the hip.

Figure 7.63 Marking the line across the corner

Figure 7.64 Marking 45°

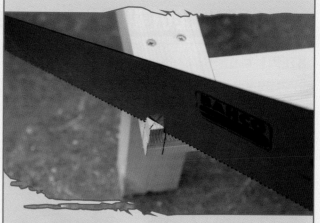

Figure 7.65 Cutting the corner of the wall plate at an angle

STEP 7 From the plumb cut mark back the allowance made for the cut off at the corner of the wall plate.

Figure 7.66 Allowing for the cut off at the corner (1)

Figure 7.67 Allowing for the cut off at the corner (2)

STEP 8 Square the lines on to the edges and make the cuts.

Figure 7.68 Squaring the lines on the edges

STEP 9 Cut the ridge back to the centre line where the hip sits against the ridge.

Figure 7.69 Cutting the ridge back to the centre line at 45°

PRACTICAL TIP

It is rare in modern construction for the backing or dihedral angle to be applied; however, its application provides a far superior fixing for slate lathes (tile battens). If the backing angle is not to be used an allowance still has to be made at the birdsmouth on the seat cut. This sits the hip down lower so that the arris of the hip is in line with the tops of the common rafters.

STEP 10 Make the reduction for the backing angle on the seat cut. Alternatively, form the backing angle on the edge of the hip using a portable powered planer. The photos show a practical method of applying the backing angle.

Figure 7.70 Making the reduction for the backing angle on the seat cut. Line back to half the thickness of the hip

Figure 7.71 Finger gauge along the edge. This can also be done with a marking gauge

Figure 7.73 Forming the backing angle on the edge of the hip

Figure 7.72 Marking centre line for the backing bevel

STEP 10 Position the hip and fix it using 100 mm round-headed wire-cut galvanised nails. (The example in the photograph is fixed with screws to aid disassembly.)

Figure 7.74 The hip in position

PRACTICAL TASK

6. MARK OUT, CUT AND FIX A VALLEY RAFTER

STEP 1 From the setting out set a bevel to valley rafter edge cut.

STEP 2 From the setting out, set a bevel to the plumb cut valley. In a roof that is regular on the plan this will be the same as the hip plumb cut.

PRACTICAL TIP

A roof that is regular on the plan will have hips and valleys with runs of 45° to the wall plate. This results in a central ridge.

STEP 3 With the crown up, mark a centre line on the top edge close to one end of the valley rafter.

STEP 4 Use the sliding bevel that is set to the edge cut to mark a point on the top edge of the valley rafter that meets on the centre line.

Figure 7.75 Setting the bevel to the valley rafter edge cut

STEP 5 From the edge cut lines mark out plumb cut lines on both sides of the valley rafter.

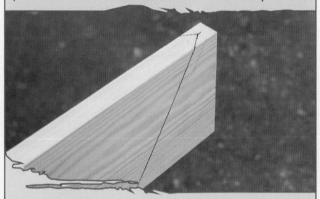

Figure 7.76 Marking the point on the top of the valley

STEP 6 Measure from the point of the edge cut along the length of the valley rafter using the length from the setting out. Mark a plumb cut line.

STEP 7 Use the height above the plate to measure down the plumb line. Use a bevel set to the valley rafter seat cut and mark the seat cut.

Figure 7.77 Measuring the height above the plate and marking the seat cut

STEP 8 Using a bevel set to the valley edge cut, mark a line from the bottom of the plumb cut line on to the bottom edge. Mark a centre line, then where the two lines intersect return the edge cut bevel to create a point.

Figure 7.78 Marking the point on the back of the birdsmouth

STEP 9 Use a bevel set to the valley rafter plumb cut and return the lines from the ends of the edge cut bevels back on to the sides of the valley rafter.

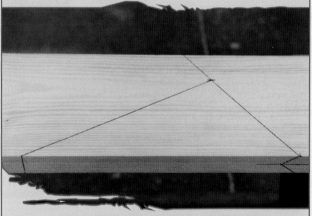

Figure 7.79 Transferring the plumb cut lines onto the sides

Figure 7.80 Reducing the birdsmouth by the depth of the backing angle

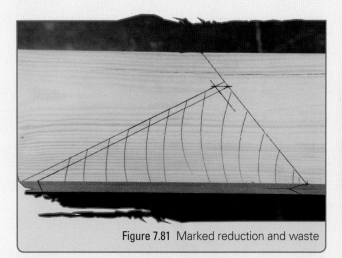

Figure 7.81 Marked reduction and waste

STEP 10 Make the cut at the ridge end of the valley rafter.

Figure 7.82 Making the cut at the ridge end

STEP 11 Make the cut at the birdsmouth.

Figure 7.83 Making the cut at the birdsmouth

Figure 7.84 The birdsmouth cut

STEP 12 Position the valley rafter and fix it using 100 mm round-headed galvanised wire-cut nails.

PRACTICAL TASK

7. MARK OUT, CUT AND FIX A JACK RAFTER

Jack rafters are common rafters that are shortened by their intersection with the hip rafter. Because they are in the same plain they share the common rafter plumb and seat cut.

STEP 1 From the setting out set a bevel to the common rafter plumb cut.

STEP 2 From the setting out set a bevel to the jack rafter edge cut.

STEP 3 With the timber crown up, use the bevel set to the common rafter plumb cut and mark a plumb cut line onto the jack rafter.

STEP 4 Use the bevel set to the jack edge cut to mark the angle.

Figure 7.85 Marking the edge cut

STEP 5 From the point formed by the two lines measure down the edge, to get the jack rafter length and mark a plumb.

Figure 7.86 Marking the plumb

STEP 6 Use the height above the wall plate to measure down the plumb line. Use a bevel set to the common rafter seat cut and mark the seat cut to form the birdsmouth.

Figure 7.87 Forming the birdsmouth

Figure 7.88 The jack marked out

STEP 7 Make the cuts at the end of the jack and at the birdsmouth.

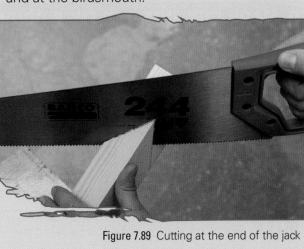

Figure 7.89 Cutting at the end of the jack

STEP 8 Position and fix the jack using 100 mm round-headed galvanised wire-cut nails. (The example in the photograph is fixed with screws to aid disassembly.)

Figure 7.90 The jack in position

8. MARK OUT, CUT AND FIX A CRIPPLE OR VALLEY JACK RAFTER

Cripple rafters are common rafters that are shortened by their intersection with the valley rafter. They are in the same plane as a common rafter and therefore share the same plumb and seat cuts.

STEP 1 From the setting out set a bevel to the common rafter plumb cut.

STEP 2 From the setting out set a bevel to the cripple edge cut in a regular roof. This will be the same as the jack rafter edge cut.

STEP 3 With the crown up, mark a plumb cut line on to the timber.

STEP 4 Measure the length of the cripple rafter on the setting out and transfer this to the timber, measuring from the point of the plumb cut. Then mark another plumb cut line.

Figure 7.91 Measuring the length and marking another plumb cut

STEP 5 Use a bevel set to the cripple edge cut and mark a line.

Figure 7.92 Making the edge cut

STEP 6 Make the cuts.

Figure 7.93 Making the cuts

STEP 7 Position and fix the cripple rafter using 100 mm round-headed galvanised wire-cut nails. (The example in the photograph is fixed with screws to aid disassembly).

Figure 7.94 The cripple rafter in position

Figure 7.95 Position of the cripple rafters

PRACTICAL TIP

The cripple rafters should sit up above the arris on the valley rafter. This is because their top edge is in line with the centre of the valley rafter.

The distance they sit up is the same as the allowance for the backing bevel on the hip in a regular roof. This also places the cripples in the same plane as the common rafters.

PRACTICAL TASK

9. MARK OUT, CUT AND FIX A PURLIN

STEP 1 Set bevels to the side and edge cuts from the setting out.

STEP 2 Mark both cuts onto the purlin at one end.

STEP 3 Measure the true length of the purlin from the setting out.

STEP 4 Measure from point to point on the purlin and mark on the side and edge cuts at the other end of the purlin.

STEP 5 Make the cuts.

STEP 6 Fix in position.

Figure 7.96 The purlins in position, carrying common rafters

Figure 7.97 All the rafters in position. Note that this roof is for demonstration purposes only. Normally, the weight of the timber would mean that it is not necessary to nail rafters in place

TEST YOURSELF

1. What is Pythagoras' theorum?

    a. $A^2 + B^2 = C^2$

    b. $A + B = C$

    c. $A = BC^2$

    d. $A^2 + B^2 = C$

2. What is a MEWP?

    a. A type of working platform

    b. A type of wire pin

    c. A type of weatherproofing

    d. A type of waste protection on site

3. What is the usual maximum span of a fan trussed shaped rafter roof?

    a. 4.5 m

    b. 11 m

    c. 16 m

    d. There is no maximum

4. What is the term used to describe the boards that are fixed underneath the eaves along the length of the building?

    a. Wall plate

    b. Verge

    c. Valley

    d. Soffit

5. Which of the following is likely to mean that there is a requirement to provide an opening in a roof?

    a. Roof light

    b. Dormer window

    c. Chimney

    d. All of these

6. What is a jack rafter?

    a. A type of rafter that reinforces wall plate joints

    b. A common rafter that is shortened by its intersection with the hip rafter

    c. Another name for a valley rafter

    d. A common rafter that is shortened by its intersection with the valley rafter

7. Which type of joint is used for a higher quality finish at the angle between the bargeboard and the fascia board?

    a. Mortise

    b. Tenon

    c. Mitre

    d. Butt

8. What type of eaves finish is used to slow down the flow of rainwater on a steep pitched roof?

    a. Flush

    b. Sprocketed

    c. Open overhanging

    d. Closed overhanging

9. What is the component used to provide intermediate support to rafters in a double roof?

    a. Purlins

    b. Gable ladder

    c. Hip rafter

    d. Restraint strap

10. What is the term used to describe the line at which two sloping surfaces meet at an internal angle?

    a. Hip

    b. Ridge

    c. Verge

    d. Valley

Chapter 8

Unit CSA–L3Occ118

INSTALL AND MAINTAIN NON-STRUCTURAL AND STRUCTURAL COMPONENTS

LEARNING OUTCOMES

LO1/2: Know how to and be able to prepare for installing and maintaining non-structural and structural components

LO3/4: Know how to and be able to install and maintain non-structural and structural components

LO5/6: Know how to and be able to install and maintain doors, windows and structural timbers

LO7/8: Know how to and be able to replace glazing

LO8/9/10: Know how to and be able to reinstate surfaces

INTRODUCTION

The aim of this chapter is to:

* help you identify maintenance needs and carry out maintenance.

PREPARING TO INSTALL AND MAINTAIN NON-STRUCTURAL AND STRUCTURAL COMPONENTS

The term 'non-structural components' covers a wide range of architectural and design features, from mouldings around doors, window frames and glazing to decorative finishes on a variety of surfaces.

Structural components are those that have a supporting function in the building's structure. These include structural timbers, such as rafters and floor joists, or the main structural features of a staircase.

Health and safety and potential hazards

The health and safety and potential hazards are identical to those that you would encounter when carrying out first fix, second fix or being involved in erecting complex structural carcassing components. You should refer back to Chapters 4, 5 and 6, which deal with these topics.

The main additions to potential health and safety issues and associated hazards is dealing with broken glass when replacing glazing and using a wide range of different materials to reinstate surfaces. Both of these issues are covered later in this chapter.

Schedules and specifications

When undertaking maintenance work, initial survey to identify defects usually begins by looking at the outside of the building. Damp patches in brickwork could suggest that there might be a problem with the guttering or downpipes. Other external problems may be more obvious, such as a cracked pane of glass or a sash window not opening.

Once inside the building, there may be several other defects. Visible holes in woodwork could suggest an insect infestation. A door may not close properly. This could be a problem with the hinges, ironmongery or the door may be twisted or actually swollen.

The normal course of action is to:

* identify the location of the defect

* note its possible cause

* suggest a remedial action to correct the defect.

This process will identify a clear way forward. It will enable a list to be compiled of the work to be carried out, with the defects prioritised, ensuring the most serious is completed first. This will form the basis of a schedule of work, suggesting how long the work will take (and its probable cost). Finally a specification can be completed, listing the detail and quality expected. It will also help to state the level of work or specification that will be needed.

The process is similar for installing components. Schedules for both installation and repair should follow a logical sequence. It makes sense to prioritise major installation and replacement work that could impact on other work required of a finishing nature. This will avoid unnecessary repetition.

The specifications for each job will reveal precisely what is required in terms of installation and maintenance. They will state the level and complexity of the work. In some cases a specification may state that an entire component will have to be removed and replaced. In other cases a partial repair may be required.

PPE

In Chapter 1 we looked at PPE in relation to collective protective measures and personal protective equipment. We also looked at respiratory protective equipment.

Dust fumes and other airborne contaminants are responsible for a wide variety of occupational diseases. At worst these particles can cause lung diseases or asthma. Typical work that generates airborne contaminants includes:

* dust from sawing, planing, sanding wood or other materials becoming more widely used in construction

* working in areas with poor ventilation such as lofts

* dust and chippings from operating a router, for example scribing kitchen worktops

* drilling structures, particularly walls

* mist, such as paint mist from spraying

* fumes from welding

* gas, such as carbon monoxide from fires

* vapour from solvents and adhesives.

An LEV (local exhaust ventilation system) should take any dust, vapour or fumes out of the air so they cannot be breathed in.

Access equipment

When you are working on repairing timber it is likely that you may need access equipment and be working at height. This means that the Work at Height Regulations (2005) apply.

In Chapter 1, there is information about Work at Height Regulations and how to ensure that any equipment and safety measures you use will protect you. You should always try to avoid working at height if possible. Always use the proper equipment and put measures in place to prevent falls if this cannot be avoided. There will always be a risk, even if the proper equipment and safety measures are taken. As there is always a risk, measures need to be put in place to minimise the distance and consequences of a fall.

INSTALLING AND MAINTAINING STRUCTURAL AND NON-STRUCTURAL COMPONENTS

Installing and maintaining structural and non-structural components in a building can involve a wide range of different components and carpentry skills. Some jobs will require replacement or repair of relatively minor parts while others may involve total reinstallation and replacement.

Different types of fixings

'Fixings' describes a range of different screws, nails, bolts and adhesives.

Nails

Nails are one of the simplest fixings that can be used to join wood or to secure other components to wood. The following diagram shows a typical range of different types of nails and fasteners.

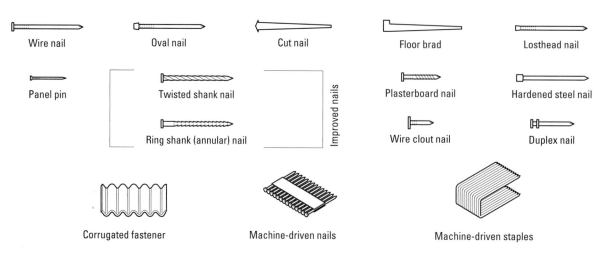

Figure 8.1 Typical range of nails and fasteners

Type of nail or fastener	Description and use
Wire nail	Usually 12–150 mm. The top part of the shank is ribbed. It is a good general-purpose nail used for first fix, carcassing and form work.
Oval nail	This can also be 12–150 mm. It has a small head that is nailed in below the surface. Useful if the timber is to be painted.
Cut nail	Available in many sizes up to 100 mm, and mainly used for fixing timber to blockwork and is made from mild sheet steel.
Floor brad	Similar to cut nails and available in lengths up to 75 mm. They tend to be used for surface fixing of floorboards.
Lost head nail	These are used mainly to fix floor boards. They are available in lengths of up to 75 mm.
Panel pin	Available in lengths of 12–50 mm. They are rather like a lost head nail but are used for mouldings.
Improved nail	Available in lengths up to 75 mm. They have a twisted shank that gives extra holding strength.
Plasterboard nail	These are galvanised and up to 40 mm in length. They are used to fix plasterboard and insulation board.
Wire clout nail	These are available between 12 and 25 mm and tend to be used to fix roofing felt and building paper. They are also galvanised.
Hardened steel nail	Available up to 100 mm these are zinc-plated steel and are ideal for fixing directly into brickwork.
Duplex nail	These are like wire nails with a double head. The lower head is driven into the surface and the upper head left proud, enabling it to be removed. Mainly used for temporary fixing.
Corrugated fastener	Available in 6–25 mm these are used to reinforce joints, such as mitres and butts.
Machine driven nails or stapler	These are driven into the timber using either a pneumatic nailer or stapler. The nails are good for structural work and the staples for plywood, plasterboard and insulation board.

Table 8.1

Slotted screw

Phillips

Pozidriv

Crosshead screws

Clutch-head screw

Figure 8.2 Screw heads

Screws

The vast majority of screws are made from steel, although brass screws can be used for decorative purposes, as can chrome-plated ones and black Japanned versions. Stainless steel screws tend to be used most often as they are more resistant to corrosion.

Screws can either be specified as being an imperial number, such as Number 4, or a metric size, such as 3.0mm. In fact this can be something of a problem, as the metric and imperial sizes are not completely interchangeable.

Screws have threads along most of their length. The top part of the screw, under the head, acts rather like a dowel and is called the shank. Screws are also identified by their head type and shape, as can be seen in the following diagrams. Note, however, that slotted heads are now less commonly used.

The following table briefly describes the various different types of screw.

Screw type	Description and use
Countersunk head	Before driving the screw into the timber a countersunk hole needs to be created. The screw is then driven into the timber and the head finished flush with the surface.
Round head	This is used for fixing pieces of material together where countersunk holes are not being used
Raised head	This has a slightly rounded head and is used mainly for fixing surface ironmongery.
Bugle head	This is flat-topped and is mainly used as a dry wall screw for fixing plasterboard.
Pan head	This has a slightly rounded head and is mainly used for fixing sheet metal.

Table 8.2

Handrail bolts

Handrail bolts are generally available in lengths of 60 to 120 mm. The longer the bolt, the stronger the connection achieved. Handrail bolts are used in the installation and maintenance of staircases.

The nut is embedded into one of the parts of timber and a wrench is used to tighten the two pieces of timber together.

Figure 8.3 Handrail bolt

Adhesives

Adhesives fall into one of two categories:

* Cold setting – the adhesive will work and bond at normal room temperature.

* Hot setting – these adhesives require heating up to transform into liquid form. As they cool down they will set and bond.

Adhesives also need to have varying degrees of durability, so their choice will depend on where they are going to be used:

* Internal adhesives should only ever be used where they will not be exposed to the weather or damp.

* Moisture resistant adhesives are weather resistant to an extent. They can cope with cold water but not hot water.

* Boil resistant adhesives can cope with boiling water and have good weather resistance, but they are not good long-term solutions if they are exposed to external weather conditions.

Weather and boil proof adhesives should be resistant to most weather conditions and temperatures.

The following diagram shows a range of different types of adhesive.

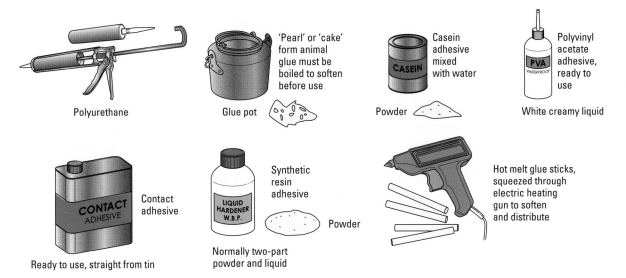

Figure 8.4 Types of adhesive

Different types of stairs and returns

There are several terms that you need to understand.

Term	Description and use
Landings	This is a platform on a flight of stairs, or it can be at the end of the flight of stairs. It is often used as means by which to change the direction of the stairs.
Staircases	This is a term used to describe the stairs and any surrounding walls or structures, including the balusters.
Tapered tread	Also known as kites, these are staircases where two or more treads can be placed in the space where usually a half landing (a landing halfway up the stairs) would be fitted. The idea is that they optimise the space available where space is restricted. They are often used for loft conversions.
Dog legs	This is a type of staircase that has a half landing before either turning or continuing upwards. These are often seen in commercial buildings.
Geometric stair	These take many forms, including a spiral stair, and are staircases that have landings with a three-quarter or 90° turn at the landing before continuing upwards.
Nosing	It is the front edge of a tread or the finish to floorboards around the stairwell opening.
Baluster	This is also called a spindle, which is a moulded piece of timber that supports the handrail of the staircase.

Table 8.3

Different types of double doors

There are several different types of double doors, which are looked at in the following table.

Type of door element	Description
Double doors with rebates	The doors need to be closed in a particular order to ensure that the rebated styles meet together properly. This arrangement is common for double casement doors and the rebate provides an overlapping seal rather than a straight joint (see Fig 8.6).
Double action	Double action doors are designed so that the door can open either inwards or outwards. Effectively they are swinging or side hung doors. The double doors consist of a pair of leaves (doors) and are particularly useful where there is a lot of traffic through the doorway; hence they are used in public spaces, such as offices, hotels and shops (see Fig 8.6).
Rising floor spring	This is a means by which the door returns to the closed position. There is a spring inside a metal box embedded into the floor. At the bottom of each of the doors there is a shoe that is located over the pivot spindle. The pivot is fixed to the head of the frame and the other to the door itself. The way in which this is constructed can be seen in Figs 8.7, 8.8 and 8.9.

Table 8.4

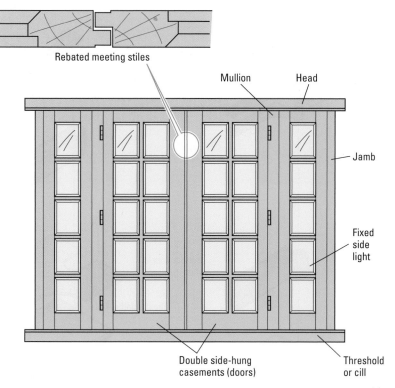

Rebated meeting stiles

Mullion

Head

Jamb

Fixed side light

Double side-hung casements (doors)

Threshold or cill

Figure 8.5 French casements

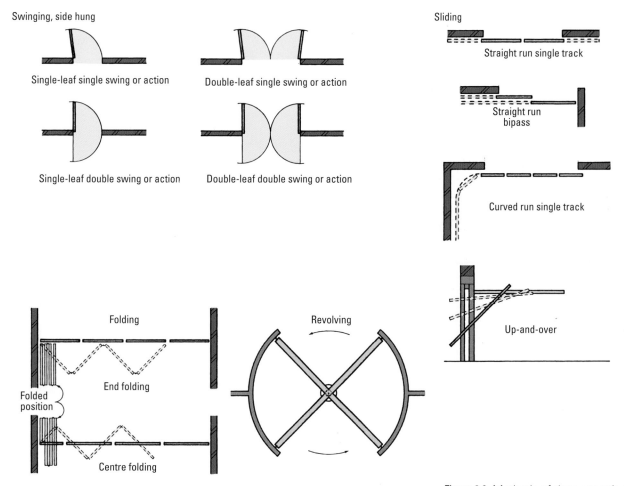

Swinging, side hung

Single-leaf single swing or action

Double-leaf single swing or action

Single-leaf double swing or action

Double-leaf double swing or action

Sliding

Straight run single track

Straight run bipass

Curved run single track

Up-and-over

Folding

End folding

Folded position

Centre folding

Revolving

Figure 8.6 Methods of door operation

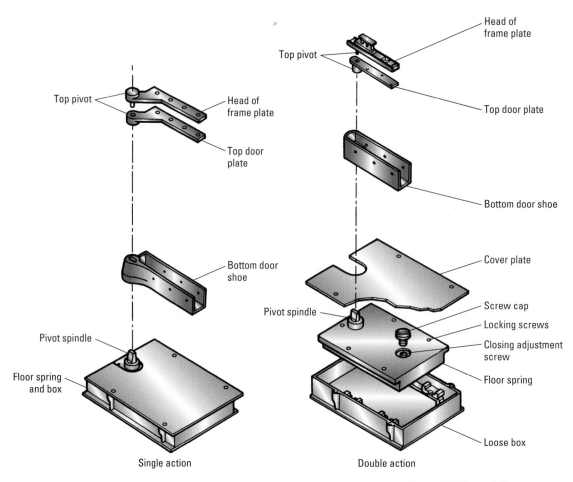

Top pivot

Head of
frame plate

Top door
plate

Bottom door
shoe

Pivot spindle

Floor spring
and box

Single action

Top pivot

Head of
frame plate

Top door plate

Bottom door shoe

Cover plate

Pivot spindle

Screw cap

Locking screws

Closing adjustment
screw

Floor spring

Loose box

Double action

Figure 8.7 Pivoted floor springs

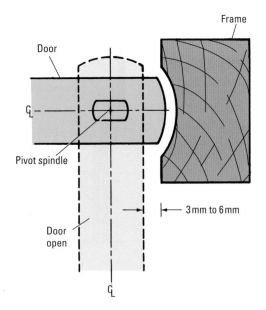

Door

Frame

Pivot spindle

Door
open

3 mm to 6 mm

Figure 8.8 Floor spring loose box positioning

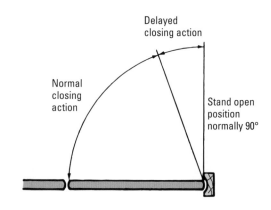

Delayed
closing action

Normal
closing
action

Stand open
position
normally 90°

Figure 8.9 Action of door with floor spring

Different types of convex and concave mouldings

Most mouldings are either Roman (based on arcs of circles) or Grecian (formed from elliptical, parabolic or hyperbolic curves).

Either setting out or identifying particular types of moulding can be important to match existing moulding. The following set of diagrams show each of the different types of moulding, but the following points should be borne in mind:

* Ovolo – this is a quarter circle.

* Scotia – this produces a concave curve and is made up of two quadrants of different radii.

* Torus – also known as a bull-nose or half-round moulding.

* Cavetto – this is the reverse shape of the ovolo moulding.

* Cyma-recta – this is more commonly known as an ogee moulding.

* Cyma-reversa – this is more commonly known as a reverse ogee.

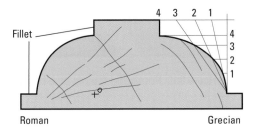

Figure 8.10 Ovolo moulding

Figure 8.11 Scotia moulding

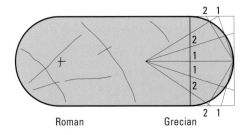

Figure 8.12 Torus moulding

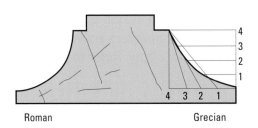

Figure 8.13 Cavetto moulding

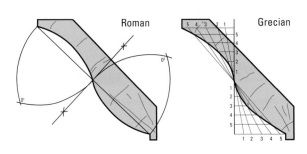

Figure 8.14 Cyma-recta cornice

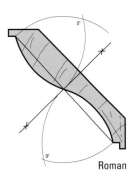
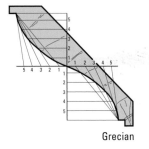

Figure 8.15 Cyma-reversa cornice

PRACTICAL TASK

1. REMOVE FIXINGS AND COMPONENTS TO CARRY OUT REPAIRS AND MAINTENANCE TO STAIRS

The following step by steps outline the remedial action that can be adopted if there are problems with stairs.

REPLACING GLUE BLOCKS

Creaking or squeaking stairs are often the result of loose or missing glue blocks and/or wedges. Glue blocks are located on the underside of the stairs at the intersection of tread and riser. They are, as the name suggests, blocks that are simply rub-glued in position. They are often cut as triangular fillets for appearances only; this does not improve the performance of the blocks.

Access will be required to the underside of the stairs. This is not always exposed and may be clad in a number of ways, such as lathe and plaster, plasterboard and skim coat or timber cladding.

PPE

For this and the tasks that follow, ensure you select PPE appropriate to the job and site where you are working. The carpenters shown are not wearing gloves for clarity. Refer to the PPE section in Chapter 1.

STEP 1 Remove any cladding from the underside of the stairs; this should be done carefully to avoid damage to the surrounding area. Dust sheets should be used to protect flooring and furnishings.

STEP 2 Using a hammer and a sharp chisel, remove any loose glue blocks. There will normally be two or three per step, depending on the width of the stair. Ensure the entire glue block is removed to allow the new glue block to seat correctly.

STEP 3 Sand any remaining fibres still stuck to the underside of the tread or the back of the riser.

Figure 8.16 Removing the old glue block

STEP 4 Apply glue to the back of the new glue blocks and rub into position; this removes the air. Rub until the block will not move. This should be sufficient to hold the block in place; however, a panel pin can be used until the glue dries if required. This will then have to be removed.

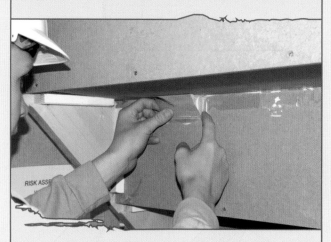
Figure 8.17 Rubbing new glue blocks into position

STEP 5 Repeat for all loose glue blocks.

REPLACING OR RE-FIXING WEDGES

The wedges are located where the treads and risers are located into the strings. Horizontal wedges are located under the treads and vertical wedges behind the risers.

STEP 1 The cladding will already have been removed to maintain the glue blocks. Whenever carrying out this type of maintenance it is good practice to carry out all necessary operations at the same time.

STEP 2 Check for loose wedges by trying each wedge in turn, starting at the bottom and working up. Work systematically so that no wedges are missed. Mark all loose or missing wedges for repair.

STEP 3 Any wedges that are still intact can be reused. Apply glue to them and, using a hammer, tap back into position until they are tight. Do not drive the wedges so hard that they split. Repeat for all loose wedges.

STEP 4 Any split or cracked wedges should be replaced. Cut new wedges and glue them into place as above.

Figure 8.18 Replacing damaged wedges

INTERSECTION OF TREADS AND RISERS

In the UK closed riser stairs are constructed with the riser sitting against the back of the tread below. In better construction this is jointed with a tongue and groove joint but is more often butted and fixed with screws or nails.

STEP 1 Check for movement at this intersection from underneath the stair by applying pressure to the underside of the tread.

STEP 2 Where there is pronounced movement, the risers can be re-fixed to the back edge of the treads. A clearance hole, pilot hole and countersink should be drilled before fixing with an appropriate sized wood screw.

Figure 8.19 Fixing risers to back of treads

STEP 3 Repeat where required.

REPLACING NOSINGS

Nosings can become worn or damaged, and can often split along the top edge, in line with the front edge of the riser housing.

STEP 1 Set a marking gauge to the depth of the nosing and mark a line across the top edge of the tread. Note that the gauge cannot be used all the way to the string; however the line can be completed with a combination square and pencil.

STEP 2 Make a vertical cut at both ends of the tread adjacent to the string; this should be to the depth of the face of the riser.

STEP 3 Make a series of cuts approximately 10 to 12 mm apart towards one end of the tread. This should extend about 100 mm in from the string. This should be on the left-hand side if you are right handed and vice versa if you are left handed, when facing the stairs from the bottom.

STEP 4 Using a hammer and a sharp chisel remove the nosing between these saw cuts.

STEP 5 Using a sharp hand saw, cut along the waste side of the gauge line and remove the nosing. Take care not to cut into the face of the string at the end of the cut.

STEP 6 Use a block plane to dress the cut back to the gauge line. Be careful not to scuff the face of the riser.

STEP 7 Using the old nosing as a template, make a new nosing. This may have been pre-made in the workshop after a survey or it could be produced on site. The method adopted could be determined by factors such as the complexity of the nosing (not all nosings are simple bull noses) or the quantity of nosings to be replaced.

STEP 8 Measure the distance between the strings and cut a length of nosing.

STEP 9 Dry fit the nosing; make sure the nosing sits tight back to the remaining tread with no gaps and that it sits tight between the strings.

STEP 10 Apply PVA glue to the back edge of the nosing and fix with nails or screws.

PRACTICAL TIP

The best finish would be produced by counter-boring and plugging the screw holes with timber plugs.

STEP 11 Ensure the nosings are dressed flush with the top of the tread, and then finish with glass paper.

PRACTICAL TIP

On quality work the nosings could be further strengthened by the use of biscuit joints or a loose tongue.

REPAIRING NOSINGS

An alternative to replacing the entire nosing is to repair parts of it where required. This is usually achieved using a simple splice joint. This could be somewhere in the middle or to one end; the method described below is for a repair in the middle of the tread but the method remains the same for a repair up to the strings where only one mitre would be required.

STEP 1 Identify the area to be repaired and mark a 45° line at both ends of the section to be replaced.

STEP 2 Gauge a line between the 45° marks to the depth of the nosing.

STEP 3 Using a tenon saw cut the two 45° angles.

STEP 4 Between the two 45° cuts make a series of vertical cuts approximately 10 to 12 mm apart. Be careful not to exceed the depth of the gauge line. These should extend about 100 mm from one of the angled cuts, provided the repair is sufficiently longer than this.

STEP 5 Using a hammer and sharp chisel, remove the timber between these cuts.

STEP 6 Use a hand saw to remove the nosing as for Step 5 in Replacing nosings.

STEP 7 Dress back to the gauge lines using a block plane and a wide, sharp chisel.

STEP 8 Cut a length of replacement nosing. This does not necessarily need to be pre-shaped but it should be the correct width and thickness.

STEP 9 Fix the replacement piece as for Step 10 in *Replacing nosings*.

STEP 10 Dress to a smooth finish using a block plane and glass paper.

BALUSTERS (SPINDLES)

Balusters sometimes require either replacement or repair. Replacing balusters can often be problematic when matching to existing profiles, especially in older properties. There are many specialist wood turners who can reproduce balusters; a sample will be required for the turner to work from. This type of work does not come cheap; however, when considered against the replacement of all balusters it can often be the most viable method.

Cracked balusters can often be repaired with glue and clamps (cramps); however, sometimes pieces may have to be spliced-in (see window repairs and nosing repairs) and the techniques are exactly the same albeit requiring slightly more delicate work.

In traditional construction the balusters were tenoned into the handrail and string. Occasionally these get broken, and in these circumstances the balusters can usually be re-fixed by either nailing or screwing. When screwing balusters they should be counter-bored and plugged using a pellet of the same timber as the baluster.

FIXING BALUSTERS

Refer to page 170 for information about fitting and fixing balusters.

2. REMOVE FIXINGS AND COMPONENTS TO CARRY OUT REPAIRS AND MAINTENANCE TO DOUBLE DOORS

There are two types of maintenance that can be carried out on doors: routine planned maintenance and remedial maintenance. The first is preferable and is usually adopted in large organisations.

PPE

For this and the tasks that follow, ensure you select PPE appropriate to the job and site where you are working. Refer to the PPE section in Chapter 1.

ROUTINE MAINTENANCE OF DOORS AND DOUBLE DOORS

STEP 1 Check the gap around the door. This should be parallel and consistent. The door should be clear of the floor and the gap should be even. Edges of doors touching rebates or doors catching the floor often indicate either that the door has dropped or that it has taken up moisture, causing it to swell and affect the fit.

STEP 2 Check the operation of the doors. Do they open and close smoothly with no squeaking hinges? Are they binding anywhere? For example, the door could be binding against the back of the rebate.

STEP 3 If door springs are fitted, are they operating correctly? Check the closing speed and the checking action. A door that is banging will usually mean that it is closing too quickly without sufficient check at the end of its sweep.

Doors that are latching incorrectly are usually either not closing with sufficient speed or are closing so quickly that the latch is unable to engage. The speed and checking action can be altered with adjustment screws usually found on the edge of the door spring.

Check for any signs of oil leaks, as this could indicate that the spring is no longer fit for purpose.

STEP 4 Check the condition of the hinges. Are all the screws tightened fully? Are any screws missing or broken? Check that there are no cracks in the hinges. Black stains on the knuckles of the hinge extending on to the face of the door and frame indicate excessive wear of the hinge or hinges and they may need replacing.

If the hinges are relatively new, consider what is causing this. It could be that the hinges are not strong enough for the door in question or they may be fitted out of line. Creaking or squeaking hinges are often an indication of this.

STEP 5 Do the handles work correctly? Does the handle return after being depressed? If not, this could be a result of the springs no longer functioning or a faulty latch.

Are the handles loose? Check that all screws are tight, but not over-tight, as this can also affect the proper functioning of the handles.

Are the handles in line? If only one handle is functioning, check the length of the spindle. If it has been cut too short, this sometimes takes time to reveal itself as a problem, as the spindle gradually works back into one of the two handles.

STEP 6 Check the operation of the lock and/or latch. Check that the key is easily inserted into the keyhole.

Check the operation of the key; first check the operation with the door open, then check from both sides. The action should be smooth with no catching or dead spots. A key that is not turning easily can often be the result of an ill-fitting or damaged faceplate to the lock. If this is OK it may be necessary to remove the lock to check that all the levers sit correctly and that their springs are located.

Check the key to make sure no parts of it are twisted and that there are no burrs of metal preventing smooth operation. Check that there is no damage to the end of the key.

Now check the operation of the latch by pressing the handles down. The latch should retract fully into the lock, without catching when released and it should return quickly to its original position without catching.

STEP 7 Close the door and check the operation of the lock. Again check that the key works from both sides and that it engages in the keep. Remember that the reason a lock is catching may have nothing to do with the lock or keep! The door may have dropped, which can prevent the lock properly engaging, or it may have twisted, which again would prevent the lock from working correctly.

STEP 8 While maintaining fire doors, ensure that all intumescent seals are seated properly and that none are broken or missing. Close the doors and make sure the gaps do not exceed the specified distance. Where smoke seals are fitted, check for wear and replace as required.

STEP 9 Check that kick plates and push plates are secure and free from damage, and check for sharp edges.

STEP 10 Check any glazing for cracks or chips, particularly on fire doors. Check that beading is undamaged and correctly fixed.

STEP 11 Check the operation of all bolts. On double doors these are often flush bolts, which are found in the edge of one of the doors or the leaf. The action should be smooth and should engage and disengage without catching.

STEP 12 Routine maintenance should include the lubrication of all moving parts. Always check the manufacturer's instructions for maintenance details.

CASE STUDY

South
Tyneside Homes

South Tyneside Council's
Housing Company

Modern communications get the job done

Gary Kirsop, Head of Property Services at South Tyneside Homes, says:

'Technology is playing a massive part in our business these days. In responsive repairs and empty homes, we're striving to be 100 per cent paperless. We also want to provide a service that is highly responsive. So, at 8am, our repairs team will turn on their smartphone while they're still at home, log on to the system, and get the details of their first job ... all before they've left the house. That means they don't waste time getting into work first, and they can go directly to the first job. Each time they complete a job, they log the job and materials used, and then the details of the next job are downloaded straight to the phone. What used to happen is that they'd be given about 15 pieces of paper and they had to figure out what order to put all the jobs in themselves.

Working in this way has had a great effect on productivity because they waste less time on admin and get to the jobs more quickly. One of our employees said, "I used to be a van driver that occasionally did a bit of plumbing" – and now he's finally doing more plumbing than driving!'

INSTALLING AND MAINTAINING DOORS, WINDOWS AND STRUCTURAL TIMBERS

Learning how to install and maintain a wide variety of different types of doors, windows and structural timbers is an important part of the carpentry trade. Many challenges face a carpenter, from defects in structural timbers, to infestations from insects and rot. It is necessary in some cases to completely remove and replace affected timbers and in others to carry out remedial work before applying a range of preservatives.

Each time a major component, such as a door, has to be replaced it may mean having to fit new ironmongery.

Identifying defects and infestations affecting timber components

Structural timbers and other timber components can come under a variety of different attacks. The main type of attack is biological. This means that the timbers are affected by either wood-boring insects or fungi. If the conditions are right then the timber can come under attack from both at the same time.

Structural timbers can also suffer from natural defects that become obvious over a period of time. One of the most common is shakes. This type of defect was actually developed before the timber even reached the site. It may have been caused when the tree was felled, or during the seasoning process. Clearly if there are shakes or cracks in the timber then this not only affects the structural strength of the timber but also leaves it open to infestation.

Splits are points where the wood fibre has separated. They usually develop along the grain of a piece of wood. Small surface splits may not necessarily represent a particular problem. Problems can occur when there are splits on the ends of timber that could develop into longer and broader splits.

Lifecycle of an insect attack

It is important to understand the development of insects that can affect timber. In fact some of the young (larvae) can live in wood for ten years. The majority of damage done to timber in the UK can be attributed to five species of insect:

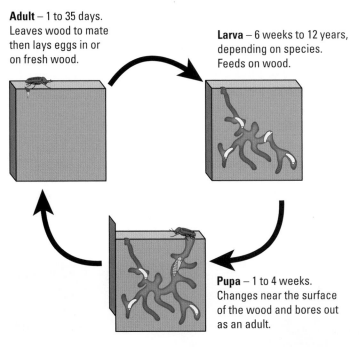

Adult – 1 to 35 days. Leaves wood to mate then lays eggs in or on fresh wood.

Larva – 6 weeks to 12 years, depending on species. Feeds on wood.

Pupa – 1 to 4 weeks. Changes near the surface of the wood and bores out as an adult.

Figure 8.20 The life cycle of a wood-boring insect

* common furniture beetle

* powder post beetle

* death watch beetle

* house longhorn beetle

* weevil.

As with rot, the ideal solution is to remove the conditions that allow the insects to thrive. The main thing to do is reduce the moisture content of the timber. Any rotten timbers are more likely to be attacked by insects, so this means looking for leaky roofs and pipes and poorly maintained guttering.

Figure 8.21 Woodworm holes

Figure 8.22 Flight holes caused by the common furniture beetle

Woodworm

Woodworm is a generic term for wood-boring insects. They create small holes and leave egg-shaped pellets in the dust they create. The larvae can live for three years and will bore into the wood. They can cause huge damage to structural timbers. If the moisture content of the timber is less than 12 per cent it is hard for the larvae to survive but if the moisture content of the timber is high and there is existing rot then woodworm can add to the structural failure of the timber.

Softwood, such as pine and fir, is particularly vulnerable to insect attack. Usually it is necessary to replace structural timbers that have been affected.

Common furniture beetle

These are the most common form of wood-boring insect. They measure 2.7 mm to 4.5 mm in length and have a brown body. The larvae will attack soft and hardwoods. Their natural habitat is broken tree branches and areas where tree bark has been damaged or removed. They will attack any type of woodwork including flooring, joinery and structural timbers. They do not like very dry wood, so are less likely to be seen in timbers that are kept dry by heating systems, preferring areas of the house where there may be some dampness. The flight holes are around 2 mm. The insects will bore deep into the wood and create many tunnels and galleries.

Powder post beetle

These will attack most types of new timber, including flooring. They produce a fine dust and holes 2 mm in diameter.

The flight holes can be seen clearly in Fig 8.22. The dust around the holes is called frass and is the waste material left by the activity of the larvae and the beetles' flight from the timber.

Figure 8.23 Larvae of the powder post beetle

Figure 8.24 A death watch beetle

Death watch beetle

This wood-boring insect is related to the common furniture beetle, but is much larger. Death watch beetles are approximately 7 mm long with larvae growing up to 11 mm long. They prefer very damp conditions, especially when there is some kind of fungal decay such as wet rot in the timbers. They attack timber that is already rotting or decaying but prefer European hardwoods, especially oak, ash and chestnut. Their larvae can live for ten years. They are often found in hard-to-see places, where the ventilation is poor. If they are allowed to establish themselves, the timber will fail. They leave holes around 3 mm in diameter.

The house longhorn beetle

These are about 25 mm long. House longhorn beetles are typically black or brown. They are principally found in roof timbers, where they attack the sapwood of exclusively softwood species, often resulting in severe structural weakness. The holes and tunnels of the house longhorn beetle are much larger than those of the furniture beetle. The damage caused by these insects can be severe.

Treatment

If an infestation is found, then it is wise to seek specialist advice. Experts will be able to advise you whether the infestation can be treated without having to replace affected timbers or whether the timbers will need to be taken out. The opinion of the specialist may have an impact on the work you are doing and whether it needs to be delayed as a result of necessary treatments.

It is sometimes necessary to use chemicals to treat the infestation. Usually, this should be carried out by a specialist. There are several options:

* Spraying – this is good against furniture beetles, but as the spray is only applied to the surface of the wood it may not be effective against those that are deep inside the timber.

* Injection – small holes are drilled into the timber, or into the flight holes of the insects and a chemical injected. The chemical penetrates deep into the timber and kills the majority of the insects.

* Paste – this is a good alternative to spraying, as the chemical will slowly penetrate into the timber.

* Smoke – this will usually kill adult insects that are emerging from the timber, but will have virtually no effect on eggs or larvae. This means that the treatment has to be repeated over several years to kill off all the insects.

* Fogging – this is a chemical fog that is used when large areas are affected. The chemicals target the eggs. The problem is that the deeper the eggs are in the timber the less likely they will be affected by the chemical fog.

Wet and dry rot

When timbers have a moisture content of more than 24 per cent they are more susceptible to wet rot. It is caused by direct contact with water, such as leaks from gutters and pipes.

DID YOU KNOW?

Death watch beetle is often found in the structural timbers of churches, hence their name. It was common for people to watch over the bodies of friends or relatives overnight while the body was awaiting burial. A knocking sound was often heard during these vigils – this was in fact the sound of the death watch beetle.

Wet rot is easy to notice because it encourages the growth of a fleshy mould. The strands of the mould are usually classed as either brown or white. This classification does not refer to the colour of the mould, but to what it does to the timber. Brown rot makes wood darken and crack. White rot affects the grains and causes the timber to lighten in colour. Both make timber weak and in most situations you will be able to pull pieces of timber away using your hand.

Wet rot can be managed in the following way:

* find the source of the dampness and cure the defect

* dry out the surroundings and remove damaged timbers, as they will no longer be strong enough and will look damaged.

Dry rot refers to timbers with a slightly lower moisture content of between 18 and 22 per cent. It is caused by high moisture content coupled with a lack of ventilation, which results in high humidity. This process can be accelerated by the addition of warmth.

Dry rot can travel through masonry in order to find more timber, for example the structural timber. Dry rot spores have the appearance of cotton wool (known in the trade as 'dead man's fingers') and they will extend along timber or masonry. Dry rot will eat any nutrients it finds in the timber. It can be stopped by:

* determining the source of the moisture and curing the defect

* cutting out and removing any affected timbers and removing up to 600 mm of the timber beyond the visible signs

* stripping the plaster back until there are no visible signs

* drying out the area if possible

* cleaning any surrounding masonry with a steriliser

* drilling and injecting a **biocide** into thick walls

* spraying any surrounding timbers with the biocide.

KEY TERMS

Biocide

– this is a chemical substance that can kill living organisms and spores.

Figure 8.25 Dry rot

Figure 8.26 Wet rot

Disposing of affected timber

It may be impossible and in some cases not desirable even to try to recycle timber that has been badly affected. This is certainly the case when dealing with timber that has had wet or dry rot. It needs to be completely removed from the building.

Normally it is taken away and burned. Do NOT start open fires on site – if this timber is to be destroyed it must be taken away. The danger of leaving any affected timber, for example, under the floorboards, is that the rot will spread once again into the replaced timbers.

Splicing new timber into structural timbers

Repairing structural timbers can be an expensive and time-consuming business. The most common types of repair that are necessary are likely to be:

* timber end repairs – as a result of the timber being in contact with damp masonry

* damage to cross sections of the timber – as a result of insect or fungal attack

* cracks – these are usually longitudinal and as a result of changes of the moisture content within the timber.

There are three different ways of carrying out the repairs, splicing being just one of them:

* like for like – this involves replacing some of the timber with a similar timber

* strapping and plating – this is known as an honest repair and the straps and plates will be clearly visible

* resins – this involves cutting out the affected area and then pouring or injecting resin into the timber.

Scarf joints are commonly used when the ends of structural timbers have decayed, such as on the ridge of a roof. The decayed portion is cut out and replaced with a similar timber that has been jointed into place. This avoids replacing an entire structural timber, which can be very complex and often involves access problems.

The process of splicing involves connecting two or more pieces of material. It is in effect a joint, but the type of splice used will be dependent on the stresses or strains that the timber is under.

Some structural timbers will be under longitudinal stress. These will require splices that can resist compression.

Joists and trusses, for example, are likely to be under transverse and angular stress, so they will need splices that can resist tension.

Horizontal structural timbers will require a splice that can resist both compression and tension.

The three main types of splice are detailed in the following table.

Type of splice	Description
Butt	Two ends of the timber are squared off and then secured with either metal fastenings or wood. These supporting pieces prevent the timber from buckling. It is also possible to create a halved splice. Half the thickness of the timber is cut away to the same length and then the two parts are fitted together. In effect the two pieces of wood overlap one another. The laps need to be long enough to be able to bear the weight that they will be subjected to. Nails and bolts can be used to fasten the half splice together.
Tension resistant	When dealing with trusses, braces and joists any splice or joint is going to be under stress in more than one direction. A square splice is when notches are cut into laps, rather like a halved splice. These provide additional locking. It is then secured with nails or bolts.
Bend resistant	Some horizontal timbers will be under stress that would crush the fibres. A bend resistant splice aims to resist both compression and tension. Laps are cut at the ends of the two pieces of timber. The upper lap, or bearing surface, is squared and butted against the square of the other lap. This will give good resistance to crushing.

Table 8.5

Preservatives for structural timbers and applying them

DID YOU KNOW?

Control of Substances Hazardous to Health (COSHH) Regulations also apply to the use of wood preservatives.

Any wood preservatives that are used on timber have to be approved under the Control of Pesticides Regulations (1986/1997). Only people who have been trained and competent to use them are allowed to apply preservatives.

The amount of protection that a wood preservative gives to the timber is dependent on:

* the quantity of the preservative that remains in the timber

* the depth to which the preservative has penetrated the timber

* how long the preservative is expected to be effective.

Timbers that are exposed to the elements, particularly ones that will be exposed to rainwater and changes in temperature, present a higher decay hazard than those used for indoor woodwork. Any exterior timber that has contact with the ground is likely to decay far quicker.

The simplest method of applying preservative is to paint it on. Soft bristled brushes are used to provide a flood coat. The timber needs to be clean and dry. Subsequent coats can be added once the previous coat has soaked in, but has not dried out. The preservative needs to be flooded into joints and on end grains for better protection.

Another method is to apply the preservative as a paste. This technique is usually used where access is difficult.

A third option is to use pressure treatment. The timber is loaded into a cylinder and then the cylinder is filled with the preservative. A pressure is then applied. The gauges on the cylinder will show just how much of the preservative has been absorbed by the timber. This is a technique that is often used to apply **creosote** substitute to timber.

A final alternative method of preservation is to inject the timber. Holes are drilled into the timber and a strong fungicide and insecticide gel is injected into the holes. This is available in a cartridge and can be applied using a sealant gun. The holes are then plugged with dowels.

Water-based preservatives

Water-based preservatives are anti-fungal, but they are not as effective on exterior woodwork as waterproof preservatives. Therefore, water-based preservatives are mainly used on interior wood, but not in areas where the woodwork may be exposed to water, such as kitchens or bathrooms.

Spirit-based preservatives

Spirit-based wood preservatives are good for overall external use. They are waterproof. Usually the preservative needs to be reapplied to keep it effective.

Installing panels into UPVC frames

Replacing double-glazed panes can be a fairly straightforward task. However it does rely on making sure that the correct size of replacement pane has been ordered.

On the exterior of UPVC units there is what is known as an exterior shuffle bead. The measurements for the replacement pane are taken to include this exterior shuffle bead, but 10 mm needs to be deducted from the measurements for the pane to fit.

The other thing you will need to know is the thickness of the double-glazed unit. The glass is nearly always 4 mm thick. So the two panes of glass together total 8 mm. But it is the space in between the two panes that determines the overall thickness of the unit. Professionals who work full time on replacing these units may have an analysis kit, which can make the measurement by placing the instrument against the glass pane. More normally, however, the unit will have to be taken out and measured.

To replace a double-glazed unit you will have to identify which bead system has been used. Each is different and requires you to handle the unit in a slightly different way.

KEY TERMS

Creosote

– this is a preservative that is commonly used to colour and protect external woods. It is a tar-based preservative that is irritating to eyes and skin so its sale is restricted under the COSSH regulations. Creosote subsitutes are available.

System type	Description	Procedure
External shuffle bead	The glazing beads are on the outside of the window and there is an internal wedge gasket inside.	The wedge gasket needs to be removed first. This will expose the external glazing bead. The beads are removed, leaving the top until last. The unit should then be removed. The new pane should sit on the bottom glazing pack before any other glazing packs are put into place. The glazing beads should be put back in reverse order to the way in which they were removed and clipped into place. On the inside the wedge gasket has to be replaced and then the outside bead locked into place.
External knock-in bead	Internal glazing tape secures one side of the glass and an external bead has been knocked into place.	This is not a common type of system. It needs a deglazing tool. This is placed between the glass and the window frame to release the glazing bead. The process is continued until all the bead has been taken off. On the inside the foam tape needs to be cut to release the pane. A scraper needs to be used to clean out all of the glazing tape, which should then be replaced. Any glazing packs need to be retained or replaced in the same position. The panel can then go in and the glazing beads replaced in the reverse order to which they were removed. They are tapped into place using a glazing mallet.
Internal clip-in bead	This is the simplest system and just has an internal glazing bead, which is clipped into place to hold the panel.	Using a flat scraper on the inside the bead is lifted out and the position of any glazing packs noted. The new pane can then be stood onto the bottom glazing packs and the bead replaced in reverse order from the way it was removed. These are clipped back into the groove in the window frame.
External clip-in bead	A glazing bead with a gasket attached to the inner side holds the pane in place.	A flat scraper is used to prize the glazing bead away from the window frame. You then need to go inside and remove any foam tape. This can be removed by using a knife or a flat scraper. The unit should be removed from the frame from the outside, noting the position of any glazing packs. The glazing tape should be replaced and the new unit sat on the bottom glazing packs. The glazing beads are then replaced in reverse order to the way they were removed.

Table 8.6

Packing toe and heel

In order to ensure that the double-glazed unit is properly positioned within the window frame it is necessary to pack in between the frame and the unit. This ensures that the pane is properly positioned and that any water that gets into the frame will not affect the unit.

The packers are hidden inside the window frame. Seep holes allow any water that does get in to escape.

The term toe and heel refers to packing around the unit at pressure points. These are usually corners. The toe and heel packers are there usually to stop the glass from falling out of the sash or door. The packers brace the pane diagonally, corner to corner. They are slipped into the gap between the glass and the frame under the beading. On the hinge side of a sash or door the packers go into the bottom corner. On the lock side of the sash or door the packers go in at the top or opposite corner. It is usually the case that packing is added to both sides.

Replacing ironmongery

Door ironmongery is sometimes called door furniture and it includes a wide range of different latches, locks, hinges and bolts. In addition to this there are other practical and decorative items, such as letter plates or finger plates.

The following table outlines some of the main different types of ironmongery, although the practical at the end of this section looks at how to replace door and window ironmongery in some detail.

Ironmongery	Description
Handles	Handles can be either left or right handed.
Mortise locks	A mortise lock is a key operated lock. The more levers it has the more secure it becomes.
Latches	There is a wide variety of different latches available. They can be seen in Fig 8.27. The purpose of the latch is to secure the door by a latching mechanism.
Letter plates	A letter plate is usually positioned centrally in a door's width and between 760 and 1,450 mm from the bottom of the door. The position on panelled doors may be different, but they are usually positioned centrally in a rail or vertically on a stile.
Aluminium thresholds	The bottom part of a door or window is known as a threshold. In order to protect this vulnerable part of a door frame they are sometimes fitted with aluminium rather than timber. This is because it is the part of the frame that is most likely to be exposed to long periods of water presence.
Casement stays	A casement stay is a basic locking mechanism for a window. It consists of a length of metal with graduated punched holes fixed to a pivot. The holes fit onto a raised prong, allowing the user to open the window to various amounts, or to lock it in place. It is usually fitted with an additional security key or toggle.
Fasteners	Sash fasteners are designed to hold the meeting rails of a sash window together. Essentially they hold the two sashes in a closed position. At ground level sash windows tend to be fitted with a pair of these.
Hinges	There is a wide variety of different types of hinge, but they all provide the opening and closing action required for doors. A butt hinge is a general purpose hinge that has two leaves joined by a pin that passes through the knuckle. Examples of different types of hinges used for doors can be seen in Fig 8.28.
Sliding door gearing	Lightweight sliding doors have top sliding gearing and heavier doors have bottom sliding gearing. The bottom of the door can be fitted into a channel using a small nylon guide. At the top of the door there will be a track. Sliding doors usually need special locks and latches that have hook-shaped bolts.
Floor spring	A floor spring is a way of controlling the action of a door. The floor spring consists of a box set into the floor at the correct position to the frame. It can determine the delayed closing action of the door.

Table 8.7

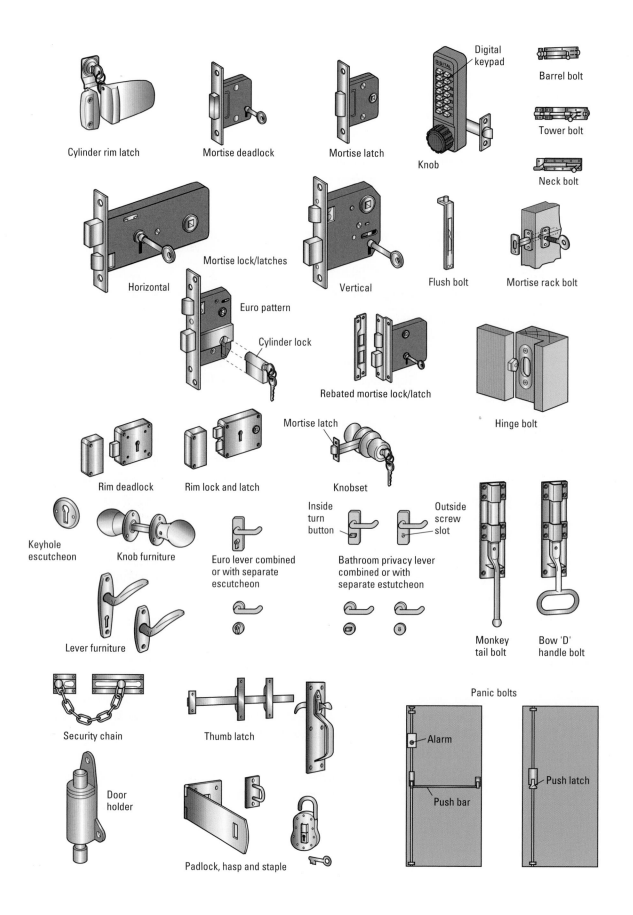

Figure 8.27 Locks, latches and other door furniture

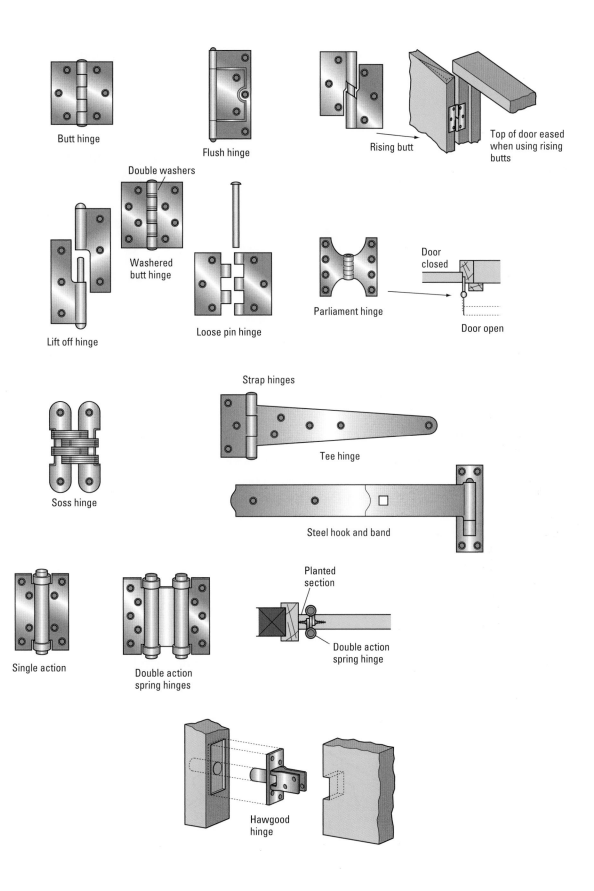

Figure 8.28 Range of hinges for doors

Repairing and replacing guttering and downpipes

Gutters are designed to collect rainwater coming off the roof. It is important to ensure that the gutters are free from debris, as their purpose is to encourage the rainwater to flow along them and into downpipes, or rainwater pipes, as can be seen in the following diagram.

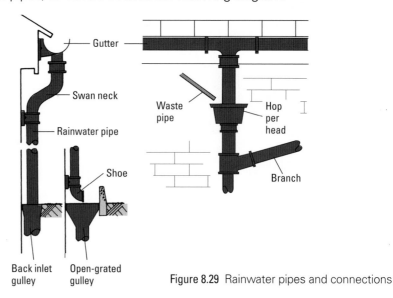

Figure 8.29 Rainwater pipes and connections

Materials used for gutters and downpipes

The majority of modern buildings have plastic gutters and downpipes. However, some in older buildings can be made from cast-iron or aluminium. Older properties may have had their original guttering and rainwater pipe systems replaced with plastic ones. However there are still many buildings (such as listed buildings or those in a town's conservation area), which are required to retain their old systems. This means it is possible to not only come across cast-iron systems but also lead, copper and even asbestos cement. In some of the very oldest buildings gutters were made from solid timber.

Guttering system components

The parts of a guttering system are designed so that they can be fixed together to fit any kind of shape or length required. Some of the fittings are designed to join longer sections together. Other parts are there to end or terminate the gutter, or to support it.

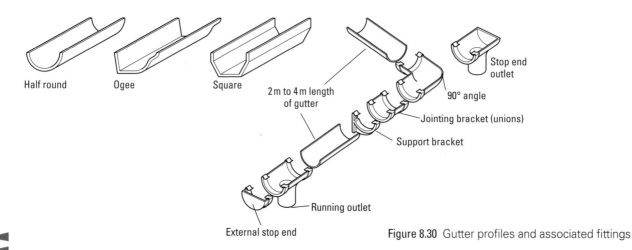

Figure 8.30 Gutter profiles and associated fittings

Gutter component	Description and purpose
Pipe	This refers to the vertical tube that makes up the downpipe.
Shoe	This is a fitting that is used at the bottom of the downpipe is angled to allow the water into the gully or drainage system.
Joint	Each time a component of the gutter or downpipe is connected it is necessary to have a joint or fixing. Many of the components are designed to slot into joints on other components or, if necessary, jointing brackets or unions can be used.
Hopper	This is also known as a hopper head, leader head or conductor head. The rainwater collected by the gutter feeds into the hopper and then passes down the downpipe and into the drain.
Elbow	This is an angled part of the piping. It is attached to the down pipe. An elbow can be square or rounded and it is used to direct water flow.
Offset	This is a pipe that directs a downpipe from the gutter. It runs under the soffit of the eaves and down the wall.
Gutter	This is a semi-circular or other shaped channel that collects the rainwater that falls onto the roof.
Clips	These are used at most joints and connectors to hold the guttering in place. They are usually wing-shaped.
Brackets	These hold the guttering or the downpipe to the building.
Running outlet	This provides an outlet to the downpipe on the length of the guttering. This means that there is guttering at either side of the running outlet.
Stop end	This closes off a run of guttering.
Angled bends	These allow the run of guttering to continue around corners.

Table 8.8

Guttering and downpipe profiles

There are several different styles and shapes of guttering and downpipes. The earliest ones were box-like channels. When metal guttering was introduced the half-round shape became the most common. Today, with new manufacturing techniques, other shapes are possible.

Square

Square gutters and matching downpipes are usually made from plastic. They are available in a variety of colours, including white, brown, grey and black.

Round

Different shaped guttering can be fitted with round downpipes. These are also available in a range of colours and materials, from traditional cast-iron through to lightweight and durable plastics.

Half round

Half round guttering is perhaps the most common type today. It is usually matched with round downpipes.

Ogee

This is a curve that consists of a pair of arcs that bend rather like an 'S' shape. Both of the ends are parallel. It is an old-fashioned style, which was introduced around 150 years ago.

Guttering joints

The ways in which guttering is jointed will depend on the material being used. Metal guttering sections, whether they are made from cast-iron or steel, are sealed at their joints and then bolts are put through for further strength. Over time the bolts can become corroded. Each of the joints will have a layer of roof and gutter sealant and the actual gutter sections overlap. The bolt holds the two sections together.

More modern plastic or PVC guttering fixes together using sections called union pieces. These have a rubber gasket with lips that hold it in place. These can be replaced or new gaskets can be fitted into the joint.

Identifying damage to gutters and downpipes

Leaking gutters are one of the major reasons why there might be isolated damp patches in a building even if it is not immediately obvious that water is leaking from the gutter. If left the water will stain the wall and there is a danger that moss and algae will grow.

Gutters can also overflow because they are blocked by natural debris. This could be moss from the roof, leaves or a bird's nest. Other common reasons for overflowing guttering are objects that have fallen from the roof and into the guttering. The water will spill out over the side of the gutter when there is a blockage.

One way of avoiding many of the problems of debris in gutters is to fit a leaf guard, or plastic grill. These can be purchased to fit most modern guttering, although in older properties chicken wire can be cut and bent to cover the top of the guttering. This would need to be secured with cable ties or wires.

Gutters and downpipes can also suffer damage in extreme weather conditions. If there is a blockage then any trapped water will expand as it freezes. This can cause downpipes to crack or joints to fail. In older properties that have cast-iron downpipes corrosion is another problem.

Metal fittings for both gutters and downpipes over time will corrode and become loose. This will allow movement that could put pressure on joints. Lead and cast-iron downpipes can crack if the protective paint layer breaks down.

Figure 8.31 A gutter with a leaf guard

Figure 8.32 A lead or cast-iron downpipe in poor condition

PRACTICAL TASK

3. INSPECT WINDOWS AND DOORS FOR DEFECTS

OBJECTIVE

To learn how to recognise defects in joinery and buildings.

> #### PPE
>
> Ensure you select PPE appropriate to the job and site where you are working. Refer to the PPE section of Chapter 1. This applies to all the tasks that follow.

When inspecting doors and windows for defects it is essential to have access to the inside of the building. An external survey will not pick up problems with opening and closing of the lights/sashes or missing items of ironmongery. Cracked or faulty glass is also easier to see from inside. However, provided there are some opening sashes, it is normally possible to inspect the outside of a window from inside the building.

Timber opening sashes – distortion and leaking

This typically occurs in older windows but it can happen at any time. It is more likely when joinery is badly maintained, or not adequately treated prior to installation, or when there is a change in the conditions to which the joinery is subjected.

Example of a typical problem

The sash does not sit against the frame on all edges. This can lead to draughts and rain penetration, both of which may be related to certain wind conditions. In extreme cases, the sash or frame is so distorted that the two parts will not fit together. The sash cannot then be properly shut and secured.

INVESTIGATION

STEP 1 Look at the whole building. Distortion caused by structural movement will normally be evident in more than one element. If no structural cracks are obvious, test for the plumbness of the walls with the trueness of floors.

Figure 8.33 Problems with joinery items such as doors and windows can often be attributed to movement within the structure

STEP 2 Is the defect weather related? Note the conditions under which it occurs. Could the defect be due to an air movement 'pulled' from an internal heating appliance, chimney or lift shaft rather than 'pushed' from outside?

STEP 3 Examine the paintwork. Do any runs or drips lead to a build-up of paint on what should be meeting surfaces? Is there cracking or unevenness in the paint film over the joints in the opening sashes?

STEP 4 In new frames, examine other sashes in similar situations to judge whether the components are poorly made or not made to adequate tolerances (purpose-made joinery is more likely to be affected by this problem).

STEP 5 Measure the diagonals of sashes and frames for square. Flex the corner of hinged sashes to test rigidity.

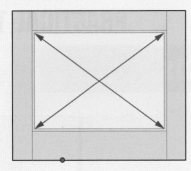

Figure 8.34 Checking the diagonals of sashes and frames

STEP 6 The detailing of the timber sections may be poor – for example there may be inadequate rebates. Throatings may be filled with paint and become ineffective, or there may be insufficient slope on the cill.

Repairs

It is obvious that if any of the problems identified are not solved, then the repair or replacement of the component will not last. It is not always necessary to replace the whole window or door – often a repair will suffice, however, the cause of the damage should always be identified and cured before a repair is carried out.

There are various options other than total replacement, such as repairing through splicing, manufacturing some of the components or replacing some or all of the ironmongery.

4. SPLICING

Splicing is the term used to describe the letting in of a new piece of timber to repair a damaged component, such as a stile on a sash or a jamb on a door. Three variations are described below. Protect the surrounding area with dustsheets if necessary. Rotten timber should be removed from the site immediately and ideally burned. Joinery in the immediate vicinity of the repair that is undamaged should be protected with MDF, plywood, corrugated cardboard or similar to prevent damage.

OBJECTIVE

To learn the practical techniques for replacing damaged timber.

METHOD 1

This could be used on the top or bottom of a door stile, window jamb or a window cill and many other applications.

STEP 1 Mark out the area to be replaced using a 45° combination square. The repair is angled to act as a key for the new timber. Mark the depth of the repair along its length using a marking gauge.

STEP 2 Remove the damaged area using a tenon or panel saw and/or chisel as required, working back to the gauge lines.

STEP 3 Cut the new piece of timber slightly longer, wider and thicker than the recess in the component.

STEP 4 Treat the area being repaired with a suitable timber preservative.

STEP 5 Drill and countersink the repair piece and fix using glue and screws.

STEP 6 Dress the spliced timber to the component size using planes.

STEP 7 Use filler and a filler knife to fill the screw holes and any minor gaps in the repair. Leave the filler to set.

STEP 8 Sand the repair to a smooth finish.

STEP 9 Apply a primer coat, two undercoats and gloss to finish.

METHOD 2

This method can be adopted when a repair is towards the centre of a component.

STEP 1 Mark the area to be removed with 2 × 45° angles, then mark the depth along the length of the repair with a marking gauge.

STEP 2 Remove the damaged area by making the 2 × 45° cuts down to the gauge lines. Then make a series of intermediate cuts, again down to the gauge lines.

STEP 3 Chop out the recess using a sharp bevel-edged chisel; this should be the widest chisel that the work will allow.

STEP 4 Mark the new piece of timber that is to be spliced in. This should be the exact length at the narrowest points between the mitres and slightly wider and deeper than the recess. Cut using a tenon saw.

STEP 5 Treat the area being repaired with a suitable timber preservative. Drill and countersink the repair piece and fix using glue and screws, then dress the spliced timber to the component size using planes. Sand the repair to a smooth finish.

STEP 6 Apply a primer coat, two undercoats and gloss to finish.

METHOD 3

This is similar to both Methods 1 and 2 but differs in that the repair does not extend on to both faces of the component.

STEP 1 Mark out as in Methods 1 or 2; use a marking gauge to mark both the depth and the width of the splice in this instance.

STEP 2 Make a series of angular cuts to the gauge lines; this includes the 45° cuts.

STEP 3 Using a sharp bevel-edged chisel remove the waste in two directions, feather the recess before removing the waste across the grain.

STEP 4 Mark out and cut a new piece as for previous methods.

STEP 5 Follow Steps 5 and 6 in Method 2.

Manufacture replacement timber sections

When carrying out maintenance it is not always possible to repair existing sections of joinery items, and in these circumstances it will be necessary to manufacture a new section, which could be a new rail, stile or cill etc. With basic hand and power tools it is possible to produce a replacement part that is fit for purpose while on site. There are occasions when this is not possible and careful site measurements should be taken and the sections produced off site in a workshop environment.

REPLACE DOOR AND WINDOW IRONMONGERY

The process of replacing ironmongery often simply involves unscrewing the component and replacing with a new part. There are, however, considerations prior to starting work as follows.

> **STEP 1** Is the component repairable?

> **STEP 2** Is the same component available in the same size or finish? If not, are the fixing points in the same position on the replacement as on the original?

> **STEP 3** When replacing locks, the insurance rating of the lock must be considered. How many levers does the original lock have? What is the depth of the lock? What is the measurement to the spindle?

PRACTICAL TIP

It is essential to gather as much information as possible when 'measuring up' to reduce the amount of work required when fitting replacement components.

PRACTICAL TASK

5. REPLACING IRONMONGERY

OBJECTIVE

To learn the techniques for replacing ironmongery on doors and windows.

> **STEP 1** Unscrew the damaged piece of ironmongery.

> **STEP 2** If required splice in a new piece of timber.

> **STEP 3** If the replacement item is a different size, shape or style it may be necessary to fill the screw holes from the original.

> **STEP 4** Rub down with glass paper.

> **STEP 5** Prime and paint the surface.

> **STEP 6** Fix the new piece of ironmongery.

Maintain structural timbers

The first thing to consider when replacing or repairing structural timbers is how to avoid collapse of the structure. In some instances a structural engineer may be required to carry out a survey and produce calculations of the forces imposed on the structure. A detailed method statement will be produced explaining how the work is to be carried out successfully without collapse or injury to operatives.

The following is an example of how to replace damaged or rotten floor joists. Most of these steps can be applied to the replacement of other structural timbers.

PRACTICAL TASK

6. REPLACE FIRST-FLOOR JOISTS

OBJECTIVE

To learn the practical techniques for replacing floor joists in this and the tasks that follow.

Note: A structural engineer must provide guidance before any structural work is undertaken.

PRACTICAL TIP

A structural engineer or temporary works co-ordinator must provide guidance for the work undertaken in Step 5. They may provide a temporary works design for you to follow.

STEP 1 Carefully survey the work, considering all drawings and the method statement.

STEP 2 Identify any plant and equipment that will be required to complete the work.

STEP 3 If possible ensure all materials are on site prior to work starting. Structural work should be carried out in the shortest time that is realistic and safe.

STEP 4 Ensure that all services that will be affected by the work are located and isolated.

STEP 5 It may be necessary to support the existing floor joists before the floorcovering is removed. This can be done using dead shores. External walls may sometimes need supporting. This can be done from the outside using a series of raking shores. A temporary work sign may be required.

PRACTICAL TIP

The propping of structural timbers should only be carried out by competent operatives and should be done in accordance with a strict method statement, risk assessment and health and safety legislation. Once the floor is shored the work can begin to remove the defective joists.

STEP 6 In order to support first floor joists it may be necessary to cut holes into the ground floor covering between the ground floor joists to allow the adjustable props to sit on to the over-site concrete. If the first floor above is deemed unsafe, some form of support will have to be rigged to allow the main support work to continue. This could include propping up the lower floor using scaffold planks to spread the load.

STEP 7 If it is safe to do so the ceiling should be removed at this stage. If the floor is deemed to be too unstable this should be left until the floor is supported.

STEP 8 The number of props will depend on the length of the joists and the number of joists that require support. The joists require support at both ends and in some instances mid-span support. Set the height of the props to the height of the room less the head timber.

STEP 9 Place the props and wind upwards until they trap the head timber against the underside of the joists. The ceiling may still be in place at this stage. Use a level to keep the props plumb. Secure the props to the head timber by nailing through the flat plates at the top. 100mm round-headed nails are ideal; these should be partially driven in and bent over.

STEP 10 Nail the head timber to the joists, leaving the heads clear to allow them to be withdrawn later.

STEP 11 Take down the ceiling if this has not already been done. Some of the ceiling will still be trapped between the head timber and the underside of the floor joists; this will not affect the removal of the floor joists.

STEP 12 Use a circular saw/jig saw, nail bar and claw hammer to remove the floor covering.

STEP 13 Cut through the first defective joist about 600 mm from both ends, removing the central section, which takes weight of the props. It will be necessary to remove the nails holding the head piece to the joist.

STEP 14 The short ends of joist may pull out of the brickwork; however, they may need to be carefully chopped out using a lump hammer and bolster. Care should be taken to damage as little of the surrounding brickwork as possible.

STEP 15 Repeat Step 13 until all defective joists are removed. Remove the shores as the work progresses.

PRACTICAL TASK

7. FIXING THE NEW JOISTS

The new joists should be of the correct structural grade, which will be specified on the drawings and in the specification. If not, stop work and ask.

STEP 1 Measure and cut the new joists.

STEP 2 Treat the ends of the new joists with a suitable preservative.

STEP 3 The pockets in the brickwork will need to be widened at one end of the joist to allow the joist to be put in on an angle. In some circumstances it may be necessary to cut holes in the external brickwork to feed the joist through from the outside of the building.

STEP 4 Place the new joists into the holes, making sure they are not sticking into the cavity at the ends.

STEP 5 Level the joists using slate to pack the joist ends.

STEP 6 Make good the brick or blockwork around the joists.

STEP 7 Fix strutting and perimeter noggins.

STEP 8 Relay the floor covering.

STEP 9 Plasterboard the ceiling.

STEP 10 Make good the ground floor.

STEP 11 Plaster the ceiling and make good the plasterwork on the walls.

PRACTICAL TIP

When working on the maintenance, repair and renewal of structural timbers it is of paramount importance to make the structure safe. The method used above is one example, but for other structural timbers such as purlins or rafters the methodology will require a slightly different approach. However, the basic rules will remain the same. If in doubt always seek expert advice.

Repairing structural timbers

The method of splicing structural timbers is very similar to the techniques used for repairs to windows frames, doors and other joinery items, albeit on a much larger scale. Support and access to these timbers are often much more problematic. Adopt correct methods of temporary support and ensure there is safe access.

PRACTICAL TASK

8. SPLICING ROOFING COMPONENTS

STEP 1 It may be necessary to expose the roofing components. To do this a scaffold must be erected; this must be carried out by a competent scaffolder.

STEP 2 Identify the damaged components, and remove the tiles or slates from around the damaged timber.

STEP 3 Cut the tile battens back around the damaged timber and remove the roofing felt if applicable.

STEP 4 Make the repair using a suitable splicing technique. The method of repair will be dictated by its location.

STEP 5 Treat the repair and the surrounding area with a suitable preservative and replace the roofing felt, making sure that overlaps are correct.

STEP 6 Measure, cut and fix replacement tile battens.

STEP 7 Replace slates or tiles.

Working from access equipment

All health and safety legislation must be complied with before any work at height is started. Only qualified card-holding operatives can erect putlog or independent scaffolding. A permit must be issued to commission the scaffold. For work of short duration, such as in maintenance operations, tower scaffolds are often used and all manufacturers' instructions should be followed when using this type of equipment. Tower scaffolds are not suitable to be loaded with heavy materials such as slates and are strictly access platforms.

PRACTICAL TASK

9. MAINTAIN JOIST COVERINGS

Removing damaged floor or flat roof coverings

TOOLS AND EQUIPMENT

Bolster	Panel saw
Lump hammer	Floorboard saw
Nail bar	Portable circular saw
Claw hammer	Floorboard clamps

PPE

Ensure you select PPE appropriate to the job and site where you are working. Refer to the PPE section of Chapter 1.

REPLACE DAMAGED TONGUE AND GROOVE FLOORBOARDS OR FLAT ROOF COVERINGS

STEP 1 Check that all services are identified and turned off. Set the depth of the circular saw to the thickness of the boards to be removed.

STEP 2 Run the circular saw along the length of the joint between the boards. The saw will have to be plunged to the depth required. Alternatively saw through the tongue using a floorboard saw.

STEP 3 Use a lump hammer and a broad chiselled bolster to ease up the back of the first board.

STEP 4 Use a nail bar to work along the joint, lifting the back edge of the board. Use a short end of scrap timber as a lever and also to prevent damage to any flooring that is to remain.

STEP 5 Now use the nail bar to lever off the floor joists to remove the board.

STEP 6 Remove all remaining damaged boards by working along each board, levering off the top of the joists.

STEP 7 De-nail the tops of the joists using either a claw hammer or nail bar.

STEP 8 Remove all floorboards.

PRACTICAL TASK

10. CONSTRUCTING INSPECTION TRAPS IN FLOOR COVERINGS

It is often necessary to form inspection/access traps into floors to provide a means to install services and repair utilities such as water, gas and electrics.

FORMING INSPECTION TRAPS IN TONGUED AND GROOVED FLOOR BOARDING

STEP 1 Check that all services are identified and turned off. Determine position and size of trap.

STEP 2 Cut through the floor boards between joists.

STEP 3 Cut through the tongue of a floorboard along the length of the board between the first two cuts.

STEP 4 Lift the floorboards out of the opening.

STEP 5 Fix 50 mm × 25 mm battens on to the sides of the joists. These should extend beyond the edges of the opening under the floor at both sides.

STEP 6 Screw 50 mm × 25 mm bearers to the underside of the floorboards to join them together.

STEP 7 Screw access panel into position, ensuring that the boards are flush with the surrounding floor.

FORMING INSPECTION TRAPS IN SHEET MATERIALS

STEP 1 Check that all services are identified and turned off. Determine the size and position of the trap.

STEP 2 Cut through the flooring between the joists.

STEP 3 Cut returns at 90° to first cuts to form a square or rectangular opening.

STEP 4 Screw 50 mm × 25 mm timber battens to the sides of the joists, extending past the length of the opening.

STEP 5 Fix 50 mm × 50 mm noggins between the battens; these should sit under the ends of the opening by 25 mm.

STEP 6 Screw the trap in position; ensure that the screws are below the surface and that the trap sits flush with the surrounding floor.

REPLACING GLAZING

It may sometimes be necessary for carpenters or joiners to re-glaze panes. In most cases the glass can be cut by the supplier to size. This requires accurate measurement by measuring the rebate size and then ordering the glass 3 mm undersized in both directions.

If it is necessary to cut glass then this should be done on a flat surface. Score the glass with a glass-cutting wheel and then put a matchstick at either side of the score mark at each end of the glass. If you apply a little pressure it will snap.

Always wear appropriate PPE when cutting glass, such as thick gloves and eye protection.

> **PRACTICAL TIP**
> Whenever you are cutting glass do NOT try to cut very narrow strips. Always make sure that you have gloves and eye protection.

Different types of glass and how to safely remove it

There are various different types of glass, which are briefly described in the following table.

Type of glass	Description
Toughened	Toughened glass is designed to be resistant to breakage. It has a broad application and is widely used for windows and glass sliding doors. It breaks in a predictable way and crumbles rather than shatters. In some areas and at certain heights toughened glass is required in order to comply with Building Regulations. This is particularly true for glass on staircases and in bathrooms.
Laminated	This is made up of two or more layers of glass. The layers are held together by a polymer. The polymer layers hold the glass together if the glass breaks. This means it has a huge range of different applications and is in widespread use in construction.
Double-glazed units	For many years double-glazed units had standard clear glass but this is now being replaced with more efficient materials. Modern glass is more thermally efficient. Any new units have to be given this type of glass in order to comply with Building Regulations. When sealed units are replaced they are now being switched to this type of glass. The only problem is that there is a slight tint, which means that they do not easily match other glass in the structure.

Table 8.9

The first stage is to remove the broken pane of glass. If it is possible then casements or sashes should be removed to allow this and the whole repair to take place at ground level.

If you are forced to carry out the work at high level then it is a necessary precaution to ensure that nobody can access the area directly below your working position. Also ensure you are working from a suitable working platform - not a ladder

You should wear goggles and, ideally, long gloves or gauntlets to protect not only your hands but also your wrists and lower arms. There are likely to be small shards of glass and this is particularly true when you get to the point of removing fragments inside the rebates.

You should start at the top of the pane and use either a wood chisel or hacking knife to remove putty or glazing beads. You will need a pair of pliers to remove the small, flat or square nails, known as glazing sprigs. You should then be able to take out the glass using a wood chisel. The procedure can be seen in the following diagram.

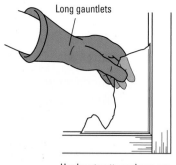

Hack out putty and remove loose pieces of glass

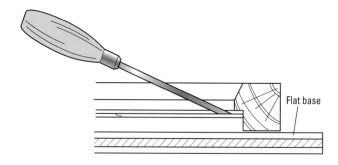

Lever out remaining glass

Figure 8.35 Remove existing glazing

Disposing of glass

Do not put glass in the general waste. Small amounts of sheet or window glass can be taken to household waste recycling centres.

Larger amounts of glass are classed as being construction waste and need to be taken to a waste transfer station.

An entirely new industry has been developing over the past few years to process glass. It is now used to manufacture bricks for water filtration and a host of other applications, including of course the manufacture of new glass.

Securing glass into frames

There are different ways of re-glazing and fixing the glass, dependent on the original method used. Ideally you should use the same method that is present in the other windows or panes. Generally you should:

* test fit or measure the pane to see if it is the right size

* prime the rebates with paint if appropriate

* put in a bead of putty at the back of the rebate

* insert plastic seating blocks at the bottom of the rebate (these will support the glass)

* put in the glass and gently push it into the rebate. You are looking for a 1 mm to 2 mm thickness of putty at the back

* tap in glazing sprigs to secure the glass. You can use either a pin hammer or the edge of a firmer chisel

* apply a bead of putty around the rebate to the front of the glass

* replace the glazing beads

* trim off surplus putty and bedding putty

* clean the glass.

A more detailed step-by-step guide to replacing glazing can be found in the following practical task.

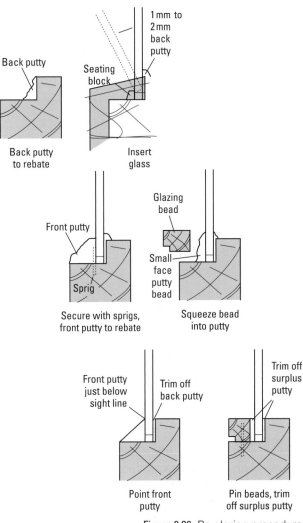

Figure 8.36 Re-glazing procedure

PRACTICAL TASK

11. REPLACE BROKEN GLASS

OBJECTIVE

To safely replace broken glass.

PPE

Ensure you select PPE appropriate to the job and site where you are working. Refer to the PPE section of Chapter 1. This applies to all the tasks that follow.

TOOLS AND EQUIPMENT

Claw hammer	Putty knife
25 mm bevel-edged chisel	Pincers
	Dust sheets
Hacking knife	
	Brush and shovel
Pin hammer	
	Glass cutter

STEP 1 The area around the broken glass should be cordoned off to prevent general access.

STEP 2 Assess the damage. Is any piece of the broken pane in immediate danger of falling from the frame or sash, with the potential to cause harm? If so, remove this immediately, very carefully, while wearing all relevant PPE. If this is too dangerous push them out from a distance using either a sweeping brush or a long length of timber.

PRACTICAL TIP

The removal of glass should always be undertaken in a controlled manner.

STEP 3 Starting at the top, remove the old putty with a hacking knife and claw hammer. Remove any loose pieces as the work progresses. It may be necessary to tap the glass with the handle of the claw hammer to loosen it from the back of the rebate.

PRACTICAL TIP

It is dangerous to place glass in with the general waste. Throw the glass in a skip if one is available or remove from site to the local waste recycling centre where there will be a skip set aside for glass.

STEP 4 Dispose of the glass in a responsible manner.

STEP 5 After removing the glass, clean the rebate of all the old putty using the hacking knife, claw hammer and a sharp chisel. Remove any old glazing sprigs with a pair of pincers.

STEP 6 Sand the rebate and prime with a quick drying undercoat/primer. On metal window frames the rebate may need treating with a rust inhibitor.

STEP 7 If the glass has not been ordered in advance, measure the opening both in length and width and deduct between 3 and 6mm from both measurements. In smaller pieces of glass, 3mm clearance will be sufficient; however in larger pieces the clearance should be increased to around 6mm. Check the diagonals of the opening for square.

For fitting glass go to Step 13.

CUTTING GLASS ON SITE

STEP 8 Place the glass on a flat surface.

STEP 9 Measure the length of the glass and place a straight edge across the glass, setting it back by the thickness of the glass cutter.

STEP 10 Run your index finger down the straight edge on the face of the glass.

STEP 11 Hold the glass cutter at 90° between your index and middle fingers. Use your thumb to support the back of the cutter. Run the cutter along the straight edge, applying a consistent pressure throughout the cut.

STEP 12 Lift the glass and place matchsticks or pencils under it at both ends of the cut. Use a firm pressure to break the glass. Repeat the process for the width.

FITTING THE GLASS

STEP 13 Open the putty and take a generous handful. Work the putty like dough, kneading it until it is workable.

STEP 14 Run a bead of putty into the rebate all around the frame, using your finger and thumb.

STEP 15 Push the glass into the frame, making sure that it is centralised. Ensure that it is evenly bedded into the putty by applying pressure around the edges of the pane.

STEP 16 Use a pin hammer to tap in glazing sprigs evenly spaced on all edges of the glass. These should be lower than the depth of the rebate. Panel pins will suffice in the absence of sprigs. These will hold the glass in place while the putty hardens. (You cannot use springs in metal frames.)

PRACTICAL TIP

When knocking in sprigs or panel pins rest the hammer head on the glass, to reduce the risk of breaking the glass.

STEP 17 Work more putty and run it into the rebate on the outside of the glass.

STEP 18 Use a putty knife to form an angled bead all around the frame. This should be in line with the depth of the rebate. Rest the knife on the edge of the frame to make the bead parallel. Carefully form a mitre in the corner. The putty finish can be smoothed with a small amount of water applied to the putty knife when finishing the putty level.

STEP 19 Remove excess putty inside and out.

STEP 20 Allow the putty to harden before applying paint finish.

REMOVING AND REPLACING TIMBER GLAZING BEADS

STEP 1 Place a chisel in the centre of the longest bead and carefully prise the bead from the rebate and gradually work the chisel along the length of the bead until it is free. Repeat for the opposite bead.

STEP 2 Remove the two shorter beads in the same way.

STEP 3 The glass is then removed in the same way as for putty pointing.

STEP 4 Re-glaze following Steps 13 to 15 above.

STEP 5 Apply a small bead of putty into the rebate on the face of the glass.

STEP 6 Push the shorter beads into place and fix with oval nails.

STEP 7 Bend the longer beads into position and allow them to snap into position. Push them flush with the shorter beads and fix with oval nails.

STEP 8 Punch the nails below the surface and fill using a little putty. Use a putty knife to trim all excess putty inside and out.

REMOVING GLASS BEDDED IN GLAZING TAPE

STEP 1 Remove left, right and bottom glazing beads.

STEP 2 Run a utility knife down the rebate between the glass and the glazing tape and gradually ease out the glass. This will usually be a double-glazed unit when glazing tape has been used.

STEP 3 Remove the top bead and lift the unit out.

STEP 4 Remove the glazing tape from the rebate using a sharp chisel, taking care not to damage the rebate.

STEP 5 Lightly sand the rebate.

STEP 6 Use scissors to cut glazing tape to length and apply to the back of the rebate, do not overlap the tape in the corners, leave a gap of 2 or 3 mm.

STEP 7 Strip the paper from the face of the strip and apply silicone to the gaps in the corners where the tape meets.

STEP 8 Place spacer blocks in the bottom of the rebate and lift the unit into place, making sure that the unit is central and place spacers in each edge.

STEP 9 Fill the gap around the frame with silicone.

STEP 10 There are two methods of beading the glass:

Method 1: Push the two shortest beads into the silicone and fix, snap in the two longest and fix.

Method 2: Apply glazing tape to the back of the beads and fix as above. This is a little trickier to execute.

STEP 11 Trim the glazing tape inside and out with a utility knife.

STEP 12 Apply a thin bead of clear silicone over the glazing tape. This should just touch the glass and the beads.

PRACTICAL TIP

When you are working on older properties the bricks will be imperial sized. The new metric sizes are smaller. New bricks can be bought in imperial sizes. To find bricks to match, you could try a reclaimed building materials specialist but if this is not possible metric bricks can be used with slightly enlarged mortar joints.

REINSTATING SURFACES

Carpenters and joiners may often be required to perform other maintenance duties and will be expected to have a wide range of skills. They may need to carry out minor brickwork, plaster and tiling repairs.

Preparing old surfaces for remedial work and reinstating surfaces

There are several different types of surface and this section looks at how to carry out remedial work on each of them.

Repairs to damaged bricks and blocks

The first thing to do is to try to ensure that any pattern, size or make of brick or block is matched. It is just as important to match the existing mortar as well. It is often a good idea to take a small piece of brick to a supplier to help them identify the precise type.

Bricks and blocks can be removed using a bolster and club hammer. The ideal is to cut out the old brick and then clean away the old mortar joints. You should clean off any remaining mortar or debris with a soft brush.

The next stage is to cut the new brick to size. You can score around the old brick using a bolster and club hammer and use that line as a guide to cut the brick. The mortar mix should usually be 1:6 but trial mixes should be made using different proportions, sand grades and lime (if applicable) to ensure you match the existing mortar. Repairs to pre-1919 buildings must be allowed to breathe. You are looking for a mix that has the consistency of softened butter. A bed of mortar should be put into the hole and then mortar applied to the top edge of the brick. The brick can then be put into place and excess mortar removed.

Any gaps in the mortar joints should then be filled. As the mortar begins to harden the joint should be raked out. It may be necessary to repoint the joints with the mortar mix to match the colour of the rest of the jointing.

PRACTICAL TIP

If you are working on pre-1919 buildings, remember that they need to breathe. The materials you use should allow for this. After 1919 the mortar would be made from Portland cement and sand.

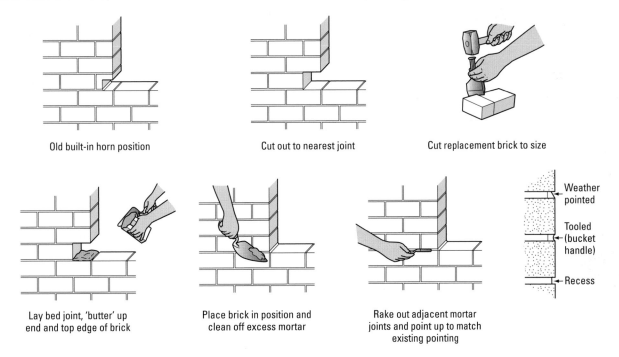

Old built-in horn position

Cut out to nearest joint

Cut replacement brick to size

Lay bed joint, 'butter' up end and top edge of brick

Place brick in position and clean off excess mortar

Rake out adjacent mortar joints and point up to match existing pointing

Weather pointed

Tooled (bucket handle)

Recess

Figure 8.37 Replacing a brick

Plasterwork

Many brick and block walls have a plastered finish, which usually consists of two layers. There is a fairly thick 9 to 12 mm backing coat and then a thinner 2 to 3 mm finishing coat.

The first thing to do is to protect the surrounding area using a dustsheet and then follow a clear procedure to deal with the damaged area of plasterwork, as can be seen in Fig 8.38.

Hack off existing loose plaster

Brush off to remove dust and loose particles

Damp down with water

Mix plaster in a bucket

Scoop up plaster from hawk and apply to wall in an upward sweep

Reinforce large areas with repair mesh or scrim

Comb or scratch area to provide a key

Brush off and apply finishing plaster

Rule off using a sideways sawing action, working upwards

Trowel up to a smooth finish

Repeat trowelling up while splashing with water

Figure 8.38 Patching plasterwork

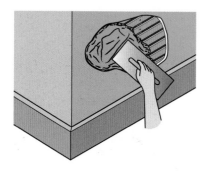

Figure 8.39 Patching a hole in a lath and plaster partition

You can tap around the damaged area to hear whether it is hollow or loose. Use a club hammer and bolster to take off any loose plaster. Extend the cutting until you are sure that you are now up against solid plaster. Be careful – there could be hidden services.

Brush off any remaining dust or loose particles. Dampen the exposed area with water. The new plaster is applied using an upward sweep. Once the hole in the plaster has been filled, you can reinforce it with repair mesh or scrim. You should then comb or scratch the area to provide a key for the finishing plaster.

Lath and plaster

The same procedure can be followed when dealing with lath and plaster partitions but use a knife to cut around the loose area and a wire brush to remove any loose particles that are around the laths and studs. The exposed area should then be dampened with water. Apply a coat of backing plaster, making sure that some of the plaster is forced between the laths. When this has started to set scratch the surface to provide a key for the finishing coat. Use only like-for-like materials, tools and techniques. Old buildings need to breathe.

Plasterboard

Small holes in plasterboard can be easily dealt with, as can be seen in the following diagram.

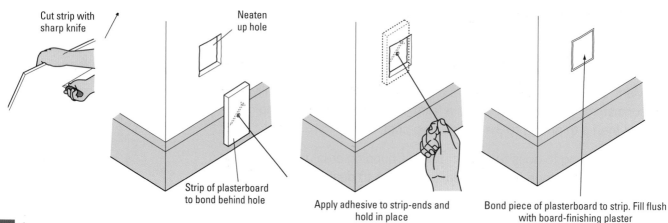

Cut strip with sharp knife

Neaten up hole

Strip of plasterboard to bond behind hole

Apply adhesive to strip-ends and hold in place

Bond piece of plasterboard to strip. Fill flush with board-finishing plaster

Figure 8.40 Patching small holes in partition walls

Neaten the edges of the hole using either a knife or a pad saw. A small strip of plasterboard, cut so that the width is narrower than the hole but about 1.5 times the size of the hole in length, is prepared. Make a hole in the middle and push a piece of string through the hole, knotting it onto a nail. Mix some plasterboard adhesive and apply it to both ends of the strip. Push the strip into the hole and use the string to pull it tight against the face of the hole. Then tie off the string to a scrap of timber over the face of the hole.

Once the adhesive has set you can cut the string. Prepare another piece of plasterboard that fits the hole and stick it in place using adhesive.

Larger holes in plasterboard may require additional support. This is particularly true if there are holes in plasterboard ceilings. The procedures for dealing with this can be seen in Fig 8.41.

Note that when dealing with larger holes it is important to square the damage off between the joists. The joists will act as the main support for the battens and noggins that will hold up the plasterboard.

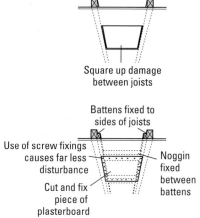

Figure 8.41 Repairing large holes in plasterboard

Stone

Any loose, flaking or unstable material needs to be removed using either a bolster and club hammer or a stiff brush and broad-bladed scraper. The material needs to be removed until you have reached a sound edge. Watch out for hidden services.

When you are replacing stonework carefully measure any replacement stone blocks or pieces by dry-fitting them first. Once you are happy with the fit then wet the gap in the stonework and the stone replacement to encourage them to bond using fillers or sealers. Depending on the type of stone and the age of the building, you can use acrylic, resin or gypsum-based fillers. In older buildings it is important not to use modern non-vapour permeable plaster systems.

Removing old tiles and fixing new ones

It is very difficult to find identical replacements for older types of tiles and it is not usually possible to do anything to damaged tiles to make good. Sometimes the customer may have spare tiles. The only other alternative is to visit a tile supplier to see if they have a match.

In order to remove the old tiles you need to follow a series of procedures, which are illustrated in Fig 8.42.

Wearing goggles, gloves and a dust mask, cover the surrounding area with a dust sheet. You should then rake out the joints around the tile. You can drill a series of holes in the centre of the tile and break out the centre using a chisel. Using this hole you can then work your way around the tile and remove it. You will then need to scrape or chip off any remaining tile adhesive.

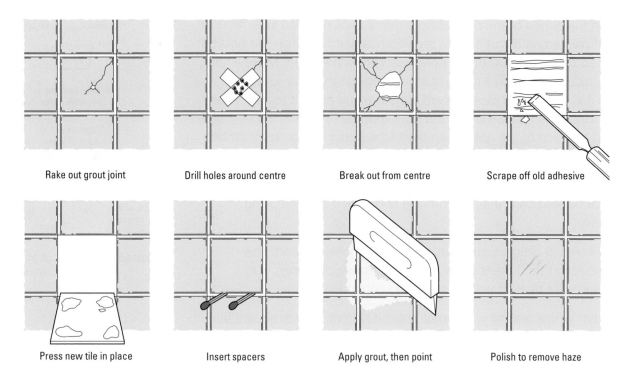

Rake out grout joint

Drill holes around centre

Break out from centre

Scrape off old adhesive

Press new tile in place

Insert spacers

Apply grout, then point

Polish to remove haze

Figure 8.42 Replacing a damaged tile

Select the new tile and give it four dabs of tile adhesive, one in each corner, or use a notched cone to give it a ribbed layer of adhesive. The tile then needs to be pressed into place and matchsticks or tile spacers pushed into the joints to support the tile. You should leave the tile for 24 hours before taking out the spacers.

The gaps around the tile are then filled with grout. You can point the joint using a grouting tool or a small, wooden dowel.

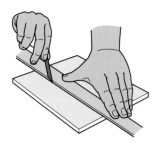

It may be necessary to cut the tiles. You can use a tile cutter, a diamond tipped wet saw or a carbon tipped tile cutting point. All that is necessary using the tile cutting point is to score the tile's surface. You then put a match under each end of the scored line and press down. The tile should snap, as can be seen in the following diagram.

If you are required to replace tiles immediately above worktops, baths or sinks, then you will need to seal the joints with a silicone sealant. The following diagram shows how this is achieved.

Remember that you should fix masking tape to either side of your sealant line and use a cartridge gun to give you a consistent bead to fill the joint.

Maintain surface finishes

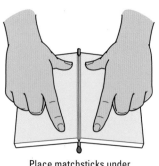

Place matchsticks under score, press down to snap tile in two

Figure 8.43 Cutting ceramic tiles

Wall and floor tiles are often ceramic or porcelain and they will splinter in a similar way to glass. It is essential, therefore, to ensure all relevant PPE is worn. Some older tiles may contain asbestos and a risk assessment should be carried out if this is a possibility.

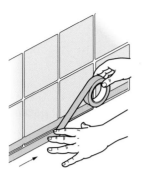

Apply masking tape
along angle to be sealed

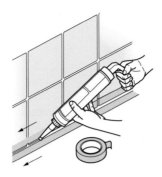

Push the cartridge nozzle
along the angle

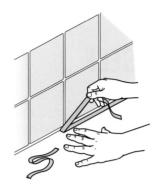

Allow sealant to skin
over, peel off tape

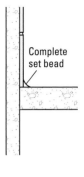

Complete
set bead

Figure 8.44 Sealing tiles to a worktop

PRACTICAL TASK

12. REPLACE BROKEN OR CRACKED WALL TILES

OBJECTIVE

To safely replace wall tiles to fit with the surrounding tiles.

PPE

Ensure you select PPE appropriate to the job and site where you are working. Refer to the PPE section of Chapter 1.

TOOLS AND EQUIPMENT

Cordless drill

Masonry bit

Bolster chisel

Adhesive

Tile spacers or matchsticks

Grout

STEP 1 Use a cordless drill and a masonry bit to drill a series of holes in the tile close to the centre.

STEP 2 Using a small bolster chisel and a hammer, chop out the broken tile or tiles; work from the centre outwards. This will reduce the chances of damaging the surrounding tiles.

STEP 3 Strip off any old tile adhesive or mortar that remains on the wall.

STEP 4 Test fit the new tile to ensure that it will sit flush and that there is sufficient room behind the tile to allow a bed of adhesive or mortar.

STEP 5 Apply a suitable adhesive to the background surface following the manufacturer's instructions.

STEP 6 Fix the new tile, space off the existing tiles using proprietary spacers or matchsticks.

STEP 7 Allow the adhesive to set.

STEP 8 Re-grout to match existing grouting.

TEST YOURSELF

1. Which type of nail is designed so that it can be driven in with the upper head remaining proud?

   a. Lost head

   b. Cut

   c. Wire clout

   d. Duplex

2. Which type of screw head is ideal for use as a dry wall screw for fixing plasterboard?

   a. Bugle

   b. Raised

   c. Round

   d. Pan

3. How should you dispose of broken or used glass?

   a. Put it in the general waste

   b. Wrap it up and leave it next to the general waste

   c. Put it in a skip or take it to be recycled

   d. Ask a specialist to remove it

4. Which structural roofing timber sits at the apex or uppermost part of the roof?

   a. Hip rafter

   b. Valley rafter

   c. Rafter

   d. Ridge board

5. For wet rot to thrive, what is the minimum moisture content in the timber?

   a. Less than 12 per cent

   b. Between 12 and 20 per cent

   c. Over 24 per cent

   d. Over 60 per cent

6. Where would you find toe and heel packing in a double-glazed unit?

   a. At the bottom

   b. At the top

   c. At the side

   d. At pressure points

7. What is a casement stay?

   a. A locking mechanism for a window

   b. A reinforcing strip for a window

   c. A moisture resistant layer around a window

   d. An air brick positioned close to a window

8. In guttering, what is the purpose of an offset?

   a. It closes off the run of the guttering

   b. It is a joint

   c. It directs a downpipe from the gutter

   d. It is a bracket

9. In laminated glass what is between the layers of glass?

   a. Polymer

   b. Adhesive

   c. Reflective transparent metal

   d. A tinting layer

10. If you are removing a broken tile, where should you begin drilling?

    a. One of the corners

    b. In the centre

    c. On the left edge

    d. On the right edge

INDEX

A

access traps
  floor coverings 147–8, 338–9
  services 183
  tongued and grooved floor boarding 148
accident books 2, 9, 17
accident procedures 8–13
alternative building methods, sustainability 96–8
alternative energy sources, energy conservation 102–4
architraves 219, 220–3
  scribe architraves 222–3
asbestos, Control of Asbestos at Work Regulations 3
assembly drawings 44
assembly points 34

B

bath panels 184
bills of quantities, planning 66
biodegradable materials, sustainability 98
biodiversity, sustainability 93
bird's mouths, trussed rafter roofs 263
biscuit jointers 237
biscuits, cutting and shaping machinery 252
block plans 42
Building Regulations
  energy conservation 100, 105
  insulation 105
  stairs 161
built environment
  activities 78–9
  client types 81
  roles and responsibilities 81–3
  work types 80
built-in frames, door frames 130, 135–6

C

carbon content, energy sources 101–2
carbon footprint, sustainability 94
charts, planning 67–9
chimney stacks, trussed rafter roofs 263
cladding, second fixing operations 176, 178–9
climate change, sustainability 95–6
colour coded cables, electricity 31
combustible materials 18, 34–6
common rafters, roofs 288–9
communication, good working practices 74–5
competent (individuals/organisations) 4
conductive materials 247
confidence, good working practices 74
construction industry
  activities 78–9
  client types 81
  roles and responsibilities 81–3
  work types 80
construction projects
  benefits 88–92
  land types 88–91

physical and environmental factors 84–7
  social benefits 91–2
contamination 18, 19
Control of Asbestos at Work Regulations 3
Control of Substances Hazardous to Health Regulations (COSHH) 2, 3, 20
cornices 219
COSHH see Control of Substances Hazardous to Health Regulations
costing materials 62–3
  see also pricing work
creosote 323
cripple rafters, roofs 296–7
cutting and shaping machinery 233–54
  bench saws 237
  biscuit jointers 237
  biscuits 252
  blades, changing 242–3
  chop saws 237, 250
  circular saws 237, 238, 244, 248–9
  cross-cut saws 249
  cutting lists 246
  drills 237
  dust extraction 247
  hazards 234–5
  jig saws 237, 251
  jigs 241
  legislation 235–6
  machinery guards 244
  machines and components 237–40
  maintaining and cleaning 244–6
  manufacturers' instructions 235–6
  mortisers 237
  personal protective equipment (PPE) 236–7
  planers 237
  pre-operational checks 241
  riving knives 244
  routers 237, 253
  safety aids 240–1
  sanders 237
  setting up 242–6
  waste disposal 247–8

D

dado rails 219, 231
dangerous occurrences 9
defects, timber 122–3, 316–21
dermatitis 20, 21, 32
design/planning, roles and responsibilities 82
detail drawings 45
diseases 9
documentation, information 40
door frames 124–6, 129–38
  built-in frames 130, 135–6
  fixed-in frames 129–30, 133–5
door linings 131–2, 136–8
doors 197–8, 204–17
  defects 331–2
  double doors 306–8, 314–15
  fire doors 217
  hinges 198–200, 207–9, 327
  inspecting 331–2
  installing 316–27
  ironmongery 175, 197–203, 211–17, 325–7, 334
  maintenance 314–27
dormer windows, trussed rafter roofs 263, 272–3
double doors 306–8, 314–15

double-glazed units 323–4
double roofs 275
downpipes 328–30
drawings and plans 40–5
  assembly drawings 44
  block plans 42
  detail drawings 45
  electronic 41–2
  elevations 51
  floor plans 50
  hatchings 55–6
  height, working at 257
  orthographic projections 52–3
  pictorial projections 53–4
  projections 52–4
  sectional drawings 44–5
  site plans 43–4
  specifications 51–2
  symbols 55–6
  traditional 42
dry lining 121
dust extraction, cutting and shaping machinery 247

E

ear defenders 20, 21, 32
eaves, trussed rafter roofs 264–72
ECOSHH Regulations, noise 20
electricity 28–31
  colour coded cables 31
  dangers 29–30
  Portable Appliance Testing (PAT) 28–9
  precautions 28–9
  voltages 30, 31
electronic drawings 41–2
elevations, drawings and plans 51
emergency procedures 8–13, 34–6
energy conservation
  alternative energy sources 102–4
  Building Regulations 100, 105
  carbon content, energy sources 101–2
  energy ratings 105
  geothermal ground heat 103
  heat sink systems 103
  sustainability 100–6
engineering, roles and responsibilities 82–3
environment see built environment; physical and environmental factors
equipment
  see also tools and equipment
  height, working at 258
  plant and equipment 64–5
estimates, job 57, 63
estimating quantities of resources 57–64
  formulae 58–61
  inaccurate estimates 63
  measurements 57–61
  requirements 57–64
eye protection 32

F

fascia boards, trussed rafter roofs 270–1
ferrous metals 109
fire doors 125, 217
fire extinguishers 35–6
fire procedures 34–6
first aid 12–13
first fixing operations 113–72
  fixings 119–22
  materials 119–22

site datum points 114–15
tools and equipment 115–19
fixed-in frames, door frames 129–30, 133–5
fixings
    first fixing operations 119–22
    maintenance 302–5
flat roof decking 143
flat roofs 276
floor (base) units 186, 189–92
floor coverings 138–48, 337–9
    access traps 147–8, 338–9
    fixing methods 140–1
    flat roof decking 143
    services openings 142, 147–8
    softwood tongue and groove floorboards
        146
    tongue and groove chipboard floors 144–6
    types 139
floor joists 334–6
floor plans 50
fluorinated gases 110
formulae
    estimating quantities of resources
        58–61
    measurements 58–61
foundries 109
frames see door frames; window frames
framing anchors, partition walls 152
framing square 284

G
geometrical solutions, roofs 286–97
geothermal ground heat, energy
    conservation 103
glazing, replacing 339–44
global warming, sustainability 95–6
goggles 32
good working practices 72
    communication 74–5
    confidence 74
    relationships, working 72–3
    trust 74
guttering 328–30

H
hand protection 32
handling materials 22–6
HASAWA see Health and Safety at Work Act
hatchings, drawings and plans 55–6
hazards 5
    creating 17–18
    cutting and shaping machinery 234–5
    height, working at 256–7
    identifying 13–18
    method statements 14–15
    reporting 16–17
    risk assessments 14–15
    types 15–16
head protection 32
Health and Safety at Work Act (HASAWA)
    2, 5, 236
Health and Safety Executive (HSE) 6, 7
health risks 21
hearing protection 20, 21, 32
heat sink systems, energy conservation 103
height, working at 4, 16, 17, 256–8
    drawings and plans 257
    equipment 26–7, 258
    hazards 256–7
    maintenance 302

hinges, door 198–200, 207–9, 327
hip rafter lengths and angles, roofs 284–5
hipped roofs 276, 287–97
    geometrical solutions 287
hours required, pricing work 70
housekeeping 14
HSE see Health and Safety Executive
hygiene 18–21

I
improvement notices 6
information
    documentation 40
    drawings and plans 42–5
    manufacturers' technical information 48–9
    organisational documentation 49
    policies 47
    procedures 46–7
    programmes of work 45–6
    schedules 47–8
    specifications 47
    training and development records 49
injuries 7, 9, 10
in situ partition walls 149–50, 152, 155–6
insulation
    Building Regulations 105
    trussed rafter roofs 265–6
ironmongery, doors 175, 197–203, 211–17,
    325–7, 334

J
jack rafter lengths and angles, roofs 285
jack rafters, roofs 294–5
jigs, cutting and shaping machinery 241
joist coverings see floor coverings
joists, floor 334–6

K
kitchen units 184–5, 189–92, 195–6
kitchen worktops 187–9, 193–5

L
labour, planning 66–9
labour rates 62
ladders 26–7
land types, construction projects 88–91
landfill, sustainability 93
lead times, planning 67
legislation
    Building Regulations 100, 105
    cutting and shaping machinery 235–6
    health and safety 2–8
    personal protective equipment (PPE) 33
    waste management 108
leptospirosis 20, 21
letter plates, doors 216–17
lifting, safe 22–3
locks/latches 200–2, 211–16

M
machinery guards, cutting and shaping
    machinery 244
maintenance 299–350
    blocks 345
    bricks 345
    fixings 302–5
    height, working at 302
    nails 302–3
    personal protective equipment (PPE) 301
    plasterboard 346–7
    plasterwork 345–6

schedules 300–1
screws 304–5
specifications 300–1
stairs 310–14
stone 346–7
surfaces, reinstating 344–9
tiles, wall 347–9
timber, repairing/splicing 321–2, 332–3,
    334–8
wall tiles 347–9
major injuries 7, 10
Manual Handling Operations Regulations 4
manufacturers' instructions, cutting and
    shaping machinery 235–6
manufacturers' technical information 48–9
mark-up 63
materials
    costing 62–3
    first fixing operations 119–22
    partition walls 150–1
    planning 66–9
    purchasing systems 62–3
MDF (medium density fibreboard) 121
measurements
    estimating quantities of resources 57–61
    formulae 58–61
method statements, risk assessments 14–15
mitring, skirting 225–9
mouldings 218–31
    architraves 219, 220–3
    types 218–19, 309
MRMDF (moisture-resistant medium
    density fibreboard) 176

N
nailed butt joints, partition walls 152
nails 302–3
near misses 5, 10, 11
noggins 141
noise 20
non-conductive materials 247
non-ferrous metals 109

O
Ordnance Survey Benchmark (OSBM) 115
organic materials, sustainability 98
organisational documentation 49
orthographic projections 52–3
over 7-day injuries 7
overheads, pricing work 71
ozone layer 110

P
partition walls 149–58
    framing anchors 152
    in situ 149–50, 152, 155–6
    materials 150–1
    nailed butt joints 152
    openings 158
    pre-fabricated 149–50, 152, 153–5
    services 151
    skew nailing 152
    terms 149–50
PAT see Portable Appliance Testing
personal hygiene 20–1
Personal Protection at Work Regulations 4
personal protective equipment (PPE) 4, 31–3
    cutting and shaping machinery 236–7
    legislation 33
    maintenance 301

physical and environmental factors
  construction projects 84–7
  planning process 85–7
pictorial projections 53–4
picture rails 219, 231
pipe casing, second fixing operations 180–1
planning
  bills of quantities 66
  charts 67–9
  labour 66–9
  lead times 67
  materials 66–9
  pricing work 66–9
  programmes of work 66–7
  stock systems 67
planning process, physical and environmental factors 85–7
plans and drawings see drawings and plans
plant and equipment, purchasing/hiring 64–5
plasterboard, maintenance 346–7
plasterwork, maintenance 345–6
plinth blocks 219
policies, information 47
Portable Appliance Testing (PAT), electricity 28–9
PPE see personal protective equipment
pre-fabricated partition walls 149–50, 152, 153–5
preservatives, timber 322–3
pricing work 62–72
  added costs 70
  costing materials 62–3
  hours required 70
  overheads 71
  planning 66–9
  profitability 71–2
  purchasing/hiring, plant and equipment 64–5
procedures, information 46–7
profiles, door frames 124
profitability, pricing work 71–2
programmes of work 45–6
  planning 66–7
prohibition notices 6
projections
  drawings and plans 52–4
  orthographic projections 52–3
  pictorial projections 53–4
protective clothing 32
Provision and Use of Work Equipment Regulations (PUWER) 3–4, 236
purchasing/hiring, plant and equipment 64–5
purchasing systems, materials 62–3
purlins, roofs 297
PUWER see Provision and Use of Work Equipment Regulations
Pythagoras' theorem 61
  roofs 280–3
  trigonometry 280–3

Q

quantities of resources, estimating see estimating quantities of resources
quotes 57, 63

R

regulations, health and safety 2–8
relationships, working 72–3
repairs see maintenance
Reporting of Injuries, Diseases and

Dangerous Occurrences Regulations (RIDDOR) 2, 8, 9–10
resources
  see also estimating quantities of resources
  sustainability 94–5, 99–100
respiratory protection 32, 33
reveals, door frames 124
RIDDOR see Reporting of Injuries, Diseases and Dangerous Occurrences Regulations
risk assessments 14–15
risks 5
  health risks 21
riving knives, circular saws 244
roles and responsibilities
  built environment 81–3
  construction industry 81–3
  design/planning 82
  engineering 82–3
  surveying 82
roof lights, trussed rafter roofs 263
roofing square 284
roofs
  see also trussed rafter roofs
  common rafters 288–9
  components 276–7
  cripple rafters 296–7
  double roofs 275
  flat roofs 276
  framing square 284
  geometrical solutions 286–97
  hip rafter lengths and angles 284–5
  hipped roofs 276, 287–97
  jack rafter lengths and angles 285
  jack rafters 294–5
  openings 262–3, 277–9
  purlins 297
  Pythagoras' theorem 280–3
  roofing square 284
  setting out 286–97
  single roofs 274
  traditional roofing 273–97
  trigonometry 280–3
  triple roofs 275–6
  trussed rafter roofs 259–63
  valley rafters 292–4

S

safety aids, cutting and shaping machinery 240–1
safety notices 36–7
saws see cutting and shaping machinery
scaffold 26–7
schedules
  information 47–8
  maintenance 300–1
screws 304–5
scribe architraves 222–3
scribing, skirting 228–30
second fixing operations 173–232
  cladding 176, 178–9
  grounds, timber 177–8
  ironmongery 175, 197–203, 211–17, 325–7, 334
  pipe casing 180–1
  services, encasing 176–7, 182–4
  tools and equipment 174–5
sectional drawings 44–5
services

access panels 183
  detecting/protecting 185
  encasing 176–7, 182–4
  partition walls 151
services openings, floor coverings 142
  access traps 147–8
setting out roofs 286–97
side hung doors 204–17
signs 36–7
site datum points, first fixing operations 114–15
site plans 43–4
skew nailing, partition walls 152
skirting 219, 223–30
  mitring 225–9
  scribing 228–30
social benefits, construction projects 91–2
social regeneration, sustainability 96
soffits, trussed rafter roofs 269–70, 272
softwood tongue and groove floorboards 146
specifications
  drawings and plans 51–2
  information 47
  maintenance 300–1
splicing timber 321–2, 332–3, 334–8
stairs 159–71
  assembling 161–5
  balusters 170–1, 313
  balustrades 159, 161, 162
  Building Regulations 161
  components 159–61
  erecting 166–7
  fixing 170–1
  glue blocks 310
  handrails 167–70
  installing 167–70
  levelling 166–7
  maintenance 310–14
  nosings 311–13
  risers 311
  terms 160–1, 306
  treads 311
  types 306
  wedges 311
stock systems, planning 67
stone, maintenance 346–7
storing materials 22–6, 31
stud partition walls see partition walls
sub-contractors 6
surfaces, reinstating 344–9
surveying, roles and responsibilities 82
sustainability 92–111
  alternative building methods 96–8
  benefits 96–111
  biodegradable materials 98
  biodiversity 93
  Building Regulations 100, 105
  carbon footprint 94
  climate change 95–6
  energy conservation 100–6
  global warming 95–6
  landfill 93
  organic materials 98
  resources 94–5, 99–100
  social regeneration 96
  waste management 107–10
  water recycling 106–7
symbols, drawings and plans 55–6

T

tenders 57, 63
terms
     partition walls 149–50
     stairs 160–1, 306
     timber frames 131–2
tiles, wall, maintenance 347–9
timber, repairing/splicing 321–2, 332–3, 334–8
timber defects 122–3, 316–21
timber floors 138–48
timber frames 124–38
     door frames 124–6, 129–38
     terms 131–2
     window frames 126–9
timber preservatives 322–3
timber stud partition walls see partition walls
tongue and groove chipboard floors 144–6
tongued and grooved floor boarding, access
     traps 148
toolbox talks 7, 8, 19
tools and equipment
     see also cutting and shaping machinery
     first fixing operations 115–19
     second fixing operations 174–5
training and development records 49

trigonometry, roofs 280–3
trussed rafter roofs 259–63
     birdsmouth 263
     chimney stacks 263
     components 261
     dormer windows 263, 272–3
     eaves 264–72
     fascia boards 270–1
     insulation 265–6
     lateral restraints 262
     openings 262–3
     roof lights 263
     soffits 269–70, 272
     types 260–1
     ventilation 265–6
     verges 264–9
trust, good working practices 74

U

UPVC units, windows 323–4

V

valley rafters, roofs 292–4
ventilation, trussed rafter roofs 265–6
verges, trussed rafter roofs 264–9

W

wall tiles, maintenance 347–9
wall units 187
walls, partition walls 149–58
waste control 25–6
waste disposal, cutting and shaping
     machinery 247–8
waste management
     legislation 108
     sustainability 107–10
water recycling, sustainability 106–7
welfare facilities 18–19
window frames 126–9
window types 126–9
windows
     defects 331–2
     double-glazed units 323–4
     glazing, replacing 339–44
     inspecting 331–2
     UPVC units 323–4
Work at Height Regulations 4
working platforms 26–7
working practices, good see good working
     practices
worktops, kitchen 187–9, 193–5

ACKNOWLEDGEMENTS

The publisher would like to thank David Wilkins for his review and feedback on this book.

The author and the publisher would also like to thank the following for permission to reproduce material:

Images and diagrams

Alamy: Building Image: 3.14, Construction Photography: 8.33, Midland Aerial Pictures: 3.3, Mike Booth: 8.25, Peter Davey: chapter 1 opener, Rory Buckland RF: chapter 7 opener, russ witherington: 4.33, Scott Camazine: 8.23, ZUMA Press, Inc.: 2.1; **BOSCH:** 5.17; **BSA:** 2.5; **2013 © Energy Saving Trust:** 3.16; **Fotolia:** 1.1, 1.2, 1.3, 1.5, 1.6, 1.7, 1.8, 1.14, 1.15, 1.16, 3.2, 3.8, 8.21, 8.26; **Helfen:** 2.4; **instant art:** table 1.15; **iStockphoto:** 1.11, 2.12, 2.13, 3.1, 3.4, 3.5, 3.10, 3.12, 3.13, 3.15, 4.7, 4.12, 4.16, 4.32, 4.36, 4.41, 8.31, 8.32; **Leeds College of Building:** 4.73, 4.74, 4.75, 4.76; **Nelson Thornes:** 1.9, 1.10, 1.12, 1.13, chapter 4 opener, 4.3, 4.4, 4.5, 4.6, 4.8, 4.9, 4.10, 4.11, 4.13, 4.14, 4.15, 4.17, 4.18, 4.19, 4.20, 4.21, 4.22, 4.25, 4.26, 4.28, 4.29, 4.30, 4.31, 4.57, 4.58, 4.59, 4.60, 4.61, 4.97, 4.98, 4.99, 4.100, 4.101, 4.104, 4.105, 4.106, 4.107, chapter 5 opener, 5.1, 5.2, 5.29, 5.30, 5.31, 5.32, 5.33, 5.34, 5.35, 5.36, 5.51, 5.52, 5.53, 5.54, 5.55, 5.56, 5.57, 5.58, 5.59, 5.60, 5.61, 5.62, 5.63, 5.64, 5.65, 5.66, 5.67, 5.68, 5.69, 5.70, 5.71, 5.72, 5.73, 5.74, 5.75, 5.76, 5.77, 5.78, 5.79, 5.80, 5.81, 5.82, 5.83, 5.84, 5.85, 5.86, 5.87, 5.88, chapter 6 opener, 7.50, 7.51, 7.52, 7.53, 7.54, 7.55, 7.56, 7.57, 7.58, 7.59, 7.60, 7.61, 7.62, 7.63, 7.64, 7.65, 7.66, 7.67, 7.68, 7.69, 7.70, 7.71, 7.72, 7.73, 7.74, 7.75, 7.76, 7.77, 7.78, 7.79, 7.80, 7.81, 7.82, 7.83, 7.84, 7.85, 7.86, 7.87, 7.88, 7.89, 7.90, 7.91, 7.92, 7.93, 7.94, 7.95, 7.96, 7.97, 8.3, 8.16, 8.17, 8.18, 8.19; **Peter Brett:** 2.3, 2.6, 2.7; **Reprinted with permission from WOODWEB - The Information Resource for the Woodworking Industry - www.woodweb.com:** 4.39; **Science Photo Library:** Peter Gardiner: 1.4; **Shutterstock:** chapter 2 opener, chapter 3 opener, 3.6, 3.7, 3.9, 3.11, 4.2, 4.23, 4.24, 4.27, 4.34, 4.35, 4.37, 4.38, 4.40, chapter 8 opener, 8.24; **Trend Machinery & Cutting Tools Ltd:** 6.9; **© Victoria and Albert Museum, London:** 4.93; **Wikipedia:** 8.22.

Every effort has been made to trace the copyright holders but if any have been inadvertently overlooked the publisher will be pleased to make the necessary arrangements at the first opportunity.